Embraci

MW00882334

Contents

Introduction

I took a job as the Director of Religious Education (DRE) at Holy Spirit Church in Huntsville, Alabama after teaching in Catholic Schools for many years. As part of my job as DRE, I was assigned to teach the Confirmation Class. I took a look at the materials that had been used to teach the Confirmation Class in previous years and began to plan my lessons. At the same time I was hearing about several high school students, who had been confirmed two or three years prior, who were leaving the Catholic Faith. I sought out those high school students and inquired as to why they were leaving the Catholic Church. Their response came as a great shock to me. These teenagers had been approached by Baptist or Evangelical teenagers at their public high schools and had been convinced by them that the Catholic Church had it all wrong. The Catholic Church calls their priests "Father," which the Baptist or Evangelical teens pointed out was directly against the Bible. The Catholic Church worships Mary and statues and isn't at all biblical. In fact most Catholics can't even quote Scripture. They were told that Catholics believe in a 'works' salvation, that again, was clearly not biblical. We even baptize babies who can't possibly accept Jesus Christ as their personal Lord and Savior, which is the means of Salvation according to the Bible.

I looked at these teenagers with amazement and said, "Hasn't anyone ever told you that the Catholic Church is the Church that Jesus founded? Don't you know that the Catholic Church gave the Bible to the world? Haven't you been taught that Jesus entered into the heavenly covenant with God the Father, at the age of eight days, when Mary and Joseph had him circumcised? This is exactly what your parents did when you were baptized as infants. You entered into the Everlasting Covenant with God." These teenagers looked at me, mouths open and wide eyed. They had never been taught this. Many had even attended Catholic School from first to eighth grade and still did not know these basic truths. This was when I decided that a much better Confirmation formation program had to take place. We simply had to teach our eighth graders the truth of the Catholic Church so that we could keep them Catholic. I began to study a great deal. And I prayed to Jesus every single day asking Him to guide me to teach what He wanted these children to know about His Church.

In my studies, I learned from great Catholic Scripture Scholars, Theologians, and Apologists such as Dr. Scott Hahn, Jeff Cavins, Father Bill Casey, Matthew Kelly, Father Larry Richards, Dr. Peter Kreeft, Stephen Ray, Father Robert Barron, Patrick Madrid, Michael Cumbie, and Father Francis Peffley. The result was a book entitled, <u>Confirmed Catholic</u> that took our Confirmation Candidates through an entire faith formation, similar to "The Rite of Christian Initiation of Adults" or RCIA. I took what I had learned and began to teach the complete faith in a way that children could understand it.

The results have been outstanding. The Confirmation Classes have responded with great enthusiasm toward the curriculum. Students are proud of their Catholic Faith and in no way want to leave it. In fact, quite the opposite has occurred. Students are now leading teenagers of other faiths into the Catholic Church. Instead of being evangelized, our students are evangelizing. More importantly, we are seeing Catholic teenagers who enthusiastically live their faith by understanding the importance of the sacraments. They have taken charge of their own souls deciding for themselves when they will go to confession and they go often. The Eucharist is truly the center of their lives. They allow the Church to guide them morally and fully embrace Catholic Doctrine. Many are wearing a scapular and praying the Rosary daily. Most importantly, they have a deep and close relationship with Jesus. They have given their lives to Him.

What I did not expect and what came to as great surprise to me was the reaction of the adults who attended each and every Confirmation Session along with the children. Because we have an average of 80 Confirmation Candidates each school year attending Confirmation Sessions, I ask for volunteers among the parents of the Confirmation Candidates to *help* by attending each session. These parents help with activities or simply crowd control, which allows me to lecture uninterrupted. Each year approximately twenty parents attend the Confirmation Sessions as helpers and learn along with the children. The reaction among the parents has been very enthusiastic. Parents explain that they are learning the Catholic Faith like never before, understanding it in terms that change their lives for the better. More and more parishioners are requesting a copy of <u>Confirmed Catholic</u> as they have heard about it by word of mouth. Some parents, who are converts to the Catholic Faith, have told me that what is taught in the Confirmation Sessions should also be taught in the RCIA Program. After reading <u>Confirmed Catholic,</u> one person said to me, "I've been Catholic for 22 years and finally I understand the Catholic Faith."

After many years of teaching the Confirmation Class, I have been asked to teach and to lead the RCIA program at Holy Spirit Church. Again, I was taking on something new; something I have never done before. I naturally wanted to do the very best job that I could possibly do to help adults inquiring about the Catholic Faith to embrace it. As I did when new to teaching the Confirmation Class, I looked at the materials that had been previously used to teach the Right of Christian Initiation of Adults (RCIA). I found that it had some good qualities and some bad qualities. Most importantly, I prayed. I was willing to do whatever Jesus wanted. I prayed, "Lord, what do you want to teach these adults who are inquiring about your Church? What is it that you want them to know?" This book is the result of that. It does contain much of the same information that is taught in the book for Confirmation, <u>Confirmed Catholic</u>, but it also contains much, much more. For new Catholics need an explanation of many things that children who have been Catholic their entire lives do not need. Both books however, use a lot of what we call 'Catholic Apologetics,' which is basically an explanation of Catholic Doctrine and why it is worthy of belief. Through the book I hope to convince you, by way of the Truth, as to why you want to be Catholic and why you want to stay Catholic. So in places, it seeks to defend the Catholic Faith against Protestant criticism, which I think many adults need. This is in no way meant to demean other faiths, but only seeks to assure you that you have indeed found the Truth of Christ's teachings through the Apostles and the guarantee that comes with Apostolic Succession.

It is my hope that you will, as the title indicates, embrace Catholicism and that this will happen as Jesus pours His grace into your hearts through His Church.

I. The Shroud of Turin

Most people have heard of the Shroud of Turin. Perhaps it has been the topic of a Discovery Channel episode they have seen. Maybe they have read an article concerning it on the Internet or in a science magazine. What exactly is the Shroud of Turin? Well, many people of faith believe the Shroud of Turin to be the actual burial cloth of Jesus Christ. Many believe that it is the actual shroud that Jesus was wrapped in when He was taken down from the cross and laid in the tomb given to him by Joseph of Arimathea. They believe that this is the cloth that the apostles, Peter and John, saw when they entered the tomb on Easter morning; the shroud that they mention in the Gospel (Luke 24:12). The Catholic Church has made no definitive statement regarding the Shroud of Turin and rightly so. The Church allows each person to examine the evidence for him or herself and decide.

The Shroud of Turin Has Been Studied for 600,000 hours

The Shroud of Turin has been in the possession of many people for 2,000 years. Currently it resides in Turin, Italy in the Cathedral of Saint John the Baptist where it is on display from time to time. The burial cloth of Jesus has been mentioned in Scripture, as all four gospels state that Joseph of Arimathea, a very wealthy man, gave Jesus fine linen in which to be buried. The Shroud of Turin could be that actual burial cloth.

The Shroud is the most studied scientific object in the world. It has been studied for 600,000 hours by scientists from all over the world. Because of this scientific study, the scientists have given us many facts about the Shroud of Turin. Scientists report that this linen is very, very fine. They report that

Cleopatra's burial linen was not nearly as fine as this one. It was a very fine and very expensive linen 2,000 years ago. This causes one to ask why such an expensive cloth was used to bury a crucified man; a condemned criminal; a man condemned to die in the most humiliating way.

Approximately two thousand scientists have studied the Shroud of Turin. The majority of them were Atheists or Agnostics. An Atheist is a person who does not believe in God at all. An Agnostic is a person who believes that there is no way that you and I can know whether or not God exists. After studying the Shroud of Turin, an overwhelming number of these scientists became Christian.

What Can the Scientists Tell us About the Shroud of Turin?

The scientists who studied the Shroud of Turin have many interesting things to tell us. First of all, what we see printed on the Shroud is a perfect negative of the man who has been buried in it. This means that the picture on the Shroud is the same type of picture that we see on film. When we take a picture and look at the film, we see a negative of the picture we took. The Shroud of Turin is a perfect negative of the man buried in it. Scientist then decided to see what would happen if they took a picture of the Shroud of Turin itself. When they took a picture of the Shroud, they got a positive image. This amazed them.

Second, after taking a picture of the shroud, they placed that picture underneath a 3-Dimensional Image Analyzer just to see what would happen. The Shroud is the only image in the entire world that comes out a perfect 3-Dimensional image of the man who was buried in the cloth. Every other 2-Dimensional photograph comes out distorted, but not the Shroud. This served to further amaze them.

What can these scientists tell us about the man who was buried in the Shroud? The Scientists say that the image on the Shroud is of a man who was 5 feet 11 inches tall. He weighed 175 pounds and he was in excellent physical condition. Scientists tell us that he was a Jewish male between the age of 30 and 35. They know he is Jewish for 2 reasons: First, he has long hair and it is worn in a ponytail, which is exactly how, religious Jewish men; men, who were devoted to prayer, wore their hair in the time of Jesus. Second, under magnification, they can see that the man wore a phylactery between his eyes. A phylactery was a little leather box which contained a parchment of Sacred Scripture. The Scripture contained in the phylactery would have been the *Shema*: "I am the Lord Your God. You shall love the Lord with all your heart, soul, strength and mind." Devout Jews would wear this on their forehead, because Scripture told them to keep this teaching before their mind and heart.

This man was laid with his feet at one end of the Shroud; his head in the middle; and the other half of the Shroud was folded over the top of him. Then he was wrapped tightly with other strips of linen and tied.

Scientists have determined that there are no pigments or paints on the Shroud. Therefore, no one could have painted the man's image onto the cloth. The Shroud of Turin has been in three recorded fires. These fires caused holes in the Shroud that were repaired, but they did not affect the image imprinted on it. These fires were extinguished with water. Water did not damage the image nor did it cause the image to fade.

Scourging at the Pillar

Scientists have determined that the man, whose image is on the Shroud, was scourged. The Shroud indicates that he had scourge marks up and down his entire body from the back of his neck to the heels of his feet. The scourge marks were made by a device that had a wooden handle. Attached to the end, were strips of leather holding 2-3 little balls made of metal. These balls would have contained spikes of some sort that hooked into his skin and tore it. Every time the man received one lash, he was actually given two to three scourge marks. The Scientists have determined that there are 120 lashes on this man's body. He was mercilessly scourged nearly to the point of death. We believe that this man was our Lord, Jesus. They know that two different Roman Soldiers must have scourged Him, because of the direction of the scourge marks being at a slant and coming from one side or the other. They can tell that one soldier was on His left and one was on His right. One soldier was shorter and one was taller. One soldier was very harsh and hit our Lord very hard. The other was a bit more lenient. There are also scourge marks on the front of our Lord's chest; abdomen; front of His legs; and some on His arms. Jesus was obviously completely naked at the time of His scourging.

This evidence of the scourging from the Shroud supports Scripture. In John 19:1 we read, "Then Pilate took Jesus and had him scourged." In fact all four Gospels say that Pilate had Jesus scourged.

Agony in the Garden

The Scientists who studied the Shroud of Turin tell us that the man who was wrapped in this cloth sweated blood prior to being scourged. They can tell that blood has flown from the skin on all parts of His body. He underwent Hematidrosis several hours before His death. Hematidrosis is the sweating of blood. It occurs when a person is facing extreme levels of stress such as facing his own death. The capillaries underneath the skin burst and the person actually sweats blood through the pours. The effect of this is that the person's entire skin becomes a bruise from head to toe.

Scripture tells us that our Lord sweat blood in the agony in the garden. In Luke 22:44 we read, "He was in such agony and He prayed so fervently that His sweat became like drops of blood falling on the ground." The scientists have determined that this is exactly the truth. Jesus must have undergone Hematidrosis. This means that His entire skin was bruised before they began to scourge Him.

Have you ever had a bruise on an arm, leg, or elbow? When you hit that bruised arm, leg, or elbow on something, the pain is much worse. Jesus was completely bruised all over His body before the Roman Soldiers hit Him even once. So He felt a lot more pain because of this than He would have otherwise.

Crowning with Thorns

The Scientists tell us that there are fifteen puncture wounds on this man's head. There are fifteen puncture wounds that penetrated his skull. These scientists have determined that a cap of thorns was placed on his head. It was not simply a crown that went around his head like a ringlet, but a cap that covered the top, sides, and back of his head. The thorns were two to four inches long. The scientists stated that someone beat these thorns into his head with a heavy stick.

Scripture tell us that the soldiers made a crown out of thorns and placed it on Jesus' head. They placed a purple cloak around Him and put a reed in His hand. They kept mocking Him, spitting on Him, and were hitting Him on the head saying, "Hail, King of the Jews." In Matthew 27:27-30 we read, "Then the soldiers of the governor took Jesus inside the praetorian and gathered the whole cohort around Him. They stripped off His clothes and threw a scarlet military cloak about Him. Weaving a crown out of thorns, they placed it on His head, and a reed in His right hand. And kneeling before Him, they mocked Him, saying, "Hail, King of the Jews!" They spat upon Him and took the reed and kept striking Him on the head."

It is true that criminals at this time in history were scourged and crucified. There has never been evidence, however, that any other person was crowned with thorns other than Christ. This was a torture that the soldiers invented just for Jesus, because He claimed to be a king. More than any other evidence on the Shroud, the evidence of the 'Crowning with Thorns' helps to prove that this cloth is truly the burial cloth of Jesus.

Swollen Right Cheek

Scientists say that the man's cheek under his right eye is extremely swollen. Both cheeks are swollen, but the right cheek is extremely swollen.

Scripture tells us that a temple guard hit Jesus when He was standing before Annas, the High Priest. This can be found in the Gospel of John 18:22. Perhaps this is when our Lord was struck on the cheek.

Evidence from the Shroud indicates that striking Jesus on the cheek caused His nasal cartilage to be separated. In order to separate His nasal cartilage, He had to have been struck extremely hard. Couple that with the fact that this image on the Shroud was made forty hours after Jesus died. Some of the swelling would have gone down and yet His cheek is still very swollen forty hours after His death.

Jesus Falls to the Ground

Scientists tell us that this man fell, face to the ground, several times. They know this because the tip of his nose is very badly scraped. His knees are completely torn up and his lips are scraped. They have determined that he was carrying the cross that was used to crucify him on rocky streets and fell under the weight of it.

Nailed to the Cross

Scientists say that a large nail was driven through each of his wrists. This man was literally nailed to a cross. When the nail was driven through his wrists, it half severed the Median Nerve. This would have sent bolts of hot fiery pain down both arms and then down his entire body. Scientists know that the Median Nerve was half severed because both thumbs have been pulled inward. This is a natural effect when the Median Nerve is half severed.

The scientists say that the right foot of the man was placed over the left foot and one nail was driven through both feet at the same time. Our crucifixes give us the image of what our Lord suffered for us.

No Broken Bones

The man who was wrapped in the Shroud of Turin had no broken bones. Instead, the evidence on the Shroud indicates that he had a wound in his side. This wound is one and a half inches wide and ¾ of an inch high. This is the exact dimension of a Roman lance. Scientists say that this wound in his side did not swell. This means that this wound was inflicted after the man was already dead. If this wound had been inflicted before death, there would have been swelling. Scientists also determined that there was no blood spray from this wound. If the man had been alive and breathing when this wound was inflicted, there would have been air in his lungs. This would have caused a spray pattern on the shroud and there is none.

This piercing by the Roman lance into the man's side came between the fifth and sixth rib and it pierced the lower part of his right lung and then his heart. According to the evidence on the Shroud, blood and clear blood serum poured out of this wound. This would have been caused when the lance punctured his lung and heart.

This corresponds to Scripture. In the Gospel of John chapter 19: 31-34 we read, "Now since it was preparation day, in order that the bodies might not remain on the cross on the Sabbath, for the Sabbath day of that week was a solemn one, the Jews asked Pilate that their legs be broken and they be taken down. So the soldiers came and broke the legs of the first and then of the other one who was crucified with Jesus. But when they came to Jesus and saw that He was already dead, they did not break His legs, but one soldier thrust his lance into His side, and immediately blood and water flowed out."

The scientists have proven that there is human blood on the Shroud and that it is the Blood Type AB. The scientists have proven that the man had to have been wrapped in this linen shroud within one and a half hours after his death. Otherwise the blood would not have transferred to the linen. The Gospel states that they took Jesus down from the cross and wrapped Him in fine linen and laid Him in the tomb. They did not wash His body, they did not have time. The Sabbath was about to begin at sundown. They had to get Jesus' body into the tomb before the Sabbath began, because they were not allowed to do any work whatsoever on the Sabbath. If they did not get Him down and buried by sundown, our Lord would have had to stay on the cross until Sunday. This is why Mary Magdalene was coming back to the tomb on Sunday morning. She was going to finish the burial process.

Rigor Mortis but No Decay

Scientists tell us that there are absolutely no signs of decomposition on the body that was wrapped in the Shroud. The man who was wrapped in this shroud was in rigor mortis, but his body at no time began to decompose. This means that the man was wrapped in this cloth for only two to three days.

Let us examine this further. The scientists can tell that the man's body entered into rigor mortis. Rigor mortis is the stiffening of the body that occurs a few hours after death. This man's body had definitely entered into rigor mortis. His left knee is higher than his right. His feet are almost pointing straight down. This was caused by the way his feet were nailed to the cross. The feet of this man were forced into this position and then nailed down. Rigor mortis caused the feet to remain in that position.

A body only remains in rigor mortis for two or three days. After that, it begins to decay. The Shroud shows no signs of decay. Therefore, scientists tell us, that the man's body never began to decay.

As Christians we know that Jesus was wrapped in a burial shroud. The Christian faith teaches that Jesus arose from the dead on the third day, Easter Sunday. It makes perfect sense to us that His body was in rigor mortis, but of course it never decayed. He arose from the dead before His body had a chance to decay. The scientists, on the other hand, were very baffled when they discovered that His body never decayed. This would mean that the cloth was removed from His body within three days of death.

So far, the scientists had discovered that everything Scripture states about Jesus' death was true of the man buried in the cloth. He did sweat blood; He was hit in the face; He was scourged; He was crowned with thorns; He was made to carry a heavy cross; He did fall to the ground, face first, several times;

He was nailed to the cross; He was wrapped in a very expensive cloth; He was laid in a tomb. Remember that the majority of these scientists didn't even believe in God. They certainly didn't believe the Christian claim that Jesus arose from the dead. However, they were beginning to discover facts that proved this man arose from the dead. Now they had proven that His body was no longer in the Shroud after two or three days. So they began to investigate exactly *how* the image appeared on the Shroud in the first place and *how* the Shroud was taken off of His body.

How Was the Image on the Shroud Made?

Upon investigating how the image was made on the Shroud of Turin, the Scientists discovered these important things: First, the image was not made by paint. There are no pigments or paints on the Shroud. Therefore some artist did not create this image. Second, the image was not made by blood. There is blood on the Shroud, but blood did not make the image. So how was the image made?

After much experimentation and reenactments, scientists can only conclude that the image on the Shroud was made by a burst of light, heat, and radiation that came forth from the man's body. This burst of light lasted less than a second in length. This light, heat, and radiation burned the image onto the Shroud.

The Scientists were amazed at their findings and perplexed because they cannot explain where the light came from. The image of the man was literally burned onto the Shroud! It was burned onto the Shroud by a burst of light! And the light came from inside of the man's body outward! Not only was the image burned onto the Shroud by light, heat and radiation, but when the man's image was burned onto the Shroud, he must have been in an upright position. In other words, the man was not laying down when his image was burned onto the Shroud. He was completely vertical in an upright position. The scientists proved this and were again, shocked at their findings. In the image on the Shroud, the man's long hair is falling straight down to his shoulders. If he were laying down when the image was made, his hair would be falling back toward the platform that his body had been laid upon. So there is no way he could have been lying down when the image was made.

Not only was the man completely upright when his image was burned onto the cloth, the science indicates that he was suspended in mid-air. The scientists proved that the man had to be completely suspended in air, with his feet off the ground, when his image was burned onto the Shroud. It was proven that there are absolutely no pressure points, no marks of pressure, on any parts of the Shroud. The scientists said that the man had to be completely weightless in order for this to happen. Otherwise there would have been pressure points where the Shroud touched his body.

The scientists then proved that not only was the man upright and suspended in the air with his feet off the ground when his image was burned onto the Shroud, but light, heat, and radiation entered the man's body from above. The scientists tried duplicating this image using light sources that came from all sides. The only way they could get the same type of image was if the light source came from above. This light, heat, and radiation that entered the man's body from above lasted less than a millisecond and it literally burned his image onto the Shroud.

Picture this: Jesus is wrapped in a linen cloth that is tied around Him. His body is completely lifted up; feet dangling in mid-air. A burst of light and heat enter His body from above and burn His image onto this linen cloth that He is wrapped in. This light bursts forth from the inside of His body outward, burning the image on all sides 3-Dimensionally. This is what the scientists proved happened. Even though it is unexplainable, this is the only hypothesis that can produce the type of image that is seen on the cloth. There are no other possibilities.

Even more interesting is the fact that Jesus did not remove the linen cloth from His body. The scientists proved that the man wrapped in the Shroud of Turin could not have removed the Shroud from his body. In other words, he did not take it off and either did anyone else. This is true because there is absolutely no smearing of the blood on the Shroud. The scientists proved that if the man had removed the Shroud from his body; if he had unwrapped himself or if someone else had unwrapped him, they would have had to pull it off all of the bloody places on his skin. The linen would have been stuck to those places by the dried blood like a bandage. All of the hundreds of wound spots on the shroud would have smeared. There is not even one smear…Not one! The Shroud was not removed from His body. It was not taken off.

Instead, the Scientists theorize that the man's body simply disappeared from the Shroud and left it laying there like an empty shell. Their only explanation is that the Shroud simply fell through the man's body.

This makes perfect sense to us who are Christian. We know that the Bible tells us that Jesus appeared to the Apostles on the evening that He arose from the dead. The Bible tells us that Jesus simply came through locked doors and walls. Quite obviously, His glorified body could pass through material elements. At the moment of Jesus' Resurrection, the Shroud simply fell through His glorified body. It remained laying there, but He was no longer in it. The Apostles found it lying there as if it were an empty shell. Still tied closed, yet His body was gone.

These scientists, many of whom didn't even believe in God; who didn't believe the Christian claim that Jesus arose from the dead; were changed after studying the Shroud. They had proven that the man who was buried in that cloth arose from the dead. They had proven that the image of His badly beaten and crucified body had been burned onto the Shroud by His Resurrection from the dead and at the moment of His Resurrection from the dead; as His soul reentered His body. In other words, Jesus' Resurrection caused the image to be burned onto the Shroud. How could they continue to be Atheists and Agnostics? They had found the Truth. Many of these scientists became Christian after studying the Shroud of Turin. They had discovered the Truth and had proven that Jesus of Nazareth was who He said He was; God's Son. Jesus, without a doubt, arose from the dead and the shroud is the proof.

The Truth

There is only one reason to believe anything and that is because it is the truth. Christians believe that Jesus arose from the dead. No one has to prove it to us. We have faith and we believe. Still, it is pretty amazing when a group of scientists have drawn the conclusion that it did indeed happen by studying the shroud that Jesus was wrapped in when He was taken down from the cross.

Before studying the shroud the majority of the scientists didn't even believe in God. After studying the shroud, an overwhelming number of them became Christian. Not only did they suddenly believe in God and believe that Jesus indeed arose from the dead, they went out and actively sought the Church so they could become members of it. Before studying the Shroud of Turin, many of these scientists thought that they knew the truth. They believed that God did not exist. That was the truth to them. After studying the Shroud of Turin, the truth suddenly changed. Now there was a God and not only was there a God, but His very own Son came to earth to save us from our sins. He was tortured and crucified and on the third day He arose from the dead. This was the truth, now.

Did the truth suddenly change? Or did the scientists change? Well, it is obvious that the scientists changed. The truth was always there. The truth always declared that not only does God exist, but His very own Son did indeed rise from the dead. It's just that now these scientists suddenly believed the truth and it became real to them.

It is important to understand that truth never changes. Just because someone refuses to believe the truth doesn't mean it's not the truth. The truth is independent of our belief. Simply put, Truth is what is real and a real thing can't be both true and false.

In the pages that follow in this book, we will be exploring the truths of the Catholic Faith. Some of the things you will know something about and some you may know nothing about. Everything that is written here is the truth. It is the truth handed to you from Christ Himself through His Church down through the ages.

Our souls long for the truth that is Christ alone. Saint Augustine said, "You have made us for yourself, O Lord, and our hearts are restless until they rest in you." We have a hunger deep inside of us that this world cannot fill, because it is meant to be filled by God. As the two disciples said after encountering the risen Christ on the road to Emmaus, "Were not our hearts burning within us while He spoke to us on the way and opened the Scriptures to us?" I pray that your heart too will burn inside of you as this book opens the Scriptures to you. I pray that the truth will enlighten you and lead you on a journey that ends with your full union with Jesus.

Why Begin with the Shroud of Turin?

I begin with the Shroud of Turin, because it clearly shows the sufferings of Christ: His swollen right cheek and separated nasal cartilage; the sweating of blood that caused a bruising effect on His body; 120 scourge marks made with a Roman flagrum; fifteen puncture wounds to His skull caused by the crown of thorns; the falls to the ground that caused His badly scraped nose, lips, and torn up knees; the wounds on his shoulders caused by the weight of the cross; and the nail marks in His wrists and feet as He was nailed to the cross. All of this gives us a clear picture of what Jesus endured in order for our sins to be forgiven. When we look upon the crucifix, we truly see the doorway to Heaven and the price that was paid for our salvation.

I read a book many years ago that gave an account of the passion of Christ as seen in the 'Visions' of Venerable Anne Catherine Emerich. Anne Catherine Emerich was a mystic who was shown, in her minds eye, vivid accounts of the life of Jesus as if she were present as they were happening. These visions were then recorded. One such image was of the Passion of Christ in all His sufferings. This book I was reading then compared her visions (account of the passion) with the scientific evidence on the Shroud of Turin for accuracy. The result was that the scientific evidence on the Shroud supported exactly what Anne Catherine saw.

Before I read that book, I knew that Jesus suffered and died for me. What I did not know was the magnitude of His sufferings. I can honestly say that reading that vision was the hardest thing I have ever read. Hard in that I was shocked at the cruelty of Christ's executioners. It was difficult to read the truth of just how badly our Lord was treated and suffered. The pain that He endured was difficult for me to swallow. I remember asking God at the time, "Why did it have to be <u>that</u> bad?" The answer, because sin is <u>that</u> bad.

Every Palm Sunday during Mass, an account of the Passion of Christ is read from one of the Gospels. As a cradle Catholic, I grew up hearing this read aloud. I understood that Judas betrayed our Lord and that Peter denied Him. Pilate had Jesus scourged. The soldiers beat Him. It was they who mocked Him and spit upon Him. Christ's executioners weaved a crown out of thorns and placed it upon His sacred head. They were the ones who kept striking Him on the head saying, "Hail King of the Jews." But as I read Anne Catherine's account of the sufferings of Christ, my childhood understanding grew up. I now understood clearly that I did this to Jesus. My sins have caused His pain. I have denied Him. I scourged Him; crowned Him with thorns; mocked Him; spit upon Him. He was pierced for my transgressions. I realized that I did this to Jesus and I knew it to be true, because my many sins of the past came to my mind like never before. I hadn't been to confession in twenty years. I was a cradle Catholic, but I certainly was not practicing all of my faith; only some of it.

A deep love for Jesus suddenly came upon me. It had to be the result of the Holy Spirit's presence, since I was deeply repenting of my past sins. My heart opened up to Christ and His love came pouring into my soul. I humbled myself and it was just enough for Him to come rushing in ready to forgive me and embrace me. To the core of my being I was sorry for all of the sins I had committed and believe me, there were a great many reaching all the way back to my middle school years. I had so much to say to Jesus. I wanted Him to know how much I loved Him and again, and again, how sorry I was for my sins.

But that wasn't all. I wanted to change. I wanted to rid my life of sin. I did not want to do anything further to hurt Him. I felt in the depths of my soul, "Lord, you have been hurt enough. I will no longer hurt you." Over time my shallow prayer life became vibrant. I slowly but surely with the help of His grace began to rid my life of the habitual sins that I committed several times each day. I asked the Lord to raise my spirituality to higher levels and to open my eyes to see as He sees. I handed my life over to Jesus and proclaimed to Him that the only will I had was His will. I began to seek that deep relationship with God that we all long for.

That was the day that my conversion toward God began. This was the beginning of the rest of my life. Saint Paul tells us that every person is called to become a saint, that is, to become holy. In Matthew 5:48 Jesus Himself said, "You therefore must be perfect as your heavenly Father is perfect." Perfect in purity of heart, perfect in compassion and love, perfect in obedience, perfect in conformity to the will of the Father, perfect in holiness. This sounds impossible and may cause us to become discouraged to the point of giving up, but take courage, because we are not alone. Left up to ourselves alone and struggling, holiness is impossible, but with God, all things are possible, even our sanctity.

God is calling each of us to a holy conversion. The reality of the Passion of Christ is what triggered mine and that is why I share it with you. What triggers each person's conversion toward Christ can be quite varied. What is important is that we turn our lives toward Him and begin to live for Him instead of for ourselves. What I have gradually come to understand about conversion is that it is a process. Some of the greatest saints of the Church, those considered to be 'Doctors of the Church' have written great insights as to the process of conversion; the process of becoming holy. They all teach that there are three stages of spiritual growth. The first stage, called the "Purgative Stage" or "Purgative Way," includes the initial phases of conversion such as turning away from sin, bringing one's life into conformity with the moral law, initiating the habit of prayer and the practices of piety or goodness, and maintaining a relatively stable life in the Church.

The second stage, the Illuminative stage, is one of continuing growth. It is characterized by deeper prayer, growth in virtues, deepening love of neighbor, greater and more stability, more complete surrender to the lordship of Christ, greater detachment from all that is not God and an increasing desire for full union with God.

The final stage or Unitive Stage is one of deep, habitual union with God, characterized by deep joy, profound humility, freedom from fears of suffering and trials, a great desire to serve God, and apostolic fruitfulness. In this stage the experience of the presence of God is almost continual.

Not every person experiences every characteristic listed in each of the stages, but we all progress through them on our way to holiness. You may be able to identify characteristics that you have already experienced in each of the stages, but if not, do not be distressed. We are all on a journey toward Christ and we can help one another a great deal in the process.

It is my desire to help bring as many people as I can into union with Jesus; into full conversion to holiness. I know no better way than through His Church. We all have two jobs to do on this earth that are of most importance. First, and foremost you want to get to Heaven. That must be your greatest desire. Second, take as many people with you as you can. So let us be on our way.

II. Our Belief in God

God Always Was

God has always existed. No one created God. He always was. A lot of people have trouble understanding that. They say, "Who created God and how did He come to be?" This is difficult for us to understand, but I offer you a bit of help with this. Think of God as "existence itself." God is existence for everything exists through Him. The Bible says that it is through God that we "live and move and have our being" (Acts 17:28). We exist through Him. We have life because of Him. God is existence itself.

Kneeling before the burning bush, Moses was commissioned by God to go to Egypt and set God's people free. The voice of God came from the burning bush saying, "I will send you to Pharaoh to lead My people, the Israelites, out of Egypt." Moses asked God, "When I go to the Israelites and say to them, 'The God of your fathers has sent me to you,' if they ask me, 'What is his name?' what am I to tell them?" God replied, "I am who am." (See Exodus 3:10-14) This name of God tells us exactly who God is, doesn't it? His name is simply, "I am" and…. He is. No one created God. He always was.

We cannot *prove* the existence of God. We cannot see Him the way we see this book. We can't place Him under a microscope and prove His existence the way we do molecules. But we also can't prove the existence of love and yet we know what it means to love and to be loved. We can easily see that believing in love is worthwhile because it enriches our lives and brings us great happiness. The same is true for God. We cannot prove His existence, but believing in Him is worthwhile. Because of our faith in Him, our lives are enriched and we find great happiness.

The point is that God is either real or He isn't. The universe must have come from God or it must have come from nothing. There are no other alternatives. For most people it is more natural to believe that the universe came from God. For if there is no creator, why does anything exist? It only makes sense that a creator that exists outside the universe created the universe. We call that creator God.

If you found a watch out in the middle of the desert, you would assume that someone created it. The watch is a complicated machine where the inner parts must sink together exactly in order for it to keep time. No one would assume that the watch came into existence by chance. It's far too complicated. It had to be created. The human eye is far more complicated and complex than a watch, yet there are people who insist that God does not exist. It only stands to reason that the universe in all its complexity had to be created. It could not have happened by chance.

Chance means that something occurs without intention or cause. For example, if I take ten coins dated 1991 to 2000 and try to draw 1991 without searching for it, I depend on chance. If so the odds are ten to one. If I try to draw 1991 and 1992 in order, the odds jump to one hundred to one. The odds of pulling out 1991 to 2000 in order are ten billion to one!

But let's up the scale a bit. There are 48 ancient prophesies about the Messiah written in the Old Testament. Every one of them have been fulfilled in Jesus of Nazareth. The prophets claimed that He would be born of a virgin; that He would be born in Bethlehem; that He would be worshiped by wise men and presented with gifts; that his birthplace would suffer a massacre of infants; that He would speak in parables; that He would be scourged and spat upon; that a friend would betray Him for 30 pieces of silver; and that his executioners would gamble for His clothes, just to name a few. A researcher named

Philip W. Stoner figured the probability of just eight of the 48 prophesies being fulfilled in one man. The result was one chance in ten to the seventeenth power. That is a ten with seventeen zeros behind it; a number so large that it doesn't even have a name. How big of a number is ten to the seventeenth power? Well if you had that many silver dollars, you could cover the entire state of Texas in silver dollars two feet deep. Now let's look at the odds for all 48 prophesies. The odds of all 48 of the Messianic Prophesies being fulfilled in just one man is ten to the 157th power. That is a ten with 157 zeros behind it. There is no way to describe how large that number is. Yet all 48 prophesies have been fulfilled in Jesus Christ.

Belief in God makes sense because it brings out the best in us. Belief in God make us better than we would be otherwise. Life doesn't make sense unless we are moving toward God. Our hearts are truly restless until they rest in God and life only has meaning because it comes from God. We are not chance happenings and we certainly are not accidents. We are children of God created in His image and likeness. We were made by God for God and we are absolutely precious to Him.

The Trinity

The children of Israel, the Jewish people, believed in the one true God. Jesus revealed God to them as Father, Son, and Holy Spirit (John 14-17). The Apostles came to know Jesus as their "Lord and God" (John 20:28). He spoke of God as Father and even taught them to call God "Father." He promised to send the Holy Spirit to them to be their advocate.

The life of Jesus began when Mary was overshadowed by the Holy Spirit and conceived in her womb the "Son of God" (Luke 1:35). When Jesus was baptized in the Jordan River by John the Baptist, the Father's voice was heard saying, "You are my beloved Son with whom I am well pleased" (Luke 3:22). The heavens were opened and the Holy Spirit descended upon Him in the form of dove.

When we speak of Father, Son, and Holy Spirit we are referring to the Trinity. This means that there is only one God, yet in that one God there are three divine Persons—the Father, the Son, and the Holy Spirit. There is only one divine nature, but there are three divine persons.

This is a mystery that we cannot fully understand, but we can gain some insight into it. The word *person* refers to "who" we are. The word *nature* refers to "what" we are. If someone asks us, "Who are you?" we respond with our name—person. If someone asks us, "What are you?" we respond that we are human—our nature. With humans there is only one person in each human nature. God however, is three divine Persons in one divine Nature.

We believe that Jesus is the only begotten Son of the Father. This means that the Father and Son are of the same nature. When parents "beget" a child, they beget someone of the same nature as themselves. When people "make" something, they make something different. When we say that the Son is "begotten" by the Father, we profess our belief that the Son is equal to the Father, "true God from true God." When we say that the Holy Spirit "proceeds from the Father and the Son," we also express the equality of the Spirit with the Father and the Son.

Theologians have tried to offer insights into the Trinity by saying that the Father knows Himself from all eternity, and this knowledge is the Son. The Father and the Son love each other with infinite love, and this Love is the Holy Spirit. I can know myself, and this idea, or mental picture, is real. I can love myself, and this love is real. But God's knowledge is so limitless that it is a Person, the Son. The love of the Father and the Son is so limitless that it, too, is a Person, the Holy Spirit.

Jesus revealed God as a Community of love because God wants to draw us into that Community. God is Father—Creator. He created everything including us. There is a relationship in God's being that we can best understand as a "Father-Son" relationship. God the Son is therefore the second Person of the Trinity. We further learn from the Bible that God the Son is the incarnate Word of God: "In the beginning was the Word, and the Word was with God, and the Word was God…And the Word became flesh and made his dwelling among us" (John 1:1-14).

That God the Son became a human being is a miracle we call the Incarnation. The Church teaches us that Jesus has a divine nature and a human nature, united in one divine Person, the "Word." We may not fully understand this, but we do believe it.

God is Holy Spirit. We as Catholics believe that the Holy Spirit is the love eternally proceeding from the Father and Son. This means "God who loves." The Holy Spirit, then, is the cause of all that is good and loving in the world. The Holy Spirit is Love, and love is power, our source of strength as we follow Christ. Just as the Spirit descended as a dove upon Jesus at the beginning of His ministry (Matt 3:16-17), so the Spirit descends upon us to guide us. The Holy Spirit is the wind and fire which strengthened the Apostles to witness Christ. We have to open our hearts and lives to the Holy Spirit so that He can accomplish mighty deeds through us. This means that we have to be open to the promptings of the Holy Spirit. We have to be willing to do the will of God and pray that we understand what He is calling us to do each and every day.

III. God's Covenant with You

Adam and Eve

God is infinitely perfect. He is love. He did not need to create, yet He created out of love. God chose not to be self-inclusive but to be creative. The Bible says that God created everything and His creation was good (Gen 1:31). He did not create the earth because He was bored. God did not create the world because He was lonely. He created the world with one thing in mind—us. God was creating a place for us to live. He created everything with us in mind. Again, we are absolutely precious to Him (CCC 288).

The first people, Adam and Eve, were created on the 6th day along with the other animals, but they were created differently than the other animals. God created man in his own image and likeness. The Bible says that God "blew into his nostrils the breath of life" (Gen 2:7). God blew His very own Spirit; His very own life, into Adam and Eve. We call this breath of God "Grace" (CCC 375). Therefore Adam and Eve had two distinct parts to them. They had a BODY and they had a SOUL.

When the Bible says that God created man in His own Image and Likeness, it means that we are like God in that we can think and reason and make choices. It also means that we are like God in that we are capable of love. We can freely worship. We can love God and we can love one another of our own free will. No other animal is capable of loving and worshiping as man is. This sets us apart from all other earthly animals.

Adam and Eve were placed on the earth and given dominion over it. God had a plan: Adam and Eve would live on the earth for a short time and then they would be welcomed into the Heavenly Kingdom to live with God for all eternity along with their children and their children's children. Body and Soul they would enter Heaven and live for all eternity with God. But first, God needed to test their love for Him. Did they truly love God more than themselves? Did they completely trust God? Were they completely committed to Him?

He said to them, "You may eat of the fruit of any tree of the Garden, especially the Tree of Life. But of the 'Tree of Knowledge of Good and Evil' do not eat. For if you eat of it or even touch it, on the day you eat of it, you will surely die" (Gen 2:16-17). Please understand that God was their Father. They were His children. Like a good Father He was saying to them, "Trust me. Don't go near this tree and do not eat anything off of it. In fact, don't even touch it. I don't want anything bad to happen to you. Trust me to take good care of you. Stay away from that tree or you will surely die." Like a good Father, God was warning His children, whom He loved, to stay away from something that would harm them. But at the same time, He was testing their love for Him; their obedience; and devotion to Him.

Satan shows up in the garden in the form of a serpent and he tempts Adam and Eve. He lies to them and they eat of the fruit of the 'Tree of Knowledge of Good and Evil.' This is the very tree that God told them not to eat of or even touch. Satan appeared to them in the form of a serpent. Going back to the original word in Hebrew which is actually closer to the word *dragon* than serpent, some say that he would have been a very scary; very menacing; very intimidating creature. He said to Adam and Eve, "God won't let you eat of the fruit of *any* of the trees in the Garden?" Eve answered saying, "No, God only said we could not eat of the fruit of the Tree of Knowledge. For if we eat of it, we will surely die" (Gen 3:1-3).

Satan replied, "You will not die. Instead your eyes will be opened and you will become like gods and you will know what is good and what is evil" (Gen 3:4-5).

Temped with the prospects of becoming like gods, Eve gave in. She and Adam ate the fruit of this forbidden tree. This means they chose to please themselves and their own pride instead of God and His will for them. This was the first or Original Sin.

Did they die as God said they would? Or did they not die as Satan said they wouldn't? Remember, Adam and Eve were two part beings. They had a body AND they had a soul. They lived a physical life AND they lived a Spiritual Life—the Life that God had breathed into them. The truth is, Adam and Eve continued to live by their physical existence after they ate that forbidden fruit, but they experienced a spiritual death the moment they ate it. Their physical bodies did not die. No, they kept right on living, but their spiritual existence died. They lost Sanctifying Grace. The very Life of God, and the right to Heaven (CCC 375-376).

The Catechism of the Catholic Church calls this a death of the soul in paragraph 403. What do we mean by "death of the soul"? We do not mean that the soul no longer exits. We simply mean that God's Life can no longer be found in the soul. God's Life inside your soul makes your soul alive! God's Life gives light to a darkened soul. Take the Life of God from your soul and it is spiritually dead. God's Life that He had breathed into Adam and Eve; His very Life; Sanctifying Grace; was immediately gone from them. Adam and Eve were in a state of grave sin that we call Mortal Sin, which is a "death to the soul" (CCC 403). This wasn't less of a death! It was much more of a death. It is the worst kind of dying! Why? Because the part of Adam and Eve that would live forever was now dead! They desperately needed the forgiveness of God and His grace upon them.

Adam and Eve were changed because of this sin they had committed. They became like you and me. No more were they in His presence. Now they had to work for a living; they could feel pain; and their physical bodies would eventually die. They were now prone to sin and they began to sin easily doing what they know they shouldn't and not doing what they know they should.

God's plan to bring them to Heaven, body and soul was lost when they ate the forbidden fruit. On account of the sin of Adam, we come into this world without the Life of God; Sanctifying Grace, in our souls and we inherit his punishment. This sin in us is called Original Sin. Because we are born without God's Life, we need Baptism. Baptism gives us the Life of God for the very first time. Baptism removes Original Sin.

Let the Covenants Begin

The First Covenant—"One Holy Couple"

God did not stop loving Adam and Eve that day. His love is unconditional. Instead, He immediately made a promise to them. God said to the serpent, "Because you have done this, you shall be banned from all the animals and from all the wild creatures. On your belly shall you crawl, and dirt shall you eat all the days of your life. I will put enmity between you and the woman and between your offspring and hers; He will strike at your head while you strike at his heel" (Genesis 3:14-15).

Adam and Eve rejected God. They chose to love themselves more than Him. They chose to sin. God promised to save them—to redeem them. God promised that one day there would come a Woman; a Woman who would bear a Son. This Son of the Woman would come and save the people of God. The Son of the Woman would crush the head of the serpent.

This has already happened. Today, we know that, 'The Woman,' was Mary and her Son, was Jesus. This promise that God made to save His people is called the "protoevangelium" (CCC410). This was no ordinary promise. This promise was a Covenant that God made with Adam and Eve. Most people think that a "covenant" is a contract or an agreement. Please understand that a covenant is not simply a contract or an agreement in which one person promises, "I'll do this for you and you do this for me." A Covenant made with God is not a situation where God simply promises to do something for us and we promise to do something for Him in return. In a Covenant we don't just make a promise. Instead, we swear an oath! We literally swear an oath. With an oath we invoke God's name for assistance in keeping the oath and also for blessing. The person swearing the oath places himself under God's divine judgment. If the person breaks the oath, he or she is subject to a curse! God has every right to curse the person who has broken this sacred oath.

In contracts or agreements we exchange services or good. In a Covenant, we don't exchange goods and we don't exchange services. Instead, we exchange people. Instead of it being, 'you do this for me and I'll do this for you,' it is, 'YOU BELONG TO ME… AND I BELONG TO YOU.' The people swearing the oath; the ones making the covenant; create a family bond with one another. You see, they become family. A family bond cannot be broken.

So when God made this covenant with Adam and Eve, He promised; He swore, "I will be your God and you will be my people. I belong to you and you belong to Me. You will worship only Me and I will Father you. I will be your Father and take care of you as a father would take care of his children whom he loves."

So God made a covenant, a family bond with Adam and Eve. This couple belonged to Him and He belonged to them. Adam and Eve truly belonged to God's family.

Now, every Covenant has a sign. The sign of this Covenant was worship on the Sabbath Day. Adam and Eve would worship only God and they would give the Sabbath Day to God in worship.

The Second Covenant—Noah "One Holy Family"

God wanted His family to grow. Adam and Eve began to have children. They had two sons named Cain and Abel. Cain was the evil one and Abel was the good one.

Abel gave to God the best animals of his flock. Sacrifice is how God wanted them to worship Him. Sacrifice is the greatest way to show worship to God. Offering to God your very best; giving to him your very self was and is the greatest act of worship. Abel gave God the very best of his flocks in sacrifice. Cain, on the other hand, gave God only what was left of the grain of his fields, but never the best. Cain never gave himself to God in sacrifice; just his leftovers.

So God looked with favor upon Abel and his offering, but he did not look with favor upon Cain and his offering. God blessed Abel who served Him, but He did not bless Cain, who did not serve Him. God asked, "Cain, why are you so resentful and crestfallen? If you do well, you can hold up your head; but if not, sin is a demon lurking at the door: his urge is toward you, yet you can be his master" (Genesis 4:6-7). But Cain did not listen and he did not do well.

Out of envy Cain killed Abel and thus he was banished from the soil and went to live in the land of Nod, east of Eden as a wanderer. Cain's descendants followed in his wickedness and did evil things. They were not a people who worshiped God. Soon they began to populate the earth. They are referred to by many biblical scholars as the Cainites.

Adam and Eve had many other children. We are told that another son was named Seth. Seth was like Adam. He worshipped God and made sacrifices to Him. Seth's descendants were a worshiping people who "called on the name of the Lord" (Gen. 4:26). They are referred to by many biblical scholars as Sethites.

So the evil Cainite people, descendants of Cain, and the God fearing Sethite people, descendants of Seth, had to live on the earth together.

The Cainite people sinned greatly. They built cities named after themselves. They were interested in material wealth and outer beauty. They were sexually immoral and violent for one of Cain's descendants was the first to take two wives, a perversion of the order of marriage God established in the garden (Gen. 2:21-24) and boasts of his murderous, vengeful ways (Gen.4:23-34).

On the other hand, the Sethites were God fearing people. They were moral and worshipped God alone. That is, until the Sethite men came in contact with the Cainite women. The Sethite men began to marry the beautiful and irresistible Cainite women. Not only did they marry just once, they married several women, having multiple wives. Soon these Sethite men were committing the same immoral acts as the Cainite men. These Cainite women, who married the Sethite men, soon had those worshipping false gods. Violence began to fill the earth.

It wasn't long before the world was filled with wicked, wicked people. God found only one righteous man alive: A man named Noah; a descendent of Seth; Son of Adam. Noah had a wife and three sons. Each son had his own wife and children. Noah was called by God to repopulate the human race. God had decided to recreate the earth. So God wiped out all of mankind with a flood, for they were all wicked committing horrible sins, many of them sexual in nature. They worshipped false gods.

Noah and his family alone were saved from the flood and the earth was repopulated through Noah.

God was recreating the earth. He was starting over, because the people had not kept His Covenant. Through Adam and Eve they had promised to worship God alone and be His children obeying what He commanded. God had promised to be their Father and take care of them, but the people had broken this Covenant. God now made a new Covenant. God renewed the creation Covenant with Noah saying to him, "I belong to you and you belong to me. I will be your God and you will be my children. Worship only me. I will be your Father and take care of you as a father takes care of his children. Serve Me and I will bless you."

Noah, upon leaving the ark, built an altar and offered a sacrifice to God. It was an animal sacrifice and the entire family took part in eating the sacrifice offered to God. Covenant union cannot take place unless the sacrifice is eaten. The sacrifice must be offered up to God, yes. But in order to seal the covenant and create union, the sacrifice must be eaten. In this way they had communion with God. This bonded their relationship and made them family. They swore an oath to keep this Covenant with God. God placed a rainbow in the sky as a sign of this Covenant promising to never destroy the whole earth by flood again. To this day, God has kept his promise. We remember this sign of the Covenant; this sacred promise; every time we see a rainbow in the sky.

Saint Paul tells us that "The Great Flood" prefigured Baptism, which cleanses us of Original Sin. As the Great Flood rid the world of sin and made it pure again, Baptism rids our souls of Original Sin and makes us pure. This is an example of how the Old Testament foreshadows the New Testament and how the New Testament boldly fulfills the Old.

The Third Covenant—Abraham "One Holy Tribe"

God's family consisted of just one couple, Adam and Eve, who entered into Covenant with Him. Now God's family had visibly grown. Because of this Covenant with Noah, God was now the Father of an entire family: Noah, his wife and his three sons: Shem, Ham and Japheth; and their wives and children. With these three sons of Noah: Shem, Ham and Japheth, the whole earth was repopulated.

With the Cainite people destroyed, the earth would be repopulated with only God fearing people; Noah's sons, right? Wrong. Sin soon reared its ugly head in the family of Noah. You see, Noah grew grapes and made wine. On one occasion, Noah drank too much wine. The Bible tells us that he became drunk and fell deeply asleep from the effects of the alcohol. While Noah was asleep, his son Ham greatly disrespected him. In Genesis 9:22 we read that Ham looked upon "the nakedness of his father." The Bible doesn't specifically say what Ham did, but we know that he committed a grave sin. The answer lies in the idiomatic meaning of the Hebrew phrase "to look upon his nakedness," since it refers to *incest* elsewhere in the Bible (see Lev 20:17; 18:6-18).

"To look upon nakedness" refers to a very sordid act. Without going into a great amount of detail we can summarize the matter by saying that Ham committed maternal incest. Noah then cursed the fruit of that union, the boy Canaan. Noah's sons Shem and Japheth "covered the nakedness of their father" and were blessed by Noah because of this.

Ham went on to have 3 more sons and they were all wicked: Cush, Egypt, and Put. All four of these sons caused much trouble for God's people, who were the descendants of Shem.

From Put came the Philistines. From Egypt came the nation of Egypt, which held the Israelites in bondage for centuries. From Cush came the country of Babylon, Assyria, and the city of Nineveh. Babylon would one day destroy the Temple in Jerusalem and take God's people into captivity. Canaan went on to occupy the land of Canaan, which became the land that God promised to give to His people through Abraham. All of these nations of people, under the sons of Ham, worshipped false gods and made sacrifices to these false gods. These were horrible, terrible sacrifices, such as throwing babies into fire, in worship of the gods.

Soon the earth was again being populated with wicked, wicked people. The good news however, was that Shem's people, the Shemites (where we get Semites), loved God and worshiped him. They kept God's Covenant. They served God and He blessed them. Shem was granted the blessing of living 500 years and some believe that Shem was none other than the High Priest Melkisedek, the King of Salem, who gave a blessing to Abraham using bread and wine. This blessing was a foreshadowing of Jesus, the High Priest, who gives us the blessing of Himself in the Eucharist using bread and wine. This is another example of how the Old Testament foreshadows the New Testament and how the New Testament boldly fulfills the Old.

God then called Shem's great, great, great, great, great grandson, a man named Abram, saying to him: "I will make your name great; so great that you will be a blessing, and by you all the families of the earth shall be blessed." God told Abram: "I will take you, (a seventy-five-year-old man), and use you to bless all of the families on earth."

God gave Abram three promises: First, God promised to give Abram his own land; a land where his people would serve God (Hence—"The Promised Land"). Second, God promised to make Abram's name great; to make of him a great nation.

Abram's descendants would become a royal power; a Kingdom that would rule other nations. And third, <u>God promised to bless all the families of the earth through Abram</u>. Through one of Abram's descendants, world-wide blessing would take place. That descendant would of course be Jesus.

But there was a problem. Abram had no children. He had only a wife named Sarah, but he had no descendants. How could Abram's descendants be so great in number that they would become a royal power, when he didn't even have one child? Just the same, God called Abram to leave his rich, powerful city and go to a land he had never seen. God called Abram to leave his people; to leave his real estate holdings; to leave his possessions; and come to a land he had never seen before. And Abram obeyed. Now that is Faith! And this is why Abraham is called, 'Our Father in Faith' today.

God raised each of these promises to a much higher level. He raised them to be Covenants. You see, each promise became a separate Covenant. Abram promised to serve only God and obey Him. God promised to be his God and the God of his tribesmen. God would be their Father and they would be His children. They would serve God and He would bless them.

Abram offered sacrifice to God. Abram's people ate of the sacrifice communing with God. Again, covenant union cannot take place unless the sacrifice is eaten. The sacrifice must be offered up to God, but in order to seal the covenant and create union, the sacrifice must be eaten. In this way they had communion with God. This bonded them as family. And like the Covenants beforehand with Adam and Eve and the Sabbath Day worship and with Noah and the Rainbow, this Covenant also had a sign. The sign of this Covenant was **Circumcision**. Every male member of the tribe had to be circumcised in order to enter into this Covenant with God. Men of all ages, even in their 20's, 30's, 40's, 50's, even 90 years of age, had to be circumcised in order to enter into this Covenant with God. Even children and babies entered into this Covenant with God. Abram's tribe began to circumcise their babies on the 8th day after their birth to show that the child indeed belonged to God.

This circumcision was a visible sign that a person belonged to God's family. It meant that he had entered into this Covenant with God; that he had sworn an oath. Every male who wanted to become part of God's family had to be circumcised. Through this Covenant, Abram's name was changed to Abraham.

Look how God's family had grown. First God's family consisted of just two people, Adam and Eve. Then through the Covenant with Noah, God's family grew to the size of a family: Noah, his wife, his sons, his son's wives, and their children. Now through Abraham, God's family has grown to the size of a tribe. A tribe is made up of many families. Abraham's entire tribe entered into this Covenant with God. God was their Father and they were His sons and daughters. They served God and God blessed them.

The Fourth Covenant—Moses "One Holy Nation"

Abraham's family became a great nation through his son Isaac. Yes, finally, Abraham and Sarah had a son. Now God's promises could come true since Abraham had a descendant. First, God tested Abraham's love for Him. Did Abraham truly love God? Did he truly trust God? Was he obedient to God? God wanted to know. So He told Abraham to take his only son, Isaac, to the top of a mountain, called Moriah, and sacrifice him. God told Abraham to kill his own son in sacrifice to Him.

How in the world are God's promises of Land; a huge nation of descendants; and worldwide blessing; going to happen if Abraham kills Isaac in sacrifice to God? Still, Abraham obeyed. Abraham gave the wood, the wood that his only son would be sacrificed upon, to Isaac to carry up the mountain. Isaac carried the wood up Mount Moriah and asked Abraham, "Father, we have the fire and we have the wood, but what will be the sacrifice?" Abraham answered, "God alone will provide the Lamb."

Abraham built an altar and piled the wood upon it. Then he tied Isaac to that wood; the wood of the sacrifice. Just as he was about to kill his only son with a knife, Abraham heard the voice of God say, "Do not lay your hand on the boy. I know now how you are devoted to Me." And just then, Abraham spied a ram caught in the thicket. God had provided the sacrifice. It was a ram, however, not a lamb. Remember that. Remember that God did not provide a lamb for the sacrifice, at least not yet.

Abraham had passed the test. This was the same test that Adam and Eve had failed. Abraham was willing to sacrifice his only son, Isaac. This sacrifice in the Old Testament foreshadows the sacrifice of Jesus in the New Testament. Let's see how.

First, Abraham was called to sacrifice his only Son, Isaac— God did sacrifice His only Son, Jesus. Second, Isaac willingly carried the wood of the sacrifice up the hill—Jesus willingly carried the wood of His sacrifice, the cross, up the hill of Calvary. Third, the hill that Isaac climbed was part of a mountain chain called Mount Moriah—Two thousand years later, Jesus climbed the hill of Calvary. Calvary was part of the same mountain chain of Mount Moriah. Finally, Abraham told Isaac that God would provide the Lamb for the Sacrifice—Jesus is the Lamb—the Lamb of God, that God provided as a sacrifice for the sins of the world in order to redeem you and me from all sin.

Here is yet another example of how the Old Testament foreshadows the New Testament. Abraham sacrificing his only son, Isaac, was the foreshadowing of God sacrificing His only son, Jesus.

Isaac married and fathered two sons: Esau and Jacob. They were twin boys. Esau was supposed to have his father's blessing passed on to him, because he was actually born first; a few minutes before Jacob. Isaac was supposed to bless Esau and Esau would be the priest of the family. But Esau traded his blessing to Jacob for a meal. He traded his blessing for food! How did this happen? Jacob was boiling pottage one day when Esau came in from the field famished. Esau said to Jacob, "Let me eat some of that pottage for I am famished!" Jacob said, "First sell me your birthright." Esau replied, "I am about to die of hunger, what use is a birthright to me?" Jacob said, "Swear to me first." So Esau swore it to him and thus sold his birthright to Jacob. Then Jacob gave Esau bread and pottage of lentils, and he ate and drank, and rose and went his way (Gen 25:29-34). Thus Esau carelessly traded his blessing for a meal. Esau cared much more about his stomach than he did his birth right. This was very foolish of him.

Several years later, when Isaac was very old and was about to die, his son, Jacob, and his mother, Rebecca, tricked Isaac into blessing Jacob instead of Esau. Rebecca favored Jacob, so she had him dress up as Esau and pretend to be him. You see, Esau was very harry, so Jacob dressed in animal skins so that his arms would feel harry to the touch. Isaac was completely blind and therefore could only feel his son; he could not actually see him. Isaac gave the blessing to Jacob thinking that he was really his first born son, Esau. When Esau found out that Isaac blessed Jacob instead of him, he was furious! Out of fear, Jacob ran away. He went to live with his mother's uncle in the northern country. It was there that he went through many trials, married several women, and fathered 12 sons. (See Gen. 27-33)

Jacob's 12 sons: Reuben, Simeon, Levi, Judah, Zebulon, Issachar, Dan, Naphtali, Gad, Asher, Joseph, and Benjamin became known as the 12 Tribes of Israel or the Israelites. This is because God changed Jacob's name to Israel and from his twelve sons came the twelve tribes. Jesus is a descendent of the Tribe of Judah. These 12 sons of Jacob (or Israel) and their wives and their children become the children of Israel; the chosen people; the Israelites; the Jews.

Remember the story of "Joseph and the coat of many colors"? Joseph, one of the youngest brothers, was sold into slavery in Egypt by his older brothers. They were jealous of Joseph because he was Jacob's favorite son. This was because Joseph was the son of Jacob's true love, Rachel. Joseph kept having these annoying dreams, in which his brothers would bow down to him, as if he were a king. The brothers were so angry with Joseph that they wanted him dead. Instead of killing Joseph, they sold him to an Ishmaelite tribe. Joseph was then taken to Egypt. Eventually he was placed in prison after being accused of a crime he did not commit. (See Gen. 37-40)

While in prison in Egypt, Joseph showed that he had a talent for interpreting dreams. He was asked to interpret the dreams of the Pharaoh. By interpreting the Pharaoh's dream, Joseph saved the people of Egypt from the devastating effects of a great famine. Through Pharaoh' dream, Joseph predicted that there would be seven years of great abundance, followed by seven years of famine. Believing Joseph to be correct, the Kingdom began saving food through the years of great abundance. This way there would be plenty to eat when the seven years of famine struck. Sure enough, things happened just as Joseph said they would. Because of this, Joseph was made the "Steward" of the entire Kingdom.

When the famine broke out, Jacob (Israel) sent his sons to Egypt to seek food from the Steward. They were starving and needed the Steward's help. Jacob's sons had no idea that the Steward of the Kingdom was none other than Joseph, their brother. They thought Joseph was dead. When the brothers came to Egypt to see the Steward, they stood before Joseph. Joseph recognized them as his brothers, but the brothers did do not recognize Joseph. The brothers bowed down to the Steward, Joseph. Joseph then revealed who he was and forgave his brothers. Thus his dream of his brothers bowing before him came to be. They left to fetch their father, Jacob, and the entire people came to live in Egypt.

Now the 12 Tribes of Israel, made of the 12 sons of Israel (or Jacob), were all living in Egypt. They were getting larger and larger and larger. They served God and God blessed them greatly. They kept the Covenant that their Great Grandfather, Abraham, had begun.

Over time, a new Pharaoh seized control of Egypt. This Pharaoh did not know Joseph. He did not care about what he had done in the past. This new Pharaoh felt threatened by the Israelite people. They were growing too great in number. He wondered, "What if they decide to take over my kingdom?" He felt that they owned too much land! The Pharaoh decided that he wanted their land! So this Pharaoh decided to make the Israelite people his slaves.

For 400 years the Israelite people were slaves to the Egyptians. In those 400 years, the Israelites forgot how to worship God. They made no animal sacrifices to God; they forgot God. They even adopted the ways of the Egyptians by worshiping false gods. The Egyptians had many false gods such as frogs, the Nile River, the sun, and many animals. Pharaoh wanted the Israelite women to marry the Egyptian men, so he ordered that the first born sons of the Israelite people be put to death. If he destroyed their male children, the Israelite girls would grow up and have to marry Egyptian men.

One Israelite son was saved from death. His mother put him in a basket and floated him down the Nile River, while his sister watched from the bank. That child was Moses. Moses was raised by Pharaoh's very own daughter and grew up in the palace. Eventually he had to flee Egypt after killing an Egyptian who was beating a Hebrew slave.

Moses fled to the desert, where he met a man named Jethro, who had many daughters. Moses became a herdsman and married one of Jethro's daughters. After forty years, God called Moses out of the desert to return to Egypt and set His people free so they could go and worship Him with sacrifice. (See Exodus 1-3)

You know the story. Moses pleaded with Pharaoh, but he would not let God's people go. Despite 9 plagues sent by God, Pharaoh would not allow the Israelites to go and worship the one true God. Finally, the 10th plague brought the death of the first born sons of the Egyptians and Pharaoh let God's people go free to worship Him.

The events of the tenth plague are extremely important to us and the details of the sacrifice that saved the Israelites from death and slavery in Egypt are even more important. The Israelite people were given exact instructions by God as to what they were supposed to do. God instructed the people, through Moses, to take an unblemished, one-year-old, male lamb; perfect; without flaw; and sacrifice it. They were to spread its blood on the doorposts and lintels of their homes using a hyssop branch. They were to roast its flesh and eat every bit of the sacrifice with bitter herbs, unleavened bread, and wine. And if they did this, the Angel of death, seeing the blood on the wood of their doors, would PASS OVER their homes.

However, upon seeing no blood on the doorposts and lintels of the Egyptian homes, the Angel of Death would not pass over. It would instead enter the homes of the Egyptians and the first born would become sick and die.

That is exactly what happened. The blood of the sacrificed one-year-old, perfect male Lamb saved God's people from death, but the first born of the Egyptians were slain. It was then that Pharaoh let God's people go.

God said to His people, "YOU MUST KEEP THIS FEAST!" Each year they must do this again. They must obtain an unblemished Lamb, roast and eat its flesh with bitter herbs and unleavened bread and wine. They must keep this feast telling their children how the blood of the Lamb saved them from death. They would not just remember, but instead make these events present as a biblical, liturgical memorial. It would be the representation of the past event so that the current generation could benefit from its saving action. It would be, for future generations, as if they were walking out of Egypt hand in hand with their ancestor from the past. The Passover became the greatest Jewish Feast.

Moses then led the Israelites out of Egypt and into the desert where they crossed the Red Sea and settled at the base of Mount Sinai. It was here that Moses received the Ten Commandments from God. The people entered into a Covenant with God promising to keep the laws of the Covenant. They even declared, "All that the Lord says, we will heed and do." The whole Israelite people entered into a Covenant with God. Moses sacrificed young bulls and the people put on clean white garments and sanctified themselves. They swore an oath to obey God; to be His people; to worship only Him. God promised to be their God; to be their very own Father. They would belong to God and He would belong to them. They would serve God and He would bless them. God would even dwell in their midst and lead them to the promise land! The people ate of the sacrifice communing with God. Again, covenant union cannot take place unless the sacrifice is eaten. The sacrifice must be offered up to God, but in order to seal the covenant and create union with God, the sacrifice must be eaten. In this way they had communion with God. This formed a family bond.

So Moses went back up the mountain. He went up the mountain to receive the stone tablets of the 10 Commandments from God and to receive instruction from God on how to build the Ark of the Covenant and the Tabernacle that God would dwell in. You see, God was going to LIVE with His people. He was going to "Tabernacle" with them; a Hebrew word meaning to "tent" a dwelling.

Moses was gone for an entire month. When Moses came back down the mountain, he found that the people had taken their gold; melted it; and created a golden calf to be their god. They were worshiping it and shouting, "This is the god who brought us out of Egypt!" Moses couldn't believe it! He was gone only a month and the people went right back to their old ways of worshiping false gods. It was certainly easier to take the people out of Egypt, than to take Egypt out of the people.

God said to Moses, "I will destroy these people with a flick of my hand. Then I will make of you, Moses, a great nation." These are the same words that God spoke to Abraham. You see, God was so upset that the people were worshiping a false god; so upset that they had broken the Covenant in just one month; that He was ready to start all over again. But Moses talked God out of punishing the people. He reminded God that these Israelites were truly His very own people and asked God to give them another chance. Of course God relented in His punishment. In his pleading with God, Moses proved to God that he was worthy of leading the people and not interested in making a name for himself.

Even though God relented in His punishment, He did say, however, that He would no longer dwell with the people, but would instead send an angel to guide them. Again, Moses begged God to stay and dwell with the people saying that it was God's presence with them that made this people different. Moses then had the Tabernacle built, which housed the Ark of the Covenant.

Inside the Ark of the Covenant, God would dwell. God then led the Israelites through the desert as a cloud during the day and as a pillar of fire by night. God's presence was truly with them. He was inside that Tabernacle. He was inside the Ark they had built and they carried it wherever they went. And how was God present inside the Ark? He was present in the stone tablets of the Ten Commandments that He had written with His mighty hand. He was present in the urn of Manna that was kept in the Ark. Remember that God fed His people, the Israelites, with bread or manna that fell from the sky. Each morning when they awoke the Israelites filled their baskets with this manna. In the tabernacle was kept an urn of this bread; manna. God was also present in the "Rod of Aaron." The Rod of Aaron was the rod that the High Priest, Aaron, used. Even though it was just a staff, it budded as if it were still alive. This is the staff or rod used by Moses to part the Red Sea. So you see God dwelled inside the Tabernacle. Moses said, "This is what sets us apart as a Nation. This is how we are different. God's presence is truly with us."

This is another example of how the Old Testament foreshadows the New Testament and how the New Testament fulfills the Old. God's true presence with the Israelites was a foreshadowing of How Jesus would be present in bodily form to us as Catholics. God dwells in the Tabernacle inside each Catholic Church. Jesus is truly present in our Tabernacle under the appearance of bread. Like the Israelites, this is one thing that sets us as Catholics apart from every other people of the World. God is present in our Tabernacle in Body, Blood, Soul and Divinity and not just in spirit.

God led the Israelites to the Land of Canaan, the land that He promised to give Abraham. There followed a period of conquests with the twelve tribes settling in various parts of Canaan. They fought with the inhabitants (Philistines and others) through a "frontier period" called the time of the Judges.

Moses died on the border of the Promised Land, and his lieutenant, Joshua, led the people into Canaan. The name *Joshua* means 'savior' or 'the salvation of the Lord.' Joshua led the people into the Promised Land, the land promised to God's chosen people. The name *Jesus* is the same name as Joshua. They sound different because the name *Joshua* has been translated from Hebrew into English (Yeshua to Joshua) and the name *Jesus* has been translated from Hebrew into Greek and then into English (Yeshua to Iesous to Jesus). Therefore the name *Jesus* means 'savior' or 'the salvation of the Lord' as well. Jesus leads us into the New Promised Land, the land of eternal life promised by God—Heaven. This is another example of how the Old Testament foreshadows the New and how the New fulfills the Old.

God's family had now grown from just a holy couple: Adam and Eve; to a family: through the Covenant with Noah; to a tribe: through Abraham; to a nation of people: under Moses. God's family was getting much, much bigger.

The Fifth Covenant—David: "One Holy Kingdom"

Next God's people grew to the size a Kingdom. Their first king was Saul; their second king was David; and their third king was Solomon, David's son. First, Soul was anointed king and began to bring the tribes together. He eventually went insane and was killed in a battle with the Philistines. David was the next anointed king. David united the 12 tribes, set up Jerusalem as the center of his government, defeated the enemies of the Israelites, and made Israel a force to be reckoned with in the Middle East. His son, Solomon, succeeded him as king and built a magnificent temple in Jerusalem. The Tabernacle that contained God; the Ark of the Covenant that the Israelites had carried with them through the desert and into the Promised Land; was in this Temple once it was built by Solomon.

In order to get the temple built in Jerusalem, Solomon had to make alliances with other nations of people. This was because he needed workers and building materials. Every time he made an alliance with a new nation, Solomon ended up getting another wife in the deal. King Solomon had over 500 wives! Most of these wives worshipped false gods. These wives, and their influence, led Solomon to worship false gods as well.

When the king worships false gods, the people begin to worship false gods also. This led to many problems including the withdrawal of God's blessing. God's people were united under King David. They stayed united under David's son, King Solomon. After the death of King Solomon however, a civil war ensued and the tribes split while Rehoboam was king. Ten tribes split to the north and made up the Northern Kingdom of Israel with its capital in Samaria. Two tribes split to the south and made up the Southern Kingdom of Judah with its capital in Jerusalem. New kings began to reign in the two kingdoms. Sometimes they were good kings, who led the people in worshiping the one true God. Sometimes they were very bad kings, who led the people into worshiping false gods.

A cycle began to emerge. First, the people would begin to worship false gods. When that happened, God would withdrawal His blessing from them. When bad things happened because of the withdrawal of God's blessing, the people would pray and ask God to help them. God would then send them a 'Judge' to guide them and get them back on the right track of worshiping Him. The people would then worship God and He would in turn bless them. When things got better because of God's blessing, the people would fall back, start the cycle all over again, and begin to worship false gods again. After all, who needs God when things are going well? Then God would withdraw His blessing once again and the whole thing would start over.

Finally in 721 the Northern Kingdom was captured by the Assyrians and taken up into Assyria where they were exiled from God's presence. In 587 the Southern Kingdom of Judah was captured by the Babylonians and taken into exile to Babylon. The Babylonians destroyed the Temple in Jerusalem. Before they did, the Ark of the Covenant was taken out of the Temple and hidden in a cave. God's people no longer possessed the Ark. God no longer dwelled with His people.

The Northern Kingdom stayed in exile. They never did return to the Promised Land. But eventually, when Persia captured Babylon, the Emperor, Cyrus, allowed the people of the Southern Kingdom to return to Jerusalem in 539 and rebuild the temple that had been destroyed. Their hopes of regaining the glory of King David, however, were doomed to disappointment. Alexander the Great conquered Palestine in 332. After Alexander's death, Egypt and Syria struggled for control of the Jewish nation, and in about 200 the Syrians launched a terrible persecution of the Jews. In 167 a family of warriors, the Maccabees, led a revolt against the Syrians and succeeded in gaining independence in 142. This lasted until 63 when the Romans conquered Jerusalem and made Palestine a vassal state (independent in internal affairs, but subordinate in foreign affairs). In 37 Herod the Great was set up by the Romans as king. It was under his rule that Jesus Christ was born.

Even though the Jews had returned to Jerusalem and rebuilt the Temple there, the Ark of the Covenant remained hidden far away and was never returned to the Temple. This means that God's presence was no longer with His people. He was not with them in the Tabernacle. All the way to the time of Jesus, God was not present with His people. That is, until Jesus came.

The New and Everlasting Covenant—Jesus

Jesus is called Emanuel, which means "God with us." When Jesus came, God was present with His people again.

At the Last Supper, Jesus began a new and final Covenant. Understand this very clearly. So far God made a Covenant with Adam and Eve "one holy couple." Then God made another Covenant with Noah, and God's family grew to the size of an entire family: Noah, his wife, his 3 sons, his son's wives, and his sons' children. Then through Noah's son Shem, God made a Covenant with Abraham, Shem's great, great, great grandson and his entire tribe. Through Abraham's son Isaac and Isaac's son Jacob, who had 12 sons, God made a Covenant with an entire nation of people. God changed Jacob's name to Israel. The 12 sons of Israel (Jacob) became the 12 tribes of Israel (the Israelites). They later became slaves in Egypt. Through Moses, God rescued his people from slavery with the blood of the Passover Lamb and led this nation through the desert to the "Promised Land." This Nation of Israel grew into a united kingdom, under King David. Because they were not completely faithful to the Lord, this kingdom divided. Each kingdom was captured separately and taken into exile. The Southern Kingdom of Judah did return to the Promised Land. They rebuilt the temple. Generations later, a 'Woman', the promised woman by God, was visited by an angel. Her name was Mary.

God was ready to extend His invitation to Covenant with Him, to the entire world. No longer would God make a Covenant with just the Israelites. Now God was inviting the entire world to be part of His very own family by entering this New and Everlasting or Eternal Covenant with Him. Please understand that God invites you and me and everyone in the entire world into His Covenant today. This Covenant is the Church.

At the Last Supper Jesus began this new Covenant: this New and Eternal Covenant; inviting the whole world to be children of God. What would the sacrifice of the Covenant be? This time God Himself provided the sacrifice. This time God Himself *was* the sacrifice. Remember what Abraham said, "God Himself will provide the Lamb." This New and Eternal Sacrifice is sealed with the Blood of the Lamb; the Blood of the Lamb of God. Jesus was and is this New Covenant Sacrifice.

You see, at the Last supper, Jesus and His disciples were celebrating Passover and partaking in the Passover Meal. At the Last Supper, Jesus and His disciples were celebrating that same memorial feast God had commanded that His people celebrate each year; the memorial of the time when the Angel of Death passed over the homes of the Israelites upon seeing the blood of the sacrificed unblemished; perfect male lamb—the Passover Lamb. At the Last Supper, Jesus proclaimed: This is the New Passover Meal. I am the sacrifice; I am the Lamb. It is My Blood that will save you from death. I am the Lamb that God will provide fulfilling what He said to Abraham, "I myself will provide the lamb".

Jesus is the Lamb; the sacrifice of this New and Eternal covenant. What did the people have to do at the Passover meal so long ago in order to enter the Old Covenant; in order to be saved from the Angel of Death? They had to kill and eat a lamb. They had to eat the flesh of the Lamb that saved them. They had to eat the sacrifice. Here is another example. The New Testament is fulfilling the Old Testament. Jesus is taking what happened in the Old Testament to a new and bolder level. The lamb of the Passover Supper saved the Israelites from slavery and death in Egypt. Jesus, the Lamb of God, saves us from slavery to sin and death in Hell. The lamb of the Passover Supper gave them life in the Promised Land. Jesus, the Lamb of God, gives us life in the New Promised Land… Heaven!

Each of us is invited to enter this New and Eternal Covenant with God for the New Eternal Covenant is the Church. We are invited to enter into a family relationship with God. He wants to be our very own Father and He wants us to be His very own children. In order to enter this Covenant, we must keep the laws of the Covenant. We must not turn our backs on God. We must give ourselves to Him fully. We must put Him first in our lives. We must open up to Him fully. And yes, we must obey the terms of the Covenant. We serve God and in turn, God blesses us.

How do you and I enter into this Covenant with God that is the Church? How do we become God's very own children? We enter it when we are baptized. If you were baptized as a baby, your parents spoke for you. You did not say that you wanted to enter the Covenant. It was done for you. Baptism washes away Original Sin and any sins we have committed. We promise that we will love God with our whole heart and soul and try to please Him in everything.

In Confirmation, however, those who were baptized as infants have the chance to enter the Covenant themselves of their own Free Will. They have the chance to speak for themselves and tell God that they truly want to be His very own child and want Him to be their very own Father. They have the opportunity to 'confirm' what their parents began for them.

As Catholics, we continue with this Covenant every time we receive the Sacraments. The first is Baptism. We cannot receive any other sacraments until we are baptized, but the rest soon follow. To stay in God's Covenant, we must strive for holiness; obey the commandments; become like Jesus. We need help with this. We need lots of help if we are going to lead a holy life. Every sacrament puts the very LIFE of God inside of us and therefore helps to make us holy. We need the sacraments in order to live in a covenant relationship with God. Confirmation seals our baptism; marks us as a witness for Christ; and gives to us the full outpouring of the Holy Spirit. This is a powerful strength that we have with us the rest of our lives. So we call on it often and use it to help us lead a holy life and reach Heaven. We will discuss these sacraments more in depth at a later time.

Jesus Established the Church

Jesus established His Church. There is no salvation without Jesus. No one gets to the Father without first going through the Son, Jesus. There is no going through Jesus without going through His Church. We cannot separate Jesus from His Church. So understand that salvation comes to us through Jesus; through His Church (CCC457).

Jesus Commissioned 12 men at the Last Supper to take His Church to the entire world. Those 12 men were the Apostles. Jesus educated these 12 men. He chose one to be the head. They understood very well what Jesus wanted; they understood very well what Jesus taught; they understood very well the purpose of the Church.

In the Gospels, Jesus spoke; acted; traveled; taught; lived; suffered; died; arose from the dead; and ascended into Heaven. Every single word He spoke and every single thing He did however, was not written in the Bible. In the Gospel of Mark Chapter 4 verse 34 it says, "Jesus taught the crowds using parables and without parables He did not speak to them, but to His own disciples, He explained everything in private." So understand that these twelve men were taught everything privately by Jesus and they understood well. What Jesus taught them in private is not written in the Bible for us to read. Jesus prepared them to bring His salvation to the world; to spread His Church to all nations.

If we read John 16: 12-14 Jesus says to His Apostles: "I have much more to tell you, but you cannot bear it now. But when the Holy Spirit comes, He will guide you to all Truth. He will not speak on His own, but He will speak what He hears, and will declare to you the things that are coming." Here we understand that Jesus did not speak everything even to His disciples even before He died, but sent the Holy Spirit to guide these twelve men as they began the Church. Therefore it is the truth, the absolute truth, that our faith, as we believe it and understand it today, was revealed to us by Jesus Christ. Jesus commissioned the 12 Apostles to lead His Church and those 12 men were guided and literally led by the Holy Spirit. Jesus chose Peter to be the head of the Apostles. Peter was the first Pope (CCC816).

The end of God's revelation to us; the end of God telling us anything new about Himself or about salvation; came with the death of the last Apostle. The last Apostle to die was John. There are no more covenants and there will never be any more covenants. Jesus established the last covenant at the Last Supper and invites the entire world to enter into it. "Then he took the cup, gave thanks and gave it to them saying, 'Drink from it all of you for this is my blood of the covenant, which will be shed on behalf of many for the forgiveness of sins.'" (Matthew 26:27-28) "And likewise the cup after they had eaten, saying, 'This cup is the new covenant in my blood, which will be shed for you.'" (Luke 22:20) "He said to them, 'This is my blood of the covenant, which will be shed for many'" (Mark 14:24) (CCC75).

IV.   Jesus, Present in His Apostles; Present in His Word; Present in His Church

The New Covenant—The Kingdom of God is at Hand

Jesus began His teaching with the words: "This is the time of fulfillment. The kingdom of God is at hand. Repent and believe in the gospel" (Mark 1:15). Jesus went to Nazareth where He had grown up and entered the synagogue on the Sabbath day. He stood up to read and a scroll of the Prophet Isaiah was handed to Him. He opened it and read the Scripture that clearly referred to Himself saying, "The Spirit of the Lord is upon me, because He has anointed Me to bring glad tidings to the poor. He has sent Me to proclaim liberty to captives and recovery of sight to the blind, to let the oppressed go free, and to proclaim a year acceptable to the Lord." Rolling up the scroll, He handed it back to the attendant and sat down, and the eyes of all in the synagogue looked intently at Him. He said to them, "Today this Scripture passage is fulfilled in your hearing" (Luke 4:16-21).

The Kingdom of God was indeed at hand. Jesus was establishing the New Eternal Covenant; His Church. God's plan for us had far surpassed that of human hope. The New Covenant would change the course of history. The time of the fulfillment of the promise made to Adam and Eve in the garden was coming to pass. God became a member of the human family, born of the woman promised in Genesis chapter three, and sent to crush the head of the serpent. Jesus had come to die for our sins and reconcile us with the Father, so that God's life could be placed into the souls of men once again, making us holy and capable of eternal life with Him.

Jesus taught in Parables

Jesus was a gifted teacher. He told wonderful stories which vividly illustrated important truths about the Kingdom of God; His Church. Jesus taught that the Kingdom of God is like a hidden treasure or a pearl of great price. It is more valuable than anything (Matt 13:44-46). To embrace the Kingdom of God and allow it to lead you through life is likened to a man who builds his house on solid rock (Matt 7:24-27). We live the Kingdom of God by seeking God's mercy like the humble tax collector and not like the proud Pharisee (Luke 18:9-14). We must accept His Word like fertile soil accepts a seed and allows it to grow (Matt 13:1-23).

Jesus proclaimed that the time of mercy was at hand. He called us to repent of our sins and turn to God for forgiveness. Jesus taught that God welcomed us back into His loving arms like the gentle father who welcomed back his prodigal son. God is like the Good Shepherd who leaves the 99 in search of the one lost sheep. And when He finds it, He rejoices! This mercy is ours for the asking, but we must also share this mercy with others. Our model is the Good Samaritan, who cared for the injured man when others passed him by (Luke 10:25-37). We cannot accept mercy from God and then deny it to one another as the servant did in the "Parable of the Unforgiving Servant" (Matt 18:23-35).

Jesus taught that the Kingdom of God cannot be destroyed. As a mustard seed, the smallest of all seeds, grows into a large bush, so the seed of the Church planted by Christ will grow sturdy and strong and many will rest in its branches. Even when the enemy sows weeds in the wheat, the crop will continue to grow and will be harvested just the same. The wheat will be taken to the barn while the weeds are bundled for burning (Matt 13: 24-30).

Jesus was and is calling us to turn toward Him and accept the gospel; the Kingdom of God; the Church. The Kingdom of God must become what is most important in our lives. We do not want to be like the five foolish bridesmaids who are invited to a wedding but do not have enough oil for their lamps (Matt 25:1-13). We are invited to the banquet of Heaven and Jesus urges us to accept the invitation (Matt 22:1-14).

Jesus Gave the Sermon on the Mount (Matthew Chapters 5-7)

Jesus begins His sermon on the mount with the "Beatitudes." The values of the secular world are literally turned on their ears: "Blessed are the Poor in Spirit for theirs is the Kingdom of God; Blessed are they who mourn for they will be comforted; Blessed are the meek for they will inherit the earth; Blessed are they who hunger and thirst for righteousness for they will be satisfied; Blessed are the merciful for they will be shown mercy; Blessed are the clean of heart for they will see God; Blessed are the peacemakers for they will be called children of God; Blessed are they who are persecuted for the sake of righteousness for theirs is the Kingdom of God; Blessed are you when they insult you and persecute you and utter every kind of evil falsely against you because of me. Rejoice and be glad for your reward will be great in Heaven."

These teachings were completely counter cultural then and remain so today. Jesus was not afraid to make serious moral demands and asked that we not turn away from these demands, but embrace them. We can overcome our tendency to sin; to become angry; to lust. We can treat others the way we want to be treated and even learn to love our enemies. We can be faithful in our marriages and generous to the poor. We can imitate God with the help of the Kingdom: Jesus and His Church.

In the Lord's Prayer, Jesus taught us to call God "Our Father." In it we ask for the grace to do God's will, so that it will be done here on earth through us, as it is done in Heaven. We place our lives in His very hands asking for daily needs; "our daily bread," but this is also a reference to the Eucharist, our "spiritual daily bread." We ask for forgiveness of our sins, but only as we forgive others. And we pray for the grace to overcome the temptations of this world.

In the Sermon on the Mount, Jesus boldly calls us to put God first in our lives. If God is not first in our lives, there will be no room for Him at all. He assures us that God is present in our lives at every moment. He is not a passive observer.

Jesus Worked Many Miracles

Jesus worked many miracles that had no natural explanation. These signs attracted large numbers of people who flocked to see Him. Some wanted to simply witness the signs. Others came to be recipients of His mercy. Because all things were created in Him and through Him, Jesus had great power over the material world. He changed water into wine; walked on water; calmed a storm; multiplied bread and fish enough to feed over 5,000. Jesus cured the sick, the lame, and the blind. He even brought the dead back to life. In working these miracles Jesus brought God's great love to the people and in the process demonstrated His great power.

Jesus Returns to Heaven to Guide His Church

After Jesus' death and Resurrection, He appeared to his Apostles numerous times in the course of a forty day period. They were ready to spread the Kingdom of God. The news of Christ's Resurrection was too good to keep to themselves. The

Apostles had been called to be the "light of the world." We do not light a lamp and then put it under a bushel basket. Instead it is set on a lampstand, where it gives light to all in the house (Matt 5:15). So too the Apostles were called to spread the Kingdom of God to all the nations. They could not keep their excitement hidden.

Jesus promised to always be with them and then ascended into Heaven in their presence. He said to them, "All power in Heaven and on earth has been given to me. Go, therefore, and make disciples of all nations, baptizing them in the name of the Father, and of the Son, and of the Holy Spirit, teaching them to observe all that I have commanded you. And behold, I am with you always, until the end of the age" (Matt 28:18-20).

Jesus promised to be with His Apostles always. He ascended into Heaven and is now seated at the right hand of the Father. This tells us that Jesus is truly God and is no longer limited by space or time. He is now where God is—everywhere (CCC 659-667).

After the Ascension, the Apostles returned to Jerusalem and gathered in the upper room with Mary, the Mother of Jesus, and the other disciples. They prayed and waited for the coming of the Holy Spirit, whom Jesus had promised to send (Luke 24:49; Acts 1:8). And so it happened on the day of Pentecost, a Jewish feast day, tongues of fire appeared, parted, and came to rest on each one of them and they were filled with the Holy Spirit. No longer timid and afraid, the Apostles came forth to preach to the crowds who had gathered in Jerusalem for the feast.

Peter proclaimed that Jesus was the long awaited Messiah; the fulfillment of the Old Testament prophesies. He told the people to repent and be baptized in the name of Jesus for the forgiveness of their sins and promised that they too would receive the Holy Spirit. With that 3,000 Jews were baptized that day.

Spreading the faith came with many trials. When Peter and John healed a crippled man in Jesus' name, they were arrested and told to stop preaching in the name of Jesus. This did not stop them. They proclaimed that they must obey God rather than the Jewish authority.

As the Apostles continued to proclaim Jesus as the Messiah, the number of believers continued to grow, but so did the opposition. A deacon named Stephen was executed. He became the first Christian martyr. Saul, the overseer of this murder, was trying to destroy the Church. He was entering houses and dragging out men and women to be handed over to the authorities for imprisonment. On his way to Damascus to arrest the followers of Jesus there, Saul was struck by a sudden bright light and blinded. He heard the words of Jesus ask him, "Saul, why are you persecuting Me?" For when Saul persecuted the Church, he persecuted Christ Himself, who cannot be separated from His Church. Saul was converted and became Paul the instrument that Jesus used to bring the Gospel to the Gentiles.

The Good News of the gospel was preached to Jews and Gentiles alike. People were being converted in the towns in all directions spreading out from Jerusalem. Another persecution broke out in 44 A.D., started by Herod Agrippa, who was the ruler of Judea. He killed the Apostle James, the son of Zebedee and arrested Peter. The people prayed to God on Peter's behalf and he miraculously escaped from prison by the help of an angel.

Despite these trials, the Apostles continued to preach and Christians continued to grow in number. They were gradually moving away from their Jewish ties because of the persecution against them and because so many Jews refused to accept Jesus as the Savior. After Herod's death in 44 A.D., Paul and Barnabus were sent by the church at Antioch to preach the gospel in Cyprus and Asia Minor. They first spoke in Jewish synagogues, but were rejected. So they turned to the Gentiles and brought many people into the Church.

Those who had converted to Christianity from Judaism expected the Gentiles to be required to observe all of the Old Testament regulations including circumcision. Their opinion was rejected by Church leaders however, at the council of Jerusalem in 49 A.D. The crucial argument was given by Peter, the first Pope: "We believe that we are saved through the grace of the Lord Jesus" (Acts 15:11) (Peter as first Pope: see page 430-432). The council of Jerusalem made clear that Jesus Christ is the Word of God and the revelation of God. Any other word or revelation must be judged in the light of Jesus' life and teaching. Salvation can only be found in Christ. Christians now clearly recognized this as the foundation of their tradition, and from that point on, the Old Testament would be judged in the light of the New Testament. Christianity was no longer seen as a Jewish sect, but as a religion for all people—a "catholic" or universal religion.

The Apostles spread the faith to Asia Minor and Europe, including the very heart of the Roman Empire, Rome itself. The Gospel was also taken to Africa, India, and Asia. This task was made easier by the Roman roads. But Rome soon became the enemy. Emperor Nero began a persecution against the Christians in the 60's and both Peter and Paul were martyred in Rome at this time. The Roman Empire should have stamped out Christianity, but the "blood of martyrs is the seed of Christians," and the Church continued to grow.

After the death of Herod Agrippa in 44 A.D., a group of Jews called the Zealots pushed for a "holy war" against the Romans. In 66 A.D. the unrest exploded into a full-blown revolt. In the year 70 A.D. the Romans besieged Jerusalem and reduced the city to ruins. The Temple was destroyed and Christianity was separated even further from its Jewish roots.

The Canon of the New Testament

The Gospel of Mark was the first to be written probably in 65 or 70 A.D. Many believe that the author is John Mark, a missionary who travelled with Paul and had some contact with Peter. It was likely intended for non-Jewish Christians.

The Gospel of Matthew was composed around the year 80 A.D. and was written for Jewish Christians as it shows that Jesus is the fulfillment of Old Testament prophecy.

The Gospel of Luke appeared about the same time as Matthew. Luke was a missionary who traveled with Paul and was a physician. He composed this Gospel as well as the Acts of the Apostles.

The Gospel of John was written ten or more years after Luke and differs from the other three gospels in language and in style. The author has been identified as the Apostle John and was probably written for the Christians who lived around Ephesus in Asia Minor.

The Acts of the Apostles takes up where the Gospel of Luke leaves off. It describes the beginnings of the Church in Jerusalem, the first missions outside Jerusalem, the conversion of Paul, the missionary journeys of Paul, and Paul's arrest and trip to Rome.

The next twenty-one books of the New Testament are called letters or epistles. Some are actually letters, but some are simply sermons. None of the letters is a complete theological explanation of Christian doctrine. They were written to meet the specific needs of the early Christians and to solve problems as they arose.

Romans was written by Paul in about 58 A.D. Paul emphasizes that we are saved by faith in Jesus Christ and not by the observances of Old Testament law or Torah. Paul devotes considerable time to an explanation of the moral duties of Christians and to the meaning of life in Christ.

First and Second Corinthians were written between 54 and 58 A.D. Corinth was a Greek city known for its lack of morals. The Christians of Corinth needed a great deal of guidance and correction from Paul after their conversion from paganism.

Galatians was written to the Christians in Galatia by Paul in about 54 A.D. In this letter, Paul reminds them that we are saved in faith by Christ and not by circumcision.

Ephesians is addressed to the Christian community in Ephesus, which was a seaport in Turkey. It proclaims Christ to be the Son of God and emphasizes that Christ and His Church are one. It lays the foundation for our understanding of the Church as "one, holy, catholic, and apostolic."

Philippians was written by Paul to the converts in Philippi, a city in northern Greece. Paul thanks the Philippians for their generous assistance, and assures them of his love for them, and encourages them to remain one in Jesus the Lord.

Colossians proclaims Jesus as the Son of God and Head of His Body, the Church. It encourages Christians to die to sinful ways and live in union with the Lord. It is addressed to the community of Colossae, a small town in southwestern Turkey.

First Thessalonians was written in 51 A.D. and is therefore the oldest book in the New Testament. In it Paul writes to the church at Thessalonica, a seaport in northern Greece. He encourages them to be faithful as they await the coming of Christ, which is apparently expected in their lifetime. Second Thessalonians was written later to answer more questions about the coming of Christ.

First and Second Timothy and Titus are called the "pastoral letters" because they are addressed to early Church leaders as guides for the pastoral care of their communities. The letters reflect the growth of the Church and emphasize the importance of faithfulness to the gospel and to the teachings of the Apostles.

Philemon is a personal letter written by Paul in 58 A.D. asking Philemon, an influential friend, to take back a runaway slave whom Paul had converted.

Hebrews is a sermon probably written late in the first century to Christians in general. It presents Christ as the Word of God, as the Priest who saves us from death, and as the Leader who opens Heaven to us. The author of Hebrews is unknown.

James is a sermon of the late first century. It teaches that a living faith must show itself in good works and a holy life. It is thought to have been written by James of Alpheus, an Apostle and relative of Jesus.

First and Second Peter were written to encourage Christians of the late first century. It is believed that sermons of Peter were used to compose these books along with baptismal liturgies and hymns. First Peter gives comfort and encouragement to persecuted Christians, while Second Peter urges them to remain faithful to Christ and to always be ready for His coming.

First, Second, and Third John are believed to have come from the Apostle John. First John proclaims that Jesus is the Son of God, but also that He is truly human. It emphasizes that God is love and therefore we are to love one another. Second John urges faithfulness to Jesus, while Third John is a short note requesting aid and hospitality for missionaries.

Jude is a short sermon, written about the year 100 A.D., warning Christians to avoid false teachers and remain faithful to the teachings of the Apostles. It is thought to have been written by Jude Thaddeus the brother of James.

Revelation uses a literary genre called "apocalypse" that was popular at this time. It uses figurative language, symbols and numbers, visions and heavenly messengers to describe the struggle between good and evil. The author calls himself John so it is commonly held that this is the Apostle John. Many people have tried to use Revelation as a 'heavenly timetable' to determine the end of the world, but Revelation was not intended for this purpose. Much of the Old Testament is referenced in this book. In symbol it describes the destruction of the Temple in Jerusalem in the year 70 A.D. The message in Revelation is that God will prevail over Satan. It describes the heavenly banquet that all are invited to attend. In symbol it describes the Mass in Heaven that we participate in here on earth.

V. Confirmed in the Church

The 12 Apostles and the Catholic Church

The Twelve Apostles began to spread the Church throughout the world. Each apostle went a separate way, but still established the same Church under one head, Jesus Christ; under one Vicar of Christ on earth, Peter, the first Pope. The Bible, as we know it today with Old and New Testaments did not exist. That would not come for another 400 years. Instead, it was by 'Sacred Tradition' that the Church was spread throughout the world. The Apostles spread the Church by teaching and preaching; by giving example living amongst the people; and by establishing institutions. The Apostles taught the same doctrine no matter where they went. They gave the same example with their very lives. They established the same institutions: The Sacraments and the Mass. The Apostles did exactly what the Holy Spirit led them to do. They established One Church; one united Church throughout the world. Soon the name catholic was used to describe this Church (CCC76).

The word catholic comes from the Greek word "Katholou," meaning "on the whole" or "universal". The Church was the same everywhere and everywhere the same. The word catholic was first written in the year 110 by St. Ignatius of Antioch in his letter to the Smyrnaens (Jurgens 25). It was certainly used orally long before it was written.

It is important for all of us to understand *when* we came to believe the doctrines of our faith. The *when* matters a great deal. We need to be able to trace our doctrinal beliefs back to the very twelve Apostles who handed us the faith directly from Christ Himself. For if we came to believe something merely 100 years ago, how could it have come from the Apostles? Understand that the true Church of Jesus must be able to trace itself and its doctrine all the way back to the time of Christ or it simply is not the Church that Jesus established.

A simple example might be the doctrine concerning the Eucharist. The Catholic Church believes that the bread and wine that we bring forward during the Offertory at Mass really and truly become the very Body, Blood, Soul, and Divinity of Jesus and remains Jesus from that point on. Should we believe this? Is it worthy of belief? What are the criteria for belief? We must ask, "Did Christ teach this?" "Did the very 12 Apostles teach this and say it is true?" If the very 12 Apostles taught it, we have no choice but to believe it. It must be true; for they walked, talked, and lived with Jesus Himself. They were led by the Holy Spirit. It was they who spread the Church throughout the world. But if the 12 Apostles did not teach this and we simply invented this idea 10, 25, 80, 100, or even 200 years ago, we simply cannot believe it. You see, the Apostles are our measuring rod. Of course we know today that the twelve Apostles did teach this to be true and every other doctrine we believe in, for we have the writings of the Early Church Fathers to prove it.

You see the Church Fathers were the second generation of Bishops who were taught by the original twelve Apostles. The Church Fathers were commissioned to take the place of the Apostles as successors. The faith was handed down to them and they were ordained and sent to lead us. At that time, many false teachers began to arrive on the scene. These false teachers began to teach what is false or what we call heresy. The Early Church Fathers wrote "apologies" or documents defending the faith and showing how these heretics taught falsely. We have all of these writings today. Many Church doctrines, including the doctrine on the Eucharist, were defended by the Church Fathers. It shows each of us that what the Church believed back then is the same as it believes today. It is proof that our doctrines truly came from

Jesus to the original twelve Apostles themselves and passed down to us never changing.

The Splits

The first Christian Church to be established was the Holy Catholic Church founded in the year 33 A.D. by Jesus Christ. The location was the city of Jerusalem. (For political reasons the East-West Schism of 1054 took place splitting the Catholic Church into two branches, but this was not a separation in doctrine. Only a political separation). There was no other separated Christian group until the year 1517. Martin Luther split from the Catholic Church and started the Lutheran religion in 1517. The location was Germany.

Next the Anglican Church split in 1534. It was started by King Henry the VIII, who pulled away from the Catholic Church and the Holy Father, the Pope. Henry the VIII claimed that the King should be the head of the Church, not the Pope. The Episcopal Church here in the United States is similar to that of the Anglican Church in England. Why did this group split from the Church? King Henry VIII denied himself nothing. He had many mistresses. Most were content with simply being mistresses except for one, Anne Boleyn, who had become pregnant with Henry's child. Anne set her sights on the crown and wanted King Henry to divorce his wife, Catherine of Aragon, and marry her. So Henry asked the Church to grant him an annulment from his wife, the queen. The Church would not grant it to him. Their marriage was deemed valid and no grounds for an annulment could be found. Henry VIII did not disagree with the Church on matters of doctrine or morals. He separated for political reasons. He wanted to be head of the Church so that he could grant himself an annulment. (Weidenkopf 75).

In 1555 John Calvin started the Calvinists in Switzerland. The Presbyterians were started in 1560 by John Knox in Scotland. The Congregationalists were started in 1582 by Robert Brown in Holland. The Baptist Church started in 1609 by John Smith in Amsterdam. The Methodist Episcopal Church was started in 1739 by John and Charles Wesley in England. The Episcopalians were started by Samuel Seaberry in 1789 in the American Colonies. The United Brethren started in 1800 by Philip Otterbean and Martin Boem in the state of Maryland. The Disciples of Christ started in 1827 by Thomas and Alexander Campbell in the state of Kentucky.

The Mormon religion was started by Joseph Smith who claimed to have had a vision in 1830 in New York.

The Seventh Day Adventists were founded by Ellen G. White in 1860 in the state of Maine. The Salvation Army was started in 1865 by William Booth in London, England. Jehovah's Witnesses started in 1874 by Charles Taze Russell in Pennsylvania. Christian Science was started in 1879 by Mary Baker Eddy in Boston, Massachusetts. Four-Square Gospel was started in 1927 by Aimee Semple McPherson in Los Angeles, California. The Church of Scientology was founded by L. Ron Hubbard in Washington DC in 1952. Calvary Chapels started in 1965 by a man named Chuck Smith in Costa Mesa, California. The Harvest Christian group started in 1972 by Greg Laury in Riverside, California. The Purpose Driven Church was started in 1982 by Pastor Rick Warren in California. And the list goes on and on and on.

Using the definition for Denomination—*a large group of religious congregations united under a common faith and name and organized under a single administrative and legal hierarchy*, we can discern that there are over 35,000 Christian denominations today (Mead Hill). Because many of them are nondenominational and are independent of a hierarchical government or leadership, the doctrine that they teach is for the most part left completely up to them. What aspects of Christianity they hold as true and those they reject become largely a matter of personal biblical interpretation and many claim that the Bible is their sole authority.

In speaking to many pastors of many of the nondenominational churches in our surrounding area, some say they align themselves with a known denomination such as the Church of Christ for example. However, they seek no guidance from the government of that denomination nor are they subject to their decisions. An overwhelming number of pastors that I interviewed believe strongly that they as individuals can interpret the Bible on their own and derive what is best for them and their congregations. When asked what guarantee they have that they are teaching what is absolute truth, their only answer is "the Bible."

New denominations are increasing at very rapid speeds. Some estimate that new denominations are being added at a rate of 100 per week. Many Protestant leaders are becoming alarmed with these numbers and speculate that they will continue to grow until finally Protestantism completely self-destructs. Some predict that each individual will eventually belong to his own church believing what he has personally interpreted from Scripture. Many have already abandoned Sunday worship stating that they don't need a church, but only the Bible. In this way, worship can easily take place at home.

I think that it's important to realize that people today are searching for the truth. They want the truth; are naturally drawn to the truth; and will not stop until they find the truth. At this point it is important for you to understand that the Catholic Church is not just another Christian Denomination. In fact the Catholic Church is not a Christian Denomination at all. The Catholic Church is 'The Church'; the holy Mother Church that can trace herself all the way back to Jesus Christ, the founder, in 33 A.D. This is a historical fact; simply a matter of history.

Another important point to note is that all Christian denominations possess some of the truth, but none of them possess the whole truth. Many are missing vital aspects of the faith that Jesus handed to the Apostles and the Apostles handed to us (CCC 838). Even more alarming is the fact that some simply teach false doctrine that can lead a person astray. This can be very dangerous, because the purpose of the Church is to lead people to Heaven. If a church teaches something false, it could lead people away from Heaven, instead of toward it.

There is only one reason to become Catholic and there is only one reason to stay Catholic. That is because we want the Truth and not just part of it. We want the entire truth. We want to belong to the actual Church Christ founded with all the Truth that goes with it, because there lies salvation. This is the road to Heaven. Remember, Jesus said, "I am the Way, the Truth, and the Life" (John 14:6). When we follow Jesus as head of the Church that He founded, we have the "Way," the "Truth," and the "Life."

The Nicene Creed

Back in the year 325 A.D. a council of Bishops was summoned. This was the first Ecumenical Council of the Christian Church. It took place in Nicaea, which is in present day Turkey. The purpose of this council was to resolve disagreements arising from within the church of Alexandria over the nature of Jesus in relationship to God the Father. The question they were trying to answer was this: Was Jesus of the same substance as God or of a similar substance? In other words, "Was Jesus one in being or consubstantial with the Father? Were Jesus and God one and the same?"

As a result of this council, the first uniform Christian doctrine, called The Nicene Creed, was created. The Nicene Creed, written in the year 325, gives us the answer to which Church is the Church that Jesus truly founded.

The Nicene Creed gives us the <u>Four Marks of the Church</u>: One; Holy; Catholic; and Apostolic. If you want to know which Church is the true Church of Christ, all you have to do is find the one that has these 4 signs; these 4 marks; these 4 Characteristics: **One, Holy, Catholic, Apostolic.**

The 4 Marks of the Church

ONE: The Catholic Church is one. This means that Jesus started one true Church. We share one faith; one set of morals; one set of beliefs under the authority of our Pope who is the successor of Saint Peter, the apostle that Jesus chose to first lead His Church. This oneness is particularly expressed each time we celebrate the Eucharist as one worldwide family. The same Mass is celebrated in every Catholic Church throughout the world. The Bible says that there will be one flock, one shepherd, one Lord, one Faith, and one Baptism. St. Paul even writes, "I urge you brothers in the name of our Lord Jesus Christ that all of you agree in what you say and that there be no divisions among you, but that you be united in the same mind and in the same purpose" (1Cor. 1:10).

Holy: The Catholic Church is holy, because the Church's founder is Jesus, who is God Himself. This means that the Church and its members have been set apart for God's purposes. It doesn't mean that the members of the Church are perfect or that they don't sin. But it does mean that through the continued presence of the Holy Spirit and the grace of the sacraments, the Body of Christ and its members are being perfected and growing in holiness. We all need the holiness Christ offers to us through His Church.

The Catholic Church is not perfect. It can't be. The Church is made up of people and people are not perfect. In fact, they're sinners. The Catholic Church has made a lot of mistakes in the past 2,000 years. But I challenge you name another institution on earth that has even lasted 2,000 years. Keep one thing in mind: The Catholic Church is not a museum for saints. Instead, it is a hospital for sinners.

Catholic: The word catholic means universal. Jesus established a world-wide Church and sent it on a mission as the means of salvation to the whole human race. Because God desired all men to be saved and come to the knowledge of the Truth, the Church is open to everyone. The Church doesn't belong to a certain nationality, race, or ethnic group. The Church is worldwide and is for all people for all times.

Apostolic: The Church is apostolic, which means it traces its beginnings back to Christ and the Apostles. It also means that the Church has remained faithful to what Jesus and His Apostles taught. In addition, it means that its members are loyal to the successors of the Apostles, the bishops. Jesus Christ appointed apostles and said to them, "Whoever hears you, hears me" (Luke 10:16). "Whose sins you forgive are forgiven" (John 20:23). "Whatever you bind on earth is bound in heaven" (Matt 18:18). The apostles, exercising the authority given to them by Christ, appointed successors called Bishops. These Bishops still exist in the Catholic Church in an unbroken line of succession. Every Bishop can trace himself historically to an Apostle (CCC 857).

Major Differences between Catholicism and Protestantism

I think that it is helpful for those who are learning the Catholic Faith to be able to compare and contrast it with the faith of Protestantism. For this reason we will begin to discuss the major differences between Catholicism and Protestantism. These are the major differences that serve to divide us. It is my objective to help you understand the Catholic view so that you can embrace it. In doing so, I will seek to defend it using apologetics. As stated in the Introduction, this is by no means meant to demean other faiths, but only to help you to embrace Catholicism as truth by presenting a reason for our faith.

Common Ground: In discussing the major differences between Catholicism and Protestantism, it is good to begin with common ground, where both agree. All of us are called Christians because we believe that Jesus Christ was and is God's only Son; that He became a man; and that He died for our sins. All of us believe that God gradually revealed Himself to us. We call this Divine Revelation. God revealed Himself to us through the covenants of the Old Testament, but when He became the Man, Jesus Christ, He spoke directly to us. He fully revealed Himself to us in the man, Jesus.

All of these covenants, and especially this New and Eternal Covenant, are God's way of granting us salvation. Unless you enter into God's Covenant, this New Covenant in Jesus' Blood, you will not be saved and you will not enter Heaven (CCC 846).

It is the Transmission of Divine Revelation that divides Catholics and Protestants. And it is the method by which we are justified or sanctified that divides Catholics and Protestants. What in the world does that mean? Well, we don't agree on *how* God transmits His message of salvation to us. And we don't agree on the method by which we become justified or sanctified in God's eyes. To put it simply, we don't agree on where the truth of salvation comes from and we don't agree on how we get to Heaven.

Scripture and Tradition or is it The Bible Alone?

Let's start with the difference between Catholicism and Protestantism that has to do with the transmission of Divine Revelation to us from God. Most Protestant denominations believe that the Bible is the ONLY source of Divine Revelation. In other words they believe that the Bible is the written Word of God and there is no other way that God reveals Himself to us. The Bible is the only source of God's revelation, period. God wrote the Bible and this is the only way He has of communicating with us today. This view is called Sola Scriptura or "The Bible Alone" (Hensley).

Most Protestant denominations hold that now that Christ and the Apostles are no longer with us, walking the earth and teaching, all we have left is what was written to fall back on. All we have left of the teachings of Christ and the teachings of the Apostles is in the Bible. There is nothing else. Therefore, if these denominations can't find a certain doctrine spelled out in the Bible, it must not be true and it cannot be proven as true. Each person is therefore allowed to read and interpret the Bible on their own and come up with their own understanding, even if his understanding differs from everyone else and differs from what the Apostles taught.

The truth is that the Bible itself doesn't even agree that it is the Bible alone that is in charge. In other words, this idea of the Bible being the sole source of authority is not even taught in the Bible. Instead, the Bible states that it is the Church that Jesus founded, that is in charge. Jesus did not leave and place a book in charge of His Christian Religion. He left and placed a Church in charge of His Christian Religion (Matt 16:18-19). Moreover, the Church existed for almost 400 years before the Bible, as we know it today, was even available to read. The truth is that the Catholic Church gave the Bible to the world. The Bible that many individuals and Protestants Denominations say is their sole source of authority was written and given to them by the very authority they reject, the Catholic Church. The bishops of the Catholic Church discerned which writings were to be included in the canon (list) of Scripture, the Bible. It was by the authority of the Church that we have the Bible (Graham).

As Catholics, however, we completely agree that God wrote the Bible. We believe that men did the actual writing, but that God inspired them to write what they wrote (CCC 105). Every man who wrote a book of the New Testament was a member of the Catholic Church. We also agree that the Bible is absolutely a source of Divine Revelation. God does indeed speak to us through His written Word. St. Jerome said, "Ignorance of the Bible is ignorance of the Faith." We must know our Bibles or we do not know our faith.

For us as Catholics, it is ridiculous to say that the Bible is the *only* source of Divine Revelation. There is no way that the Bible could be the *only* way to know God's Church, because the Church existed for 400 years without the Bible. If is it the truth that we are to rely on the Bible alone, as many Protestant denominations claim, then how did the Christian Church exist and spread throughout the world for 400 years without it? The Christian Church was spread all over the world before the Bible even existed. Yes, there were writings from the Apostles that were read, at Mass, to the people, but there was no book. Also note that there were many writings that did not end up becoming part of the Bible. By the end of the first century there were between 250 and 350 books that all claimed to be written by the Apostles. Hundreds of these writings were rejected and not included in the canon or list of books chosen to become the New Testament. Only 27 books were determined to be "inspired by God". Who determined that 27 books were inspired by God and the other 200 to 300 plus were not? It was the Bishops of the Catholic Church, led by the Holy Spirit (CCC120). So anyone who accepts the authority of the Bible has already accepted the authority of the Catholic Church, because it was the Catholic Church that gave the Bible to the world.

Even when the canon, or official list of books, was put together and the New and Old Testament was made into a book form, very few people knew how to read. The average person did not know how to read until the 18ᵗʰ century. How could Jesus build a Church, solely based on a book, when very few people even knew how to read (Graham)?

Even for those who knew how to read, most could not afford to own their very own Bible. This is because the printing press would not be invented until the 1400's. The Bible had to be copied by hand one at a time. It took at least one year to copy a Bible by hand therefore making a new copy. That would mean that the cost of a Bible was a whole year's wages. Who could afford to pay someone a year's pay to get a copy of the Bible? That would be the equivalent of tens of thousands of dollars by today's standards. Only the very rich owned a Bible. Even with these facts, many, many Protestant denominations maintain that Christ built His Church on the Bible even when the New Testament did not come into existence for the first 400 years of the Church; when only a few people could read; and when only the rich could afford one. I think one can easily see that one reason why Catholics do not believe that God communicates to us solely through the Bible is because He was communicating to us long before the Bible even existed; long before the majority of people could even read; long before the average person could afford a Bible (Graham).

Still individuals will quote 1Timothy 3:16 as their proof text that the Bible alone is the sole authority: "All Scripture is inspired by God and is useful for teaching, for refutation, for correction and for training in righteousness." Well, Catholics completely agree with this, but it doesn't say Scripture alone.

Also when you read the verse in context you see that verse 15 says, "Remain faithful to what you have learned and believed because you know from whom you learned it and that from your infancy you have known the Sacred Scriptures." What Scriptures is Paul talking about? Much of the New Testament wasn't even written when Paul said this, including the Gospel of John. The only Scriptures that Timothy could have known from his infancy are the Old Testament Scriptures. So this verse taken literally is not even referring to the Christian Bible as we know it.

The Bible simply doesn't teach Sola Scriptura. On the contrary, the Bible clearly demonstrates the need for a teaching authority. In Acts 8:26-40 an Ethiopian Eunich is reading from the book of Isaiah. Philip asks if he understands what he is reading. The Eunich answers, "How can I unless someone instructs me," which Philip proceeds to do. Peter says of Paul's letters, "There are some things in them hard to understand which the ignorant and unstable twist to their own destruction" (2 Peter 3:16). In 2 Peter 1:20 he writes, "First of all you must understand this, that no prophesy of Scripture is a matter of one's own interpretation."

Sacred Tradition and Sacred Scripture

As Catholics we believe that our Christian Faith comes to us in two ways. The first way is by Apostolic Tradition—the teaching of the Apostles handed down to us from generation to generation by an unbroken line of Apostolic succession—our popes and bishops. The second way is by the Word of God—the Bible. So understand, many Protestant denominations rely on the Bible alone and the Catholic Church relies on Sacred Tradition through Apostolic succession and the Bible (CCC 82).

In other words, the Catholic Church teaches that our Gospel has been handed down to us in two ways. First, it was handed down to us **orally and by example**. Then it was handed down to us in **writing**.

Many people, including Catholics, do not understand exactly what we mean by "Sacred Tradition" or Apostolic Tradition. It is good to understand this so that you can explain it and defend it if need be. When we speak of *Sacred Tradition*, we mean three things: First, we mean that the apostles **preached** to us. They handed the faith to us by teaching **orally**. Every word that Jesus preached was not written down. How could it have been? Second, we mean that the apostles lived with us and gave us **direct example** by their very lives and actions. The Christian community lived together and saw firsthand the faith lived out. Third, we mean that the Apostles **established institutions** in the Church at that time. These institutions continue to be a very large part of our faith. Examples would be the Sacraments and the Mass. Eventually people began to write down the teachings of the Apostles. These writings later became the New Testament (CCC 76).

In the Gospel of Matthew chapter 18:19-20 Jesus said, "Go therefore, and make disciples of all the nations baptizing them in the name of the Father and of the Son and of the Holy Spirit, teaching them to observe all that I have commanded you. And behold, I am with you always, until the end of the age". Notice that Jesus did not say, "Go therefore and write a book and send it all over the world and use it as the sole means of your faith." It is the absolute truth that only five of the Apostles ever wrote anything that went into the Bible. Only Matthew, John, James, Jude and Peter wrote anything that was considered the "Inspired Word of God." It is equally true that these Apostles had no idea their writings were going to end up as part of the Bible in a new section called the *New Testament*. To them, the only Scripture that existed was the Old Testament. Instead the apostles did what Jesus commanded. They went to all the nations of the world and baptized the people "In the Name of the Father and of the Son and of the Holy Spirit" and they taught the people to observe all that Jesus had commanded as part of His Church. Jesus gave them the authority to act for Him; to make decisions; and to hold those decisions bound. And Jesus was with them through the Holy Spirit guiding them the entire time.

The apostles taught by preaching to the people; they taught by the example of their very lives—living with the people and directly showing them a moral Christian life; and thirdly they established institutions within the churches; the same everywhere and everywhere the same. Some of the twelve wrote and the next generation wrote as well. Mark, Luke, and Paul were all of the second generation that came after the original twelve Apostles. They themselves were not one of the original Twelve. This shows how the Church was handed down to the next generation. It was handed down orally and the oral teaching began to be written by the second generation. The Church learned its Doctrine by this preaching and teaching; by the example given to it by the Apostles; and by the institutions established by the Apostles that the people participated in.

The Bible says that Saint Paul taught the Church in Ephesus night and day for three years (Acts 20:31). The Christians in Ephesus, after learning from Paul night and day for three years, would have known about God, Christ, the Holy Spirit, salvation, Heaven, Hell, Purgatory…you name it. After learning from Paul night and day for three years, they would have lived a sacramental life. They would have been Baptized, Confirmed, had their sins forgiven, received the Eucharist, been married by St. Paul, and participated in the Holy Sacrifice of the Mass. Their sick would have been anointed. Some of them would have become priests and even bishops ready to take Paul's place. Paul would have ordained some of them as he did Timothy, whom Paul writes to in First and Second Timothy.

You see, the people would have learned from Paul's preaching day and night for three years; from Paul's example—the example of his life; and they would have experienced the faith by participating in the institutions that Paul established among them.

The preaching of the Apostles became the Church's Doctrine. The Apostles' example became the Church's manner of life. And the institutions that the Apostles established became the Church's Sacraments, Liturgy, sacramentals, rites, and practices. Put all this together and you have a Church passed down by Sacred Tradition through Apostolic succession. When you add the writings of the Apostles you also have the Sacred Scriptures to go along with it. This is what has been passed down to us.

The Apostles passed down the whole Church; not just part of it; not just the writings; not just the Bible. They passed down all of it: their preaching, their example, and a sacramental life. That is what we mean when we say that the Catholic Church possesses the 'Fullness of Faith'.

I have had some individuals say to me that Scripture condemns all traditions. They quote Mark 7:8-9 in which Jesus says, "You leave the commandment of God and hold fast to the traditions of men." They may also quote Matthew 15:3 which says, "You break the commandment of God for the sake of your tradition." The truth is that the Bible does condemn the bad traditions of men, but it also upholds good traditions. St. Paul commands the Thessalonians to keep Apostolic Tradition in 2 Thessalonians 2:15 "Therefore brothers, stand firm and hold fast to the Traditions that you were taught either by an oral statement or by a letter of ours." This verse also shows us that the Apostolic Teaching was oral as well as written. Saint John goes so far as to say, "There are many other things that Jesus did, but if these things were to be described individually, I do not think that the whole world could contain the books that would be written" (John 21:25). In 1 Corinthians 11:1 St. Paul writes to the Church at Corinth, "I praise you because you remember me in everything and hold fast to the Traditions just as I handed them on to you." Paul understands clearly that he is handing Traditions down to the people of Corinth and he is pleased because they are following them. So you see that the Catholic Church obeys the Apostolic Teaching and bases her doctrines on both Scripture and Tradition.

Justification as a Process or is it Justification by Faith Alone?

The second major difference between Catholicism Protestantism has to do with how we get to Heaven or how we are made righteous before God. Many Protestant denominations teach their members that God legally imputes or credits the very righteousness of Christ to all those who believe in Him. In other words, if a person believes in Jesus Christ, God will legally transfer all of Christ's own righteousness to that person. Simply say that you believe that Jesus saved you from your sins and you are guaranteed a place in Heaven. Your ticket is punched and you have a seat in Heaven, guaranteed. You do not have to do another thing. There is no requirement to care for the poor; no requirement to be faithful to your family. Your sins no longer matter. There is nothing more for you to do. You are guaranteed a place in Heaven and there is no way that you can lose your place in Heaven. Some even believe that once you are saved you are always saved. There is no way that you can lose your salvation no matter what you do; no matter what you say. No sin can keep you out of Heaven. You only need to believe and Christ will take His own righteousness; come to you; and simply clothe you in it as with a cloak (Hensley).

In Protestantism this is called following the "Roman Road" or the "Highway of Salvation" and it basically refers to four verses from the book or Romans. Romans 3:23 says, "All have sinned." Romans 6:23 says, "The penalty for sin is death." Romans 5:8 says, "Jesus died for our sins." And Romans 10: 8-10 says, "To be forgiven of our sins we must believe and confess that Jesus is Lord because salvation comes through Jesus." In addition, Romans 3:28 says, "For we consider that a person is justified by Faith and apart from the works of the Law." Thus many Protestant denominations conclude that we are saved by "Faith Alone."

Why do many Protestant denominations teach that this is true? Quite honestly they believe it is true. They believe it is true because Martin Luther, in the year 1517, came to believe this for himself. He then wrote a doctrine on his own and launched the Reformation with it. Later he broke with the Catholic Church and convinced others to follow him (Hensley).

How did Martin Luther come to believe this was true? Martin Luther was a Catholic Monk who considered himself to be a "Gabrielist," a follower of the theologian Gabriel Biel, who himself had adopted Ocklamism as part of his theology. In Ocklamism, justification is God's work of grace, but human activity only becomes salvific by God's recognition of it; by His act of acceptance. This meant that grace comes only as a result of human activity and our desperate need for God to pay attention to it in order to save us (Adam). Luther, believing this theology, overemphasized the role of good works in salvation to an extreme. Let me say boldly that this theology was not held by the Catholic Church. In contrast, the Church taught that grace was a movement of divine life and love entering into our souls and thus leading us toward holiness. Grace cannot be earned, but is instead freely given by God.

To make matters worse, Luther read the works of John Wycliff and Jan Hus, pronounced heretics from centuries before, and he became indoctrinated into their views. These men had denied core Church doctrines such as the Primacy of the Popes; the sacraments; and the True Presence of Christ in the Eucharist just to name a few (Lord).

The biggest tragedy in Luther's life, however, was the very hurtful relationship that he had with his own Father. No matter what Martin did, it was never good enough for his dad. His father was furious that Martin became a Monk; furious that he never lived up to what he wanted Martin to do and be. Because of this hurtful relationship with his own father; the Ocklamism view he held; and his alliance with Wycliff and Hus, Martin Luther saw God the same way he saw his own father. He saw God as an angry, vengeful God who is never pleased with us. "No matter what we do," Luther said, "It is never good enough for God." According to Martin Luther, we can fast; we can try to avoid sin; we can do acts of penance; we can work, work, work, to be the best person we can possibly be; but no matter how hard we work, we will never be able to please this angry, vengeful God who requires perfect holiness from us in order to enter Heaven. Luther had reached the breaking point (Hensley).

According to Martin Luther, the Catholic Church taught that this was the nature of God. That is simply not the truth. Instead, the Catholic Church taught then, as it does now, that God receives us in the same way that the Loving Father in "Parable of the Prodigal Son" received his son who came back to him full of sorrow for his sin. Do you remember the story of the Prodigal Son? The boy asks for his inheritance, completely separating himself from his father, and then leaves home never intending to return. He then wastes his money on sinful things and finds himself broke. Out of money, he begins to hire himself out, but even so he is still starving to death. He comes to his senses, decides to go home, and tell his father how truly sorry he is. So the boy heads home and as soon as he sees his father he says, "Father forgive me; I've sinned. I've sinned against you and against God." The boy can hardly get a single word out, because his father has already forgiven him. The boy returned home full of sorrow for his sins and that was all that was needed in order to be forgiven (Hensley).

Martin Luther even had mentors at the time who were trying to help him. They would say to him, "Martin, God does not hate you. God is not angry with you." But Luther refused to listen to anyone. Then it happened. While reading through Paul's letter to the Romans, Luther came upon chapter 3 where he read: "No human being will be justified in His sight by works of the law, since through the law comes knowledge of sin. For we hold that a man is justified by faith apart from works of law. But now the righteous of God has been manifested apart from the law, the righteousness of God through faith in Jesus Christ for all who believe" (Hensley).

Luther read this passage over and over and over trying to make sense of it. He rolled it over in his mind night and day, day and night trying to understand exactly what it meant. He did not consult the Church for help or clarification. He did not try to discover what Paul himself meant by this. Martin Luther interpreted this Scripture passage completely on his own, apart from the Church that was right there to guide him. Martin decided that this Scripture was saying the following: *God is perfectly holy and God therefore requires perfect holiness of those who would enter Heaven. Since you and I are sinners, we cannot produce the kind of holiness needed to enter Heaven. Our works will never be good enough. But Christ's works are good enough. The "Good News", according to Luther, was that we must turn from our own efforts and look only to Christ on the Cross. If we will only do that, God will forgive our sins and will legally credit Christ's own righteousness to our account. Even though we remain sinners, God will declare us to be just and righteous in His sight and welcome us into Heaven.* Luther began to write this and teach this until he finally broke with the Church (Hensley).

Luther Found Relief

Martin Luther found relief for his own problem with this new interpretation of Paul's Letter to the Romans. Luther hated God the same way he hated his own father and openly declared this. He thought that God demanded perfection, a perfection that no person could obtain; the same way his own father had demanded perfection of him that he could never live up to. On top of this, Ocklamism had demanded his perfection and he was tired of working his way to Heaven. Luther found a way to relieve his pain. He invented a brand new interpretation of Paul's letter to the Romans that had never, ever, been taught in the previous 1600 year existence of the Church. Luther invented a brand new interpretation of Roman's chapter 3 that the Church had never before taught, but Luther was convinced that he was right (Hensley).

"Luther's great mistake in creating his doctrine was that he took his own highly personal convictions, based on a very exceptional experience and made them into a binding requirement for all" (Lortz, vol. I, p.408). He taught that unless a person accepts this doctrine; the doctrine that we are "Justified by Faith Alone," a person cannot enter Heaven. Luther's doctrine states that all we have to do is believe in Christ and God will legally credit Christ's own righteousness to our account. He then launched the Reformation with this doctrine (Hensley). I have personally had many Protestants come up to me and ask me, "Have you been saved?" or "Have you accepted Jesus Christ as your personal Lord and Savior?" This is why they ask this question. In their minds if I have not outwardly professed Jesus as my Savior, I cannot be saved.

To those who believe this, there are only two choices. Either Heaven is a free gift from God to all those who believe, or you must work your way to Heaven. If you are working your way to Heaven, then you must be *earning* your way to Heaven all by yourself. This means that you would get all the credit for saving yourself and Jesus would get no credit for saving you. This would mean that you don't even need Jesus in order to get to Heaven. That cannot be true. So we must be saved by "Faith Alone" and not by "works" (Hensley).

Tradition is the Lens

Sacred Tradition is the lens through which we interpret Sacred Scripture. You and I can read the same Scripture verse from the Bible and come up with a different meaning very easily. Which one of us would have the correct interpretation? Which one of us would have the correct understanding and how would we know?

The correct understanding is the "Apostolic Understanding". The first Apostles of the Catholic Church wrote the New Testament. Therefore they are the ones who understood its meaning and taught that meaning to those with whom they passed down the faith. Only their interpretation can be the correct one. When a person reads a book, any book, but has trouble understanding it, to whom should he turn? Wouldn't turning to the author of that book be the correct thing to do? The Catholic Church, guided by the Holy Spirit, is the author of the New Testament. So it is through the eyes of "Sacred Tradition" that we must look at Scripture. If my own interpretation does not match the interpretation that the Church has always held since the time of the Apostles, then I must have it wrong. If you and I were to come up with an interpretation that differed from that which the Apostles taught, then we must recognize that our interpretation did not come from Jesus! How could our opinion hold more weight than the meaning given to it by the very Apostles who walked with Christ? How could my interpretation hold the same authority as the "Apostolic Interpretation?" And remember, no new revelation from God has or could have taken place since the death of the last Apostle. This means that there can be nothing new taught since the death of Saint John. Yet Martin Luther came up with a brand new interpretation more than 1,500 years after the death of the last Apostle. How could it possibly be accepted as true? We must ask ourselves—"If this were true, why didn't the Apostles teach it?" They did not teach it, because it is not the Truth of Jesus Christ.

These are the facts: In 1,517 years, this doctrine of "Sola Fidei" which states that we are justified by <u>faith alone,</u> had never, ever been taught. This doctrine that God legally credits us with Christ's own righteousness and clothes us in it at the moment we profess that we believe in Him—had never, ever been taught or even suggested by any apostle or priest in the entire 1,517 year history of the Church. Martin Luther had come up with a brand new doctrine, completely on his own. Even more amazing is the fact that this teaching is nowhere to be found in the Bible. Yet many Protestant denominations teach that the Bible alone is the sole source of authority (Hensley).

When asked, "Martin, why hasn't the Church ever taught this?" He simply stated that the Church did not understand the Gospel of Jesus Christ until he, Martin Luther, came along to explain it (Hensley).

Martin Luther was saying that The Church, which the Apostles had spread all over the world, did not understand the Gospel of Jesus Christ until 1517; one thousand five hundred and seventeen years later, when Martin Luther came along to explain it to each of us (Hensley).

Countless Contradictions

The Truth is that in Romans 3:28 Paul is teaching that Christians are saved apart from the "works of the law" or the Torah. That is to say, apart from the Old Testament Laws of circumcision, dietary restrictions, and hand washing rituals. Faith, provided that it is "Faith working through love" as it says in Galatians, does save us. We cannot be saved without faith, but at the same time we cannot be saved by faith alone. According to the Bible, to be saved a person must repent (Matthew 4:17), believe in Jesus (Acts 16:21), be baptized (John 3:5), keep the commandments (Matthew 19:16-17), live a life of charity (1Corinthians 13:1-3), and perform good works (James 2:24). Even the Book of Romans says that each of us will be judged according to our works.

There are countless texts, chapters, and whole books of the Bible that do not support this teaching of Martin Luther called "Sola Fidei". In fact Scripture contradicts this teaching throughout the Bible. The Catholic Church taught then and always has taught that we are saved by both our faith and belief in God AND by the good works that we perform here on earth because of that faith. We do not get to Heaven by "Faith Alone," by simply believing in Christ as many Protestant denominations teach. Moreover, we do not get to Heaven by working our way there. It is not Faith OR Works that get us to Heaven. It is FAITH AND WORKS that get us to Heaven. It is both.

In the book of James we read, "What good is it, my brothers, if someone says he has faith but does not have works? Can that faith save him? If a brother or a sister has nothing to wear and has no food for the day, and one of you says to them, 'Go in peace, keep warm, and eat well,' but you do not give them the necessities of the body, what good is it? So also faith of itself, if it does not have works is dead. Indeed someone might say, 'you have faith and I have works.' Demonstrate your faith to me without works, and I will demonstrate my faith to you from my works. You believe that God is the Holy One. If you believe this, you do well. But even the demons believe that and tremble. See, a person is justified by works, and not by faith alone" (James 2:14-19; 24).

The Bible itself, right here in the Book of James completely contradicts what Luther was teaching. James says, "A person is justified by works, and not by faith alone." What more proof do we need to refute the Protestant teaching of "Faith Alone—Sola Fidei?" (Hensley). Because of this, Luther wanted the entire book of James thrown out of the Bible. The Book of James completely contradicted his new teaching, so he wanted to remove it from the Bible. Luther said, "Away with James! His authority is not great enough to cause me to abandon the doctrine of Justification by Faith Alone. If other interpreters will not agree with my interpretation, then I shall make rubble of it. I almost feel like throwing Jimmy into the fire. I do not want James in my Bible" (Althaus). He went so far as to remove the Book of James and the Book of Revelation from the New Testament and place them in an appendix. He also added the word "alone" to Paul's letter to the Romans so it would read, "We are justified by faith (alone)" (Hensley). How can we trust any person who adds words to the Bible in order to *sell* his own interpretation and also has the nerve to remove whole books from the Bible that do not match his interpretation? Later these two books were put back where they belong. However, Luther did manage to remove 7 books from the Old Testament adopting the Palestinian Canon rather than the Alexandrian Canon that had always been used by Christians. This is why the Protestant Bible is missing 7 books of the Old Testament. (We will discuss this in more depth later.)

Sanctification is a Process

How do we get to Heaven? To answer that question we have to ask, "What did the Apostles teach?" Wouldn't their teaching be the correct one; the Truth of Jesus Christ? The truth is Jesus gave us the Church to guide us so we could get to Heaven. We enter Heaven through The Church; through the New and Eternal Covenant that Jesus made with all mankind at the Last Supper; sealed with His death on the cross the very next day. We get to Heaven through The Church (CCC 824). All through the New Testament we hear Jesus speak of the 'Kingdom of God'. He tells us that the Kingdom of God is at hand. Please understand that the 'Kingdom of God' is the Church; the Church that Jesus established; the Catholic Church.

The Catholic Church has always taught that sanctification or justification is a process. God works inside of us to make us holy and we are therefore, made holy. It is in that holiness that we can enter Heaven. This is why the seven sacraments are so very, very important. It is through the seven sacraments that God touches our souls. It is through the seven sacraments that God puts His very Life inside of each of us. He puts His Holy Life inside of us and He makes us holy as He is holy (CCC 1127).

We have to avoid sin in our lives, because sin breaks down our relationship with God. We are made holy by prayer; by worship; by humbling ourselves and confessing our sins; by professing our belief in Him; by handing our life over to God and especially when Jesus gives us His very Body to eat and His precious Blood to drink. At this we are filled with His Grace; filled with His life and love. This gives us the power to go out and live the way He taught us to live. Yes, we must believe. We must have faith. But we must also do good works.

Allow me to make another point very clearly. When speaking of our good works, understand that we can accomplish nothing without the grace of God. God gives us grace, His very life, Sanctifying Grace. He also gives us 'Actual Grace, which is His help in our lives. We therefore must cooperate with this grace and therefore live of life of prayer, of holiness, of compassion, of mercy and forgiveness toward others, and of service to Him. But these good works are not accomplished on our own. In fact, we can do nothing outside of God. He accomplishes every one of our good works through us as we cooperate with the grace that He gives to us. So Catholics do not believe in working our way to Heaven; absolutely not. For we know that God produces all good works in us and through us. Therefore if we do anything worthy of praise, it is not us who accomplished it, but God.

No we are not guaranteed a place in Heaven, because you and I could turn our backs on God at any moment and begin to commit horrible Mortal Sins that literally kill God's Life in our souls. No we are not guaranteed a place in Heaven. We must persevere all the way to the end, which means to cooperate with His grace. If we do, we have the hope that we will live with God in Heaven for all Eternity (CCC Glossary Mortal Sin page 889).

It is by Faith and the Good Works we do cooperating with grace; because of that faith, that we get to Heaven. That is what has *always* been taught. That is what Jesus taught. That is what the Apostles taught. And that is what the Bible teaches (CCC 2044).

What does the Bible Say?

It's not just the Book of James that teaches salvation by faith, and works working through faith. The entire Bible from Genesis to Revelation teaches this consistently. For Catholics, the Bible does not contradict itself. We read the Bible as a whole, not one verse at a time. One book or one chapter after another contradicts both Protestant teachings: "Sola Scriptura"—the

Bible Alone; and "Sola Fidei"—Faith Alone. Literally there are whole books and whole chapters in the Bible that the many individuals avoid because these writings contradict the Protestant faith that they have been taught. It is the same reason Martin Luther wanted books removed. For Catholics, we avoid nothing, because there are no contradictions when you look at the entire message.

Let's look at a couple of things in the Old Testament beginning with Noah. God called Noah and wanted to enter into Covenant with Him. Did Noah simply have to believe in God to be saved or did he have to believe <u>and</u> do something? Noah had to trust God. He had to believe that God would send the flood. He had to have faith! AND…He had to act on that faith… He had to build an Ark. What if Noah had only believed, but did not act? What if Noah believed, but did not build the Ark? Would he have been saved from the flood? No.

Let's take Abraham. Did Abraham simply have to believe in God and trust that all three promises would be fulfilled or did he have to act? He had to believe AND he had to act on that belief. Abraham had to leave his country and go to a new one. He had to be circumcised and so did all of the men of his tribe. He had to take his only son, Isaac, to the top of Mount Moriah and sacrifice him. Even though God stopped him just before he sacrificed Isaac, Abraham still acted. Did Abraham have to believe? You bet he did. Did Abraham have to act? Yes, he did.

What about Moses? Did Moses only have to believe that God would free the Israelites from slavery in Egypt or did he have to act? Moses had to believe that God would free the Israelites, but he had to go and speak to Pharaoh. Moses had to cooperate with the grace of God and God accomplished mighty deeds through Moses. Did Moses have to believe? Yes, he did. Did Moses have to act? Absolutely!

Let's move to the New Testament to the Gospel of Matthew chapter 7. Let's look at the parable Jesus told of the house built on rock and the house built on sand. It says, "Everyone who listens to these words of mine **and acts on them** will be like a wise man who built his house on rock. The rain fell, the floods came, and the winds blew and buffeted the house. But it did not collapse; it had been set solidly on rock. And everyone who listens to these words of mine, **but does not act on them** will be like a fool who built his house on sand. The rain fell, the floods came, and the winds blew and buffeted the house. And it collapsed and was completely ruined" (Matt 7:24-27).

Straight from the mouth of Jesus we are told that we must not only listen to His words, but we must also **act** on them or the storms of life will cause us ruin. Jesus tells us that if we do not hear His words **and put them into practice, we will not enter Heaven.**

Also in the Gospel of Matthew chapter 25, Jesus says that the Son of Man will sit in judgment with all the nations in front of him and He will separate the good people from the bad, as a shepherd separates the sheep from the goats. He will say to the ones on His right, "'Come you who are blessed by my Father and enter Heaven. For I was hungry and you gave me food; I was thirsty and you gave me drink; a stranger and you welcomed me; naked and you clothed me; ill and you cared for me; in prison and you visited me.' And the people will say, 'Lord, when did we do these things for you?' The Lord will answer, 'When you did them for the least of my brothers, you did it for me.' But to those on his left he will say, 'Depart from me you accursed, into the fire prepared for the devil and his angels, for I was hungry and you gave me no food; I was thirsty and you gave me no drink; a stranger and you did not welcome me; naked and you did not clothe me; ill and in prison and you did not care for me.' And the people will say, 'Lord, when did we **not** do these things for you?'

'When you did not do them for the least of my brothers, you did not do them for me'" (Matt 25:31-44).

Moreover, Jesus says in the Gospel of Matthew, "Not everyone who says to me, 'Lord, Lord' will enter the Kingdom of Heaven, but only the one who does the will of my Father in Heaven (Matt 7:21).

In Paul's letter to the Philippians Saint Paul says, "Work out your salvation with fear and trembling" (Phil 2:12).

Even in Paul's letter to the Romans, the very book that Martin Luther quoted, there is contradiction. In Chapter 2 of Romans we read, "God, will repay everyone according to his works: Eternal Life to those who seek glory, honor and perseverance in good works. But God will repay with wrath and fury those who selfishly disobey the truth and instead obey wickedness" (Rom 2:6-8).

Martin Luther taught that our sins no longer matter. He taught that we can sin and our sins will never keep us out of Heaven once we have accepted Jesus as our Savior. He assured people that we never have to worry about our sins; we don't have to confess our sins; and we don't have to be sorry for our sins. Yet, this is not supported by Scripture (Hensley).

In First John chapter one John teaches: "Children, I do not want you to sin, but if you do, we have someone who will speak to the Father in our defense if only we will confess our sins and repent." Saint John pleads, "I don't want you to sin." If our sins do not matter, why is Saint John so concerned and telling us to confess our sins (1 John 2:1)?

Martin Luther taught that there was no way a person can lose his place in Heaven once he believes in Jesus. But Paul's letter to the Corinthians says, "Our ancestors all ate the same spiritual food and drank the same spiritual drink, but God was not pleased with most of them. Therefore, whoever thinks he is standing secure should take care not to fall" (1Cor 10:12).

There are so many contradictions to this Doctrine of "Sola Scriptura"—the Bible Alone and "Sola Fidei"—Faith Alone, that it would take hours just to go through it all. Read for yourself and you will find more at every turn. Reading the entire book of Romans will help you see that Saint Paul was speaking of all the ritualistic works of the Jewish Law that had to be practiced, such as the ceremonial hand washings. He was not referring to good works of Christianity as Martin Luther suggests.

The Cause of Leniency

The sad truth is that once Martin Luther split the Church, it was easy for others to break away. In interpreting the Bible on their own, others began to disagree with Martin Luther's newfound religion and it began to split again and again and again. As I mentioned, the Protestant church has split over 35,000 times, while the Catholic Church remains one in Doctrine and Faith. The other sad truth is that once a church splits, anything goes. They are free to add to or take away from the very teachings of the Apostles. By saying that the Bible alone is the only source of revelation from God, most Protestant churches reject all of the sources of holiness that God wishes to offer them. For them there are no sacraments. What's more is that they believe that when they accept Jesus Christ as their personal Savior, they are then and there converted and are reborn. This takes the place of Baptism in the Catholic Church where we are recreated and reborn of the Spirit. Many Protestant denominations teach that there is no need for God to enter them and make them holy in any sacrament, because they are already guaranteed Heaven. There is no need to become holy if one is already destined for Heaven. So there is no confession of sins and no need for forgiveness. Most teach that they don't even have to be sorry for their sins or even think about them.

If your Church taught that no matter what you did you were going to Heaven, would you worry about receiving the sacraments to help you to lead a holy and good life? Would you confess your sins and ask for forgiveness? According to much of Protestant teaching, Jesus died and took our sins away and we do not have to do another thing. Can you see what a dangerous doctrine this is? To teach that my sins don't matter and that no matter what I do, my sins can never keep me out of Heaven once I have accepted Jesus as my personal Lord and Savior…is very dangerous.

Instead, the Catholic Church teaches that there are two types of actual sins, Mortal and Venial. We correctly teach that Mortal Sins, if not confessed; if you have not repented of them; Mortal Sins kill God's Life in your soul and can indeed keep you out of Heaven. This means that many people who *think* they are saved and going to Heaven, may not be going to heaven at all! Their soul is in grave danger and by their actions they have rejected God. What a dangerous doctrine to teach (CCC 1033).

Moreover the second Doctrine of "the Bible Alone" is equally as dangerous. Each person becomes his own Pope and his own church; possessing the right to decide for himself or herself what the Bible is teaching. It matters not what has always been taught. Many don't even know what was always taught. They simply apply the interpretation that they feel is correct or the one that works best in their lives and that is the one they believe and profess. Many people shop from one church to another until they find the church or the pastor that interprets the Bible to their own personal liking or one they can agree with. Still others get angry and leave a church because they believe that their own interpretation of Scripture, which differs from their Pastor's interpretation, is the correct one.

The minute Martin Luther began to teach "Sola Scriptura"—the Bible Alone— there was an explosion of denominations. His new church began to splinter and split until it spiraled out of control. Martin Luther began to complain about this saying, "There are as many sects and beliefs as there are heads. This fellow will have nothing to do with Baptism. Another denies the sacrament. Some even teach that Christ is not God. There is no end to their divisions!" Luther realized what a disaster this had caused! He went on to say, "People no longer belong to churches; they cease to honor God. After throwing off the Pope, everyone does as he pleases" (DeWette, op.cit.III.61).

Pray for Unity

The reason to learn all of this is so that you will understand the sacredness and holiness of the Catholic Faith and learn to trust it. It is important to belong to the Church that Christ founded, not a church founded by mere men. Many Catholics have left the Catholic Church because they did not understand these teachings. They were led astray by very convincing Protestants and did not know their own faith well enough to defend it. You need to know the Truth so that you are not so easily fooled. We are all called to help as many Protestants as we can to come home to the true Church so that they can find true salvation. We as Catholics must first learn the Truth and then we must spread this Truth. We are all called to evangelize. The Sacrament of Confirmation marks us as a witness for Christ. Gently and kindly bring others back to the Mother Church, back to the Catholic Church, by sharing the Truth with them. Pray that one day Jesus' Church will be united in one faith once again.

VI. Prayer and Sacraments

Part I: Prayer

I think that a lot of people have trouble praying. I think there are a lot of people out there that simply don't know how to pray and they need someone to help them develop their prayer life. Once we develop our prayer life, everything changes. It becomes easy and natural and ongoing. Prayer is of most importance in helping us to develop a deep and close relationship with God. That is what we all seem to want; a deep and close relationship with God. So I'm going to do my best to help you to understand some key things that will help you to learn to pray better and deeper and in a more meaningful way. Hopefully this will be a blessing in your life.

Prayer: Lifting One's Heart and Mind to God

Let's start with the definition of prayer: *Prayer is the lifting of one's heart and mind to God in adoration, thanksgiving, reparation, and petition.* I think that this definition is very important to ponder. Realize that when we pray, we are lifting our entire being to the God of the universe; the God who made the moon and the stars and the sun and the animals and us! We are lifting our minds and our hearts to Him who created everything out of nothing. We must, however, keep one very important thing in mind. When we lift our hearts and minds to God, He is already there waiting for us. God is there gazing upon us and simply waiting for us to respond to Him. Knowing that God is already there is vital. With this knowledge we realize that the first step in prayer is to simply acknowledge God's presence and understand that He is eagerly waiting for us to respond to His invitation to a close relationship with Him. With this in mind, I think it is good to possess the correct disposition that each of us should have when we pray. We should possess the disposition of humility. The virtue of humility is the key to learning to pray in a more meaningful way.

Humility

What is humility? Humility is honesty. It is Truth. What do I mean by that? Well, we have to learn to see ourselves as we truly are. We have to learn to see ourselves in Truth. We have to learn to see ourselves the way God sees us. When we can truly be honest about ourselves and see ourselves as we truly are; the way God sees us; our prayer life will change.

With God there can be nothing false. He knows us completely. He knows the truth about us. God wants to change us; to transform us; from the inside out. He wants to bring us into a deep relationship with Him. He wants to make us holy. He wants to make of us a new creation—a saint. For in Heaven there are only saints and He desires greatly that we join Him in Heaven. We should want this too. Becoming holy and reaching full union with God will bring us complete happiness. Prayer is a key way to do this, but we have to want to change. We have to want God to change us; to change us for the better. If we cannot see ourselves as God sees us, He cannot change us. Why? Because we are not willing to change. We are not open to the grace He is freely offering us. So it is very important that, when we pray, we pray with humility. See yourself as you truly are. See yourself as God sees you. And begin there.

The Pharisee and the Tax Collector

The perfect Bible story to illustrate this disposition of humility in prayer is the Parable that Jesus told of the 'Pharisee and the Tax Collector'. The Parable goes like this: "Two people went up to the temple area to pray; one was a Pharisee and the other was a tax collector. The Pharisee spoke to God saying, 'O God, I thank you that I am not like the rest of humanity—greedy, dishonest, adulterous—or even a sinner like this tax collector. I fast twice a week, and I pay tithes on my whole income.' But the tax collector stood off at a distance and would not even raise his eyes to Heaven, but prayed, 'O God, be merciful to me for I am a sinner.'" Then Jesus said, "I tell you, the latter went home justified and not the former" (Luke 18:9-14).

The truth is this: That Pharisee was a good man! He was! He went above and beyond what was required of him. He fasted much more often than what was required. He paid more money to the Church than what was required! He was a very good man! The tax collector, on the other hand, was a sinner! He cheated people out of their money in order to give to himself more than he deserved. He was a cheater! He was a thief! He was not a good man! So why does Jesus say that the Tax Collector is more justified; more holy; than the Pharisee? How could this cheating, stealing, sinner of a tax collector, be more holy than this Pharisee, who was a very good man?

It all has to do with humility. It all has to do with honesty. The Pharisee was not honest with himself and therefore not honest with God. He did not see himself as he truly was. He did not see himself as God saw him. Therefore his prayer was not honest. This Pharisee claimed that he did not sin. According to his self-evaluation, he was about as perfect as you can get and simply thanked God for his perfection. That just wasn't the Truth. He was a good person, sure, but he was a sinner, and God knew it.

The Tax Collector on the other hand was a sinner, and God knew it, but so did he. The Tax Collector was completely honest with God and therefore honest in his prayer. In his honesty and humility, he couldn't even raise his eyes to Heaven. He truly saw himself the way God saw him. In doing that, he was able to talk to God with complete honesty saying, "O God, be merciful to me—a sinner." In his honesty, he was able to open up his heart to God and receive the grace that God so desperately wanted to give him; grace that would transform him and change his life for the better. We all need to learn from this parable. When we talk to God, we have to be honest. We have to be honest with God and honest with ourselves. A deep relationship with God is truly based on humility. We simply have to see ourselves in truth. We have to see ourselves the way that God sees us. We can then receive the grace He offers us; a grace that will bring about our holiness.

Mean What You Say

Once we are honest with God and speak with honesty and humility, the next step is to mean what you say and say what you mean. Prayer should always come from the heart; not just the head. When you mean what you say to God, and you mean it with your whole heart, everything changes in your prayer life. I remember when I was six years old my dog got hit by a car. My dad rushed her to the vet and the vet began to do what he could to save her life. All the while, I had to wait at home and see what would happen. I don't think I had ever prayed before, like I did that day. I begged God, through sobbing tears, to save my dog's life and He did. The point is this, my prayer was real and I meant it. It came from the depths of my being. I meant what I said to God with my whole heart that day. It was a fervent prayer.

I also remember coming home from school on a Friday evening when I was 16 years old. My next door neighbor was sitting at our kitchen table with my sister who was in college. I walked in the door and was told that my dad was in the hospital and that he was not expected to live through the weekend. I ran to my bedroom and begged God, again through sobbing tears, not to take my dad away from me. My prayer was real and I meant what I said to God with my whole heart that day. Again, from the depths of my being I prayed and my dad lived through that weekend and lived another four years.

And I remember an evening, back in 2000; when I got a phone call from my sister in Indiana telling me that my sixteen year old niece had cancer. Again I begged God, through sobbing tears, not to take my brother's baby away from him. And I meant what I said to God that day. I meant it with my whole heart and my prayer was real.

We should pray like that to God every day. We should mean what we say to God every day and our prayer should be that meaningful. It should come from the depths of our being. Even when things are good, we need to talk to God that deeply…that deeply… every day. And remember, God is reaching out to you in prayer even more than you are reaching out to Him. When you speak, He is attentive. He gives you His full attention and He hears every word you say.

It is equally important to mention that we don't always get what we ask for in prayer. I can remember plenty of times when I have prayed for something to happen and it did not happen. I can look back on many of those occasions and see that it is a very good thing that God did not grant what I wanted. The point is that God knows what is best for us and we have to be open to His will in our lives. We must pray for His will for our lives to be done and trust Him to lead us in the right direction.

Memorized Prayer and Prayer Books

There are many prayer forms and they are all equally good. The key is to simply mean what you say when you talk to God. When I say that there are many prayer forms, what I mean is that we can pray candidly, or in other words, we simply talk to

God in our own words. We can pray using memorized prayers that the Church has taught us or we can use prayer books. One prayer form is not better than another and I recommend using all of them. The key is to mean what you are saying and deeply talk to God.

Let's start with "Memorized Prayer" and use the "Our Father" as an example. We can *say* the "Our Father" or we can *pray* the "Our Father." Believe me, there is a difference. When we say the "Our Father" we simply say the words to that prayer, but when we *pray* the "Our Father" we actually talk to God. The point is that we can recite a memorized prayer or we can actually pray it. When we pray it, we are talking to God and we mean what we are saying. When we simply recite the prayer, we are just saying words; words that mean nothing at the time.

Remember, the key to prayer is to be humble; to be honest; to see yourself as God sees you; and to mean what you are saying to Him. Using a prayer book is another fantastic way to pray. Sometimes these prayer books give us the words we want to say when we can't seem to come up with those words on our own. There is a prayer in one of my prayer books that is a perfect prayer for praying after communion. It does a better job of saying what I truly want to say, than I can come up with by myself. It says, "Jesus, I firmly believe that You are present within me as God and Man, to enrich my soul with graces and to fill my heart with the happiness of the blessed. I believe that You are Christ, the Son of the living God! With deepest humility, I adore You, my Lord and God; You have made my soul Your dwelling place. I love You with my whole heart, my whole soul, and with all my strength. May the love of Your own Sacred Heart fill my soul and purify it so that I may die to the world for love of You, as You died on the Cross for love of me. My God, You are all mine; grant that I may be all Yours in time and in eternity."

That is a beautiful prayer! Don't let anyone tell you that you don't need to learn prayers or that you don't need prayer books. Sometimes prayer books such as these, can give you the perfect words for what you truly want to say. Moreover, these types of books can teach you how to pray. When you use them well and often, you learn how to pray. After a while, you are able to put into words exactly what you are feeling and you may not need the book quite as often. I encourage you to purchase and use a good Catholic prayer book. They are well written and can truly help you to develop a meaningful prayer life. The one that I recommend is simply called "Catholic Book of Prayers."

The Mass

Along with the prayers we as Catholic memorize and the prayer books we use, there is also the greatest prayer of all—The Holy Sacrifice of the Mass (CCC Glossary p. 887). The Mass is one long continuous prayer. In the Mass, we talk to God, and God talks to us. But more than a prayer, it is also a Sacrifice. Jesus offers Himself to God and we offer ourselves to God right along with Him at every Mass. We actually give our lives; our beings; ourselves to God. Jesus, the perfect sacrifice, is also offered to God on our behalf. The Graces that flow from the Mass are infinite! The Mass will become much more meaningful to you, when you begin to understand what it is and what it does. Second, when you begin to participate in the Mass and truly mean what you are saying, it is the most powerful prayer you can pray. When we get old enough and mature enough to realize that at Mass we are there to worship God and then we actually spend that entire hour worshipping God; everything changes in our lives. When each of us goes to Mass and we truly give ourselves to God, as we are supposed to, and we mean what we are saying to Him; everything changes. The Mass becomes the greatest prayer we could possibly pray. At the end of the Mass, God puts

His very Life inside of us in the Eucharist and sends us on our way with the power to go out and change the world. At Mass God puts His very Life inside of us and changes us from the inside out. He makes us Holy.

The Rosary

Now the second most important prayer, next to the Mass, is the Rosary. The Rosary is a very powerful prayer, because when it is prayed, we reflect upon the entire life of Jesus. In the Rosary, we pray for the intercession of Mary, our Spiritual Mother, through the fruits of the Mysteries that we reflect upon. In praying the Rosary, we reflect upon the announcement from the Angel Gabriel that the Savior will be born unto the Virgin Mary. We reflect upon the visitation between Mary and Elizabeth and how Elizabeth recognized that Mary carried in her womb, the Son of God. Even the child that Elizabeth carried in her womb, John the Baptist, recognized the Mother of God who carried the Savoir of the World, at the sound of her greeting. In the Rosary, we reflect upon the Birth of Christ; the Presentation of Jesus in the Temple; and the time when Jesus was lost for three days and found in the Temple teaching the elders—The Joyful Mysteries.

In the Rosary, we reflect upon the life of Christ during His ministry: As he performed His first miracle at the wedding in Cana; when He was Baptized by John in the Jordan River; when he proclaimed in the synagogue that the Kingdom of God was at hand; at His Transfiguration on the mountain; and when He instituted the Eucharist at the Last Supper—The Luminous Mysteries.

In the Rosary, we reflect upon Christ's Passion: The agony in the Garden; the scourging at the pillar; the crowning with thorns; the carrying of the cross; and His crucifixion—The Sorrowful Mysteries.

In the Rosary, we reflect upon Jesus' glorious Resurrection and Ascension into Heaven; the Descent of the Holy Spirit upon the Apostles; and how Jesus took Mary, body and soul, into Heaven and crowned her as Queen of Heaven—The Glorious Mysteries.

These reflections allow us to contemplate the entire life of Jesus. They help us to grow in holiness as we try to discern their meaning in our life today.

When prayed, the Rosary gives us many graces and blessings. St. Francis de Sales said, "The Rosary is the ladder to Heaven." Pray the Rosary daily. All you need is 20 minutes; a Rosary; and a little book telling you how to pray the Rosary in case you don't know. Today you can even download an App for your iPhone or iPad called "iRosary." This App is a great way to pray the Rosary, especially for those who don't know how. It even has pictures of each Mystery and provides the prayers in written form. Think about who and what you give 20 minutes of your time to each day. Think about whether you have 20 minutes that you can give to the praying of the Rosary before you go to bed at night. I bet you could do it if you really wanted to.

Our lives change when our habits change. Create good habits that will change your life for the better and bring you into a closer relationship with God.

Scripture

Besides memorized prayer; prayer books; the Mass; and the Rosary, reading the Bible and reflecting upon it is also a form of prayer. It is very important that you have your own Bible and that you read it regularly. It is great to read the Bible from beginning to end in order to get the whole picture of Salvation History, but it can also be read by skipping around. In that case I suggest starting with the Gospels and reading the entire New

Testament straight through. Keep in mind however, that when doing this; it is like beginning a book in the middle and skipping the entire beginning. You will understand the New Testament much better if you read and study the Old Testament first. That is true because once you understand the Old Testament; you can see how the New fulfills it and then it gets very interesting. The key when reading the Bible is to stop and reflect upon it and ask how you can live what it teaches. Taking the adult Bible Study Programs that are offered at many parishes will also help you a great deal. At Holy Spirit, we offer the "Great Adventure" Bible Study that is produced by Ascension Press. It is excellent!

If you want to get into deep prayer with the Bible, pray the book of Psalms. They are beautiful and are perfect for every mood and situation. They can help you learn to pray very well. They are just like a prayer book.

Remember that the Bible is the Word of God. This is both a book and a person, because Jesus is the incarnate Word of God. So the Bible is a living book that truly speaks to your heart. God communicates to you through it. Open up your heart and let Him speak to you in this way.

If you decide to read the Bible through from beginning to end, I suggest that you begin with the Historical Books first and read them straight through. Then you can go back and read the supplemental books that support the history. This will keep you moving through the story and that is very important. Follow the following pattern:

Read the Bible in this order:

- Genesis
- Exodus
- Numbers
- Joshua
- Judges

- 1st Samuel
- 2nd Samuel
- 1st Kings
- 2nd Kings
- Ezra
- Nehemiah
- 1st Maccabees
- And then read the Gospel of Luke
- Acts of the Apostles
- Then read the remaining Gospels and the rest of the New Testament in order.

Supplemental Books:

- Leviticus is a supplement to Exodus. It is a guide book for the Levite Priests.
- Deuteronomy is a supplement to Numbers. It repeats the story.
- Ruth is a supplement to Judges.
- The Book of Psalms; 1st Chronicles, Proverbs, Ecclesiastes, and the Song of Solomon are supplements to 1st and 2nd Samuel.
- 2nd Chronicles, Obadiah, Job, Amos, Jonah, Hosea, Isaiah, Micah, and Tobit are supplements to 1st Kings.
- Nahum, Habakkuk, Daniel, Ezekiel, Judith, Lamentations, Jeremiah, Zephaniah, and Baruch supplement 2nd Kings.
- Zechariah, Haggai, and Esther supplement Ezra.
- Malachi supplements Nehemiah.
- 2nd Maccabees, the Wisdom of Solomon, and Sirach supplement 1st Maccabees.

Candid Prayer

Memorized prayer; prayer books; the Mass; the Rosary; and reading Scripture are all very important prayer forms that we should all practice and use to develop our prayer life. Keep in mind, however, that it is also very, very important to simply talk to God candidly. It is very important to talk to God just like you are talking to your very best friend. You see, God knows everything. He knows everything that you are doing and everything that is happening to you. He has given you every talent and ability you possess. He accomplishes every good thing you do. Tell Him your problems; your worries; your exciting achievements. Praise Him and thank Him for blessing you and giving you all that you have. Even thank Him for the things that are not going as well as you would like. They are opportunities for you to grow closer to Him. In short, talk to God about everything. He should be your most intimate friend.

You have an outside world where you interact with the world around you. It all happens... out there. But don't you also have an inner life as well; a life on the inside of you that is private where all your thoughts take place? This inside world is where God dwells. This is where we talk to God. Develop your inside life and begin to talk to God very often. You can literally talk to God all day long and no one would know it but you. Talk in your inside life to God, all day long. If you gradually work on this, you will develop a deep and strong relationship with Him that will be a huge blessing to you.

Here are some key things that you should ask of God every single day as you casually talk to Him in your inner life: 1) Tell God that you love Him. 2) Tell God that you want to know what His will is for your life and that you are devoted to doing His will. You see, you can come up with your own plan for your life, but God's plan for your life is far better than anything you could possibly come up with on your own. So seek to know

His Will for your life and you will find happiness here on earth. 3) Ask God to increase your love for Him; to help you love Him more. 4) Ask God to make you holy, because you cannot do this on your own. 5) Ask God to guide your life and to help you not to sin. 6) Tell God that you want to give your life to Him; that you truly want to belong to Him and live for Him. 7) Pray for others: those in your family; those who are sick; deceased relatives and friends; those who are going through a rough time. 8) Pray for your priests; your bishop; and our Pope. 9) Pray for morality and for God's will to be done in the secular world. 10) Pray for peace.

A Prayer Routine

It is really important that you establish a prayer routine. This means that you have a set time every day that you pray. It also means that you pray in much the same way every day. People who have a set prayer routine tend to stick with it. They are far more likely to pray every day. Our lives change when our habits change and until we get into the habit of praying, we will only do it randomly. So I strongly encourage you to develop a prayer routine if you haven't already done so.

For an example, I'll share my prayer routine with you. This is not to say that the way I do it is best. It is just important to have a routine and I can share mine with you as an example.

Each morning as I get out of bed, I pray the prayer "The Morning Offering." I pray this prayer without fail every single day and it is always the first prayer I pray. As I get ready for work, which takes me an hour, I pray candidly. I speak to Jesus the entire time. I pray first for the souls in Purgatory, especially those who no one is praying for. Next I pray for my deceased relatives and the deceased relatives of my husband. I literally name each person by name. Then I pray for deceased friends of the family, again naming names. Next I pray for the holiness of my husband and my children and I ask God to help them with all of the hard things they are facing. Then I pray for the holiness of my brother and my five sisters, their spouses, children, and extended families. Then I do the same for my husband's mother and his brothers. Next, I pray for all those who are sick and I name every person who needs my prayers. After that, I pray for every priest I know, by name, and all the other priests of our diocese and the world including all bishops, cardinals and our Holy Father, Pope Francis. I pray for their holiness; that they will do only God's will; for an increase in vocations to the priesthood; and for God's grace upon all of them. I then pray for all deacons and religious. At this point I pray an "Our Father," a "Hail Mary" and a "Glory Be" for all of them and for the Pope's intentions. Next I ask Jesus to bless my efforts to lead others to Him; not for my glory, but to genuinely lead people to Christ for His sake and theirs. I thank Jesus for letting me, a person of great unworthiness, help Him by teaching the faith. At this point I begin to pray for morality in the world; for abortion, euthanasia, and all other destruction of life to end. I pray for God's will to be done. Then I ask for help for anything difficult happening in my life. Next I pray for holiness, something I know that I cannot accomplish on my own. After that, I tell Jesus that I am sorry for my sins and I usually name them. I tell Jesus again and again that I do not want to sin; that I do not want to hurt Him and to please help me and protect me. Then I usually pray the "Prayer to the Guardian Angel" and the "Prayer to St. Michael."

On the way to work, I pray the Rosary. I have a twenty-five minute drive so this works out well. I have the Rosary on CD so that it can be played in my car if I want to use that. I also have it on my phone so that it can be streamed in using Blue Tooth.

I usually arrive to work (the church) by 7:15 AM. Daily Mass begins at 7:30 AM. So I head to the church in order to attend Mass. If I arrive to work by 7:00 AM, which happens on good days, I go around and pray the "Stations of the Cross" before Mass begins. I pray the Stations of the Cross for my deceased relatives and seek to gain an Indulgence for them. (More about Indulgences later).

The rest of the day, I just speak to Jesus whenever I feel like it and every time I think of Him. I just talk. Mostly I tell Him that I love Him or say a word of thanks for the help I'm getting.

In the evening, once I am home and dinner is over, I engage in spiritual reading. I constantly have a book on the Catholic Faith that I am reading so that I am in a constant state of learning. I also read the Bible. I don't always get to do this, so I cherish this time when I do get to.

When I get in bed at night, I pray candidly and just talk to Jesus about my day. I tell Him that I really want to be with Him forever in Heaven. I pray for mercy. This is a very brief prayer.

In this way, I have developed a prayer routine. It is easy, once it becomes habit, to stick with it. In fact, it becomes very strange when something causes my routine to get messed up. I can honestly say that a developed prayer routine will help you to grow closer to Jesus and to grow in holiness. It is a must!

Part II. The Sacraments—A General Understanding

Sacraments by Definition

There are seven sacraments: Baptism, Reconciliation, Eucharist, Confirmation, Matrimony, Holy Orders, and Anointing of the Sick. The following is the definition of a Sacrament from the Adult Catechism of the Catholic Church: *A Sacrament is an efficacious sign of grace, instituted by Christ and entrusted to the Church, by which divine life is dispensed to us by the work of the Holy Spirit (CCC Glossary p.898)*. This definition may sound technical, but it is really a good one. When we break the definition down, we see that it is really quite simple; and not only simple; but we are able to understand more fully what a Sacrament actually is. Knowing what Sacraments are can change your life, especially when you seek them with a purpose and gain from them the holiness you desire. So let's break the definition down and look at the five aspects of it:

A Sacrament is an EFFICACIOUS SIGN OF GRACE
Let us begin with 'Sign of Grace' before we go to Efficacious.

Sign of Grace

In every single sacrament, we experience something on the OUTSIDE of our bodies. It might be as simple as the WORDS we hear, "I absolve you from your sins in the Name of the Father and of the Son and of the Holy Spirit," as we hear in the Sacrament of Reconciliation. It may be something that we *FEEL* as when we feel water poured over us in the Sacrament of Baptism. Again it might be something that we *FEEL* as in the oil of the sick; the holy oil that is used to make the sign of the cross on the hands and forehead of a sick person being anointed in the Sacrament of the Anointing of the Sick. It could be something we *TASTE* when we eat the Body of Christ and drink from the cup His Precious Blood. This is the sign of Grace that we receive.

We experience this sign on the *outside* of our bodies in some way, but that *outside* experience only serves to help us to understand the *Internal Reality* that has taken place. Sacraments *penetrate all the way through our bodies and into our souls.*

In every sacrament, we experience a taste or a sound or a touch and we see with our eyes, but what we experience with our senses serves to help us to understand what happens to us on the spiritually; on the inside. A Sacrament is an external *sign* of an *Internal Reality. God touches our souls in every sacrament.* We come face to face with Jesus in every single sacrament and He takes His very hand and imparts Grace to each of us. Jesus places His very Life inside of us. His Life; this Grace is called Sanctifying Grace (CCC2023).

Adam and Eve lost the indwelling of Divine Life that God had given them when they ate of the fruit of the "Tree of Knowledge of Good and Evil." Everything changed when they ate of it. They experienced a spiritual death. Their physical bodies kept on living, but God's Divine Life, was no longer present in their souls.

This helps us to understand why the sacraments are so important. In the sacraments, Jesus places His Life and Love, Sanctifying Grace into our souls. So you see that through the Sacraments the Divine Life of God, that Adam and Eve lost, is placed into our souls! So it is through the Sacraments that Jesus makes each of us holy (CCC 375-376; 1212). Moreover, Jesus is the Only Begotten Son of God. Through the sacraments we are able to share in His "Divine Sonship". This *Sonship* is not something that Adam and Eve had a share in even before their sin took place.

The Sacraments are not superficial. They are not just an outside experience. They are deep. They penetrate all the way to our souls.

Do you want to be holy? Receive the Sacraments! Receive them in faith as often as you can. As you cooperate with His Grace, you can and will attain holiness. The sacraments that we are allowed to receive often are Reconciliation and Eucharist. We are allowed to receive the Eucharist daily at Mass. We can receive Reconciliation any time by making an appointment with a priest or by coming when the sacrament is being offered. That is normally every Saturday evening before Mass.

Efficacious

Now let's tackle the word "*Efficacious*." Sacraments always DO what they INTEND to do....every time. We desire that God puts His life inside of us to make us holy... and what happens? God does put His life inside of us to make us holy...every single time. Sacraments are efficacious. They do what they intend to do...every single time. They bring about the desired result. Sacraments are an Efficacious sign of grace. It is a sign, that we experience through one or more of our 5 senses, which imparts Grace..., God's Life... on the inside of us every single time.

If the intention of Baptism is to wash away Original Sin and fill us with the Holy Spirit... then that is exactly what happens at every Baptism. If the intention of Confirmation is to mark us as witness for Christ; seal our Baptismal Graces; and give to us the full outpouring of the Holy Spirit, therefore strengthening the Gifts of the Spirit... then that is exactly what happens when we receive the Sacrament of Confirmation....every time for every person who receives the sacrament worthily.

Instituted By Christ

Who gave us each Sacrament? Remember—these are the Institutions that the twelve Apostles began all over the world; the same everywhere and everywhere the same. If they came from the original Twelve, where did they get them? They got them from Jesus, Himself (CCC 1114).

Every single Sacrament can be found in the Bible. Some are found explicitly in the Bible, which means they are shown directly to us in a very obvious way. An example would be Baptism. We see the Baptism of Jesus in the Gospel as He was baptized by John in the Jordan River. We're told that Jesus baptized people in John 3:22. Then later Jesus tells the Apostles to "Go therefore and make disciples of all nations baptizing them in the name of the Father and of the Son and of the Holy Spirit" (Matt 28:19). He even says, "Unless one is born again of water and the Spirit, he cannot enter the kingdom of God" (John 3:5). Of course Jesus was speaking of Baptism.

Another example would be the Sacrament of Eucharist. In John chapter 6 Jesus says that He is going to give us His Flesh to eat and His Blood to Drink. Then at the Last Supper He does exactly what He said He was going to do. Paul goes on to tell us in 1 Corinthians 10:16 that receiving the Eucharist is participating in the Body and Blood of Christ. In 1 Corinthians 11:23-29 Paul warns us that receiving the Eucharist unworthily makes us guilty of profaning the Body and the Blood.

Other sacraments are implicitly found in the Bible. That means they are implied; mentioned as if we already know what they are and are very familiar with them. And as Catholics, we are familiar with them and live them as part of our faith.

An example would be the Sacrament of Reconciliation. The Book of James tells us, "Confess your sins and be forgiven." In the gospels we hear how Jesus appeared to the Apostles on the evening of His Resurrection saying to them, "Whose sins you forgive are forgiven. Whose sins you retained are retained" (John 20:23). We as Catholics know what that means. It means to avail of the Sacrament of Reconciliation and receive Absolution from a priest.

The point is this: Jesus gave each sacrament to the Church. He established each one and they are important, because Jesus works through the Sacraments in order to give us His very Life and Love so that we can become holy or holier. It makes perfect sense doesn't it? If God puts His life inside of a person, wouldn't that person then become like God—holy as He is holy? (CCC 1127). I have often heard theologians say, "God became man so that man might become God." This means that through the sacraments, we truly share in His Divine Life.

Entrusted to the Church

What do we have to do in order to receive a Sacrament? We have to come to the Church. Jesus left a Church in charge. Jesus gave His authority to The Church. Jesus gave us a Church to guide us to Heaven. That Church has been entrusted to give or to dispense the Sacraments to us (CCC 1118).

By Which Divine Life is Dispensed to Us

Sacraments place Sanctifying Grace, the Life of Jesus, into our souls. The only way to receive a Sacrament is to come to the Church and the Church will dispense the Sacrament to you. You cannot sit in your living room and receive Sanctifying Grace; God's very Life, into your soul. There is no way that can happen. You must come to The Church and receive it from The Church because that is who Jesus entrusted the Sacraments to (CCC1129).

By the Power of the Holy Spirit

Our God is a Triune God. This means that He is one God, but three separate and distinct Persons. He is God the Father, who created all; who loves us and wants to be our very own Father. He is God the Son, who became a Man and died for our sins redeeming us so that we can become the adopted sons and daughters of God. He is the Holy Spirit; God's very Breath of Life; God's Love; that enters our souls and makes us holy. He is the Sanctifier.

It is by the Power of the Holy Spirit, that these Sacraments become a reality. God's power makes them an internal reality instead of simply an outside symbol. Sacraments are not just something we experience on the outside of our bodies, making them mere symbols. The outside symbol only serves to help us to understand the internal reality that is taking place. It is what happens to us on the inside that counts. This is what makes us holy. And it is the Power of the Holy Spirit that we are made holy (CCC 1116). In order to actually become holy, we must cooperate with this grace, this Life of God that has been placed into our souls.

Prayer and Sacraments

A life of prayer in which we lift our hearts and minds to God in complete humility will make us holy. Likewise, leading a sacramental life will fill us with the Grace of God—His Life and Love will truly dwell within our soul. Lifting our hearts and minds to Him and filling our soul with the very Life of God gradually sanctifies us throughout our life. It prepares us to reach the kind of holiness that is needed to enter Heaven for all eternity. This is the life of a Catholic. This is the job of the Church—to help us reach Heaven through her guidance and love for each of us.

VII. The Sacrament of Baptism

The Beginning of Life

A newborn baby comes into the world with a soul that has the fullness of *natural life*. He has all the capabilities and powers that belong to the nature of human beings. He has the ability to see and to hear and to feel. As he grows and develops, he will have the power to think and to remember and to love. He has all that is due to human nature and nothing more.

The reason that he has nothing more is because his forefather, Adam, failed to earn it for him. God imparted to Adam a *supernatural* life in addition to his natural life. This means that God Himself dwelt in Adam's soul. Simply put, Adam possessed God's Life and Love in his soul. Adam possessed Sanctifying Grace. Whatever Adam did, God was acting in him and with him. God's plan was for Adam and Eve to enter eternal happiness with Him in Heaven at the end of their lives.

Sanctifying Grace was a heritage that Adam would pass down to the rest of the human race. For Adam to make Sanctifying Grace secure for himself and his descendants, only one thing was necessary: He must obey God's command not to eat of the fruit of the Tree of Knowledge of Good and Evil, a certain tree located in the Garden of Eden.

Adam failed to obey God's command. He ate of the forbidden fruit committing the first human sin, the *original sin*. He chose himself over God. In rejecting God, Adam cut himself off from union with God. The supernatural life that God had placed in his soul was now gone. Adam lost Sanctifying Grace. He lost it not only for himself, but for the whole human race. Why? Because at this time, Adam *was* the human race. In him all of mankind was potentially present. Sanctifying Grace was not something that man was entitled to. It was and is an undeserved gift of God's Life to us; a gift of unimaginable worth.

God did not reject Adam because of his great sin. In the depths of God's love, He chose to give each individual a chance to gain for himself this gift of Sanctifying Grace; this gift of God's Life and Love. By becoming the man, Jesus Christ, God suffered and died for our sins making infinite atonement for Adam's sin and consequently the sin of the entire human race. Because He was both God and man, Jesus bridged the gap between humanity and divinity.

This is why a newborn comes into this world with a soul that has the fullness of natural life, but does not possess the *supernatural life* of God. We say that the child is "in the state of original sin."

Original Sin

Original Sin is not something that is in the soul. Rather, it something that is *not* in the soul. With Original Sin, the soul is darkened when it should be lit. Original Sin is therefore the absence of light; the absence of Sanctifying Grace; the absence of God's very Life.

Jesus instituted the Sacrament of Baptism in order to restore Sanctifying Grace to our souls. Jesus applies to each individual soul the atonement which He made on the cross for Original Sin and all sins. Jesus will not force His gift upon us; His gift of supernatural life, but it is His will that we each accept it. We accept it by receiving the sacrament of Baptism. In Baptism, Original Sin disappears as God becomes present in the soul, and the soul is caught up into that sharing of God's own Life which we call Sanctifying Grace.

Infant Baptism

As Catholics we bring our infants to the parish church to receive the Sacrament of Baptism. We do this when our baby is very young, perhaps only a week or two weeks old. This is because we understand Baptism to be of the upmost urgency. Because of our faith, we accept this gift on behalf of our child.

As Catholics we are sometimes criticized for this by people of other faiths. They point out that the child never accepted this gift of divine life. A baby is not capable of doing so. It is true that their acceptance of Sanctifying Grace was a passive one, but they will have the chance when they become older to decide whether they want to confirm what took place at their Baptism. This happens in the Sacrament of Confirmation. At Confirmation, their baptismal graces will be sealed and confirmed and they will receive the full outpouring of the Holy Spirit as the Apostles did on the day of Pentecost. Until then they are safe in the Eternal Covenant of God.

You see Baptism is also the entrance into the Eternal Covenant; the covenant that Jesus established at the Last Supper. The Eternal Covenant is the Kingdom of God—the Church. So in Baptism, the child gains entrance into the Church and becomes a Catholic. This is the day that this baby becomes a child of God a member of God's own family.

This is no different than the way Jesus entered into the Old Testament Covenant and became a child of God; a member of God's own family. When Jesus was just eight days old, He was circumcised and given entrance into the Covenant. And at the Temple He was presented to God and a sacrifice of two turtle doves was offered by His parents (Luke 21-24). Remember, circumcision was the external sign that marked a person's entrance into the Old Covenant. Today however, we enter the New Covenant through Baptism. Jesus Himself passively accepted entrance into the Old Covenant, but as He grew and matured He accepted the faith of His parents like every other Jewish boy.

We also know through Apostolic Tradition that the Apostles baptized infants. In Acts Chapter 16 the entire household of Lydia was baptized. No one was excluded. There is every reason to believe that children and even babies were present. Moreover, Christ wants to take into his arms the little children of today, just as He embraced the children of His time (Mark 10:13-16). It also shows that we don't have to do anything to earn Sanctifying Grace: God's Life and Love, which is freely given to us, and infants, as a gift.

A Parent's Obligation

Parents who have their children baptized should take seriously their obligation to bring their children up in the faith of the Catholic Church. In the baptism ceremony, Catholic Parents make solemn promises to do just that. Parents should pray for and with their children and be the first teachers of the faith to their children in word and in example. They are obligated to lead their children to receive the other sacraments of the Church and guide them along a path to holiness. If parents have their children baptized and then do not raise them as Catholics, they are denying their children the very Life of God begun in baptism. They are cutting their children off from the supply of Sanctifying Grace that flows from the other sacraments.

The Effects of Baptism

A baby is not capable of committing sin, but as he develops and grows he will begin to commit what we call "Personal Sin" or "Actual Sin." Baptism takes away not only

Original Sin, but all sin. Moreover, it takes away all punishment due to sin. Sin and its consequences disappear when God enters the soul just as darkness disappears when the light is turned on. So when an adult is baptized, their soul is made perfect; ready for Heaven at that very moment (that is until they commit sin again).

Two things happen to us when we are baptized. First, we receive the supernatural Life of God, called Sanctifying Grace, which removes Original Sin (the darkness) from our soul. Second, our souls receive a permanent mark or the character of baptism.

If we commit Mortal Sin after Baptism, God's Life is removed from our soul. The flow of Divine Life is cut off from us. We lose Sanctifying Grace, but we do not lose the baptismal character. Because we possess the baptismal character, it is easy for us to regain the Sanctifying Grace that was lost. In that case we turn to another sacrament, Reconciliation. It is only by a sacrament that Divine Life or Sanctifying Grace can be placed in our souls.

The Symbols used in Baptism

Jesus said, "No one can enter the Kingdom of God without being born of water and the Spirit. What is born of flesh is flesh and what is born of spirit is spirit" (John 3:5-6). In baptism, **water** is used as the symbol of *washing away* Original Sin and all sin. Water is used to cleanse and is therefore the perfect symbol for Christ to use for Baptism. Remember, the external symbol or sign only serves to shows to us the internal reality that is taking place. As we feel the waters of Baptism being poured over us, the darkness in our soul is being removed or washed away. Our soul becomes lit with the light of Christ. For this reason a **Baptismal Candle** is another sign used in

Baptism. It reminds us that "Christ is the light of the world (John 8:12).

St. Paul wrote that "We were indeed buried with Him (Christ) through Baptism into death" (Romans 6:4). This means that we have died of our old life of sin, because baptism brings 'death' to sin—Original Sin and Personal Sin. If we are buried with Christ than we also rise to new life with Christ. Through the waters of Baptism we die to our old life of sin and rise up out of the water into a new life of grace.

The **oil of catechumen** is used in Baptism as well. It is a blessed oil or chrism used to signify the comfort and strength given by the Holy Spirit. The priest or deacon dips his finger into this chrism and then makes the Sign of the Cross on the person being baptized.

In Baptism a **white garment** is placed on the person being baptized signifying that we have truly "Put on Christ." (This is usually a white stole that is place around our shoulders or a white bib placed around an infant.) This recalls the words of Paul when he said, "For all of you who were baptized into Christ have clothed yourself with Christ" (Galatians 3:27). We must take this very seriously. If we have been "clothed with Christ" then we must take Him to the world. We therefore have a serious obligation to share His love with others; to evangelize; and spread the gospel. In the Sacrament of Confirmation, we are given further strength to carry out this mission.

If someone were to ask you, "What is the most important thing in life for everyone without exception?" What would you say? If your Catholic training has been sufficient, you would respond, "Baptism." Baptism places the very Life of God, Sanctifying Grace, into our souls. This is a free gift of God's Life and love. It is God's will that you accept it and embrace it.

VIII. The Sacrament of Reconciliation

The Sacrament of Reconciliation is a sacrament that we may receive as often as we like. You may hear it called 'Penance' from time to time, because it has been called 'Penance' in the past. Children and adults alike tend to simply call it the 'Sacrament of Confession' or simply 'confession' for short. Reconciliation, however, is the correct title for this sacrament. This is true because the word Reconciliation means 'the act of being reconciled' or 'the state of being reconciled.' To be reconciled means to 'reestablish a close relationship with.' In the sacrament of Reconciliation, we as Catholics confess our sins and receive Absolution for them. Our sins are completely forgiven and we therefore reestablish a close relationship with Jesus; with the Church; and with one another.

I think that this is a sacrament that people coming into the Catholic Church might tend to feel a bit apprehensive toward. But let me assure you that we will calm all of your fears and help you to realize that the confession of sins is very, very easy and also very natural. In fact, it is liberating! There is an old saying, "confession is good for the soul" and there is much truth in that saying. People tend to carry around a lot of guilt, which can eat at them causing physical and emotional problems. Nothing brings more peace than to hear a priest tell you that your sins are forgiven. For you see, when a priest says these words he is only acting for Christ and it is truly Jesus who speaks to you in this sacrament and forgives your sins.

Jesus came to call sinners (Mark 2:17); he welcomed them and even ate with them (Luke 15:2). He spoke the words of healing and peace, "Your sins are forgiven" many, many times as recorded in Scripture. Jesus came so that our sins could be forgiven. He even suffered and died for them. He wanted to extend God's mercy to all sinners, but He did so by calling people to repentance. He wanted them to call to mind their sins and to ask for God's healing and forgiveness. He said, "This is the time of fulfillment. The Kingdom of God is at hand. Repent, and believe in the gospel" (Mark 1:15).

A woman came to Jesus while He was dining at the house of Simon the Pharisee. She was so deeply sorry for her sins that she knelt down at Jesus' feet, bathed them with her tears, dried them with her hair, and anointed them with ointment. She was sorry for her sins to the point of being distraught over them. Jesus spoke the exact words that she so desperately needed to hear, "Your sins are forgiven. Go in peace" (Luke 7:48,50). I know for certain that I have been just as distraught over my personal sins as this woman was. Hearing the words "Your sins are forgiven, go in peace" are true words of healing and are just as much needed today, if not more so, than 2,000 years ago.

A man named Zacchaeus wanted to see Jesus. The crowd was large and he was short in stature. So he climbed a sycamore tree in order to have a better look as Jesus walked by. Zacchaeus was a sinner. He was a tax collector for the Romans. These people were known for being extortionists. They collected more money than the people owed in taxes in order to line their own pockets. Zacchaeus wanted to see Jesus for one reason that day. He had feelings of guilt. He was seeking forgiveness and Jesus knew it. As the Lord passed under the sycamore tree, He looked up and saw Zacchaeus. In his eyes Jesus saw the need for forgiveness and the desire to change. Zacchaeus repented of his sins right then and there. He declared, "Half of my possessions, Lord, I shall give to the poor, and if I have extorted anything from anyone, I shall repay it four times over." Zacchaeus was deeply sorry for his sins and desperately in need of a forgiveness that heals. So sorry in fact, was Zacchaeus, that he wanted to turn from his sinful life and begin to live a new life in the Lord.

Zacchaeus had a conversion experience: a turning away from sin and a turning toward a life in Christ. Jesus responded, "Today salvation has come to you!"

No sin is too big for Christ. He came to forgive every sin, no matter how grave. As Jesus died on the cross, He prayed even for those who had Him crucified. He said, "Father, forgive them, they know not what they do" (Luke 23:34). Judas Iscariot, who betrayed Jesus for thirty pieces of silver, did not think that he could be forgiven. In his grief and despair over his great sin, he hung himself. This was a great tragedy. None of us should ever think that our sins are too great; too grave to be forgiven. Christ's loving arms are wide enough to embrace every person. He wants to extend God's mercy to all people, through His Church's healing Sacrament of Reconciliation.

Confession of Sins from the Old Testament to the New Testament

In the next few paragraphs, I would like to show you that the confession of sins dates far back into the Old Testament so that you can see its progression into the New Testament.

When an Israelite sinned in Old Testament times, he had to do something. When he committed a grave sin, he was required to make up for his sins in a very real and outward way. The Israelite had to take a bull, a goat, a ram, or a sheep and take it to the Temple in Jerusalem. This animal was part of his property. He owned it. If he did not own such an animal, he had to purchase it. The larger the sin, the bigger the animal he must bring or purchase and the more costly it was. The Israelite then brought the animal to the high priest and confessed his sin. The high priest then sliced the throat of the animal; drained its blood; and offered it up as a sacrifice for the man's sin so that it could be forgiven. Then, and only then, did he receive forgiveness (See Leviticus Chapters 4-7).

You see, the Israelite was making a sacrifice, and a rather costly one at that, in order to make up for his sins. This was the only way his sins could be forgiven.

Why did the Israelites of the Old Testament do this? This was a law given to Moses by God. This is how God instructed Moses to have the people make up for their sins. God instructed Moses and Moses instructed the people.

There was also a feast day where the people would have communal confession. Once each year, on the Feast of *Yom Kippur*, the Jews would come to the High Priest and confess their sins to him. The High Priest would then say those sins while placing his hands on the head of a goat, thereby laying the sins upon the goat. The goat would then be led into the desert and abandoned all the while taking the peoples' sins with it. This is where the term scapegoat comes from (See Leviticus 16:21-22).

When John the Baptist came to pave the road for Jesus, by preaching repentance, people would confess their sins to John and be baptized. John did not baptize anyone until they first confessed their sins to him (Matt 3:1-6).

So the idea of confessing sins was nothing new to the Jews, who then became the first people of the early Christian Church. This was how it was done in the Old Testament times. Always remember that the Old Testament practices were but a shadow of the way that the New Covenant or New Testament would be fulfilled. Jesus did not come to abolish the Old. He came to fulfill it (Matt 5:17). In other words, Jesus did not come to abolish the practice of confessing one's sins; He came to bring the confession of sins to a new and bolder height. He raised it to the level of a sacrament in which He could place God's very Life and Love; Sanctifying Grace into our souls.

There was one big difference between confessing sins by the Old Law, the Old Covenant, and confessing sins in the New Covenant. The confession and forgiveness of sins in the New Covenant did not involve an animal sacrifice. Instead, the people simply confessed their sins to the Apostles and they were given Absolution by them. You see, there was no need for animal sacrifices anymore, because Jesus' sacrifice on the cross paid the debt for all sins that had ever been committed or ever would be committed. Jesus is the *Lamb of God*. He is the Lamb that was sacrificed for our sins. He was the PERFECT sin offering. He was the only sacrifice that truly pleased God and could completely make atonement for our sins. Nothing else was needed (CCC 1851).

When you and I confess our sins to a priest, we are simply continuing to do today, what the people did back in the early years of the Church after the Resurrection of Jesus. People then confessed their sins to the Apostles. The Apostles were ordained ministers, commissioned to act for Jesus. They were His hands; His feet; and His mouth here on earth. Through the Sacrament of Holy Orders, the Apostles commissioned more Apostles or bishops and also presbyters or priests. Today, we confess our sins to a priest, an ordained minister, who has been commissioned to act for Christ. The people then were given a penance and received absolution of their sins, the same as it is done today. But remember that Jesus raised the confession of sins to the level of a sacrament. This means that when we call to mind our sins and are truly sorry for them; come to the Church; confess them; and receive forgiveness, Jesus places His very life into our souls. We receive Sanctifying Grace (CCC 1468).

What's the Big Deal about Sin?

Sin is a really big deal. It must be or Jesus would not have had to suffer so greatly and die for our sins. It must be or Jesus would not have established the Sacrament of Reconciliation. It must be or God would not have commanded Moses to require the people to offer up animal sacrifices for their sins.

God spoke to our first parents, Adam and Eve. He made it very clear, "You can eat from every tree except one. And if you eat of it," God said, "On the day you eat of it, you will surely die" (Gen 2:16). God was very specific.

The serpent lied and said, "You won't die" (Gen 2:16).

Adam and Eve went ahead and ate and what happened? Did they die or did they continue to live? We know that Adam and Eve experienced a spiritual death that day. In disobeying God, Adam and Eve committed a Mortal Sin causing them to lose the Divine Life that God had given them. God's Life left their soul right then and there. The closeness they felt to God; the personal relationship they had with God was gone! The ability to live forever was gone! God had actually breathed into Adam's nostrils the *Breath of Life*. God had breathed into Adam His very own Spirit and Adam became a living soul. God had truly put His own Life into Adam.

There are two ways to live. Of course we live by our bodies, but understand, we also live by our spirits. If there are two ways to live, then there are two ways to die. Our bodies can die and they will. But our spiritual lives can die inside of us too; even though our bodies go right on living as if everything is just fine. When we deliberately commit Mortal Sin, a very serious deadly sin, God's own Divine Life is snuffed out, even though our bodies are in good health (CCC 1861).

After the sin was committed by Adam and Eve, God showed up in the garden. The Bible tells us that Adam and Eve heard the sound of the Lord God walking in the garden in the cool of the day and they hid themselves from the presence of the Lord.

God asked Adam, "Where are you?" (Gen 3:9)
Understand that God was not asking Adam for his geographical
whereabouts. God knew where Adam and Eve were. When God
asked Adam, 'Where are you?' He was asking Adam, "Where are
you, in your relationship with me?"

Adam replied, "I heard the sound of you in the garden and
I was afraid, because I was naked and so I hid myself" (Gen
3:10). Adam gives four responses to one question and he doesn't
even seem to answer the question God asked. If Adam had only
said, "I'm over here behind the bush. I'm hiding; I'm naked; I'm
ashamed; because I really messed up! Can you please forgive
me?" Perhaps he could have changed the course of history.

Instead, Adam shows no remorse for what he has done.
He shows no sorrow for the sin he has just committed. Instead,
Adam says—"I heard you coming. I heard the sound of you in
the garden and I was afraid so I hid myself."

How many times do we feel afraid when we have been
caught doing something wrong? Instead of feeling sorry and
admitting what we have done and seeking forgiveness, we just
feel afraid. We quickly think of a way to get ourselves out of the
trouble we are in. Who can I blame for what I have done? Who
can take the blame for this so that I don't have to? What kind of
excuse can I come up with so my actions look justified?

God knew Adam and Eve had eaten of the forbidden fruit
and so He said, "Have you eaten of the tree of which I
commanded you not to eat?" (Gen 3:11) What was God doing by
asking this? Understand that God was not trying to get a
confession out of Adam. He was trying to get an *act of Contrition*
out of him. He wanted Adam to admit his sin and say he was
sorry. Instead of an act of contrition; instead of admitting his sin,
his fault; Adam said, "The woman who you put here with me; she
gave me the fruit of the tree and I ate it" (Gen 3:12).

Adam blames Eve. After all, Eve gave him the fruit! It's her fault. But look at the words carefully. Who else is Adam blaming when he says, "The woman that *you* put here with me; she made me do it." He's not just blaming Eve. He is blaming God! He is saying in essence, "God, you are the one who put her here with me and look what she's done!"

God, in his infinite patience, turned to the woman and said, "What is this that you have done?" And the woman gives the shortest answer, but it is a truthful answer. She said, "The serpent tricked me and I ate it" (Gen 3:13). And that was the simple truth. Eve admitted it was her fault. That simple truth was just enough for God to work with. The next word from God's mouth was the promise of world redemption. God promised that through a Woman; through her seed; redemption would come and would crush the head of the serpent. That redemption came through Jesus. The *Woman* was Mary (Gen 3:14-15).

There is a lesson to be learned here, isn't there? When we sin, we should not feel threatened or get defensive and we should not make excuses for ourselves. Instead, we should repent of our sin and admit that we have done wrong. Many times we feel resentment and we make excuses trying to show that we were not wrong after all. We feel strongly that it couldn't have been our fault. Instead of feeling sorry for our sins, we blame others. Instead of accepting the blame, we try to drag others down. Instead of accepting the punishment, we try to get out of it.

This disposition is called *Original Sin*. This is what we have inherited from Adam and Eve. They acted this way after they sinned and we sometimes act this way when we sin. Adam and Eve died that day, absolutely. God's Divine Life left their soul and look how they acted once it happened. They lost all integrity.

This is why there is such a need for the Sacrament of Baptism, which puts God's life; God's Divine Life; into our souls for the very first time. Before Baptism, our soul is darkened. There is no light. That is Original Sin. Once we are baptized, our soul becomes lit with the Life of God; no longer dark (CCC 1262-1266).

But what about the sins we commit after we are baptized? What do we do about them? These sins can completely darken our soul once again. This is why there is such a need for the Sacrament of Reconciliation.

We go to Jesus. We go to God in the Sacrament of Reconciliation and we do what Adam should have done. We humble ourselves and we admit that we have made mistakes. We go to God and admit that through our own fault, we have done things that are wrong and we tell God that we are truly sorry. In doing that, God's Divine Life rushes into our souls and makes our souls beautiful as they were meant to always be; as they are just after we are baptized. Why do we need our sins to be forgiven? Because they remain with us until we desire forgiveness. This creates a barrier between us and God.

Why Do I Have to Confess My Sins to a Priest?

Why can't we just confess our sins to God in prayer at home and be forgiven of our sins right then? Why do we have to confess our sins to a priest? Well, we can confess our sins to God in prayer at home and be forgiven of our sins. We can and we should. Devout Catholics are aware of their sins the moment they commit them and ask for forgiveness from God right then. Others examine their conscience each and every night; confess their sins to God in prayer; and pray the *Act of Contrition*, a beautiful prayer that exhibits our true sorrow for our sins; our desire to make restitution; and our commitment to try our best not to sin in the future. In doing this, the person's sins are forgiven. Keep in mind, however, that no grace from the sacrament is received in this case. A sacrament cannot be received at home. We must come to the Church to receive a sacrament. We would never consider baptizing ourselves. In the Sacrament of Baptism no one ever asks, "Why do I have to be baptized by a minister, why can't I just baptize myself at home?" Similarly, we cannot absolve ourselves of grave sin. We must be reconciled by another; the Church.

Remember, all sacraments place God's very Life and Love into our souls. If we do not receive the sacrament, we do not receive the grace. The grace given to us in the Sacrament of Reconciliation is a strengthening grace. It strengthens us and helps us to resist temptation and sin. With this grace, we simply sin less often than we would otherwise. It sharpens our spiritual vision. This is why people who go to confession often tend to sin very little (CCC 1468-1469).

Understand that our sins separate us from God. Every sin we commit moves us further and further away from God. We build a wall between Him and us. How can we have a deep and close relationship with God when we are constantly pushing Him away with our sins; constantly building a wall between us? When you and I take a moment to actually think about the wrong we do, because we desire a close and deep relationship with our God, beautiful things happen. We can more deeply share God's Life.

We must also understand that there are two types personal of sins, Venial and Mortal. Understand that going to God in prayer at home and confessing our sins to Him directly is fine as long as our sins are only Venial. Venial Sins are less serious sins and are more easily forgiven. This is because Venial Sins only *wound* the Life of God in our souls. They do not *destroy* the Life of God in our souls.

When we are baptized, our darkened souls becomes lit and brightened with the Life of God. A permanent Character is marked on our souls. Original Sin, that is the darkness, is removed and our souls are lit up; bright; beautiful. When we commit a Venial Sin, our souls becomes wounded and dull. It is easy to brighten again such a soul. It only takes repentance and sorrow for sin.

Mortal Sin is different though. Mortal Sin does not merely wound God's Life in our souls. It *destroys* God's Life in our souls. Once we have committed Mortal Sin, God's Life no longer dwells in our souls. There is only one way to replace God's Life in our souls once it has been destroyed by Mortal Sin. We must receive a sacrament. Only a sacrament can place God's Divine Life, Sanctifying Grace, into our souls (CCC 1855).

Just as a sacrament, **Baptism**, places God's Life into our souls for the very first time, it takes a sacrament, **Reconciliation**, to replace God's Life in our souls once we have removed it by committing Mortal Sin. Because of the 'Permanent Character' that we received in Baptism, a person does not have to be re-baptized in order to replace God's Life in their soul, after committing Mortal Sin. Repenting of the sin and receiving the Sacrament of Reconciliation takes care of this matter. This sacrament restores beauty to our souls (CCC 1856).

As we mentioned earlier, the Israelite in Old Testament times had to bring an animal sacrifice to the Temple in order to atone for his grave sins. These sins being atoned for would have been Mortal Sins. The Israelite did not have to offer an animal sacrifice for Venial Sins or lesser sins. He was called to do something much greater and more costly to atone for Mortal Sins and so are we.

Even though sin can be classified as "serious" and "less serious," it is never trivial. Sin is always an offence against God.

Sin crucified our Savior. Moreover, sin is not just a personal matter. The Church is the Body of Christ, so every sin against Christ offends the Church. Therefore, reconciliation with Christ requires reconciliation with the Church. Confessing one's sins brings about reconciliation with Christ and with the Church because the priest is a representative of the Church.

The Nature of Mortal Sin

What exactly is a Mortal Sin? It is a sin that involves grave moral matter. It is done with full knowledge, or in other words, we knew it was wrong and we knew it was serious. Thirdly, we freely choose to commit this sin (CCC 1857-1859). We could have chosen not to commit it, but we did it anyway. It is hard to list specific Mortal Sins because many times whether a sin is Venial or Mortal depends on the circumstances. Saint Paul gives a list of Mortal sins in the Bible, but today people tend to laugh and ignore this. It is true that there are many actions that the Church defines as sin that our American society simply does not define as sin. Sadly, many of those actions are Mortal Sins, yet our society portrays them as acceptable behavior. Examples of this would be missing Mass on the Sabbath due to laziness; having an abortion; engaging in sexual relations outside of marriage; engaging in pornography; and homosexual relations (See 1Cor 6:9-10).

We should never let society tell us what is right and wrong. Instead, we must seek to understand what is right and wrong from the expert, the Catholic Church. Why would the Catholic Church be the expert? Because the Church speaks for Christ today and has for the past 2,000 years. It is God's morality that we must understand and obey; not societies. There can be grave consequences for following the morality of society or the lack there of. It is important that we build our consciences; our morality; from the teachings of the Church and the Bible. These are the only sources that can truly be trusted as the truth because they are from God (CCC 2246, 2420).

These are life and death realities. If we commit Mortal Sin and do not repent of it, we will die with that Mortal Sin still on our soul. No one enters Heaven with Mortal Sins (they are not sorry for) on their soul. This is Truth (CCC 1861). Again, three conditions must be met for a sin to be considered Mortal. If only one or two conditions are met, but not the third, the sin is simply not a Mortal Sin. Again, the three conditions are: 1) The sin involves grave moral matter. 2) We know the sin is wrong and very serious; very grave. 3) We freely choose of our own free will to commit the sin anyway. Keeping this in mind, many people commit sins that are grave in matter, and of their own free will, but do not understand how serious they are or that they are even grave at all. In this way they do not commit Mortal Sin. We do however, bear responsibility to learn what Christ and His Church communicate to us as grave sin. Ignorance can only become an excuse for a time.

So let us ask the question: Is the Sacrament of Reconciliation needed? You bet it is. Can we go our whole lives without committing a Mortal Sin? I wouldn't count on it. But just as importantly, the Sacrament of Reconciliation is needed because we need the grace of this sacrament to lead a holy life; to grow in holiness, so that we can enter Heaven. It is good for us to think critically about ourselves; humble ourselves; and admit that we do wrong; come to the parish church and go to confession, even if our sins are only Venial. We should be sorry for hurting God and other people. God desires repentance. He wants us to seek a close relationship with Him. We cannot be close to Him with sins on our souls for sin separates us from the love of God. The saints teach us that the first step in growing in holiness is the desire to rid one's life of sin. The Sacrament of Reconciliation is a tremendous help with this. The more often we receive this sacrament, the less we sin. The grace from it is simply that strong.

Satan does not want us to think critically about our sins. He does not want us to give our sins a second thought. Satan wants us to think that every sin is a venial one. Better yet, he wants us to think that we do not sin at all. Moreover, Satan wants us to think that anything goes; that we can determine what is right or wrong for ourselves far better than God can. Do not be deceived. Satan is the 'father of lies.' He works against God and is very good at fooling many people. He preys on the part of us that is most vulnerable…our pride. Be careful. Be very careful. Learn to love the Sacrament of Reconciliation. This sacrament causes us to do something. This sacrament causes us to take a step back and really look at ourselves critically. It causes us to humble ourselves and to see ourselves the way that God sees us. We are so busy with our day to day lives that we get completely wrapped up in them. Our jobs, our children's activities; their friends and our friends, our family commitments, our desires; all of this takes up our time. Weeks, months, and even years go by. We commit sin, after sin, after sin, after sin, without giving them a thought; without going to confession. We drift along life, spiritually lazy, failing to see *little* sins like selfishness, gossip, impatience, anger outbursts, you name it.

Jesus knows that you and I will go long periods of time without even recognizing that we sin. After all, we had a reason for yelling at that co-worker; we had a reason for slamming that door and putting fear into the eyes of our children; we had a reason for picking that fight with our spouse; we had a reason for lying about what we did. If someone asks us about our sins we tend to say, "I don't sin. I'm a good person. I don't do anything wrong." This is simply not true. While we are sinning and thinking that we don't sin, we are pushing Jesus further and further out of our souls making it impossible for us to have a deep and close relationship with Him. People who confess their sins regularly look to God for the forgiveness and help that He alone can give.

Our God desires that we do something! He wants us to do something that will cause us to stop and recognize the sin in our lives; not ignore it and keep doing it. He wants us to recognize our sin; repent; and do penance. Then and only then can we have a deep and close relationship with Him. Only then are we a changed person. Only then do we make great gains in holiness.

The Curing of the Paralyzed Man

One of the gospel stories that is relevant to the Sacrament of Reconciliation is the story of a paralyzed man who was taken on a stretcher through the streets to a house where Jesus was preaching (Matt 9:2-8). This man's friends were carrying him to Jesus so that Jesus would cure him and he would no longer be paralyzed.

Upon arriving at the house, the crowd was so large that they couldn't get through the door. So the friends cut a hole in the roof. Their faith was so great; they were so convinced that Jesus could cure their friend; that they actually lowered him down from the opening in the roof and placed him right in front of Jesus.

When Jesus saw the man and recognized the faith of his friends, He did something very surprising. He said, "My son, your sins are forgiven." The Gospel tells us that the people were thinking, "Forgive his sins? Only God can forgive sins! You're not God! You can't forgive sins." Jesus could read their minds and said to them, "So that you may know that the Son of Man has authority to forgive sins on earth, I say this, rise, pick up your mat and go home."

Immediately, the man got up; picked up his mat; and walked out of there. In essence Jesus proclaimed, "You say that I do not have the authority to forgive sins. Let me prove to you that I do indeed have the authority to forgive sins, "Rise, pick up your mat and go home." Understand this: Jesus' enemies said, "Only God has the authority to forgive sins," and Jesus is proclaiming, "I agree… Only God has the authority to forgive sins… I am God… I am God who has come down from Heaven and become a Man. My purpose for coming is to forgive sins. I came to do this." It is equally important to note that Jesus was fully human. Besides being fully God, He was fully human. The forgiveness of the man's sins came through Jesus as a human being. This foreshadows how the Apostles, mere human beings, will soon be the instrument through which God forgives sins. So Jesus cured the man's paralysis in order to prove that He had the power and the authority to forgive the man's sins. And Scripture tells us that "the crowd was struck with awe and glorified God who had given the authority to forgive sins to a human being."

Another important thing to keep in mind is that Jesus did not perform just one miracle that day. He performed two. Jesus healed the man's soul by forgiving his sins. Then he healed the man's body by curing his paralysis. From God's point of view, the healing of the man's paralyzed body was a lesser miracle. Think about it. Who cares if the body doesn't work properly? We're only going to be on this earth 70, 80, 90 years, right? That is nothing compared to eternity! It is our souls that matters much more to God. It is our souls that are going to go on living forever long after our bodies are dead and buried. Healing the man's soul; forgiving his sins; was the greater and more important miracle.

From this gospel story we learn three very important things: First, Jesus has the power and the authority to forgive sins. Second, God will forgive sins through human beings. And third, the health of our soul is much more important to God, than the health of our physical bodies. God wants our souls to have His Life in them!

Jesus Works Through the Priest (CCC 1088)

Who forgives sins in the Sacrament of Reconciliation? Answer: Jesus does. Jesus works through the priest to forgive our sins. Priests and bishops are ordained ministers. They received the Sacrament of Holy Orders. They have been marked with a permanent character; an anointing of the Holy Spirit, that is special just to them. When a man becomes a priest, he becomes "another Christ". He acts for Christ when he offers the Mass; when he forgives sins in Christ's name; when he anoints the sick. A priest acts in "Persona Christi," Latin for, "The Person of Christ." When a man becomes a priest he loans his lips; his hands; his voice; his whole body to Christ. In certain instances, Christ acts through him. In the Sacrament of Holy Orders, the authority that Jesus gave to the Apostles is passed down to the next generation of Apostles, the bishops, and to the priests. The priest is the chief sign or symbol in the Sacrament of Reconciliation. He is a symbol that Jesus is truly present and it is He who forgives our sins.

Jesus Gives the Apostles the Authority to Forgive Sins (CCC 553, 976, 1441-1442, 1461)

Where in the Bible, does Jesus give the Apostles the authority to forgive sins in His name? It is found in the gospel of John Chapter 20 beginning with verse 21. It is the evening of the Resurrection. Jesus has just risen from the dead. The Apostles found the empty tomb that morning. That evening, the Apostles locked themselves in a room. They were afraid of being arrested as Jesus was, and they were confused. They did not yet understand that He had risen from the dead. As they sat together in this locked room, Jesus appeared to them and said, "Peace be with you. As the Father sent me, so now I send you." "As the Father sent me... I am now sending you."

Let us examine Jesus' words for a moment. How did the Father send Jesus? God sent Jesus with all the authority in Heaven and earth. Why did the Father send Jesus? God sent Jesus to forgive our sins; to even die for them; to redeem us and place Divine Life into the souls of men as it once was. Jesus says to the Apostles: As the Father sent me... I am now sending you. I am sending you with the authority of Heaven and earth. I am sending you to forgive sins so that my Divine Life can be given to all men.

Then He breathed on them and said, "Receive the Holy Spirit, whose sins you forgive are forgiven them. Whose sins you retain are retained" (John 20:23).

These words of Jesus are very powerful indeed. Our Lord gave the apostles the authority to forgive sins when He said, "Whose sins *you* forgive are forgiven them; whose sins *you* retain are retained." People had already been confessing their mortal sins to the Jewish High Priest and offering the prescribed sacrifice for atonement. Now they would be confessing their sins to the High Priests of the New Covenant; to the Bishops and Priests of the Catholic Church.

In the Book of James we read, "If anyone among you is sick, summon the priest and he will pray over you and the prayer of faith will save you and the Lord will raise you up and if you have committed any sins, he will forgive you. So confess your sins to the priest that you may be healed" (James 5:13-16).

When we go to confession and hear the words of absolution, we must realize that those words are more powerful than the words Jesus spoke outside the tomb to his friend,

Lazarus, when he said, "Lazarus come forth!" Jesus only brought Lazarus' physical body back to life. What Jesus does through the priest in the Sacrament of Reconciliation is to restore Divine Eternal Supernatural Life to our souls; the same souls that are going to live not just 70, 80, or 90 years, but forever; for eternity.

Preparing for the Sacrament of Reconciliation

The Sacrament of Reconciliation is a meeting with Christ. We should begin preparation for it by asking the Holy Spirit for the grace to see ourselves as God sees us: to recognize our sins; and to understand how they offend God and others. This will help us to humble ourselves and be able to call to mind the sins of our past. We also pray for the grace to be able to confess them honestly. The basic requirement of a good confession is to have the intention of returning to God.

Next we examine our conscience. We try very hard to make a mental list (or on paper if you prefer) of the sins we have committed. It is most important to search our souls for Mortal Sins. We are obligated to confess them as well as the number of times they were committed. An approximation is sufficient: "Because of laziness, I missed Sunday Mass about 15 times since my last confession." Venial Sins should also be confessed to the best of our abilities. They can be great in number and difficult to remember. Most importantly, it is important to pray for God's help to turn away from our sins and to lead a life of holiness. Most people need help examining their conscience or in other works calling to mind their past sins and use a prepared one for that purpose:

An Examination of Conscience Based on the Ten Commandments:

1. **I am the Lord your God. You shall have no other gods besides me.** Do I give God time every day in prayer? Do I

seek to love Him with my whole heart? Are there other 'gods' in my life such as money, power, possessions, people, success, etc…? Am I superstitious or involved in astrology or the occult?

2. **You shall not take the name of the Lord, your God in vain.** Have I used God's name in vain: to show my anger; irreverently; or carelessly? Have I cursed or swore? Have I insulted or cursed God? Have I wished evil upon any other person?

3. **Remember to keep holy the Lord's Day.** Have I missed Mass on Sundays or Holy Days of Obligation without a good reason? Have I tried to observe Sunday as a family day and a day of rest avoiding unnecessary work?

4. **Honor your father and your mother.** Do I honor my parents? Do I give respect to those in authority over me? Have I neglected my duties to my spouse and children? Am I a good religious example to my children and spouse? Do I try to bring peace to my home life or do I cause turmoil in the house?

5. **You shall not kill.** Have I physically or emotionally harmed someone including my spouse and children? Am I kind and courteous to others? Do I show compassion for others? Am I enraged when I drive? Is my anger under control? Have I purposefully injured myself? Have I harmed others by hatred, unjust anger, resentment, or an unwillingness to forgive? Have I abused alcohol or drugs? Have I committed any sins against the sacredness of human life such as abortion?

6. **You shall not commit adultery.** Have I been faithful to my marriage vows in thought and action? Have I engaged in any sexual activity outside of marriage? Have I sinned by masturbation, impure actions, or by the use of

contraceptives or other means of artificial birth control? Have I indulged in pornographic movies, television, or Internet sites?

7. **You shall not steal?** Have I stolen what is not mine? Have I returned or made restitution for what I have stolen? Do I waste time at work? Do I gamble excessively thereby denying my family of their needs? Do I pay debts promptly? Do I seek to share what I have with the poor? Have I cheated anyone out of what is justly theirs? Have I destroyed the property of another? Do I let Christ's teachings guide me in business matters?

8. **You shall not bear false witness against your neighbor.** Have I lied? Have I gossiped? Do I speak badly of others behind their back? Have I harmed others by my false witness? Am I critical, negative, or uncharitable in my thoughts of others? Do I keep secrets that should be kept in confidence?

9. **You shall not covet your neighbor's wife.** Have I consented to impure thoughts? Have I caused them by impure reading, movies, television, conversation or curiosity? Do I pray at once to banish impure thoughts and temptations? Have I behaved in an inappropriate way with members of the opposite sex: flirting, treating them as objects, etc…? Do I have a healthy respect for modesty and purity? Have I led others to sexual sin? Do I desire to have for myself another's spouse?

10. **You shall not covet your neighbor's goods.** Am I jealous of what other people have? Do I envy the families or possessions of others? Am I greedy or selfish? Do I desire more and more material possessions? Do I make myself and others unhappy by my complaints, my self-

pity, or my selfishness? Am I generous with my time, talent, and treasure?

Celebrating the Sacrament of Reconciliation

In most Catholic churches there are reconciliation rooms furnished with a kneeler, screen, and chairs. The person who goes to confession is called the 'penitent.' The penitent has a choice of kneeling behind the screen and confessing anonymously or sitting in a chair and confessing face to face with the priest. Reconciliation is celebrated as follows:

1. **Reception of the penitent.** Normally the priest and penitent greet each other with a simple hello. The penitent normally says, "Hello Father" and the priest returns the greeting. Then the two make the Sign of the Cross. The Priest prays a short prayer such as: "May the grace of the Holy Spirit fill your heart with light, that you may confess your sins with loving trust and come to know that God is merciful." The Penitent responds, "Amen."

2. **Reading the Word of God.** The priest may read or recite a brief passage of Scripture or the penitent may do so. Often times this step is omitted.

3. **Confession of Sins.** The penitent tells approximately how long it has been since their last confession and then confesses their sins. At the conclusion it is important for the penitent to say, "For these and all my sins, I am sorry." In this way any Venial Sins that have been forgotten are included. The priest may then offer words of advice or encouragement. Then the priest gives the penitent a penance to carry out.

4. **Prayer of the Penitent "The Act of Contrition":** Then the penitent expresses sorrow through a prayer called the 'Act of Contrition.': "My God, I am sorry for my sins with all my heart. In choosing to do wrong and failing to

do good, I have sinned against you, whom I should love above all things. I firmly intend, with your help, to do penance, to sin no more, and to avoid whatever leads me to sin. Our Savior Jesus Christ suffered and died for me, in His name, my God, have mercy.

5. **Absolution.** The priest then says the prayer of absolution: "God, the Father of mercies, through the death and resurrection of his Son has reconciled the world to Himself and sent the Holy Spirit among us for the forgiveness of sins; through the ministry of the Church may God give you pardon and peace, and I absolve you from your sins in the name of the Father, and of the Son, and of the Holy Spirit. Amen.

6. **Proclamation of Praise of God and Dismissal.** The priest says, "Give thanks to the Lord for He is good." The penitent answers, "His mercy endures forever."

After confession, we should thank God for the grace of the sacrament and carry out the penance given to us by the priest. The penance may consist of a prayer, service, or self-denial. It helps make up for the harm done by our sins, and it more closely joins us to Jesus, who suffered for us. If the penance is a prayer, most people kneel in the church and immediately pray. Rest assured at this point that your sins are forgiven for you heard the voice of the priest say so loud and clear.

The Church requires that we confess our sins once per year, but this is a bare minimum. Confessing only once per year is not much of a help on your road to holiness. As a follower of Jesus, we should look beyond what we are required to do and instead do what we should do. As a minimum, we should be celebrating the Sacrament of Reconciliation at least once per month. Jesus has given us the Sacrament of Reconciliation as a gift. Our response to Jesus should not be, "Do I have to go to confession?" but instead, "Thank you for the opportunity to grow closer to You."

The Role of the Priest in Confession

As mentioned before, the priest acts in "Persona Christi" the person of Christ, when he forgives sins in the Sacrament of Reconciliation. The priest is a sign of Christ's Real Presence in the sacrament. So it is true that Jesus forgives our sins and gives us absolution. The priest therefore has a serious responsibility to show the same compassion and understanding that Christ showed to sinners. Most priests understand this very well and therefore, confessing our sins to them is very easy. Moreover, they are very helpful and can give us compassionate advice.

Some people worry that the priest will look down on them because of their sins. They tend to want to confess to priests who do not know them. Nothing could be further from the truth. A priest who acted in this way would be committing a terrible sin of pride, worse than anything the penitent might have confessed to him. Keep in mind that priests have heard every sin imaginable. There was only one *Original* sin and Adam committed that one. The rest of us tend to do the same things over and over. Our priests have heard it all. Furthermore, priests are sinners too. They too confess their sins to other priests. When a person confesses their sins, most priests are in awe of the honesty and humility with which they confess. They are like fathers bursting with pride that their children can admit their faults and lovingly turn back to God. A priest never thinks ill of a penitent.

Priests are also bound to observe the "seal of confession." They may not disclose what is told to them in confession and may not use it against a penitent in any way.

IX.   The Sacrament of Eucharist

The Catholic Church has boldly and unceasingly proclaimed for the past two thousand years that the bread and wine, brought up in the offertory at Mass, really and truly become the Body, Blood, Soul and Divinity of Jesus Christ. We believe in the True Presence of Christ in the Eucharist; that it is Jesus Himself.

We worship the Eucharist. We adore the Eucharist. We have perpetual adoration chapels connected with some parishes where parishioners take turns adoring Christ in the Eucharist twenty-four hours a day, seven days a week.

If the bread and wine do not really and truly become the Body, Blood, Soul and Divinity of Jesus during the Consecration at Mass, then we, our entire Church, is worshiping mere bread; mere wine. If it is *not* true, then we are committing a horrendous act of idolatry.

But we don't have to worry about that, because it *is* true. The bread and wine really and truly become Jesus Himself at every Mass. We come forward and take and eat the Flesh and Blood of our Lord and Savior, Jesus Christ. We place His divine Life directly inside of us and we become one with Him. Each time we receive it, we become more unified with Him. If you want to have a deep and close relationship with Jesus, receive the Eucharist as often as you can; even daily.

The Catholic Teaching

The official Church Teaching concerning the Eucharist is this: *Under the appearance of bread and wine, Christ is completely present in His Body, Blood, as well as His Soul and Divinity. The moment the priest says the words of Consecration,*

"This is my Body" and "This is my Blood," God miraculously changes ordinary bread and wine into the Body and Blood of our Lord Jesus Christ. All outward appearances and sensible qualities of the bread and wine remain, but the substance changes.

"All outward appearances and sensible qualities of the bread and wine remain, but the substance changes." What does this mean? It means that the Body of Christ still looks, smells, and tastes like bread and His Precious Blood still looks, smells, and tastes like wine. But that is all that remains of the bread and wine. Only the sensible qualities remain. The substance is Christ Himself. This transformation of substance is called **Transubstantiation** (CCC 1373-1377; 1413).

This is the core Catholic Teaching. We cannot be Catholic and persist in unbelief. We must embrace this teaching and avail of it often. Jesus wants to commune with us. This is how He does it. This was God's plan from the beginning.

The Paschal Lamb Exodus Chapters 7-12

Where in the Bible can this teaching on the Eucharist be found? Starting in the Old Testament, we can look at the events that led up to Jesus becoming present in the bread and wine. This was God's plan all along so there is plenty of evidence found in the Old Testament. First we must go back to the Exodus out of Egypt.

God Sent Moses to free the Israelites from slavery in Egypt. God sent nine plagues to Egypt. Despite these nine plagues, Pharaoh would not let the Israelite slaves go free. Finally God sent the tenth plague: the death of the first-born male child of the Egyptians. God gave Moses these instructions: Each family must take for itself an unblemished; a perfect male lamb. With everyone present they must slaughter it. They must then spread its blood onto the doorposts and lintels of every house using a hyssop branch. Then they were to roast and eat the flesh of the lamb with bitter herbs and unleavened bread standing up with staff in hand wearing their traveling clothes. If the Israelites followed these directions exactly, the 'Angel of Death' would **pass over** the houses of the Israelites and their first-born sons would be spared. The first born of the Egyptians, however, would become sick and die (See Exodus Ch. 7-13).

This is a matter of history. The Israelites did as God commanded and the Angel of Death passed over them, but it did not pass over the first-born sons of the Egyptians.

Because of this tenth and final plague, the Israelites were set free. The Israelites left Egypt; went out into the wilderness; crossed the Red Sea; and went to Mount Sinai where Moses received the Ten Commandments and made the Covenant with God.

The details of God's instructions were very important and Moses ensured that the Israelites followed them exactly. Had they not followed the instructions, their first born sons would not have been saved. God's people had to sacrifice an unblemished lamb and spread its blood; they had to roast the lamb; and then they had to eat the lamb. God required them to eat the sacrifice that saved them (Exodus 12:8-11).

Do you see the foreshadowing taking place here? The lamb that was slaughtered was without flaw—perfect. It was sacrificed in order to save God's chosen people from slavery and death. The people had to eat the sacrifice that saved them.

This lamb that the Israelites sacrificed became known as the "Passover Lamb" or the "Paschal Lamb." God commanded the Israelites to celebrate and to re-present this Passover Feast every year from then on (Exodus 12:14). He commanded it through Moses and the people obeyed. Every Israelite family had to do this exact same thing every single year to make present the very first Passover Meal. Every year they had to sacrifice a lamb that was without flaw. They had to roast and eat the lamb. They had to tell the story of how the lamb saved them from slavery and death to their children. They did not have to spread its blood onto their door posts and lintels, because they had already been saved. It was still a sacrifice, but it was an 'unbloody sacrifice.'

The Israelites did not just remember what happened. The Jews were told by God to make this saving sacrifice present again. In Greek, the word used for this is "anamnesis," which is the process by which an abstract idea moves into the material world, making present an object or person from the past. It is a *reactualization*; a representation; a participation in an event from the past. Why did God command this? So that the current generation could participate in the saving action of this sacrifice of the past. So understand that this was not simply a mental recollection as our Thanksgiving holiday is or even the Fourth of July. This event of the past was brought to the present and so was its saving action.

Manna—the Bread from Heaven

While Moses and the Israelites were wandering in the desert waiting to go into the *Promised Land*, the land promised to Abraham by God, they were hungry. God fed them with *Manna*; bread that literally fell from the sky. Each morning when they awoke, the families gathered this bread into baskets and ate it. God fed his people with bread that came down from Heaven (Exodus 16:4). Do you see any foreshadowing taking place? God fed his people with bread that came down from Heaven; bread which sustained them and gave them physical life. (CCC 1094). We now turn to the New Testament to fulfill this. We look for bread that gives us more than physical life, but instead gives us *Spiritual Life.*

New Testament—John the Baptist—John 1: 29-34

In the New Testament, John the Baptist begins preaching in the desert and baptizing in the Jordan River. One day he catches sight of Jesus and points Him out to the crowd saying, "Behold, the Lamb of God who takes away the sins of the world."

John calls Jesus, "The Lamb of God." Why didn't John say, "Behold, the King of kings!"? Why didn't John say, "Behold the Lion of Judah!'"? Wouldn't that have been more dramatic? After all, the Jesus is sometimes referred to as "the Lion of Judah," because His lineage can be traced to the Tribe of Judah. John called Jesus a lamb and does so on purpose. He said, "Behold, the Lamb of God."

This put a mental image into the minds of the Jews. It recalled for them the Paschal Lamb. John was explaining to the people, "Here is God's Lamb...*the Lamb*. John is proclaiming: Here is God's sacrifice; the Lamb that God will sacrifice for his people; the Lamb that will save you from the slavery of sin; the Lamb that will save you from eternal death and set you free! (CCC 523, 536).

We must understand as the Jews understood. Jesus is the Lamb of God that will save us from slavery to sin and eternal death. If Jesus is the Lamb of God, what must take place? The same thing that happened to the Passover Lamb that saved the Israelites from slavery in Egypt must also happen to the Lamb of God; Jesus. The Paschal Lamb had to be sacrificed to save the people—Jesus was sacrificed to save us from our sins. The Lamb's blood had to be spread on the wood of their doors— Jesus' blood was spread on the wood of the cross; the door to

Heaven. The flesh of the Lamb had to be eaten—therefore, we must eat the Flesh of Jesus. They ate the sacrifice that saved them—we must eat the sacrifice that saves us (CCC 608).

We, God's people, must eat the sacrifice. We must eat the flesh of the Lamb that saves us from sin and death so that we may enter the *New Promised Land*—Heaven. Jesus became the *New Paschal Lamb*. The Mass became the *New Passover Supper*. These are the terms of the New Covenant that fulfilled the terms of the Old Covenant.

The Gospel of John Chapter 6:22-71

In the Gospel of John chapter 6 we read about two great miracles. First Jesus feeds 5000 people with five barley loaves and two fish. The people were amazed that He feed that many people with such little food! More amazing is the fact that there were twelve baskets full of fragments leftover once the people had eaten their fill. We learn from this story that Jesus is going to feed us with bread. Just as God fed His people with bread; Manna; Jesus feeds us with bread. We also learn that Jesus has no problem manipulating the things of this earth to suit His Will. These are two very important lessons.

The second miracle is that of Jesus walking on top of the water; quite an amazing thing to do. Quite obviously, Jesus is trying to tell us that He is capable of doing the impossible. Can we have any doubt?

These two miracles prepare us for what Jesus is about to say to the people in the gospel of John chapter 6. Jesus tells us in His own words that we are going to eat His Flesh and drink His Blood. Not only are we going to eat His Flesh and drink His Blood, but He tells us that His Flesh is bread! He tells us that His Flesh is true food and His blood is true drink.

Jesus said, "I am the bread of life. I am the bread that came down from Heaven. Not like the bread that your ancestors ate and still died. If you eat this bread you will live forever."

Jesus is comparing Himself to the Manna that fell from the sky that the Israelites ate in the desert. And He is saying: Your ancestors ate the Manna, but they still died. In other words, this bread did not help them spiritually. Jesus explains that if we eat the Bread of Life; the Bread that He is; we will live forever; we will go to Heaven.

The people responded, "Give us this bread so we can eat it and live forever." And Jesus said, "The bread that I will give you is my flesh for the life of the world." This is worth repeating. Jesus said...THE BREAD THAT I WILL GIVE YOU IS MY FLESH!

What more do we need in order to believe? Jesus said in His own words, "The bread that I will give you is my flesh!" He gives us this bread, that is His Flesh, at every Mass. What more can we want? What more can Jesus say so that we will believe Him?

The Jews, who were His disciples, had a really hard time with this teaching. They understood what Jesus was saying, but they refused to believe. They began quarreling among themselves saying, "How can this man give us his flesh to eat?" They doubted. They had no real faith in Him.

So Jesus continued and said to them, "Truly, I say to you, unless you eat the Flesh of the Son of Man and drink His Blood, you do not have Life within you. But whoever eats My Flesh and drinks My Blood has Eternal Life, and I will raise him on the last day. For my flesh is TRUE FOOD and my blood is TRUE DRINK. Whoever eats My Flesh and drinks My Blood remains in me and I in him."

To those of us who understand what a sacrament is, these words have a very strong meaning. "Unless you eat the Flesh of the Son of Man and drink His Blood, you do not have Life within you." The word "life" has great meaning in terms of a sacrament. It is the "Life of God" or Sanctifying Grace.

Jesus repeated the teaching over and over and over and over. It did not help. Some would not accept the teaching. They said, "This saying is hard. Who can accept it?" <u>And they walked away</u>. They refused to believe His words and they walked away.

What Jesus did next was even more amazing. When the people walked away and refused to believe and refused to follow Jesus anymore, what did Jesus do about it? He did nothing. Jesus let them go. He did not stop them. **He did not say**, "Wait! You misunderstood. You don't really have to eat My Flesh and drink My Blood. You misunderstood. I meant it was just a *symbol* of My Flesh and My Blood. Come back! Let me explain it again." No, Jesus did not say that. He let them go. He let them go because He meant what He said and He said what He meant.

Today thousands of Christians do not believe the Catholic teaching that the bread and wine become the Body and Blood of Jesus at every Mass. They believe that what we eat is only a mere symbol of Jesus' Body and Blood. Where do they get the understanding that it is merely a symbol? It is not found in the Bible. If Jesus meant that the people would only be eating just a symbol of Himself, why were they so upset and why did they walk away in anger? If Jesus had said, "The bread that I will give you is a symbol of My Flesh," the people would not have been upset and they would not have walked away. The problem was that they were going to have to eat Jesus' true Flesh and drink His true Blood and they couldn't handle that idea. It was too much for them. They found it repulsive. But Jesus went on to say, "It is the Spirit that gives life, while the flesh is of no avail."

Jesus was explaining that we will never believe this using only our bodily senses, we have to believe it spiritually, in faith.

Jesus then turned to His Apostles and He asked them, "Are you leaving too?" Peter answered, "Master, to whom shall we go? You have the words of Eternal Life. We have come to believe and are convinced that you are the Holy One of God." Peter and the other Apostles did not understand *how* Jesus was going to give them His Flesh to eat and His Blood to drink, but they believed He was going to do it. Peter could see with "eyes of faith." He did not understand, but he still believed. Sometimes you and I have to use our eyes of faith too. We don't always understand, but we still have to believe.

The Last Supper (Matthew 26:26-30; 36-39)

Jesus, as a good Jew, celebrated the Passover Supper with his disciples three times. A perfect male lamb was sacrificed and roasted. It was eaten with bitter herbs and unleavened bread with wine to drink. The third time they celebrated the Passover Supper was the meal that what we call, "The Last Supper" (CCC 1339).

This third Passover supper was different. It was time for Jesus to fulfill the Old Testament Passover Meal by establishing the New Covenant that very night. Jesus did this by establishing the New Passover Meal—the Holy Sacrifice of the Mass. This time Jesus would be the Lamb; the sacrifice offered to God to save the people from sin and death and lead them into the New Promised Land—Heaven. This marked the ending of the Old Testament Law; the Old Covenant; and the beginning of the New Eternal Covenant.

In the Old Covenant Law, the High Priest sacrificed the Passover Lamb. At this New Covenant Supper, Jesus is the Eternal High Priest who willingly sacrifices Himself for our sins.

Jesus freely offered His life to God so that you and I could live. Jesus became the new victim...The New Paschal Lamb.

He took bread into His sacred hands and said, "Take this all of you and eat of it. For this is My Body, which will be given up for you." Likewise, He took the chalice full of wine and said, "Take this all of you and drink from it. For this is the chalice of My Blood; the blood of the New and Eternal Covenant. It will be shed for you and for many for the forgiveness of sins." Jesus then gave the same command that God gave to Moses: "Do this in memory of me." In other words, "This is the New Passover; the New Feast; and you must continue to make this present until I come again" (CCC 1340).

At the Last Supper, Jesus fulfilled what He promised in John chapter 6 when He said, "The bread that I will give you is My Flesh," and "My Flesh is true food and My Blood is true drink." At the Last Supper Jesus gave to us what He promised He would give. Jesus instituted the Sacrament of Eucharist and the Holy Sacrifice of the Mass. Jesus commanded His Apostles to keep offering this same sacrifice for the forgiveness of sins until He comes again. He commissioned the Twelve Apostles as priests of the New Covenant. Through their hands this sacrifice would continue to be offered so that all generations could continue to participate in it (CCC 1337).

Please understand the importance and meaning of this command. Our English Bible is a translation of the Latin. The Latin is a translation of the Greek. Sometimes the meaning gets lost in the translations. The words "Do this in memory of me" do not give justice to the actual meaning. It sounds as if we are simply asked to get together and remember this event, similarly to how we remember the first Thanksgiving when we celebrate Thanksgiving Day. That is not at all the meaning. This command from Jesus to the Apostles was the same command given to the Israelites when God commanded them to continue the Passover

Feast. In this way all generations could be saved through the covenant just as their ancestors were saved. Again, I emphasize that they did not simply remember the Passover as we remember the first Thanksgiving. They did not simply celebrate the Passover as we celebrate Thanksgiving in our homes. This was a memorial feast! The Jews were to make this saving sacrifice present again in an unbloody manner. As I mentioned previously, the Greed word *anamnesis* is a process by which an abstract idea moves into the material world, making present an object or person from the past. It is a re-actualization! A representation! It is a real participation in an event from the past. This is far different from a mental recollection as our celebration of the Fourth of July.

What Jesus commanded at the Last Supper is no different. The Apostles were Jewish men, so they understood the connection between the meal of the Last Supper and the Passover Meal. Jesus commanded them to make this saving sacrifice present again (anamnesis). All generations would need to participate in this same sacrifice so that they could be saved by it; so that they could receive the grace if offered them. Far from a remembrance, the Mass is a re-actualization! A representation! It is our participation in that event from the past. When we go to Mass, we are participating in the very sacrifice that took place at the Last Supper and on the cross the next day (CCC 1341, 1362-1367).

The Last Supper A Traditional Passover Meal

As Catholics we must understand that Jesus' sacrifice began at the Last Supper. It was at the Last Supper that He gave Himself; offered Himself to God to be the sacrifice for our sins. This sacrifice took place in anticipation of His death on the cross the next day. Jesus took bread and wine and declared it to be His

Body and Blood. He took the bread and wine and consecrated them separately thereby separating His own Body from His Blood. This separation of His Body and His Blood was the beginning of His sacrifice. This sacrifice that Jesus began at the Last Supper was not finished until He said His last words on the Cross the very next day. Therefore, the Last Supper, the New Passover Meal, did not end until Jesus said His last words on the cross. The meal continued all through the next day until He died (CCC 1329).

To understand this, we must first understand a little something about the Jewish Passover Meal. It was organized around four cups of wine, which were essential to the celebration. The meal began with the pouring and mixing of the first cup of wine. This cup was known as the cup of sanctification or in Hebrew, the *Kiddush* cup. Once the first cup was poured and mixed, the head of the family began the meal by saying a formal blessing over the cup of wine and the feast day. The first cup was then passed around and all those present drank from it.

The food was then brought to the table. It consisted of at least four key dishes: several cakes of unleavened bread, a dish of bitter herbs, a bowl of sauce known as *haroseth*, and the roasted Passover Lamb. At this point a preliminary course would begin. The bitter herbs were dipped into the haroseth sauce and eaten. This ended the opening ritual of the meal.

Next the second cup of wine would be mixed, but not yet drunk. This cup was known as the cup of proclamation or in Hebrew the *Haggadah* cup. It was called the cup of proclamation because the head of the family would read or recite the Passover story from Exodus and Deuteronomy of how God delivered His people from slavery with the blood of the lamb in response to specific questions asked by a son. To express a spirit of thanksgiving they sang Psalms 113-114, which praised the Lord for His goodness and thanked Him for saving Israel from Egypt.

The second cup was then passed around and all participants drank from it.

Next a third cup of wine would be mixed. This signaled the beginning of the actual supper, when the Passover Lamb and the unleavened bread would finally be eaten. Once the meal itself was finished, the head of the house would say another blessing over the third cup of wine. This third cup was called the Cup of Blessing or in Hebrew the *Berakah* cup. When this cup was drunk, the third stage of the Passover was complete.

It was then time for the climax of the meal. This is when the "Hallel Psalms" or psalms of praise are sung. They sang Psalms 115-118. Psalm 118 was known as the "Great Hallel." These psalms indicate that they are offering to God the "sacrifice of thanksgiving," the new "thank offering" (*zebah todah*), what Greek-speaking Christians would call the "thanksgiving" (*eucharistia*). After the singing of Psalm 118, the fourth cup of wine would be drunk. This fourth cup of wine was known as the cup of praise or in Hebrew the *Hallel* cup. This cup consummated the meal. It finished it grandly (See Pitre, 150-158).

What Happened at the Last Supper?

Upon examining the Gospels of Matthew, Mark and Luke, we see that Jesus and His disciples begin the Passover meal with the "first cup" as it was prescribed.

They are already eating when the story picks up with the "third cup," *The Cup of Blessing* and the main course of the meal. At the Last Supper, Jesus uses sacrificial language indicating that He, Himself is the sacrifice. Jesus took bread; gave thanks; broke the bread; and gave it to His disciples saying, "Take this all of you and eat of it. This is My Body which will be given up for you." After supper He took the cup of blessing, (the third cup of wine), and again He gave thanks. He gave it to his disciples and said, "Take this all of you and drink from it, this is the chalice of My Blood, the Blood of the New and Eternal Covenant, which will be shed for you and for many for the forgiveness of sins." At this Jesus commanded, "Do this in memory of me" (Matt 26:26-28).

Then after drinking from this cup, the third cup, this Cup of Blessing; the cup of His Blood; He said to them, "Truly I say to you, I will not drink of the fruit of the vine until I drink it new in the Kingdom" (Matt 26:29). Jesus declares that He will not drink wine again until His Kingdom has come!

So Jesus and the Apostles go on with the Passover Meal and sing the Hallel Psalms, the singing of Psalms 115-117 and the Great Hallel, Psalm 118. Scripture tells us that they sang the hymn and departed and went out to the Mount of Olives (Mark 14:24-26). Did you catch it? They go out to the Mount of Olives after singing, but without drinking the fourth cup. Jesus doesn't drink the fourth cup! They sing the Great Hallel, but He doesn't drink the fourth cup and either does anyone else.

This is very significant because this means that Jesus did not finish the Passover Meal. We know Jesus did not finish the meal on purpose, because after drinking the third cup, He declared, "Truly I say to you, I will not drink of the fruit of the vine until I drink it new in the Kingdom." This is extremely significant. Jesus not only altered the meal by focusing on His own Body and Blood rather than the flesh of the Passover Lamb. He also seems to have deliberately left the Passover liturgy incomplete by vowing not to drink of the "fruit of the vine" and by leaving the Upper Room without doing so. So we have to ask, 'Why didn't Jesus drink from the fourth cup? Why didn't He finish the meal?"

Jesus then goes to the Garden of Gethsemane to pray. Scripture says that He fell on His face and prayed, "Father, if it is possible, let this cup pass over me; yet not as I will, but as You will" (Matt 26:39). "Let this cup pass over me"? Jesus prayed to the Father three times about the "cup" that He must drink. Why? Isn't this a rather strange way to refer to a crucifixion? Why did Jesus describe His death through the metaphor of drinking a cup? To what cup did He refer?

Given the Passover context of His prayer (it is still Passover night), and given the fact that He had just left the Upper Room, by now, the answer seems clear: Jesus is praying to the Father about the fourth cup, the final cup of the Passover liturgy.

He has just celebrated the Last Supper in which He identified His own Body as the sacrifice of the New Passover. He has also just identified one of the cups of wine as His own Blood, about to be poured out for the forgiveness of sins. In other words, Jesus implicitly identified Himself as the New Passover Lamb. Jesus has woven His own fate into the completion of the Jewish Passover meal. When the meal is finished, and the final cup, drunk, it will mean His own death has arrived. That is why Jesus did not finish the Passover. That is why Jesus did not drink the fourth cup (CCC 612).

Next, Jesus is arrested and taken away. He is beaten, crowned with thorns, and made to carry His cross. On the way to Calvary, the soldiers offered Him wine mixed with myrrh (Mark 15:23). Myrrh was used to deaden pain. It was a numbing agent. Jesus refused to drink it. He refused to drink it because He said, "Truly I say to you, I will not drink again of the fruit of the vine until I drink it new in the Kingdom." He couldn't drink it. It wasn't time to finish the meal.

He is then nailed to the cross. Near the end of the crucifixion, Jesus said, "I thirst" (John 19:28) and He said it deliberately. So the soldiers took a hyssop branch; the same kind of branch that had been used to spread the Passover Lamb's blood on the door posts and lintels in Egypt; and they attached a sponge to it and dipped it in sour wine and lifted it up to Him.

Jesus drank the wine and said, "It is finished." What is finished? The Passover Meal is finished. Finally, Jesus drank of the fourth cup...the fourth cup of the Passover Meal. Jesus finished the Passover Meal, not in the Upper Room where it began, but on the cross at the moment of His death.

What Does this Mean to Us?

Jesus did not finish the Passover Meal until He drank that sip of wine while on the cross moments before His death. Why is this important to us? This proves that the Last Supper was a true sacrifice and that the bread the Apostles ate was truly Jesus' Body. The cup they drank from was truly Jesus' Blood. The Last Supper actually set Jesus' passion and death in motion. By praying three times in the Garden of Gethsemane for the "cup" to be taken from Him, Jesus revealed that He understood His own death in terms of the Passover sacrifice. For when the final cup of the meal was drunk, His own sacrifice would be complete, and His blood would be "poured out" like that of the Passover Lambs. Moreover, by waiting to drink the fourth cup of the Passover until the very moment of His death, Jesus united the Last Supper to His death on the cross. By refusing to drink of the fruit of the vine until He gave up His final breath, He joined the offering of Himself under the form of bread and wine to the offering of Himself on Calvary. Both actions said the same thing: "This is my Body, given for you" (Luke 22:19). Both were done "for the forgiveness of sins" (Matthew 26:28). Both were done "as a ransom for many" (Mark 10:45). By means of the Last Supper, Jesus transformed the Cross into a Passover, and by means of the Cross, he transformed the Last Supper into a sacrifice. Jesus gave the command to the Apostles telling them to continue that same sacrifice. We as Catholics continue this same sacrifice at every Mass. Therefore the Mass that we celebrate is a true sacrifice.

How can any one of us doubt that the bread we eat at Mass is truly the Body of Christ? How can any one of us doubt that the wine we drink at Mass is truly the Blood of Christ? From the Old to the New Testament, this was truly God's plan.

The Fathers Know Best

From the earliest days of the Christian Church the belief in the True Presence of Christ in Eucharist was upheld. The Church Fathers defended this belief unanimously. Here are just a few of their ancient words to us:

St. Ignatius of Antioch a disciple of St. John the Apostle wrote in 110 A.D. "Take note of the heretics and see how contrary their opinions are to the mind of God. They abstain from the Eucharist and from prayer, because *they do not confess that the Eucharist is the Flesh of our Savior Jesus Christ,* Flesh which suffered for our sins and which the Father, in His goodness raised up again. I have no taste for corruptible food nor for the pleasures of this life. I desire the Bread of God, which is the *Flesh of Jesus Christ*, who was of the seed of David; and for drink I desire *His Blood*, which is love incorruptible."

St. Justin Martyr was instructed by the disciples of St. John. Around the year 150 A.D. he wrote: "We call this food Eucharist; and no one is permitted to partake of it, except one who believes our teaching to be true. For *not as common bread nor common drink do we receive these;* but since Jesus Christ our Savior was made incarnate by the word of God and had both flesh and blood for our salvation, so too, as we have been taught, the food which has been made into *the Eucharist* by the Eucharistic prayer set down by Him, and by the change of which our blood and flesh is nourished, *is both the Flesh and the Blood of that incarnated Jesus."*

St. Irenaeus, a Bishop and great theologian of the post-apostolic period wrote: "Jesus has declared the cup, a part of creation, to be *His own Blood,* from which He causes our blood to flow; and the bread, a part of creation, He has established as *His own Body,* from which He gives increase to our bodies."

St. Cyril of Jerusalem wrote in 350 A.D.: "Jesus Himself, therefore, having declared and said of the Bread, "This is My Body," who will dare any longer to doubt? And when He Himself has affirmed and said, "This is My Blood," who can ever hesitate to say it is not His Blood." Do not, therefore, regard the bread and wine as simply that, *for they are,* according to the Master's declaration, *the Body and Blood of Christ.* Even though the senses suggest to you other, let faith make you firm."

Guidelines for Receiving the Eucharist

It is a serious obligation for Catholics to offer the Sacrifice of the Mass every Sabbath Day and every Holy Day of Obligation. We are not permitted to miss Mass due to laziness. Receiving the Lord in Holy Communion is a sign of unity with the Church in sacramental life, belief, and morals. By receiving communion, the Catholic is saying that he or she believes all that the Catholic Church teaches and holds true. It is a renewal of the Eternal Covenant with God each time it is received.

In addition, we must be *properly disposed* in order to receive Communion. In order to be properly disposed, the faithful should not be conscious of grave sin, have fasted an hour, and seek to live in charity and love with their neighbors. Those who are conscious of grave sin must first be reconciled with God and with the Church through the Sacrament of Reconciliation.

X. The Sacrament of Holy Orders and the Priesthood

What is a Priest?

The simple answer to this question is to say that a priest is "another Christ." A priest, by his ordination, acts for Christ when he consecrates bread and wine to become the very Body, Blood, Soul, and Divinity of Jesus. A priest acts for Christ when he forgives sins in Jesus' name. The priest acts in "Persona Christi," Latin for "The Person of Christ."

To fully understand what a priest is, we have to know what a sacrifice is. A sacrifice is the offering of a gift to God by a group, through the action of someone who has the right to represent the group. The purpose of such an offering is to give *group* worship to God. This worship is the acknowledgement of God's supreme lordship over mankind; to thank Him for His blessings; to atone for human sin; and to pray for His assistance. God does not *need* our gifts. Everything that exists was made by God in the first place. In reality any sacrifice we offer to God is simply giving back to God something that already belongs to Him. Until Jesus gave us Himself as the perfect gift of the sacrifice of the Mass, nothing that man could offer to God was really worthy of God.

Nevertheless, it pleased God, from the very beginning of human history, to have His children "act out" their love for Him by means of a sacrifice. God's children would take the very best of His blessings upon them whether it was a lamb, a bull, or fruit, or grain, and offer it back to God. They destroyed it upon an altar to symbolize the act of giving. These were only "token" gifts, but they expressed the deepest sentiments of the human heart toward God. "Almighty God," the gift would say, "I know that all I have, I have from you. I thank you for your bounty. I beg your forgiveness for not serving you better. Please be merciful to me anyway." Sacrifice, in short, is prayer in action. It is the prayer-in-action of a group. And the one who offers the sacrifice in the name of the group is the priest.

Since men have offered sacrifice to God from the very beginning of the human race, so also have there been priests from the very beginning. In the first period of Biblical history—the age of the Patriarchs—it was the father of the family who was the priest. It was the father of the family who offered sacrifice to God for himself and his family. Adam was priest for his family; so were Noah and Abraham. All of the other family heads were priests for their families. In the time of Moses, however, because the Israelites made the golden calf and worshiped it, God directed that the priesthood of his chosen people, the Israelites, should from that point onward, belong to the family of Aaron of the tribe of Levi. The oldest son in each generation of Aaron's descendants, would be the high priest and the other Levites would be his assistants.

When the Old Law ended with the establishment of the New Law by Christ, the priesthood of the Old Law also came to an end. The New Law of love would have a new sacrifice and a new priesthood. At the Last Supper Jesus instituted the Holy Sacrifice of the Mass. In this new sacrifice, the gift offered to God would not be a mere token gift, such as a sheep or an ox or bread and wine. The gift now, for the first time and always, would be a gift worthy of God. It would be the gift of God's own Son; a gift of infinite value, even as God Himself is infinite. In the Mass, under the appearances of bread and wine, Jesus would renew daily, the once-and-for-all sacrifice He made of Himself to God, upon the cross. In the Mass He would give to each of us, His baptized members, the opportunity to unite ourselves with Him in that offering.

But who would be the human priest who would stand at the altar—the human instrument whose hands and whose lips Christ would use for the offering of Himself? Who would be the human priest to whom Christ would give the power of making the God-man present upon the altar, under the appearances of bread and wine? There were eleven such priests to begin with. This is true because we believe that Judas was not present at the time the Apostles were made priests (he had already left to make his arrangements to betray Jesus). At the Last Supper, Jesus made His Apostles priests when He gave them the command, and with the command, the power, to do what He had just done. "Do this," He said, "in remembrance of me" (Luke 22:20).

It was this power, the power to offer sacrifice in the name of Christ and in the name of Christ's mystical body, His Church, which made the Apostles priests. Jesus then appeared to them on the night of His Resurrection (Easter Sunday night) and further gave to the Apostles the power to forgive sins in His name. "Receive the Holy Spirit," He said; "whose sins you forgive, are forgiven them and whose sins you retain are retained" (John 20:22-23).

This is the power of the priesthood that Christ conferred upon His Apostles. This power was not to die with them, because Jesus came to save the souls of *all* people who would ever live, down to the end of the world. Consequently, the Apostles passed their priestly power on to other men in the ceremony which we now call the Sacrament of Holy Orders. In the Acts of the Apostles we read of one of the first ordinations by the Apostles: "The proposal was acceptable to the whole community, so they chose Stephen, a man full of faith and of the Holy Spirit, also Philip, Prochorus, Nicanor, Timon, Parmenas and Nicholas of Antioch, a convert to Judaism. They presented these men to the Apostles, who prayed and laid hands on them" (Acts 6:5-6).

These men were ordained deacons, but not yet priests. But it gives us the picture of the Apostles sharing, and passing on to others, the sacred power which Jesus had bestowed on them. As time went on, the Apostles consecrated more bishops to carry on their work. These bishops in turn ordained other bishops and priests, and these bishops in their turn, still others. So that the Catholic priest of today can truly say that the power of his priesthood has come down, in the Sacrament of Holy Orders, in an unbroken line from Christ Himself.

What is Holy Orders?

There are two distinct ways in which the Sacrament of Holy Orders differs from the other sacraments. One is the fact that Holy Orders can be administered only by a bishop. Only a bishop has the power to ordain priests and deacons. An ordinary priest cannot pass his power on to another. The second way in which Holy Orders differs from other sacraments is that Holy Orders is not received all at once. When we are baptized, we are completely baptized by the single pouring of water. When we are confirmed, we are completely confirmed in a single ceremony. Holy Orders, however, is given by degrees, by successive steps.

The Catechism of the Catholic Church defines Holy Orders as "the Sacrament of Apostolic Ministry by which the mission entrusted by Christ to His Apostles continues to be exercised in the Church through the laying on of hands. This sacrament has three distinct degrees or 'orders': deacon, priest, and bishop. All three confer a permanent, sacramental character" (CCC Glossary p. 890). So deaconship, priesthood, and bishopric are the three stages in the Sacrament of Holy Orders as it was instituted by Christ. At each stage, as in every sacrament, there is an increase in Sanctifying Grace. At each stage there is the imprinting of a *character* upon the soul. Each successive *character*, like a progressively brighter sun, envelopes and contains the one that has gone before it.

Rooted in each *character*, is the right and power that belongs to the order being received. For the deacon it is the right to baptize, to preach, and to administer Holy Communion. For the priest it is the power to change bread and wine into the Body and Blood of Christ and to forgive sins. For the bishop, who alone has the complete fullness of the priesthood, it is the power to confirm and to ordain—to pass the power of the priesthood on to others in the sacrament of Holy Orders. Then, besides the increase in Sanctifying Grace and the priestly *character* with its accompanying power, there is a special sacramental grace given by God that will confer whatever actual grace may be needed by this ordained man as he faithfully serves his office.

The Office of the Priesthood, an Ordained Minister

Some deacons are "permanent deacons," which means that it is his intention to serve as a deacon permanently and not to become a priest. This is not to say that a permanent deacon cannot become a priest. An unmarried permanent deacon may apply and be ordained as a priest if the bishop so chooses. It is just that his intention at the time is to remain a deacon. Other deacons are "transitional deacons," which means that he is a deacon at the present time and is continuing his studies in the seminary until he completes them and can be ordained into the priesthood. Either way, the deacon receives the same ordination by the bishop.

On the day that a transitional deacon is ordained into the priesthood, the bishop again places his hands upon this same head and prays, "We beseech thee, Almighty Father, invest this thy servant with the dignity of the priesthood." This time the Holy Spirit imparts that tremendous and almost unbelievable power to call Jesus Christ down upon the altar changing bread and wine into His Body, Blood, Soul and Divinity—and the power to forgive, in Christ's name, the sins of men.

It is, of course, this power to offer sacrifice, this power to offer the perfect gift of Jesus in the name of God's people that distinguishes a priest from a Protestant minister. It would not be incorrect to call a priest a minister; he is a minister, a servant of Christ. He is a preacher, too, and could also be called a preacher, as he delivers God's message of salvation Sunday after Sunday. However, while it would be correct enough to call a priest a minister or a preacher, it would not be correct to call a Protestant minister a priest. The Protestant minister does not have the power to offer sacrifice, which is precisely what makes a priest a priest. Protestant ministers, except the clergy of the High Episcopalian Church, do not even believe in such a power. The High Church, or Anglican, clergy do consider themselves priests, but unfortunately they are mistaken. There is no one who can impart to them the power of the priesthood.

The line of succession by which the power of the priesthood has come down to us, from Christ to the Apostles to bishop to bishop, was broken centuries ago when the Anglican Church rejected the whole idea of the Mass and a sacrificing priesthood. Centuries later, high churchmen revived the idea of the Mass, but they no longer have bishops who are true successors of the Apostles, no bishops who themselves have any of the power which the sacrament of Holy Orders gives. This is not meant in any way to be criticism, nor is it said in any spirit of prideful disdain. It is just a sad fact of history; one that should move us to renewed prayers that our separated brethren may return to the one true fold.

Bishop

The third and top step of the Sacrament of Holy Orders is that of bishop. When a new bishop is needed, either to head a diocese or to perform some other high-level work of the Church, the Pope, as Peter's successor, designates the priest who is to be raised to the episcopacy (bishopric). This priest then receives his third "laying on of hands" from a bishop and himself becomes a bishop. To his previous power to offer Mass and to forgive sins there is now added the power to administer Confirmation in his own right and the exclusive power which only a bishop possesses: the power to ordain other priests and to consecrate other bishops.

The Power to Consecrate more Bishops

The essence of the order of bishop lies in his power to ordain priests and to consecrate other bishops. This is a power that he can never lose. Just as a priest can never lose his power to change bread and wine into our Lord's Body and Blood, even if he leaves the Church, so too, a bishop can never lose his power to ordain other priests and bishops, not even if he were to abandon the Catholic Church. It is here that we find the principal difference between the Orthodox churches and the Protestant churches.

The Protestant churches do not believe in the Mass or in a priesthood empowered to offer sacrifice; and therefore do not believe in the sacrament of Holy Orders. We noted that High Church members of the Episcopalian and Anglican faith do believe in the Mass and the priesthood. However, real priests and bishops ceased to exist in the Anglican church back in the sixteenth century. At that time the leaders of the Anglican church eliminated all reference to the Mass and the power of sacrifice from their ordination ceremony. Without the intention of ordaining sacrificing priests, the Sacrament of Holy Orders is invalid; it is *not* Holy Orders. In fact, that is true of any sacrament. If a priest speaks the words, "This is my body....This is my blood," in the presence of bread and wine (at dinner in a restaurant, for example), the bread and wine are not consecrated unless the priest has the *intention* of consecrating. Whoever gives a sacrament must have the intention of doing what the sacrament is supposed to do, or the sacrament is invalid. That is how true priests and bishops died out, in the Anglican church. Once the intention of ordaining sacrificing priests and bishops was taken out of the ordination service, sacrificing priests and bishops ceased to exist in those churches. When they again embraced the idea of sacrifice, they no longer had consecrated bishops able to ordain priests and consecrate new bishops.

This is different, however, with Orthodox churches. More than a thousand years ago, when all the Christian world was Catholic, the church leaders in some countries broke away from their union with Rome. They refused to obey the Pope as the head of the Church. When this happened, it was because of political rivalry and bitter personal resentments. However, as the church leaders of these nations turned their backs on Rome, they still continued to believe all the truths which the Catholic Church taught. They still believed in the Mass and all the sacraments. Their bishops remained true bishops, even though they had severed their allegiance to the Pope. These bishops continued to ordain priests validly, and to consecrate other bishops as their successors. Because they continued to pass down the power of the priesthood, the Orthodox churches still have the Mass and the sacraments. Because of their rejection of the Pope, they are non-Catholic churches. We term them "schismatic" or separated churches.

The Pope—Our Holy Father (CCC 551-53, 880-82, 888-92)

The Pope is a sign of unity and purpose for the members of the Catholic Church. The word *pope* is a word that can be traced back to the Latin *papa* and the Greek *pappas*, both of which mean "father." We believe that Jesus placed one of the Apostles in charge of the others to be that sign of unity and purpose. The Apostle that our Lord placed in charge was Peter.

Jesus and His Apostles went out to the area of Caesarea Philippi, a pagan region. In this region stood a rock that was enormous. It was 100 feet straight up and over 500 feet wide. On top of this rock was built a shrine or temple honoring the current Caesar as a god. The Romans had many false gods, but one of the gods that they were obliged to worship was their leader, the Caesar. Jesus and His Apostles went out to this region on purpose, for it was not an area that they would just happen by. Instead, it was quite a journey out of their way. This enormous rock with a pagan *church* sitting upon it, served as their backdrop for the conversation that Jesus began with the Apostles.

He said to them, "Who do people say that the Son of Man is?" When they responded with the answers John the Baptist, Elijah, Jeremiah, or one of the prophets, Jesus asked, "But who do you say that I am?" Simon, the brother of Andrew; the son of Jonah, replied, "You are the Messiah, the Son of the living God." Jesus immediately acknowledged that Simon's answer had been inspired by God and that this indicated a special role for Him. Jesus said, "Blessed are you, Simon son of Jonah. For flesh and blood has not revealed this to you, but my heavenly Father. And so I say to you, you are Rock, and upon this Rock I will build my Church, and the gates of the netherworld shall not prevail against it. I will give to you the keys to the Kingdom of Heaven. Whatever you bind on earth shall be bound in Heaven; and whatever you loose on earth shall be loosed in Heaven" (Matt 16:13-19).

Jesus had just given Simon, the brother of Andrew, son of Jonah, a new name. Jesus had named him "Rock". In Jesus' language of Aramaic, He named Simon, *Kepha* (rock). The name *Kepha* was translated into the Greek word *Petra* and then translated into English as *Peter*. So in English we call him Simon Peter or simply, Peter. But understand clearly, his name is "Rock—Kepha" and the word *Peter* is a translation of a translation.

In naming Simon "Rock," Jesus has placed Simon Peter at the head of the Apostles. Jesus has declared that He will build His Church upon the man Peter; that the gates of Hell will never prevail against His Church; that Peter possesses the "Keys" or the authority of the Kingdom; and that he possesses the power to make binding and lasting decisions that will be honored in Heaven. This was all done against the backdrop of the huge rock with a *church* resting upon it. Peter was named the "Rock" that Jesus would build His Church upon.

The Church was passed down by Apostolic Tradition: by the preaching of the Apostles, their examples, and the institutions they established. Even though this understanding of the primacy of Peter was passed down orally and by example, many New Testament passages reinforce it. One cannot read the book of Acts without coming away with the understanding that Peter was in charge. Peter is always named first in the list of the Apostles (Mark 3:16-19). In fact, his name is mentioned 195 more times than all of the other Apostles. Peter is the central figure in gospel events such as the Transfiguration (Matthew 17:1-8). An angel sits in the empty tomb and tells the women to go and announce the resurrection of Christ to Peter (Mark 16:7). After His resurrection, Jesus appeared to Peter before the other Apostles (Luke 24:34). Even after denying Jesus, Peter is singled out by the Lord to shepherd His flock (John 21:15-19). On the day of Pentecost, Peter is the first to proclaim the gospel publicly and is the chief spokesman for the Apostles. At his preaching, 3,000 Jews were converted (Acts 2:14-40). Peter headed the meeting that elected a new Apostle, Matthias, who would take the place of Judas Iscariot (Acts 1:13-26). Peter received the first converts into the Church (Acts 2:41); performed the first miracle after Pentecost (Acts 3:6-7); inflicted the punishment on Ananias and Sapphira (Acts 5:1-11); and excommunicated the first heretic (Acts 8:21). Peter alone receives the revelation that gentiles should be allowed entrance into the Church (Acts 10:44-46). Peter even leads the first council in Jerusalem (Acts 15:7) and pronounces the first dogmatic decision (Acts 15:19).

Peter was martyred in Rome at about 67 A.D. Linus was immediately elected to take his place and was recognized as the leader among the bishops. The Catholic Church has a complete list of every pope. Pope Francis is the 266th pontiff of the Church. Most have been good men and effective leaders. Many have been saints. Some have sinned gravely and have failed miserably in their roles as spiritual leaders. Such failures should not surprise us. Jesus chose twelve Apostles, and Judas turned out to be a traitor. Even Peter denied Him.

There is no further spiritual power that God gives to men above the order of bishop. The Pope does not have more spiritual power than an ordinary bishop. However, he does have more authority. Because he is the bishop of Rome, the successor of Saint Peter, the Pope has authority over the entire Church. He designates the priests who are to become bishops, and assigns bishops to their dioceses.

The pope also enjoys a very special privilege, which Jesus conferred on Saint Peter and Saint Peter's successors: the privilege of papal "infallibility." Catholics believe that Christ will not allow the Church to be misled in essential matters of faith and morals. This means that God preserves the Holy Father from teaching error whenever he makes a definitive pronouncement to the universal Church on matters of Christian faith or morals. This applies only when certain conditions are met: 1) the pope is speaking *ex cathedra*, that is, as leader of the whole Church; 2) he is dealing with faith or morals; and 3) he is expressly defining the doctrine as a matter of faith. It is very rare that infallible declarations are made by the pope. One example would be the formal definition of Mary's Assumption by Pope Pius XII in 1950.

Catholics believe that truths can be infallibly expressed when they are believed by the universal Church or taught by the College of Bishops in union with the pope. When the doctrine of the Assumption was defined, it was not a brand new doctrine. It had been the object of belief by Catholics from ancient times.

Solemnly defined doctrines of the Catholic Church are called dogmas. These are beliefs that must be accepted by all who wish to be members of the Church. They include such truths as the Holy Trinity, the Incarnation, Christ's divinity, the Real Presence of Jesus in the Eucharist, Mary's Immaculate Conception, her Assumption, and the beliefs that we profess in the Nicene Creed and the Apostles' Creed.

The doctrine of infallibility is seen as a great blessing for the Church. It gives us the assurance that God will not allow the powers of the "netherworld" to lead the Church astray. A clear understanding of infallibility and its limits may also be seen as a safeguard against the misuse of authority. Where there is no doctrine of infallibility, those in authority can easily claim their teachings to be infallible. Some who criticize the Catholic Church because of its doctrine of infallibility are the very same individuals who insist that their interpretation of the Bible is the only correct one and that their church members can only be saved by that interpretation. (Such was the case with Martin Luther.) Where there is no doctrine of infallibility, there is the temptation for leaders to claim infallibility in everything!

The Papacy is not just an institution, but Christ's gift to His Church. The successor of Peter is not just the pope, but our "Holy Father." We do not see him as a tyrant who tells us what to do. Far from it! He is seen as a "good shepherd" who lovingly leads his flock, keeping it safe from the wolf. With great love we say that he is our Holy Father; our Papa. This has become even more evident to the entire world because of television and Internet. The whole world could easily see how we as Catholics loved Pope John Paul II and how the people cried out for his sainthood moments after his death. The world can clearly see the love we already have for Pope Francis and how impressed we are by his great humility and wisdom.

Cardinal

The office of cardinal has nothing to do with priestly power. It is a position of honor independent of Holy Orders. The cardinals are simply the Pope's personal advisers; they are the Papal "cabinet officers." It was Pope Nicholas II in the year 1059 who made the College of Cardinals pretty much what it is today, giving the cardinals the right to elect a new Pope when his chair becomes vacant.

Monsignor

At this point someone might say, "What about monsignors? Where do monsignors fit it in?" The title *Monsignor*, is an honor given to a priest by the Holy Father, usually at the request of the bishop in whose diocese the priest labors. The priest who receives such an honor is usually a member of the bishop's "official family"—chancellor, secretary, vicar general, Propagation of the Faith director, and so on; or he is a pastor whose exceptional work seems to merit special recognition. This priest, in being named "Monsignor," has received the bishop's high approval, but it does not give any increase of priestly power or authority.

The Priesthood—A Call to Holiness

All priests are called to witness Christ by the manner of their lives. They are our spiritual "fathers." Throughout the centuries we have seen many, many great examples of this witness. So many priests have become saints that it is impossible to name them here. Simply purchase any book on saints and you will see the pages filled with the heroic lives of priests. Father Maximilian Kolbe is one such example.

A prisoner had escaped from Auschwitz. In retaliation, the Nazi commandant summoned the other prisoners and chose ten to be starved to death. One of them sobbed, "My wife, my children!" A forty-seven-year-old Catholic priest, Father Maximilian Kolbe, stepped forward. "I want to die in place of this prisoner," he said. The commandant hesitated, then snapped, "Request granted." Father Kolbe prayed with the other nine and cared for them until one by one they all died.

Father Damien of Molokai is another great example. In his day, all those who had the disease of leprosy were placed on the island of Molokai in Hawaii. They were simply deserted there and waited to die from their horrible disease. Father Damien volunteered to live among the lepers and care for them. He organized them and began building homes for them. Together they built a Catholic Church. Father Damien administered the sacraments to the people and treated them with dignity. Each day when Father Damien would celebrate the Mass with the lepers, he would address them saying, "My beloved lepers." Father Damien cared for their needs; nursed them at their death beds; and prayed with them in all things. After many years of this, he addressed them one morning at Mass with the words, "My fellow lepers." With that the colony began to weep. For their beloved priest was now a leper too.

Again, priests are our spiritual "fathers." We even address them as "Father" in our parishes. This title shows the family relationship a priest should have with the members of the Church, as well as the attitudes of sacrifice and generosity with which the priest serves his people. As a good father sacrifices for his children, our priests sacrifice for us.

Some people criticize Catholics for calling priests "Father," stating that Jesus forbade this when he said, "Call no one on earth your father" (Matt 23:9). People who say this have taken this passage out of context. In reading the entire passage it is clear that Jesus was speaking against the false attitudes of pride and superiority that was present in the Jewish leaders of His day. If this passage should be taken in a literal sense, then "father" could not be used even in reference to our own parents! Even Saint Paul said to the Corinthians: "I became your father in Christ Jesus through the gospel" (1 Cor 4:15).

Diocese

The whole world is divided up into dioceses. Each diocese has a definite geographical boundary just as states and countries have definite boundaries. Everyone living within the boundaries of a certain diocese, belongs to that diocese. Each diocese is divided into parishes. Each parish also has its own geographical boundary. Each person living within those boundaries belongs to that parish.

At the head of each diocese is a bishop. The bishop who rules over a diocese is called the ordinary of the diocese. Several adjacent dioceses are grouped together to form a *province* in the Church. The principal diocese of the province is called an *archdiocese*, and the ordinary of that principal diocese is called an *archbishop*. The archbishop is not the "boss" over the other dioceses in his province; each bishop is the ruler of his own diocese. But the archbishop does have precedence in honor and does have certain duties, such as calling meetings of the bishops of the province and presiding over such meetings.

Most dioceses are divided into several deaneries, each deanery comprising several adjacent parishes. One of the pastors within that territory is appointed as dean by the bishop. The bishop then delegates to the dean many of his lesser tasks of supervision.

This is then the hierarchical organization of the Church: several parishes make a deanery; several deaneries constitute a diocese; several dioceses comprise a province; and all the provinces of the world make up the Universal Church.

XI. The Holy Sacrifice of the Mass

There has always been a particular way to worship God and we can sum up that particular way with just one word: sacrifice. God has always required His people to worship Him in sacrifice. The evidence for this goes all the way back to Genesis. The very first sons of Adam and Eve, Cane and Able, offered sacrifice to God. Abel was an animal herder and he offered to God the best of his animals in sacrifice. Cane was a farmer and offered a sacrifice of grain to God, but not the best that he had to offer. We learn immediately from the Bible that God wishes us to offer Him a pure sacrifice from the heart and trust Him to take care of us.

Jesus said, "I have come not to abolish the Old Covenant, but to fulfill it" (Matthew 5:17). If this is true, then we need to realize that sacrifice is still the means through which we worship God. Beginning with the Last Supper, Jesus showed us what the New Covenant worship would look like. Led by the Holy Spirit, the original twelve apostles began what we call today "The Holy Sacrifice of the Mass." The Mass is a 'holy and living Sacrifice' and not only a sacrifice, but the greatest sacrifice that has ever or could ever be offered to God. Why? Because the sacrifice we offer to God at the Mass is the only sacrifice that has ever pleased Him fully; that has ever been good enough to truly take away our sins and reconcile us to God. It is the only completely pure sacrifice that can be offered. Why? Because what we offer to God at the Mass is His very own begotten Son, Jesus.

The Last Supper

Let's begin with the very first Mass, "The Last Supper." What you and I call, "The Last Supper," was actually a Jewish Passover Meal. Jesus was celebrating the great and holy Feast of

Passover with His disciples for the third time. This was the great feast of the Old Covenant which made present to the current generation the liberation of the Israelites from slavery in Egypt. In other words, God's people celebrated the day and sacred meal in which they were saved by the blood of the Passover Lamb! They remembered and made present again the night when the Angel of Death passed over their homes seeing the blood of the Passover Lamb on their door posts and lentils. Each year, the Jews sacrificed a perfect male lamb and ate this sacrifice with bitter herbs and unleavened bread making present the long ago event that saved their ancestors (and therefore them) from slavery and death.

At the Last Supper however, Jesus began the "New Passover Sacrifice" of the New Covenant! In other words, Jesus began "The Holy Sacrifice of the Mass." This time, however, Jesus made it clear that He was the victim; that He was the *Lamb* being sacrificed. He proclaimed the unleavened bread to be His Body and the wine to be His Blood. Jesus had replaced the Passover Lamb of the Old Covenant with Himself, the Lamb of God. Jesus became the New Passover Sacrifice of the New Covenant which He established that night and continued all the way until His death on Calvary the next day. Jesus said, "I have not come to abolish the Old covenant. Instead I have come to fulfill it!" (Matt 5:17). So you and I must remember the requirements of the Old Covenant and bring them with us into the New Covenant. It was required in all covenant sacrifices that the Israelites eat the sacrifice that they offered to God. Eating the sacrifice allowed them to be in communion with God; to become one with Him. This sealed the covenant and made it binding. The Israelites were now part of God's family. They had a family bond with Him that was binding and could not be broken.

The Mass is the New Passover Meal! We, like the Israelites, celebrate God liberating us from slavery; slavery to sin.

Jesus died to take our sins away so that we could be reconciled to God once and for all. This opened the gates of Heaven that had been closed since the sin of Adam and Eve; the 'Fall' of mankind. We celebrate Jesus' saving act; His Passion; Death; Resurrection and Ascension into Heaven. We have been saved and set free by the Blood of the New Passover Lamb, Jesus Himself. Jesus said, "I have not come to abolish the Old Covenant. Instead I have come to fulfill it!" (Matt 5:17). Jesus did not throw away the ancient Jewish worship. He brought it to new heights. So we, like the Israelites, must eat the sacrifice that saves us; the very Body, Blood, Soul and Divinity of Jesus, the Lamb of God, who becomes present on our altar at every Mass.

Jesus proclaimed the bread to be His Body at the Last Supper. Jesus proclaimed the wine to be His Blood at the Last Supper. Then He gave us the same command that was given to the ancient Israelites at the time of their very first Passover Feast, "Do this in memory of Me." He said to them in essence, "Continue to make present this sacrifice that saves you until I come again."

At Mass we celebrate and proclaim His Death! At Mass we celebrate and proclaim His Resurrection and His Ascension into Heaven. Why? Because this is what saves us!

Saint Justin Martyr (Jergens 50-56)

Saint Justin Martyr wrote a description of the Mass in the year 150 AD. He wrote this in order to try to convince the Roman Emperor to accept Christianity as truth so that he would stop his persecution of the Christians. Even though Saint Justin did not succeed, we can learn from his writings that the celebration of the Mass in the year 150 AD is the same as it is today. This proves that the Mass has always been the way Christians worship God.

Saint Justin began by saying, "No one may share the **Eucharist** with us unless he believes that what we teach is true, unless he is washed in the regenerating waters of baptism for the remission of his sins, and unless he lives in accordance with the principles given to us by Christ." So you see here that the Mass was called **Eucharist** in the year 150 AD as it is still called today. The word Eucharist means "Thanksgiving". In using the word Eucharist, we understand that we come to Mass to offer God thanks for everything He has given us, especially His only Son who has redeemed us by His blood. First and foremost the Mass has the spirit of "Thanksgiving"; "Thanks be to God!"

Saint Justin Continues by saying, "We do not consume the Eucharistic bread and wine as if it were ordinary food and drink, for we have been taught that as Jesus Christ our Savior became a man of flesh and blood by the power of the Word of God, so also the food that our flesh and blood assimilates for its nourishment becomes the Flesh and Blood of the incarnate Jesus by the power of his own words contained in the **Eucharistic Prayer**, the prayer of thanksgiving." These simple and straight forward words of Saint Justin tell us that the bread and wine truly become the Body and Blood of Jesus during the **Eucharistic Prayer** and by the words of the **Eucharistic Prayer**. Again, Justin wrote this in the year 150 AD. It proves the Catholic belief in the "True Presence" of Christ in the Eucharist; that we truly take and eat His Body and Blood at every Mass. We even learn that the Eucharistic Prayer was being used from the very beginning in Catholic Christian worship.

St. Justin Continues saying, "The apostles, in their recollections, which are called **Gospels**, handed down to us what Jesus commanded them to do. They tell us that He took bread, gave thanks and said, '*Do this in memory of me. This is my body.*' In the same way He took the cup, He gave thanks and said, '*This is my blood.*' The Lord gave this command to them alone. Ever since then we have constantly reminded one another of these things. The rich among us help the poor and we are always united. For all that we receive we praise the Creator of the universe through his Son Jesus Christ and through the Holy Spirit." Saint Justin is quoting the 'Words of Consecration' used during the Christian worship of his day and we can easily see they are the same words used at Mass today.

Saint Justin then begins to describe the parts of the Mass saying, "On Sunday we have a common assembly of all our members, whether they live in the city or the outlying districts. The recollections of the apostles or the writings of the prophets are read, as long as there is time." Here Justin is describing "The Liturgy of the Word," which is the first of the two main parts of the Mass. During the Liturgy of the Word we begin with "The First Reading," which is taken from the Old Testament. Then we read "The Second Reading" taken from the New Testament. Saint Justin describes this "as from the recollections of the Apostles or writings of the prophets." Saint Justin also states that some of the recollections of the apostles are called **Gospels**. This is the next reading that takes place during the Liturgy of the Word at Mass.

Saint Justin continues saying, "When the reader has finished, the priest of the assembly speaks to us. He urges everyone to imitate the examples of virtue we have heard in the readings." At this Saint Justin is describing the priest's homily that is still preached today. Saint Justin even states that the purpose of the homily is to urge everyone to imitate the examples of virtue found in the readings that were just read at the Mass. This is exactly what our priests do at Mass.

St. Justin then continues by saying, "Then we all stand up together and pray." Here, Justin is describing the part of the Mass that you and I would call the Petitions or "General Intercessions." We stand up and pray. Notice that Justin does not mention the

Nicene Creed. This is because it was not written until the year 325. It was added to the Mass after that year.

St. Justin then goes on to say, "On the conclusion of our prayer, bread and wine and water are brought forward." Here, Saint Justin is of course describing the part of the Mass that we call the "Offertory Procession and the Presentation of Gifts." We too bring forth bread, wine and water today.

Justin then writes, "The Priest offers prayers and gives thanks to the best of his ability, and the people give assent by saying, "Amen". Notice Justin's wording here, "The priest offers prayers of thanks." He is referring to the Eucharistic Prayer, because the word Eucharist means 'thanksgiving'. Next Justin describes the "Great Amen" that comes at the end of the Eucharistic Prayer. This "Amen" states that we believe all the sacred mysteries that have taken place on the altar as the word "amen" means, 'I believe'.

Justin then goes on to say, "The Eucharist is distributed, everyone present comes forward to receive it, and the deacons take it to those who are absent." This is exactly what we do today. We all come forward and go to communion as we call it. After Mass is over we take the Eucharist to those who are unable to come due to illness or immobility. And notice that Saint Justin not only calls the Mass the Eucharist, but he also calls the Body and Blood of Jesus the Eucharist, as we do today.

Justin continues his description saying, "The wealthy, if they wish, may make a contribution of money, and they themselves decide the amount. The collection is placed in the custody of the priest who uses it to help the orphans and widows and all who for any reason is in distress, whether because they are sick, in prison, or away from home. In a word, he takes care of all who are in need." This is a description of the collection of money that takes place at our Sunday Masses for we are all called to stewardship. We must take care of those who are in need. This has always been a basic Christian belief.

Justin then describes why the worship of the Church takes place on Sunday rather than on the traditional Jewish Sabbath of Saturday. "We hold our common assembly on Sunday because it is the first day of the week, the day on which God put darkness and chaos to flight and created the world, and because on that same day our savior Jesus Christ arose from the dead. For He was crucified on Friday and on Sunday He appeared to His apostles and disciples and taught them the things that we have passed on for your consideration." Saint Justin is very straightforward in his reasoning here. Sunday is the first day of the week. It is the day that God began the creation of the world. It is the day that Jesus arose from the dead. It is therefore the most appropriate day to be the new Sabbath day; the Sabbath day of the New Covenant.

We can learn from Saint Justin's words that the Mass is not a made up, man-created worship service that we can change and manipulate. The Mass was handed to us by Jesus through the Apostles. We received it from their hands and have not changed it. God designed His own worship service. Why? Because it is identical to the worship that takes place in Heaven. It is the worship that Jesus gave to us at the Last Supper; the sacrifice of the New and Eternal Covenant.

We can easily see from the words of St. Justin that the main focus of the Mass in his day was the Sacrifice that took place upon the altar. That it was the Eucharist; the bread and wine, which became the Body and Blood of our Lord Jesus Christ, that was the center of the worship. The homily given by the priest was just a small part of the overall worship and certainly not the main thrust. Saint Justin proves to us that the ancient Christian worship given to us by the apostles focused on the Eucharistic Sacrifice; the offering of Jesus to God in Sacrifice and then partaking of that same sacrifice by eating His very Body and Blood. We know that it is the same today for all Catholics.

The Mass as Sacrifice

As I mentioned earlier, the Mass is often called "The holy Sacrifice of the Mass". But how is the Mass a sacrifice? This is not easy to understand because Catholics do not come to Mass like the ancient Jews went to the temple, bringing animals to be cut up, burned and offered to God by a priest. Even though the sacrifice taking place at Mass is not one of sheep, cattle, or goats, it does involve a real sacrifice—the sacrifice of Jesus Christ, the Son of God, who in His death on the cross offered His life as a total gift to the Father and redeemed the world.

The Mass does not merely recall or symbolize Jesus' death on the cross. It sacramentally makes present Christ's redeeming sacrifice on Calvary, so that its saving power may be more fully applied to our lives today. In other words, what happened THEN happens NOW on our altar at Mass. When Jesus said, "Do this in memory of me," He was commanding the apostles to make present the sacrificial offering of His Body and Blood at the Last Supper. Remember that the bread and wine become Jesus' Body and Blood at Mass. Remember that Jesus told us that we would have to eat His flesh and drink His blood or we would not have Life within us (John 6). Remember that Jesus is the New Passover Lamb. He IS the sacrifice. In the ancient Jewish Passover, it was not enough to simply have the animal killed in sacrifice. Eating the sacrifice was an essential part of the Passover celebration. The people simply had to eat the sacrifice that saved them. It was true of them then; it is true of us today. We simply must eat the sacrifice that saves us.

The Introductory Rites of the Mass

The Sign of the Cross

We begin the Mass with the "Sign of the Cross". Please understand that the Sign of the Cross is not simply a way to begin praying. People will ask, "Why do Catholics make the sign of the cross?" Most Catholics answer by saying, "Well, it's just how we begin our prayers." Please understand that the Sign of the Cross is much, much more than that. It is a prayer all by itself!

When you and I make the sign of the cross, we are invoking or calling upon God's presence and we are inviting Him to bless us; to assist us; and to guard us from all harm. The sign of the cross is a powerful prayer all by itself. We are saying to God, "Be present to me; bless me; assist me; and guard me from all harm."

Saint John Chrysostom said of the sign of the Cross, "Never leave your house without making the sign of the cross. It will be your staff and your weapon. No man or demon will dare attack you, seeing you covered with such powerful armor. Let this sign teach you that you are a soldier, ready to fight against the demons. Don't you know what this cross has done? It has destroyed sin and death! It has emptied Hell. It has dethroned Satan! And it has restored the universe! Do not doubt its power."

In addition, when we make the sign of the cross, we are calling upon the name of the Lord. We are calling on the Lord in order to praise Him; to thank Him, and also to seek His help in our lives. When we make the sign of the cross and speak the words, "In the name of the Father and of the Son and of the Holy Spirit," God immediately comes to us. He is present.

It is appropriate then, that the very first thing we do at Mass is to make the sign of the Cross. We invite God into our lives in a powerful way and invoke His presence and power as we consecrate the next hour of our lives to the Lord, saying that everything we do in the Mass, we do in His name.

The Lord Be with You

After the sign of the cross, the priest greets us with the words, "The Lord be with you." Have you ever wondered why that is? Believe me, it is not just a simple greeting. Nor is it a greeting that can be changed. In other words, the priest can't change this greeting to say instead, "Hey everyone! It's nice to see you. I'm glad you are here!" Nearly every word of the Mass can be found in the Bible and has a specific meaning. The priest is literally asking the Lord to be with every person present and he is doing this for a reason. Why at the beginning of Mass do we need the priest to call upon the Lord to be with us in such a formal way? It is because the Mass, by its very act, brings about a huge change in each person present. The Mass changes us from the inside out and makes us one with Christ; holy; and able to fulfill the mission on this earth that we have been called to fulfill. The Mass is our spiritual strength.

The words, "The Lord be with you" remind us of the calling we each have. As God's children, we each have a particular mission to fulfill in the Kingdom of God according to the Father's plan. This mission is a difficult one as we are all called to be saints; to reach holiness; and to help lead others to Heaven. The words, "The Lord be with you," assure us that God is right there to support us through the trials and challenges of life. These words help us to be faithful to the mission we have been called to. At Mass, this greeting also points us toward the sacred mysteries that are about to take place on our very altar right in front of us—the mysteries of Christ's death and Resurrection and communion with Christ's Body, Blood, Soul, and Divinity. None of us are worthy of such a close encounter with Christ, but the priest's words remind us that we can do all things through Christ who strengthens us (Phil. 4:13).

You can be called to the highest heights and yet be fearless if the Lord is truly with you. Picture Moses kneeling before the burning bush; God's voice bellowing forth from it saying, "Go back to Egypt and confront Pharaoh. Convince him to let My people go so that they can worship Me." Moses, completely overwhelmed, does everything he can to convince God that he has chosen the wrong man for the job. "They are trying to kill me in Egypt! Who am I that I should go to Pharaoh? The people will not believe me. I'm not even a good speaker!" God responds to all Moses' doubts with the words, "I will be with you." I ask you, what else could Moses possibly need?

After the death of Moses, God called Joshua to lead the Israelites into the Promised Land. Joshua would have to confront many large armies and fight many battles. Yet God told Joshua to be of good courage and to be confident that he would succeed saying, "I will be with you" (Joshua 1:5)

Gideon was called by God to rescue the people from the Midianites, who had taken over the land of the Israelites, with the words, "I will be with you, and you shall smite the Midianites as one man" (Judges 6:16).

David slew Goliath with a slingshot and a single stone (1 Samuel 17). Do you doubt that God was with him?

Remember the words spoken by the Angel Gabriel to the Blessed Virgin Mary, "Hail, full of Grace. The Lord is with you" (Luke 1:28). Mary was called upon to birth, raise and educate the Savior of the world only to give Him up and watch Him die. As she held the lifeless body of her beloved Son in her arms as He was taken down from the cross, God was most definitely with her. She could not have fulfilled her mission without His Grace.

"And With Your Spirit"

The priest greets us with the words, "The Lord be with you" and we respond, "And with your spirit." We are not simply being polite; reciprocating the greeting… "Hey Father! Right back at you! The Lord be with you too." Do you understand that the Holy Spirit is truly acting inside of the priest during Mass? The priest loans his hands, lips and very body to Christ and acts for Him during the Mass. This is why the priest's street clothes are covered with the garments of priestly service and authority. As the people say, "And with your spirit," they are addressing the interior spirit of the priest where he has been ordained precisely to lead the people in the sacred action of the Mass. The people realize that by the priest's hands ordinary bread and wine will become the very Body, Blood, Soul, and Divinity of Jesus; our spiritual nourishment.

Penitential Rite—I Confess

During the Penitential Rite of the Mass, the priest invites us to "prepare ourselves to celebrate these sacred mysteries" by calling to mind our sins. By now, in reading this book, you have come to understand that where there is sin, God cannot be. Yet very soon we will all come forward to place God into our souls. We will literally place Christ's Body and Blood into our bodies. Can we do this with sin in our souls? The answer is 'No,' we absolutely cannot. If we have committed Mortal Sin, it must be confessed prior to receiving communion. But let's be realistic. The majority of us come to Mass with our souls full of Venial Sins. We cannot come forward to take and eat the bread that is Jesus and drink of His Precious Blood with our souls stained with Venial Sin. These sins must first be forgiven. The Penitential Rite of the Mass allows us to express our contrition or sorrow for our sins and thus be forgiven of them allowing us to first listen to His

Word and then to come forward with a pure soul to receive Him sacramentally.

As Catholics, we encounter Jesus Christ on our altars every time we go to Mass. He is there in Body, Blood, Soul, and His Divinity. Not only is He present on our altar, but soon we will come forward and place His very Life inside of us. We are not worthy of such a close encounter with our Lord. Our sinfulness stands in stark contrast to what we are about to do in the Mass. Through the Penitential Rite, by humbly confessing our sins publicly to Almighty God and to each other, we are made worthy to approach the altar and receive Him.

Just as the people of Israel needed to wash their garments before approaching the Lord at Mount Sinai, so we need to cleanse our souls from sin before we approach God, right there on our altar in the Mass (Exodus 19:10).

The first writing ever written by the Apostles is called the Didache. Written in the year 60 AD, the Didache was the first teaching of the Apostles. In it is written, "Assemble on the Lord's Day, break bread and offer the Eucharist; but first make confession of your sins, so that your sacrifice may be a pure one." It also says, "Let a man examine himself before partaking of the Eucharist, lest he do so in an unworthy manner."

Lord Have Mercy

We then pray with the priest, "Lord, have mercy; Christ have mercy; Lord, have mercy." When you and I truly repent of our sins and call on God's mercy in all sincerity, God is overjoyed at our change in heart. So overjoyed is God, that He forgets our sins altogether. He not only forgives them…He forgets them.

Why do we repeat three times, "Lord, have mercy; Christ, have mercy; Lord have mercy"? This can be viewed as praying to the Trinity, as we are asking each of the Divine Persons of God for mercy: Lord = God the Father; Christ = God the Son; Lord, = God the Holy Spirit. It can also be viewed as praying to Jesus as our brother; our Redeemer; and our God.

Gloria

At this point the tone of the Mass changes from sorrowful repentance to joyful praise. In the Gloria we praise and thank God for His forgiving love and His merciful kindness. The words, "Glory to God in the highest and on earth peace to people of good will" comes from the angels who announced the good news of Christ's birth to a group of shepherds outside of Bethlehem (Luke 2:14). It is very fitting that we sing these words at the beginning of the Sunday Mass, because the Mass makes present the mystery of Christmas once again. As God was made present to the world in bodily form as baby Jesus 2,000 years ago, the resurrected Jesus is made present in bodily form sacramentally upon our altars at the **Consecration** in every Mass. We prepare ourselves to welcome the resurrected Jesus by repeating the same words of praise that the angels used to herald Christ's coming in Bethlehem.

In the Mass we continually proclaim our faith. The Gloria is an excellent example of this as it praises God as Trinity; Father, then Son, and then Holy Spirit. First we praise God as "Almighty Father" and "Heavenly King," two titles of God that can be found throughout the Bible. We recognize God as our very own Father. Seeing God as our loving Father who chooses to share His goodness with us, we cannot help but to worship Him and give Him thanks and praise. In the Gloria we express our love and gratitude to God.

The Gloria also tells the story of Christ's coming; His redeeming death; and His triumphant Resurrection and Ascension into Heaven. We truly recognize Jesus as God Himself. We also recognize Him as the Lamb of God; the New Passover Lamb sacrificed on our altar at Mass, who gave His life freely for our salvation.

In the Gloria we recognize that Jesus is now seated at the right hand of God the Father. In the Bible, the right hand of God is a position of authority. We boldly proclaim Jesus to now be reigning over the Kingdom—the Church—and we humbly ask Him to receive our prayer and to have mercy on us. We express our gratitude for having received salvation from Jesus. We come to Mass with the understanding that we are in great need of redemption and that Jesus has already saved us.

Jesus is praised in the Gloria as the Holy One; the Lord; and the Most High. Jesus is Lord! He is God and we profess it boldly. We are therefore called to be loyal to Jesus and His commandments above anything else in the world: above our jobs; our friends; money; sports; etc.! "You alone are Lord."

The Gloria finishes in praise of the Holy Spirit. Thus we have praised and paid homage to the entire Holy Trinity.

The Opening Prayer or Collect

Next, we pray the opening prayer from the Sacramentary or Roman Missal. This prayer gathers together the intentions of the people participating in the Mass and concludes the Introductory Rites.

The Liturgy of the Word

Think of the Mass as two banquet tables: The Liturgy of the Word and the Liturgy of the Eucharist. God's people are nourished from the table of Holy Scripture, which is proclaimed in the Liturgy of the Word. Then they are fed with the Body of our Lord at the table of the Eucharist. Hearing the Scriptures read to us leads us into that deeper communion with Jesus that happens when we come forward to take and eat His very Body and drink His Precious Blood. Sitting attentively at only one of these tables without the other simply will not do. We need both the inspired Word of God in Scripture and the Word of God made Flesh—Jesus Himself—present in the Blessed Sacrament. This is why the Mass is so fulfilling!

The Mass is the greatest Bible study on earth. In three years' time the Bible is completely read at Mass. When we listen to the Scripture Readings at Mass or read Scripture on our own, we must understand that God is speaking to us personally. God is literally talking to each one of us. All Scripture is inspired by God. The Bible is God's own speech to us. Therefore, we must prepare ourselves to hear the Word of God. At Mass we prepare ourselves for this holy encounter with God's Word through the Introductory Rites: The Sign of the Cross; the Greeting; the Penitential Rite; the Lord Have Mercy; the Gloria; and the Opening Prayer that we have just examined. The Introductory Rites of the Mass help us to prepare our souls and make them pure so that we are able to listen well and hear God speak to us through His Holy Word.

The order, of the readings at Mass, moves from the Old Testament to the New Testament. It is the same order as God's redemptive plan; from Israel to The Church.

The First Reading

The First Reading is taken from the Old Testament (except during the Easter Season when it is taken from the Acts of the Apostles). Understanding the Old Testament is vital to understanding the New Testament. Our salvation is hidden in the Old Testament and revealed in the New. We cannot understand

Jesus and the New Testament Scriptures without knowing the history of Israel in the Old Testament. In the Mass, the Old Testament Reading generally matches in theme or prefigures Jesus or the events of the Gospel Reading. For example, the First Reading, on the Feast of the Epiphany (Three Kings), from Isaiah predicts the coming of kings who will worship God bringing forth Gold and Frankincense. The Gospel then tells the story of the three Wise Men who travel to Bethlehem in search of a new born king. Upon finding Jesus, they pay Him homage bearing gifts of God, Frankincense, and Myrrh.

"The Word of the Lord '

At the end of the First Reading the Lector proclaims, "The Word of the Lord." How profound this statement is! This should be heard in absolute amazement! God is speaking directly to us! Who are we that God should speak to us? And yet, He does. We, in utter amazement of this fact, cry out from the depths of our hearts, "Thanks be to God." Thanks be to God that He would actually want to speak to us. What a loving Father we have. Our God is truly and awesome God!

The Responsorial Psalm

Immediately following the First Reading, the Responsorial Psalm is sung. The Responsorial Psalm is taken from the Book of Psalms which is a collection of 150 sacred hymns. These were used for private devotion and public worship in the Temple liturgy in Jesus' day. The verses of the psalms would be sung by two alternating groups with a common refrain. These sacred hymns continue to be used in the same way in the Mass.

The Second Reading

The Second Reading is taken from the New Testament: one of the epistles (letters); the Acts of the Apostles; or the Book of Revelation. The Second Reading teaches us how to live the life of a Christian. It helps us to live by our spirit and avoid the temptations of sin.

The Gospel

The Gospel is our principal source for the life and teaching of Jesus Christ. Therefore, the Gospel is treated with great reverence in the Mass. First, the congregation <u>stands</u> for standing is a more reverent posture than sitting. Second, we sing <u>Alleluia</u>, which means "Praise God!" Third, while the Alleluia is sung, the priest (or deacon) begins a procession in the sanctuary, which transports the Book of Gospels from the altar to the lectern, where it will be proclaimed. The altar servers carry candles lighting the way and sometimes incense is used. The Gospel is also illuminated by candles as it is read.

Before reading the Gospel the priest quietly prays, "Cleanse my heart and my lips, Almighty God, that I may worthily proclaim your holy Gospel." If a deacon reads the Gospel, the priest prays a similar prayer over him.

The Gospel begins with another greeting dialog, "The Lord be with you." We respond, "And with your spirit." Again, this greeting alerts us to the greatness of the event that is about to take place. For in the Gospel, Jesus speaks directly to us. We are not simply listening to someone tell us what Jesus once said or once did. Jesus Himself is speaking directly to us. He is talking to you! He is talking to me. What He has to say is always relevant in our present lives.

The priest (or deacon) announces the Gospel Reading and traces the Sign of the Cross on his forehead, mouth, breast, and the book. We, in turn, make a three-fold Sign of the Cross over ourselves asking that God's Word in the Gospel be always on our minds, on our lips and in our hearts.

The Homily

The practice of explaining Scripture is rooted in ancient Jewish custom. Jewish leaders gave an explanation of Scripture so that the people understood what was read in the synagogue. Jesus Himself practiced this custom as we see in the fourth chapter of Luke's Gospel. From the earliest days of the Christian Mass, the Word of God was not read on its own. It was accompanied by a homily, which explained the meaning of the Scriptural readings and showed people how to apply these meanings to their very lives. The word *Homily* is a Greek word that means—explanation.

The Homily can only be given by an ordained minister: a deacon, priest, or bishop (canon 767). The same is true of the reading of the Gospel at Mass. You see, the bishop is the true successor of the Apostles and the priests and deacons share his authority. It is they and only they who have the responsibility to proclaim the Gospel and pass it on from generation to generation. Since the Homily is given only by an ordained minister, it is meant to be a sign or a guarantee that the preaching is truly passing on the Church's apostolic faith and not merely the private thoughts and experiences of an individual. Lay people can certainly teach the faith in classroom settings. It's just that they cannot do it at Mass. It is the particular responsibility of the bishop as a successor of the apostles to teach the apostolic faith. His union with the Pope and other bishops throughout the world gives us visible, concrete proof that the teachings are being passed down from one generation to the next by our modern day apostles.

The Creed

The Creed is a summary statement of what we as Catholics believe. It was written in the year 325 AD at the Council of Nicaea. It was very important to firmly place in writing our basic Christian beliefs. This was true because of all the false teachings that were going on at the time, and quite frankly, continue today.

At the time of Jesus devout Jews also recited a creed known as the Shema. The Jewish Shema stated: "Hear, O Israel—The Lord our God is one Lord; and you shall love the Lord your God with all your heart, and with all your soul, and with all your might." Devout Jewish men wore these words in a leather box, called a phylactery that was tied around their heads. The people stopped throughout the day to recite the Shema.

The Jews lived in a world where the majority of the people worshipped many gods. For the Israelites there was only one God; the true God. Therefore, this Shema caused the Jews to live a life that was very counter cultural. Our creed causes the same for us. We live in a society that claims the world happened by chance and was not created at all. We are even told that God does not exist. We live in a society that increasingly embraces the views of Relativism. We are told that there is no real right or wrong, but only what individuals think or feel. Your truth is right for you and my truth is right for me; no matter how different they may be. Society tells us that we can believe what we want about God. In fact, most people mold God into what they want Him to be, rather than discovering who He really is. The Nicene Creed that we profess at Mass speaks the very opposite, but that is of no surprise. God's people have always been countercultural. The Creed assures us that we are created beings loved into existence by God. We are not here by random chance. The Creed tells us that God became a man for our salvation to bring the forgiveness of sins. The Creed reminds us of the intense battle between good and evil; between God and Satan. It does not allow us to get caught up in societies claim that there is no clear right or wrong. Instead, it reminds us that at the end of our lives, we will stand before Jesus who "will come again in glory to judge the living and the dead."

The Prayer of the Faithful

We have always prayed for one another in the Mass as was noted earlier by St. Justin Martyr in his description of our Liturgy. The Bible notes that the Church in Jerusalem prayed for Peter when he was imprisoned by Herod. That very night an angel came to release him from his chains (Acts 12:5-17). Moreover, St. Paul gave instructions to his disciple, Timothy, telling him to intercede for all people (1Tim 2:1).

Jesus poured out his heart to the whole human race. At Mass we call on Christ to intercede for us to the Father. If we are in tune with God's heart, we naturally want to pray for others in need. These intercessions train us to look not only after our own interests, but also to the interests of others. Remember too that prayer is very powerful, especially when great numbers are praying. When we think about the Mass being said throughout the world in many different languages, we can begin to realize that our prayers at Mass are very powerful.

Liturgy of the Eucharist

In the second half of the Mass, called the Liturgy of the Eucharist, Jesus' sacrifice on the cross is made present by the priest. The priest carries out what Jesus did at the Last Supper and what He commanded the apostles to do in His memory. The bread and wine are offered as gifts by the people and then consecrated and changed into the Body and Blood of Christ, which we receive in Holy Communion.

The Preparation of the Gifts

The first thing to happen during the Liturgy of the Eucharist is what we call the 'Preparation of the Gifts.' People bring forward the gifts of bread and wine to the priest. We also call this the "Offertory" because it is based on the Latin word Offerre, which means to present, to bring or to offer. These gifts of bread and wine typically come from the work of human hands; for the grapes had to be grown and made into wine. The wheat had to be grown and processed into flour and then made into dough and baked as bread. These gifts are the fruits of hard labor, which call us to view them as a sacrifice in nature. When the bread and wine and water are brought forward…these items symbolize us; the people participating in the Mass. As they are given to the priest, who acts for Jesus, it symbolizes us giving ourselves to God. This is so very important to understand, because at every Mass we literally give our lives to God.

These gifts absolutely must be unleavened bread and wine. They cannot be crackers and grape juice or any other substitute. Why? Because it was bread and wine that was used at the Jewish Passover and therefore at the Last Supper. We must do the same. The fact that bread is used is very important. Bread and wine were common items offered up in Israel's sacrifices.

In the presentation of the gifts, we bring our entire lives and all our little sacrifices to the hands of Jesus Himself, who is represented by the priest. The priest then brings our gifts to the altar, which is the place where Christ's sacrifice is made present. Our gifts are combined and made one with Christ's offering to the Father. Therefore, Christ is offered to God and we are offered to God along with Him.

Mixing Water and Wine

Now the priest mixes the water and wine together. The wine symbolizes Christ's divinity and the water symbolizes our humanity. The mixing of the water and wine therefore points to the Incarnation: The mystery of God becoming man. And it also points to our call to share in Christ's Divine Life, to become "partakers of the divine nature."

May We Be Accepted by You

Now the priest prays: "With humble spirit and contrite heart <u>may we be accepted by you</u>, O Lord, and may our sacrifice in your sight this day be pleasing to you, Lord God." Again, this sacrifice the priest speaks of is not some "thing" being offered to God, like bread and wine. Instead it is the people assembled who are being offered. The priest prays, "May WE be accepted by God." I can't stress this enough. YOU are being offered to God at Mass! Our lives our bound up with the bread and wine offered to the Lord and the priest cries out on our behalf to God with a humble spirit and a contrite heart asking that WE be accepted as a pleasing sacrifice.

Entering the Holy of Holies—Washing of the Hands

Next the priest washes his hands. Does this mean that he did not wash them before Mass? No! This is a signal to us that a dramatic event is about to take place. Long ago before the Jewish priests could enter the sanctuary they had to undergo ritual washings. They washed their hands and feet before entering the tabernacle. Psalm 24 states: "Who shall ascend the hill of the Lord? And who shall stand in His holy place? Only he who has clean hands and a pure heart." At Mass, the washing of the priests hands indicates that he is about to stand in a most holy place— one that is even more holy than the tabernacle or temple of the Israel. In the Mass, God is about to come to the people in an intimate way. On our altar at our own parish church, the gifts of bread and wine will soon be changed into Christ's very Body and Blood and our Lord will soon dwell within us as we receive Him in Holy Communion. Jesus, the one true High Priest, will accomplish this through the priest's hands. The priest echoes David's humble prayer of sorrow: "Wash me, O Lord, from my iniquity and cleanse me from my sin." The washing of the hands also symbolizes the purifying of the priest's soul.

Now the priest turns toward us and he begs us for our prayers as he is about to begin the Eucharistic Prayer saying, "Pray brethren, that **my** sacrifice and **yours** may be acceptable to God the Almighty Father." The "my" part of the sacrifice points to Christ's sacrifice, which will be made present through the ordained priest who acts in the person of Christ. The "your" part of the sacrifice refers to the entire Church offering itself in union with Christ in the Mass. We respond with a prayer that recognizes how both sacrifices—Christ's and our own—will be united and offered to the Father through the hands of the priest: "May the Lord accept the sacrifice at your hands for the praise and glory of his name for our good and the good of all his holy Church." Present to God all of your worries, joys, and praises during the offertory so that these things are there on the altar. Remember to tell Him that you desire to give your life to Him.

The Eucharistic Prayer:

The Preface

Again the priest says, "The Lord be with you" and we respond, "And with your spirit." Remember as we said before, many biblical characters have been called by God to do very difficult acts such as Moses freeing the people of Israel from Pharaoh. But God told them not to worry because He would be with them. Here again is one of those difficult tasks. The priest and the people need the Lord to be with them as they prepare to enter into the mystery of that holy sacrifice on the altar.

Lift Up Your Hearts

The priest replies "Lift up your hearts." What does it mean to "lift up" our hearts? The heart is the very center of your being. It is from the heart that your thoughts, emotions and actions flow. Therefore when the priest says, "Lift up your hearts" he is calling on you to give your fullest attention to what is about to unfold! This is a wake-up call! Set aside your other concerns and focus your mind; your will; and your emotions on what is happening on this altar! Lift up your being to God in Heaven and do not allow your heart to come down again. Let no earthly thoughts remain; put aside all cares of this life and focus on that altar as you respond: "We lift them up to the Lord."

Let us Give Thanks to the Lord Our God:

The priest now says, "Let us give thanks to the Lord our God." And we respond, "It is right and just." God is coming down upon our altar and He is going to make Himself present. God sent His Son to save us from sin and Satan. This redemptive act of Christ's death and Resurrection is about to be made present to us on the altar. What a gift! What can we possibly give Him in return? Well, we can give Him our thanks. Thanksgiving is the one thing that we can actually offer God that he does not already possess. We can give Him our gratitude right from the heart. We should be thankful for the miracle about to take place in our midst, as the bread and wine on the altar will be changed into the Body and Blood of Jesus. Taking and eating this spiritual food will transform us and make us holy. Our hearts should truly be filled with gratitude. Yes, it is right and just to give Him thanks.

Holy, Holy, Holy Lord

Now we begin to pray, "Holy, Holy, Holy Lord God of hosts. Heaven and earth are full of your glory. Hosanna in the highest. Blessed is he who comes in the name of the Lord.

Hosanna in the highest." We the people are now lifted up into Heaven. We have joined with the angels and saints in their hymn of praise that takes place unceasingly in Heaven. How fitting that we do this! The King of Kings, the all holy divine Lord, is about to become present on our altar.

In the second half of this prayer we say, "Hosanna" and "Blessed is he who comes in the name of the Lord." These were the words of the people who welcomed Jesus into Jerusalem on Palm Sunday! And just as the crowds welcomed Jesus into the holy city of Jerusalem, we welcome Jesus into our Catholic Churches; for He is about to become present in the Eucharist on our altars.

Send the Holy Spirit

With us on our knees, the priest prays that the Father will send the Holy Spirit so that the gifts of bread and wine will be changed into the Body and Blood or our Lord, Jesus Christ. Just like the ancient Jews pleaded with God to send the Messiah, the priest at Mass asks God that the Messiah be made present once again, this time under the appearances of bread and wine.

The Words of Consecration:

Recall that the Israelites celebrated the annual Passover as a liturgical memorial. For the ancient Jews, this involved much more than simply remembering a past event. A memorial such as Passover was very different from modern holidays such as the Fourth of July, when we simply call to mind the founding of our country. In a biblical memorial, the past was not merely recalled; it was RELIVED! The past event was mystically made present to those celebrating the feast. It was as if the Jews themselves were walking out of Egypt with their great ancestors from the Exodus generation.

At the Last Supper, Jesus very clearly replaces the Passover Lamb with Himself as the Sacrifice. He speaks of His Body being given up and His Blood being poured out. Jesus speaks of His blood as the Blood of the New and Eternal Covenant. Jesus identifies Himself as the sacrificial lamb being offered for <u>this</u> Passover. He willingly offers up His own Body and Blood for the forgiveness of sins. All that was left for Jesus to do was to carry out that sacrifice in a bloody manner on Good Friday. Understanding this connection between the Last Supper and the Cross helps us to understand the Eucharist that we celebrate today. For the Mass commemorates or brings to present Christ's sacrifice on Calvary. Why? So that the present generation can participate in Christ's saving sacrifice just as the generation 2,000 years ago did.

Jesus concluded the institution of the Eucharist at the Last Supper with the words, "Do <u>this</u> in memory of me." What is the "this" that Jesus commands the apostles to do? They are to celebrate the 'New Passover Sacrifice' of Jesus' Body and Blood, but as a biblical memorial. Remember a liturgical or biblical memorial brings the past and the present together, making the long-ago event mystically present for the current generation. By commanding, "Do this in memory of me," Jesus is instructing the apostles to celebrate the Last Supper again and again; to perform the sacrificial offering of Christ's body and blood—and make it present to worshipers in the celebration of the Eucharist. This sacrificial offering of the Eucharist is made present to us today. It happens again and again and we are present. And this sacrifice is made present for a purpose. It is made present so that its saving power may be applied to our lives for the daily sins we commit and so that we can unite ourselves more deeply to Christ in His act of total self-giving love.

The Mystery of Faith

With the words of Consecration, Jesus is now present upon our altars. Jesus, under the appearance of Bread and Wine, is now present in our midst! In wonder and awe we proclaim the mystery of faith: "When we eat this Bread and drink this Cup, we proclaim your Death, O Lord, until you come again." Or "Save us, Savior of the World, for by your Cross and Resurrection you have set us free." Or "We proclaim your Death, O Lord, and profess your Resurrection until you come again."

Through Him, With Him and in Him, O God, Almighty Father, in the unity of the Holy Spirit, all glory and honor is yours, for ever and ever.

The priest holds up the host and the cup for everyone to see. He holds up Jesus! And he says, "Through Him, with Him and in Him, O God, Almighty Father, in the unity of the Holy Spirit, all glory and honor is yours, for ever and ever!" We are in awe! There is our God lifted up before our very eyes. We respond "Amen!" And it is no ordinary Amen. It is called the "Great Amen"! We are proclaiming that we believe all of the mysteries that have taken place upon this altar in our midst. We truly declare that "we believe that this is truly Jesus and that we are going to come forward and place Him; His very Life into our souls!"

This 'Great Amen' is a powerful Amen. Let's consider for a moment what the word "Amen" actually means. The word 'Amen' is Hebrew and we can trace its roots all the way back to the days when the Israelites were wondering in the desert. It has never been translated into any other language. I suppose this is true because of its actual literal meaning. When the Israelites were wondering in the desert for 40 years, waiting to go into the 'Promised Land,' they lived in tents. Because the desert is a harsh environment where it is hot during the day and cool at night, violent wind storms are common. Strong winds could easily pull the tent pegs out of the ground and cause a tent to go hurling through the desert. If a person happened to be inside the tent when this happened, he or she could be wrapped tightly and suffocate as the tent rolled away. So the Israelites found it very important to find solid soil to drive their tent pegs into; soil that would hold the tent peg securely into the ground and not allow it to be lifted by the wind. For this was a matter of life and death. With this in mind, the word "Amen" literally means: "Now that… I can drive my tent peg into." Today we might say, "Now that… I can stake my life on! It is true! I believe!"

Communion Rite—The Lord's Prayer

Next we pray "The Lord's Prayer" or 'The Our Father.' In this prayer, we dare to call the God of the universe; the God who created everything out of nothing; the God who makes the stars twinkle and the sun shine; we dare to call Him—"Father." God was Father to the Israelites too, but they did not dare to call Him Father. Yet this is exactly what Jesus taught us to do. He taught this prayer to the disciples and He was speaking in His native language, Aramaic. He used the word "Abba" for Father. Abba was an intimate, affectionate term for father. It is actually closer to the word "Daddy" than Father. Through Jesus, we have truly become sons and daughters of God our Father. God loves us as a father love his child. We are truly children of God and rightly and affectionately call Him "Father."

At this point in the Mass, with Jesus present on our altars, we address our God as Father and ask Him for all that we need; praying for His will to be done; praying for us to be protected from the devil and his temptations; praying for forgiveness as we forgive others; praying for our daily needs; our daily bread. Keep in mind that the daily bread we ask for is the food that we need to live each day and all of our other basic needs, but it also refers to our spiritual food present on the altar—the Eucharist itself.

After the Lord's Prayer, the priest prays for us to be delivered from evil and that God may grant us peace. Please understand that we are not necessarily asking for a world free of war, but instead peace in our own hearts. We are asking for the kind of peace that comes when a person entrusts their entire lives to God. For in the Mass you gave yourself to God. Now you can possess the kind of inner peace or inner wholeness that is free from distress.

The people respond: "For the Kingdom, the power and the glory are Yours now and forever." At this point we echo the words of King David as he humbly recognized that all the good that came through his kingship came from God. At every Mass, we acknowledge God as the Lord of our lives and praise Him for all the blessings he bestows upon us. Whatever good we might do; whatever success we might experience; ultimately comes from God. "For the kingdom, the power, and the glory are Yours now and forever."

The Rite of Peace

Now the priest says, "Lord Jesus Christ, You said to your apostles, peace I leave you, my peace I give you, look not on our sins, but on the faith of your Church, and graciously grant her peace in unity in accordance with your will." The priest is asking Jesus to grant us peace, but understand, Christ offers us a different kind of peace than the world gives. Christ's peace is not a peace of everything going well with lots of money; no problems and no suffering. Christ offers us a deeper, longer lasting peace. When we allow Jesus to be the foundation of our lives and live according to His plan for us, He gives us an internal spiritual peace that can withstand life's many disappointments, trials, and sufferings. Look at the life of the Blessed Virgin Mary as an example and this makes complete sense. She trusted in God, but suffered too. This is the kind of peace the priest offers us as he turns to the people and says, "The peace of the Lord be with you always."

The Sign of Peace

Next we offer our neighbors a gesture of peace. This can be a handshake; a hug; a kiss. This gesture expresses communion with one another and charity. We are one—one body in Christ. This gesture expresses our unity with one another just before we come forward to eat of the Body of Christ and drink of His Precious Blood. For we all eat of the same loaf and drink from the same chalice.

The Breaking of the Bread

Next the priest breaks the bread which has become the Body of Christ. This is referred to as "The Breaking of the Bread" or "Fraction." This is an ancient, ancient tradition for it used to be loaves of bread that were used at Mass. Today we have a much neater form of the unleavened bread. This is more efficient and allows for a lot less crumbs. Because every crumb is Jesus, fewer crumbs are better; for great care must be taken that they are all consumed.

The Apostles referred to the Mass as the "Breaking of the Bread" in the earliest days and in the Acts of the Apostles it says that they were committed to this or in other words, committed to the Mass in which we break the bread. The Gospels themselves report that Jesus broke bread and gave it to His disciples in four instances: In two accounts He miraculously multiplied loaves of bread to feed a crowd of 5,000 men. He took the loaves; blessed them, broke them, and gave them to the disciples to distribute to the large crowd. This is a huge foreshadowing of what takes place at Mass where the priest, acting in the person of Christ, takes the bread, blesses it, breaks it, and gives it to us, the disciples of Christ. A Third instance of Jesus breaking the bread is at the Last Supper where He again, took the bread, blessed it, broke it, and gave it to the disciples. Then a fourth time on the Road to Emmaus on the night of Easter, Jesus went into the home of two disciples, took break, blessed it, broke it and gave it to the disciples. Before the breaking of the Bread, these disciples did not recognize that this man was Jesus. When He broke the bread, the disciples suddenly recognized that it was the Lord Jesus who was sitting there with them! We too must recognize that it is Jesus who is present in the breaking of the Bread just as the two disciples recognized Him.

Commingling

After breaking the Host, the priest places a small piece into the chalice while quietly saying, "May this mingling of the Body and Blood of our Lord Jesus Christ bring eternal life to us who receive it." This ritual is called commingling, and it is a symbol that reenacts Christ's Resurrection. You see the Mass celebrates the Paschal Mystery of Jesus: The Death; Resurrection; and Ascension of Jesus into Heaven. These three things brought about our salvation, so of course this is what we celebrate at Mass. When the Priest consecrates the Body of Christ separately from the Blood of Christ, this symbolizes Jesus' death. His Body is separated from His Blood. But when the two are placed back together by placing Christ's Body into the chalice of His Blood, it represents Christ's Resurrection.

Lamb of God

While the Breaking of the Bread and the commingling is taking place, the people sing or say, "Lamb of God, you take away the sins of the world, have mercy on us. Lamb of God, you take away the sins of the world, have mercy on us. Lamb of God, you take away the sins of the world, grant us peace." The Lamb of God is another prayer that takes us right up to God's throne in Heaven. When we recite these words, we join all the angels who worship Jesus as the victorious Lamb in the heavenly liturgy that St. John describes in the Book of Revelation: You see, St. John was taken up into Heaven and he described what he saw there. John saw Heaven's Mass taking place. He saw the angels and saints worshipping the Lamb of God. So it is fitting that we address Jesus, saying, "Lamb of God, you take away the sins of the World," because the New Testament reveals Jesus as the New Passover Lamb who was sacrificed for our sake.

Holy Communion

When we think of the Mass we think of words such as: liturgy; communion; real presence; or sacrifice. Have you ever thought of the word, *marriage*? In the Gospel, Jesus speaks of being ready when the Bridegroom arrives at the marriage feast. One of the parables that Jesus tells is of the "Ten Bridesmaids." Five were ready when the groom arrived and five were not. The Mass is also a wedding feast and Jesus is the Bridegroom! Jesus is married to His Church. Therefore, the Church is Jesus' bride. And at this wedding feast we eat from the Banquet Table. Jesus is not only the Bridegroom; He is also the meal of which we partake. He is the food that we eat. So the priest holds up the Body and Blood of Christ and we hear him say, "Behold the Lamb of God; behold Him who takes away the sins of the world. Blessed are those called to the Supper of the Lamb" And truly, truly blessed are WE who are called to this Supper of the Lamb! In the Book of Revelation, the end chapters describe this heavenly banquet; this Supper of the Lamb.

But how can we, mere human beings—and sinful ones at that—dare to approach the all-holy, Almighty God and dare to take and eat His Body and drink His Blood? In response to this invitation to the marriage supper of the Eucharist, we say a prayer that on one hand, acknowledges our complete unworthiness to receive our Lord, and at the same time, expresses confidence that Jesus calls us and can heal us: "Lord, I am not worthy that you should enter under my roof, but only say the word and my soul shall be healed."

These words are an exact match to the Gospel story of the centurion who asked Jesus to cure his servant. Jesus responded to the centurion with the words, "I will come at once to cure your servant." But the centurion replied, "Lord, I am not worthy for you to enter under my roof. Only say the word and my servant shall be healed." With that Jesus said, "Your servant is healed." And he was. We echo the centurion's words here. To enter under my roof, we are meaning that the Lord will be placed into our bodies. We will take and eat His very Life and He will enter our bodies.

The Concluding Rite

Greeting, Blessing, and Dismissal

Again, the Greeting exchange takes place: "The Lord be with you," "and with your spirit." Remember, whenever we make this exchange we are being called to go forth on a mission for God just like Moses, Joshua, Gideon, or King David. This is a mission in which we will need God's help. The Mass is nearly over and we are going to be sent out. We are going to be sent out on a difficult mission to serve God by giving of ourselves in love to all the people of the community and world in which we live. This is a very difficult task. We have heard God speak directly to us in the Scripture Readings and we now possess the Life of Jesus inside of us in the Eucharist. Now we are sent to take Him to the rest of the world. We are called to be Jesus for others; to live as He lived; to love as He loves.

The priest blesses us making the Sign of the Cross. We make the Sign of the Cross invoking God's presence upon us; to help us; to guide us; and to protect us. And then the words come: "Go forth, the Mass is ended" be off on your heavenly mission! And we reply, "Thanks be to God."

This is where we get the name for our Sacred Liturgy. This is where we get the name "Mass". It comes from the Latin phrase, "Ite Missa est," which means "Go, you are dismissed." The Mass is a "sending forth." You have received your strength. You have heard the Word of God read to you and explained to you. You have taken and eaten from the Table of the Lord. You have placed the very Body and Blood of Jesus inside of your soul. With His Word on your mind; on your lips; and in your heart; and His very Life dwelling within you, you should be a changed person! You are not the same person you were when you walked in the door. With His Life inside of you, go forth! And make the world a better place.

God Changes the World Through the Mass:

Have you ever wondered why God just doesn't fix all the problems going on here on earth? Have you ever wondered why God just doesn't go ahead and defeat the devil once and for all? God is God after all. He could simply defeat the devil in an instant and then there would be no more bad stuff in this world. Why doesn't God just do that?

God is truly glorious and He does not want any more glory. He is not interested in gaining more glory for Himself. Instead, He wants to give His glory to us. He is going to defeat the devil. Satan is not going to win. But instead of defeating Satan all on His own with a swoop of His mighty hand, God wants to defeat Satan through us. He wants us to put forth the effort to defeat Satan and when we put forth the tiniest bit of effort, God takes our effort and makes great things happen through us. God wants to give us the glory for defeating Satan. He wants to defeat him through us.

The Mass is our biggest weapon against Satan. Why? The Mass is our worship of God. In the Mass we proclaim who God is and we give Him glory and praise. We sing: "Glory to God in the Highest!" In the Mass we profess what we believe. We boldly state who Jesus is and what He has accomplished. We offer the greatest sacrifice that could ever be offered. We offer Jesus, the Lamb of God, as a sacrificial offering to God and we offer ourselves right along with Him. There can be no greater offering than that.

At Mass we partake of the Sacrifice that saves us. We eat the Body and Blood of the Lamb. Therefore, we are in Communion with God. You see, this changes the world. When you and I pray; when you and I profess our belief in Jesus, God acts. How can we defeat Satan? If you were going to do battle with Satan, how could you defeat him? Can we use bullets against him? Can we use bombs or spears against him? Can we use poison gas? Will that defeat him?

No. Satan is an evil spirit; a fallen angel. None of those things will defeat him. The only way you can defeat the devil is by telling the truth; professing the Truth about Jesus. Think about it. Satan is the leader of those who do not believe in God. He is the leader of those who reject God and turn away from Him to a life of sin. Wouldn't professing your love of God; wouldn't professing your faith in Jesus; wouldn't proclaiming that Jesus is God; bring Satan down? Every time we proclaim Jesus as Lord and Savior; as the Lamb of God; Satan loses power. He gets a little smaller every single time. That is what the Mass does! That is what all of Heaven is doing in their worship. When we go to Mass, we join with all the choirs of angels in Heaven and proclaim with them: "Holy, holy, holy, Lord God of hosts.

Heaven and earth are full of your glory; hosanna in the highest. Blessed is He who comes in the name of the Lord. Hosanna in the highest." When we say to God, "We praise you, we bless you, we adore you, we glorify you, we give you thanks for your great glory," God acts upon our words and we help to bring Satan down. When you and I say, "Lord God, Lamb of God, You take away the sins of the world," God acts upon our words and we help to bring Satan down. When we say, "I believe in one God the Father almighty and in one Lord Jesus Christ the only begotten Son of God," God acts upon our words and we help to bring Satan down.

This is why we must actively respond at Mass and mean what we are saying. We are the instruments through which God changes the world. Allow God to use you to help bring Satan down. Be His servant; His steward; and let Him glorify you. At Mass we worship God. We are not spectators. We are not the audience. We are not there to be entertained. At Mass we are active participants in the Sacrifice that is taking place. We willingly give ourselves as part of the Sacrifice offered to God along with Jesus. We praise and glorify God; we boldly state what we believe! We become the instrument through which God changes the world.

This is God's plan. This is God's worship service. This is what has always been done! This is what Jesus commanded us to do when He said, "Do this in memory of me!"

You can go to all kinds of church services out there at all of the 35,000 separate Protestant churches….but there is only one Mass. The Mass is the worship that God commanded us to do. This is the same worship that takes place in Heaven. So when you get to Heaven, you will be completely at home. You will know exactly what is going on, because you have been there many times.

There is a heavenly battle going on. Come, join the battle. Understand, if you are not participating in the Mass; if you do not come, you are not joining in the battle. Moreover, you are not offering the sacrifice that Jesus commanded us to offer. The Mass will change your life. Allow God to place His Life in your soul.

XII. The Liturgical Year

Just as we have a calendar and seasons in the secular year, so too the Church has a calendar and seasons in the Church year. The "Liturgical Year" is the Church year or the Christian calendar. It includes a cycle of seasons that begins in late November or early December and runs all year until the end of November. The Church year consists of six liturgical seasons: Advent, Christmas, Ordinary Time One, Lent, Easter Triduum, Easter, and Ordinary Time Two. The purpose of the liturgical year calendar is not to mark the passage of time, but to celebrate and understand more fully the entire mystery of Jesus Christ, from his incarnation and birth until his ascension, the day of Pentecost, and the expectation of His return in glory. During the course of a year, the paschal mystery—the passion, death, resurrection, and ascension of Jesus—is viewed from different angles and in different lights.

Advent

Advent is the Season that includes four Sundays preceding Christmas. The Advent Season marks the beginning of the Liturgical Calendar. It always begins in late November, on November 30th, or on the Sunday that is the closest to this date. Advent ends on December 24th before the evening prayer of Christmas.

The Advent season is the time of waiting and preparing for the coming of Jesus. This refers both to the anniversary celebration of the Incarnation, as well as the second and final coming for which we are waiting and preparing.

The liturgical colors of Advent are Purple and Rose, with Rose being used only on the third Sunday of Advent. Each week a new candle on the Advent Wreath is lit. For the first and second weeks of Advent, a purple candle is lit. A rose colored candle is lit on the third week, while the final purple candle is lit on the fourth Sunday of Advent. Purple symbolizes penitence and preparation, while rose symbolizes hope.

Christmas

The Christmas season begins with the celebration of the birth of Jesus, Christmas day, or as a vigil on Christmas Eve. The *Feast* of Christmas lasts 12 days, until Epiphany. However, the time from Epiphany until the Baptism of the Lord is also included in the Christmas Season. Traditionally, Epiphany had been fixed to January 6th, and the Baptism of the Lord celebrated on the octave of Epiphany, which was January 13th. In most countries, the Epiphany is now celebrated on the Sunday closest to January 6th, and the Lord's Baptism is celebrated the following Sunday. The Christmas season is a time of rejoicing in the Incarnation.

The word "Christmas" comes from "Christes Maesse," which means "Christ's Mass." This is the Old English name for the Eucharistic Celebration that commemorates the birth of Christ. Christmas is one of the three great feasts that are celebrated by the Catholic Church. The other two are Easter and Pentecost. The liturgical color of Christmas is white, which symbolizes expressive joy and the purity of the Christ child.

Included in the Christmas Season is the Feast of the Holy Family of Jesus, Mary, and Joseph. This takes place the Sunday after Christmas Day and reminds us to strive for holiness in each of our families. January 1st is the Feast of the Solemnity of Mary, Mother of God. This is one of the six Holy Days of Obligation, which means that Catholics are obligated to attend Mass on this feast day.

In addition, the Feast of Epiphany celebrates the many ways that Christ made Himself known to the world. The Feast of Epiphany of the Lord places emphasis on the visit of the Magi or the three wise men (Matt 2:1-12).

The following Sunday is the Feast of the Baptism of the Lord (Mark 1:9-11). This feast is an excellent opportunity for the faithful to be reminded of their rebirth as children of God in Baptism.

Ordinary Time One

After the celebration of the Feast of the Baptism of the Lord, "Ordinary Time One" begins and lasts until the Tuesday prior to Ash Wednesday. Ordinary does not mean plain. The name comes from "*ordinalis*" meaning "showing order, denoting an order of succession." It is used in this sense to refer to the order of the counted weeks of the year. There are 34 weeks in Ordinary Time and we simply number these weeks as they are counted. Ordinary Time focuses on the early life and childhood of Christ, and then on His public ministry. The liturgical color of Ordinary Time is green. Since green is the color of springtime and new growth, it symbolizes the hope of eternal life.

Lent

Lent begins with Ash Wednesday. On this day, Catholics attend Mass and receive blessed ashes on their foreheads in the shape of a cross. The priest or minister says, "Remember that you are dust, and to dust you will return." The act of putting on ashes symbolizes fragility and mortality, and the need to be redeemed by the mercy of God. Far from being a merely external act, the Church makes use of the blessed ashes to symbolize that attitude of internal penance to which all the baptized are called during Lent.

Lent prepares us for Easter. It is a time of conversion, in which we turn away from sin, turn toward our Lord, and ask for His mercy. It is a time when we focus our attention on the poor and those in need and away from our own selfishness. It is a time of enhanced prayer, alms giving, and fasting. During Lent we abstain from eating meat on Ash Wednesday and all Lenten Fridays. In addition, we fast on Ash Wednesday and Good Friday. Abstinence and fast are forms of prayer. They are a discipline that we undertake. When we abstain from meat during Lent, we focus on Christ and our souls, rather than on ourselves.

Lent is a 40 day Liturgical Season that initiates the most sacred part of the Christian year. It covers six and one half weeks (Sundays are not included in Lent) and ends at the Mass of the Lord's Supper on the evening of Holy Thursday. During Lent, Catholics are called to meditate with awe and thanksgiving on the great Paschal mystery, which is the salvation God offers to us sinners through the suffering, death, and resurrection of Jesus Christ. Because the Season of Lent is a time of penitence, reflection, and prayer that is solemn and restrained, flowers are generally removed from the sanctuary. Songs of praise such as the "Gloria" and the "Alleluia" are removed from the Liturgy. The color of Lent is violet or purple, which again symbolizes penitence and preparation.

The Stations of the Cross devotion is offered to all the faithful each Friday evening during Lent and at 3:00 PM on Good Friday in most Catholic parishes. The Stations of the Cross is a popular devotion used by the faithful who wish, through prayer and reflection, to accompany Jesus Christ on His way to Calvary. What matters most in the Stations of the Cross is to follow Jesus Christ in His passion and to allow ourselves the opportunity to walk with Him. By accompanying Him on the Way of the Cross, we gain His courageous patience and learn to trust in God who delivers us from evil. We begin to see how much our sins truly hurt our Lord, which helps us to rid sin from our lives.

Easter Triduum

"Triduum" is Latin for "Great Three Days." The Easter Triduum recalls the events of the first Holy Thursday, Good Friday, and Holy Saturday. These are three days which take place during Holy Week. During Holy Week, the holiest time of the liturgical year, the faithful gather to relive the final week of our Lord's life.

Holy Week begins with **Palm Sunday**, or 'Passion Sunday,' which unites the royal splendor of Christ with the proclamation of His passion. It begins with a procession which commemorates Christ's triumphant entry into Jerusalem. The faithful are given blessed palms and sing as they walk in the procession. The Passion or our Lord is read from one of the gospels during Mass. The readings show how Jesus was joyously welcomed into Jerusalem and in a matter of a week condemned to death. It reminds us of how we too welcome Him into our lives one minute and turn our backs on Him through our sins the next. Even though Palm Sunday takes place during Holy Week. It is not part of the Easter Triduum or "Great Three Days."

On Holy Thursday, the first day of the Sacred Triduum, we commemorate the "Mass of the Lord's Supper," (the Last Supper) during which Jesus instituted the Eucharist and the priesthood. Good Friday, the second day of the Sacred Triduum, is the solemn remembrance of the death of Jesus on the Holy Cross. There is no Mass on Good Friday, but instead a liturgical celebration takes place that venerates the cross in the evening with Stations of the Cross in the afternoon. On Holy Saturday, the third and last day of the Sacred Triduum, the Church pauses at the Lord's tomb, meditating upon His Passion and Death; His descent into Hell, and with prayer and fasting, awaits His resurrection. The color for Holy Thursday and Holy Saturday is white symbolizing the purity of Christ, while the color for Palm Sunday and Good Friday is red symbolizing the blood of Christ.

Easter

The Easter season begins with the Easter Vigil, which is celebrated after night falls on the evening before Easter Sunday. This is the night when those preparing to enter the Catholic Church are fully initiated and become members by receiving the Sacraments of Baptism, Confirmation and Eucharist.

The season of Easter is a joyous, celebratory season. It begins with celebrating Christ's resurrection and ends by celebrating the descent of the Holy Spirit upon the Apostles at Pentecost fifty days later. Christ's Ascension into Heaven is celebrated forty days after Easter on Ascension Thursday. Here in the United States that feast is normally celebrated on the following Sunday. The liturgical colors of Easter are white, for most days, and red for Pentecost. The color white symbolizes expressive joy, while the color red symbolizes the fire of the Holy Spirit.

Ordinary Time Two

The second period of Ordinary Time is the longest Liturgical Season. Ordinary Time resumes on the Monday following Pentecost Sunday and runs until the final Saturday before Advent in November. Again, "Ordinary" does not mean plain. Instead it denotes order in succession. This period of Ordinary Time focuses on Christ's reign as King of Kings, and on the age of the Church. This is the age we live in now, which is the time between the age of the Apostles and the age of Christ's second and final coming for which we are ever preparing.

On the First Sunday following Pentecost Sunday, the Church celebrates the Feast of the Holy Trinity. On this Sunday, the Church rejoices in the revealed truth that God is triune, three Persons in one God: the Father, the Son and the Holy Spirit.

"The Solemnity of the Body and Blood of Christ" or *Corpus Christi* in Latin, is observed on the Sunday following the solemnity of the Most Blessed Trinity. On this feast the Church solemnly declares the true presence of Christ in the Eucharist.

The final Sunday in Ordinary Time, week 34, is the Feast of Christ the King. The Solemnity of Christ the King commemorates the closing of the liturgical year. It reminds us that over and above being the universal King, Christ is the Head of the Body, the Church. His Divine reign stretches out from the alpha of time to the omega. Again, the liturgical color of Ordinary Time is green.

Additional Colors

As stated earlier, the colors of purple (Advent and Lent), white (Christmas and Easter), green (Ordinary Time), and red (Palm Sunday, Easter Triduum, and Pentecost) are used for the Liturgical Seasons, but these colors may also be used for certain feast days throughout the year regardless of the season. The priest will wear white vestments for all feasts honoring our Lord and the Blessed Virgin, Mary; for the feast of saints who died of natural causes; and for funerals. White is a symbol of purity and holiness. The priest will wear red vestments on the feasts of saints who died as martyrs for the faith, as red is a symbol of blood.

Holy Days of Obligation

Throughout the Liturgical Year, The Catholic Church honors certain feasts of Jesus, Mary, and the saints. During these special feasts, we are called to remember a special event in the life of Jesus or Mary or the holy lives of the saints and to ask them to pray for us. While most days of obligation fall on Sunday, such as Easter and Pentecost, there are special feasts in the Liturgical Calendar that can fall during the week, such as Christmas. Holy Days of Obligation are these special holy days or feast days that fall during the week for which the faithful are obligated to celebrate by attending Mass. The number of days of obligation may vary from country to country. In the United States, the following six days of obligation are observed: Christmas Day (December 25); The Solemnity of Mary, Mother of God (January 1); the Ascension of Jesus into Heaven (40 days after Easter, but usually moved to the following Sunday); the Assumption of Mary into Heaven (August 15), All Saints Day (November 1); and the Immaculate Conception of Mary (December 8). Again, these are "Holy Days of Obligation" meaning that we are obligated to attend Mass on these feast days.

XIII. The Sacrament of Confirmation

While Confirmation is a distinct and complete sacrament in its own right, its purpose is to perfect in us that which was begun in Baptism. We might say, in a sense, that we are baptized in order to be confirmed.

Jesus baptized the Apostles (John 3:22) giving them the Life of God. Even though they were filled with love for Jesus, they lacked something. They ran and hid when Jesus was arrested. They denied knowing Him. But they seemed to possess the ability to love Jesus and the desire to live for Him. Peter even professed this at the Last Supper, "Even though I should have to die with you, I will not deny you, and the others spoke likewise" (Matt 26:35). In reality however, he and the others lacked courage. They did not have the spiritual strength to profess Jesus to the Jewish leaders or the mob that had gathered to condemn Him. They ran away and hid themselves.

On the day of Pentecost however, the Apostles lacked nothing. They had all of the *spiritual muscles* needed to take the gospel to the ends of the earth. On that day, they received a special strengthening of the Holy Spirit. They received the Sacrament of Confirmation. The Holy Spirit came upon the Apostles in power, symbolized by fire and wind, bestowing on the Apostles a grace that allowed them to accomplish what they could not do on their own.

On the day of Pentecost, the City of Jerusalem was packed with devout Jews from every nation who had come for the feast. The Apostles were all together in a room with Jesus' mother, Mary, and many other disciples. Suddenly they heard a sound like a strong driving wind. This noise came from the sky. Everyone outside and everyone inside could hear it plainly. In fact it was so loud, that the Jews, who had gathered in Jerusalem, began to gather around the place where the Apostles were. *Tongues of Fire* appeared to those in the room. They could see them clearly as they parted and came to rest on each person. The Apostles were filled with the Holy Spirit (See Acts 2:1-4).

They had just been confirmed. They were a new creation; no longer timid; no longer shy; no longer lacking in confidence; no longer scared. No, they were BOLD! The Apostles came forth from that room and they preached to the crowd outside that had gathered.

All the Jews who had gathered in Jerusalem for the feast of Pentecost had come from different countries and they spoke different languages. Yet no matter what the apostles spoke, each person could hear them in their own native language. It was a miracle! (See Acts 2:5-13) Peter, the first Pope, managed to convert 3,000 devout Jews that day and convince them to become Christians. He convinced them to enter into the New and Everlasting Covenant and believe in Jesus as the Christ; the Savior; the Anointed One of God, who had been sent to redeem them. Those 3,000 Jews entered into the New Eternal Covenant that day by being baptized (Acts 2:14-41).

It was now the job of the Apostles to pass the Sacrament of Confirmation on as well and that is exactly what they did. The Apostles did this by 'laying hands' on the people thereby giving them the full outpouring of the Holy Spirit. In the eighth chapter of the Acts of the Apostles we see a very specific story about Confirmation. The people of Samaria were evangelized and baptized by Philip. When the news reached Jerusalem, the apostles, "sent them Peter and John, who went down and prayed for them, that they might receive the holy Spirit, for it had not yet fallen upon any of them; they had only been baptized in the name of the Lord Jesus. Then they laid hands on them and they received the Holy Spirit" (Acts 8:14-17).

Similarly, Paul traveled to Ephesus where he found some disciples. He asked them if they had received the Holy Spirit at the time that they became believers. They answered that they had never even heard of the Holy Spirit. Paul then asked if they had been baptized. He learned that they had been baptized by John the Baptist in the river Jordan. These were people who considered themselves Christians because they believed what was taught to them about Jesus, yet they had not received the Sacrament of Baptism. Paul proceeded to baptize them and then Scripture tells us that "when Paul laid his hands upon them, the Holy Spirit came upon them and they spoke in tongues and prophesied" (Acts 19:1-6).

The Apostles laid hands on the people and they received the Holy Spirit in a distinct way, apart from its reception in Baptism. The apostles passed to the people what they themselves had received, the 'Full Outpouring of the Holy Spirit.' By laying hands on the people, a sign seen and felt by the senses on the outside, an Apostle could pass the Holy Spirit onto the baptized person, the reality taking place spiritually on the inside. Their Baptism was not complete until they received the full outpouring of the Holy Spirit (CCC 1285).

Our bishops are modern day Apostles. They are the ordinary ministers of the Sacrament of Confirmation. In The Right of Christian Initiation of Adults (RCIA), all adults coming into the Church throughout the world receive Confirmation on the same night at the Easter Vigil. Because the local bishop cannot be in every Catholic Church on the same night in order to confirm, the priest acts as representative of the bishop and administers the Sacrament of Confirmation.

The Signs of Confirmation

Chrism is one of the signs of Confirmation. **Chrism** is a blessed oil used to signify the strength of the Holy Spirit. The bishop or priest dips his thumb into the sacred chrism and then makes the sign of the cross on the forehead of the person being confirmed. As he does this he says, "(Name), be sealed with the gift of the Holy Spirit." The term *sealed* indicates that Confirmation bestows a special character, a permanent change in the person being confirmed, (as does Baptism). Because of this, these sacraments may only be received once. This special character marks the newly confirmed as a witness for Christ.

As was mentioned earlier, the **laying on of hands** is one of the signs of Confirmation. As the bishop or priests lays hands upon the individual being confirmed, he or she receives the full outpouring of the Holy Spirit just as the Apostles received it as tongues of fire.

The Effects of Confirmation

Confirmation brings forth a deepening of baptismal graces. We receive a special grace by which our faith is deepened and strengthened, so that it will be strong enough not only for our own needs, but for the needs of others with whom we try to share it. We have been marked as a witness for Christ. We have all the strength we need to witness our faith to others. This can be done openly by teaching others directly about the faith. Or it can be done by giving quiet example. In our souls there is an unending supply of strength to call upon, as we seek to do the will of God and grow in holiness ourselves, but also as we seek to help others grown in holiness. Confirmation intensifies our bond with the Church to help us spread and defend the faith.

Confirmation also strengthens our relationship to God the Father and draws us nearer to Jesus. The effects of the Spirit's grace in our lives have traditionally been expressed as the Gifts of the Holy Spirit. These gifts are: Wisdom, Understanding, Reverence, Knowledge, Courage, Right Judgment, and Wonder and Awe. The Holy Spirit increases these gifts in us and as He does so, we are able to "produce good fruit;" we are able to live a life centered on others and away from ourselves. This has been traditionally expressed as the "Fruits of the Holy Spirit" which are: Charity, Joy, Peace, Patience, Kindness, Goodness, Generosity, Gentleness, Faithfulness, Modesty, Self-Control, and Chastity. These are qualities that spring forth as we cooperate with the grace given to us in this sacrament. We are no longer alone when we try to be kind, for example; Jesus models kindness for us, and the Holy Spirit helps us to imitate Jesus. What we could not achieve by our own efforts, we can achieve with God's help as kindness becomes a "fruit" of our relationship with the Holy Spirit.

God the Father, God the Son, and God the Holy Spirit, love us personally (John 17:23) and want us to be filled with divine Life, Sanctifying Grace. Confirmation is a sacrament that should "confirm" our love for God. This sacrament can have lasting effects in our lives, but we must nurture our relationship with God. This requires a commitment on our part to learn more, pray much, read Scripture, receive the other sacraments, and worship at Mass.

Witnessing our Faith with the Strength of the Spirit

The Apostles were changed by the coming of the Holy Spirit. The Holy Spirit moved them to do Christ's work. Pentecost got the gospel out from behind locked doors and into the world. Confirmation should help us continue the work of Christ and minister to others.

We should begin the work of the Spirit in our homes with our own families and friends. It is true that sometimes we treat complete strangers on the street better than we do the members of our own families. After a difficult day at work, parents sometimes take out their frustrations on their children. We lose patience with our own family members much more quickly than anyone else. We should call upon the Spirit's help in our everyday situations at home, practicing charity, kindness, faithfulness, gentleness, patience, and self-control.

Next become involved in the work of the parish. Most parishes offer many, many opportunities for service. Getting involved in volunteer opportunities will help you to meet and get to know fellow parishioners. This helps you to feel that you belong to the family of the Church. It is true that ten percent of the people do eighty percent of the parish work, but it doesn't have to be that way. People who become active parishioners find great joy and a sense of belonging.

Don't be afraid to bring the Church to the world. Often times when people find out that you are Catholic, they will begin to ask you questions. This is the perfect opportunity to help spread the faith. Spreading the faith also involves acts of charity and alms giving. We take seriously our call to help the poor of the world and to ease the suffering of those in need. It is true that the Catholic Church is the largest charitable organization in the world and that is as it should be. Most parishes have their own ministries to the poor that help those in need in their own communities. In addition, most of the larger parishes have adopted a special mission that is located in another country such as Haiti. Parishioners get involved by joining these groups or by giving money to the cause.

Confirmation is a life changing sacrament that permanently changes each one of us. The Holy Spirit gives us the strength to do the things that we do not have the ability to do on our own. With God, all things are possible!

XIV. The Sacrament of the Anointing of the Sick

God Continues to Touch our Lives even to the End

In His great mercy and effort to bring each of us safely to Himself in Heaven, God has gone to great lengths. Jesus has given us the Sacrament of Baptism, in which Original Sin and all pre-baptismal sins are cleansed from our souls. His divine Life is placed into our souls for the very first time. Jesus then confirms our Baptism and seals its graces in the Sacrament of Confirmation. We are given the strength to witness the faith and share it with others. Sin can weaken us spiritually and even extinguish the Life of God in our souls. For this reason, Jesus has also given us the Sacrament of Reconciliation so that post-baptismal sins can be forgiven. On our spiritual journey, we can partake of the Eucharist, giving our souls what they hunger for, the Life of God. The Eucharist nourishes the soul giving it life and making it spiritually stronger just as food nourishes the body giving it life and making it physically stronger. It is our "bread for the journey."

As we grow older, the body naturally grows weak. Unexpected illness can also weaken our bodies prematurely. For these times in our lives, Jesus gives us the Sacrament of the Anointing of the Sick. The Sacrament of the Anointing of the Sick confers a special grace upon the Christian who is experiencing the difficulties of grave illness or old age. At a time in our lives when we most need His help, Jesus is there to comfort and strengthen us.

The Sacrament of the Anointing of the Sick in the Bible

The Sacrament of the Anointing of the Sick can be found in two main places in Scripture, the Gospel of Mark and the Book of James. In the Gospel of Mark, Jesus summoned the twelve Apostles, sent them out two by two, and gave them authority over unclean spirits. Jesus instructed them to take nothing for the journey except a walking stick. The Apostles were to take no food, no sack, and no money in their belts. They were instructed to wear sandals, but not to take a second tunic. Jesus said to them, "Wherever you enter a house, stay there until you leave from there. Whatever place does not welcome you or listen to you, leave there and shake the dust off your feet in testimony against them." The Gospel then tells us that the twelve "went off and preached repentance. They drove out many demons, and they anointed with oil many who were sick and cured them" (Mark 6:7-13). This portion of Mark's gospel gives us a clear picture that Jesus instituted the Sacrament of the Anointing of the Sick. The Apostles were sent on a mission to preach and to anoint and to heal.

In the book of James, we are given clear instruction as to what we should do if we are sick, "Is anyone among you sick? He should summon the Presbyters (priests) of the Church, and they should pray over him and anoint him with oil in the name of the Lord, and the prayer of faith will save the sick person, and the Lord will raise him up. If he has committed any sins, he will be forgiven. Therefore confess your sins to one another and pray for one another, that you may be healed. The fervent prayer of a righteous person is very powerful" (James 4:14-16). These words in the book of James shows that the priests of the early Church were administering this sacrament to the sick of their day.

The Signs of the Sacrament of the Anointing of the Sick

The oil used in administering the sacrament of the Anointing of the Sick is called the "oil of the sick." As in Baptism (the oil of catechumen), and in Confirmation (oil of chrism), this anointing is the sign of great strengthening and healing of the Holy Spirit.

In the administration of the Sacrament of the Anointing of the Sick there are certain introductory and follow-up prayers, which the priest recites. The essence of the sacrament however, lies in the actual anointing and the short prayer which accompanies that anointing.

The priest confers the sacrament by anointing the sick person on the forehead and on the hands. The first part of the prayer is said while the forehead is anointed, while the last part of the prayer is said while the hands are anointed. As he anoints the priest prays, "Through this holy anointing may the Lord in his love and mercy help you with the grace of the Holy Spirit. Amen. May the Lord who frees you from sin, save you and raise you up."

The Effects of the Anointing of the Sick

God has given each person a strong attachment to life. We call this the instinct of 'self-preservation.' So it is only natural that people may experience feelings of anxiety when facing the prospects of their own death. To counteract this fear of death, when it needs to be counteracted, and to remove all *cause* for fear, Jesus has given us the Sacrament of the Anointing of the Sick.

As with all sacraments, Anointing of the Sick places the Life of God, Sanctifying Grace, into our souls. It is an increase in Sanctifying Grace that this sacrament gives, because it is assumed that the person is free of Mortal Sin and is therefore in a state of grace. Supernatural life is therefore intensified in the soul. The goal of the sacrament is to confer oneness with God. This oneness is the source of all spiritual strength.

Besides this increase in Sanctifying Grace, Anointing of the Sick gives its own special sacramental grace. This special grace comforts and strengthens the soul of the sick person. This is the grace that quiets anxiety and dispels fear. It is a grace which enables the sick person to embrace God's will and to face the possibility of death without fear and apprehension. Moreover, it is a grace which gives the soul the strength to face and conquer whatever temptations to doubt, hopelessness, or even despair Satan uses to seize the soul for himself. This sacrament imparts great peace of mind and confidence in God.

A second effect of the Sacrament of the Anointing of the Sick is the preparation of the soul for entrance into Heaven. This is done by the forgiveness of Venial Sins and the cleansing of the soul from the remains of sin (temporal punishment). In this sacrament, the soul is cleansed from all that might keep it from entering Heaven. It is cleansed of Venial Sins and of the temporal punishment due to sin. (More on temporal punishment later). If we are so blessed as to receive the sacrament of the Anointing of the Sick in our last illness, we may have every confidence that we shall see the face of God shortly after our soul leaves our body.

Since Reconciliation is the sacrament in which our Mortal Sins are forgiven, a sick person who has Mortal Sins to confess must receive the Sacrament of Reconciliation prior to receiving the Sacrament of the Anointing of the Sick. It is comforting to know however, that the Anointing of the Sick does forgive Mortal Sin if the critically ill person is unable to receive the Sacrament of Reconciliation. This could happen, for example, if anointing were administered to an unconscious person.

The purpose of the sacrament therefore, is to prepare a person for death or to strengthen a person who is in danger of dying. A person in danger of dying may be someone who is scheduled to undergo serious surgery that is potentially life threatening. It may also be a person in need of this strengthening by the Holy Spirit prior to undergoing cancer treatment.

It happens in rare instances that the person who has been anointed experiences a full recovery of bodily health. We might ask why in some instances, and not in others, does the sick person receives the grace of a full recovery. Our forefathers at the Council of Trent gave an answer to this question: "When it is expedient for the soul's salvation." In other words, if it will be *spiritually* good for the sick person to recover, then his recovery can with certainty be expected. This recovery can be a sudden miraculous recovery, but more often this recovery will be the result of natural causes over time. In this case the recovery will be the result of the powers of nature, stimulated by the graces of the sacrament. By eliminating anxiety, abolishing fear, inspiring confidence in God, with resignation to His will, Anointing of the Sick works with the bodily processes for the physical improvement of the patient.

Who Can Receive the Anointing of the Sick?

Every Catholic, who has reached the age of reason, should receive the sacrament of the Anointing of the Sick when in danger of death due to sickness, serious life threatening surgery, a serious accident, or weakness from old age. Again, the purpose of the sacrament is to comfort the soul in anxieties, heal the effects of sin, and to strengthen the soul against the possibility of sin. Therefore this sacrament is not needed for infants for they have not reached the age of reason. This is true because an infant is incapable of committing sin and would be unaware of a life threatening illness.

In order to receive this sacrament, the danger of death must be present in the body of the person, whether the danger is due to illness or wounds or to the advancement of years.

Therefore, Anointing of the sick cannot be administered to a soldier before he goes into battle, even though he does face the danger of death. Nor can it be administered to a criminal before his execution.

It sometimes happens that a person who should be anointed dies without it because of the carelessness or the misdirected love of those who are in charge of him. This is unfortunate. This sacrament is not just for those who are gasping out their last breath. It is for anyone whose condition is such that death is possible or for any type of sickness or injury which a doctor might term critical or serious.

Anointing of the Sick will have its spiritual effects as long as the soul is still present in the body. We never can be sure when the soul separates itself from the body. The fact that breathing and heart action have stopped is no guarantee that the soul is gone. For this reason the Church allows the priest to administer the sacrament up to several hours after apparent death has occurred. In the case of sudden death, therefore, as by accident or heart attack, the priest should still be called.

It is important to make your wishes known to your loved ones while you are healthy and able to do so. If your loved ones know that it is very important to you that a priest is called if your life were in danger, they will certainly heed your wishes.

The Sacrament of the Anointing of the Sick is a sacrament that shows the great mercy and love that Jesus has for each one of us. Let us give thanks to Him for this great blessing.

XV. The Sacrament of Matrimony—Holy Marriages

God Made Marriage

Marriage is not merely a human institution; it comes from God: "God created man in His image; in the divine image He created Him; male and female He created them. God blessed them, saying: 'Be fertile and multiply'" (Genesis 1:27-28). It is God's design that man and woman should complete each other, draw strength from each other, and contribute to one another's spiritual growth.

Jesus clarified God's design for marriage. First, He was born into a human family. This shows the holiness of ordinary family life (Luke 2). He worked His first miracle at the wedding feast of Cana (John 2:1-11). Jesus' first miracle could have been anything, yet God chose for it to take place at a wedding, thereby putting His seal of approval on marriage. Jesus taught that married love must be faithful: "You have heard that it was said, 'You shall not commit adultery.' But I say to you, everyone who looks at a woman with lust has already committed adultery with her in his heart" (Matt 5:27-28). Jesus further proclaimed that married love should last forever: "From the beginning of creation, 'God made them male and female. For this reason a man shall leave his father and mother and be joined to his wife, and the two shall become one flesh.' So they are no longer two but one flesh. Therefore what God has joined together, no human being must separate…Whoever divorces his wife and marries another commits adultery against her; and if she divorces her husband and marries another, she commits adultery" (Mark 10:6-12).

Up to the time of Christ, marriage, although a sacred union, was still only a civil contract between a man and woman. Jesus, however, took this contract, this exchange of marital consent between man and woman, and made the contract a conveyer of grace. Jesus raised marriage to a new level. He made marriage a sacrament, the Sacrament of Matrimony among Christians. By participating in family life, by His presence at the wedding feast of Cana, and by his solemn declarations concerning the fidelity and permanence of marriage, Christ touched marriage with the grace of God in such a way that Paul could describe it as a great mystery "in reference to Christ and the church" (Ephesians 5:32). So marriage is not just an arrangement between husband and wife. Every marriage affects many others. It is especially important to the children. A stable, loving marriage gives children an environment where they can mature into happy, loving adults. A marriage that is unhappy or shattered by divorce will be often times traumatic to them.

It is not hard to understand why Jesus made marriage a sacrament. From man's beginning, marriage was a sacred union. It was God's instrument for the begetting, the rearing, the education, and the moral training of successive generations.

It is no exaggeration to say that Jesus depends largely on married couples for credibility in the world today. When a man and a woman stand before God on their wedding day and pledge their lives to each other, and then are faithful to their promises year after year, people take notice. They see Christ as the couple's source of strength and love. Christ's words at the Last Supper are verified: "This is how all will know that you are my disciples, if you have love for one another" (John 13:35).

Marriage as a Sacrament—Matrimony

The Catholic Church takes marriage very, very seriously. After all, Matrimony is a sacrament established by Jesus. Because marriage has such important implications for the Church and for society as a whole, the Catholic Church has developed laws to safeguard the sacredness of marriage. Husband and wife must intend to be faithful, to make their marriage permanent, and to be open to the possibility of children.

The bride and groom are the "ministers" of the Sacrament of Matrimony. The couple who are getting married administer the sacrament of Matrimony on each other. So it is not correct to say (even though we do) that "John and Karen were married by the priest." More correctly we should say, "John and Karen married each other in the presence of the priest." The priest cannot administer the sacrament of Matrimony; only the contracting couple can do that. The priest is simply the official witness, representing Christ and His Church. Don't get me wrong. The priest's (or Deacon's) presence is essential; without him there is not sacrament and no marriage. But he does not confer the sacrament. Two additional witnesses must also be present. But it is through the vows and the presence of the community that Christ joins the husband and wife in love.

Since Matrimony is a sacrament, we know that it imparts grace. Like every sacrament, it imparts two kinds of grace. First of all there is the increase in Sanctifying Grace, imparted at the very moment that the sacrament is received. At this moment the couple's souls are spiritually stronger, spiritually more beautiful than when they came to the altar a few moments earlier. Besides this increase in sanctifying grace, Matrimony gives its own special grace, its *sacramental* grace. This consists in a claim upon God for whatever actual graces the couple may need, through the years, to make a happy and successful marriage. For its full effectiveness, this grace needs the cooperation of both partners to the marriage. The sacramental grace of Matrimony perfects the natural love of husband and wife; elevates this love to a supernatural level which far surpasses mere mental and physical compatibility. It gives to marital love a sanctifying quality, making it an instrument for growth in holiness and marriage a path to sainthood.

This special grace of Matrimony also imparts conscientiousness in the begetting and rearing of children and foresight in the many problems resulting from family life. It enables husband and wife to adjust to one another's shortcomings and to bear with one another's faults. The couple administers the grace of Christ to each other by every loving word and action. Their sacrament continues in all they do: work, play, communication, prayer, sexual intercourse, raising children, forgiveness, healing, social activities, and all aspects of life. Married life, therefore, is a means by which Christ enters the home and fills it with His grace and love. Every Christian family should be a "little Church," so that family life can be the path of grace walked by most people to eternal life.

Five hundred years ago the Council of Trent said, "The grace of Matrimony perfects the natural love of husband and wife and confirms that indissoluble union Christ Himself merited for us by His Passion; as the Apostle Saint Paul indicates, saying, 'Husbands, love your wives as Christ loved the Church.'" It should be a wonderfully inspiring thought to a Christian husband and wife to realize that Jesus was thinking of them as He suffered His Passion; to realize that one of the things for which Christ died was the graces they would need in marriage. So if a husband or a wife is having a bad day, perhaps weighed down by the pressures of a job or the difficulties of child rearing and begins to feel that it was a mistake to ever get married—that is a good time to remember that Matrimony is a sacrament. It is a good time to remember that he or she has an absolute right to whatever grace may be needed in this emergency; whatever grace may be needed to strengthen human weakness and to guide them to a solution of the problem. To Christian spouses who do their human best to make theirs a truly Christian marriage, God has pledged His grace, when needed and as needed. God will not default on His pledge. Marriage is difficult and God knows this. But if couples appreciate the beauty and holiness of marriage, they are likely to do the practical things that make a marriage work. A good marriage does not just "happen." It is built by love, prayer, attention, and constant effort.

In addition to the conferring of grace, another effect of the Sacrament of Matrimony is the forging of the marriage bond, a moral change formed in the souls of the married couple. Two properties of marriage, *unity* and *indissolubility*, result from this matrimonial bond. The *unity* of marriage means that a man can have only one wife and a woman only one husband. They are *two* in one flesh, not many in one flesh. The *indissolubility* of marriage means that marriage is a *permanent* union. Once a man and woman are completely united in a consummated Christian marriage, there is no power on earth, not even the Pope, who can dissolve the bond. "What therefore God has joined together, let no man put asunder" (Matt 19:6).

Living a Marriage in the Real World

Most marriages go through what might be called "stages of development." First, there is the *honeymoon* stage. These are the months when husband and wife see each other as perfect. They are full of romantic feelings toward one another. Eventually, however, comes the second stage called *disillusionment*. The couple begins to see each other's faults. These faults can sometimes be exasperating. This is followed by the third stage, *unhappiness*. The husband and wife begin to wonder if it was a mistake to marry. They quarrel and try to change each other into the ideal person they thought they had married in the first place. Many marriages break up at this point often because unhappy couples do not realize that all people struggle with these very same problems. Couples who are realistic come to terms with the fact that no one is perfect, and each spouse learns to love the person he or she married and not the imaginary ideal of the romantic stage. This is the fourth stage of *acceptance*. The husband and wife realize that their love is genuine, that they can depend on each other, that they are accepted and loved just as they are. This then makes possible the fifth stage, *happiness*. The couple can enjoy the happiness that they both hoped for on their wedding day. These stages may be repeated throughout the life of the marriage. Couples who expect such patterns will not be surprised by them and can work through these stages to achieve real happiness.

Another fact basic to a successful marriage is that real love goes beyond emotions. It goes beyond the emotions of warmth and affection that we equate to "falling in love." Real love is a decision that endures even when romantic feelings are absent. Real love is the decision to put the good of the other in front of our own good. It requires us to love as we want to be loved. It includes the decision to be patient and kind, to put away selfishness, rudeness, and pride, to forgive and endure (1 Cor 13).

For a successful marriage there must be good communication and mutual respect between husband and wife. The Bible says: "Be subordinate to one another out of reverence for Christ. Wives should be subordinate to their husbands as to the Lord. Husbands, love your wives, even as Christ loved the Church and handed Himself over for her" (Ephesians 5:21-25). This passage is sometimes construed to mean that the husband has the right of dominance over his wife. Not so. If wives are to be "subordinate to their husbands," then husbands are encouraged in Ephesians to give of themselves, generously and lovingly, in imitation of Christ.

When husband and wife are blessed with children, they have the first responsibility to teach them the gospel by word and example. Parents must spend time with their children, pray with them, talk to them about Jesus, instruct them about right and wrong, and live according to their beliefs. Parents must set priorities for important activities like family meals, working and playing together, and family discussions. In these and other ways, parents bring Christ into the home.

It is of most importance that married couples pray together. Research has shown that couples who worship together, read the Bible together, and pray together have an extremely high success rate in their marriages. There are many reasons for this. First, couples who seek from God the joy and peace that only God can give will not expect a spouse to be God. Human beings have longings in their souls that can only be filled by God alone. Those who expect them to be filled by a spouse will be disappointed. Second, marriage is built on love, and God is the source of all love. Married couples who do not pray together pass up the opportunity to receive the grace that only prayer can give to them. Third, couples who pray together express feelings that strengthen marriage and family life: gratitude, sorrow, forgiveness, praise, hope and love.

Marriage and Sexuality (CCC 1652-53, 2331-2365)

The book of Genesis teaches that God created man and woman, commanding them to "be fertile and multiply." The sexual nature of human beings, like all of God's creation, is "very good" (Genesis 1:28). The beauty of marital love is expressed in such books of the Bible as Ruth, Tobit, and the Song of Songs.

But if sexuality has great power for good when properly directed, it has the potential for creating tragedy and pain when misdirected. Sexuality then loses its connection with love and produces lust, which has wreaked havoc on human lives in every age. Lust was the motivation which caused David to murder Uriah in order to steal his wife, Bathsheba (2 Samuel 11-12). Sexual activity, therefore, must be guided by God's laws, clearly expressed in the Bible.

"You shall not commit adultery." "You shall not covet your neighbor's wife." The sixth and ninth commandments (Exodus 20:14, 17) forbid sexual activity outside of marriage in the Old Testament. In the New Testament, Jesus gave His followers even higher standards. He forbade divorce, teaching that husbands and wives must be faithful to each other (Mark 10:1-11). He said that "everyone who looks at a woman with lust has already committed adultery with her in his heart" (Matthew 5:28); He thus prohibited even lustful desires. Paul wrote: "Do not be deceived; neither fornicators nor idolaters nor boy prostitutes nor practicing homosexuals... will inherit the kingdom of God" (1 Corinthians 6:9-10). Paul further warned, "Be sure of this, that no immoral or impure or greedy person, that is, an idolater has any inheritance in the kingdom of Christ and of God" (Ephesians 5:5; 1 Corinthians 6:15-20; Hebrews 13:4). These passages are very blunt in saying that sexual activity outside of marriage excludes one from the Kingdom of God. Therefore, the Catholic Church rightly holds to these truths and teaches us that sexual activity outside of the institution of marriage is a grave sin.

The Bible forbids sexual activity outside of marriage, not because sexuality is bad, but because it is so good that it can have its fullest meaning only in marriage. Sexual intercourse is a means of communication, and God wants it to say: "I love you totally, faithfully, forever, and with openness to new life. You are the only person I love in this way." But intercourse can say many other things, like "I hate you" in rape; "Let's do business" in prostitution; "I like you, but let's not get serious" as in casual sex; or "I think I love you, but let's try it for a while to make sure" in a living-together arrangement. Intercourse can communicate the very opposite of love, or less than it should, and so lose its power to express what God wants it to say.

Many people today find that this approach to sexual morality is outdated. Nothing could be further from the truth. It is sexual *immorality* that is outdated. The Greeks of Old Testament times and the pagans of New Testament times stumbled and fell victim to their own immorality. Historians have observed that they, and all other societies that followed their example, were weakened and destroyed by the erosion of morality. Sexual immorality weakens individuals. Just think of how many of our leaders have fallen as a result of sexual indiscretions. Sexual immorality weakens families, and when the building blocks of society fail, society crumbles. Sexually transmitted diseases threaten civilizations today more than ever. History reveals that those who have been hurt by sexual immorality are countless. We will search in vain for any who have been helped by it. Countless are those who have benefited from following the standards of Christ. We will find no one hurt by them.

But tragically the modern media is largely controlled by individuals who mock the standards of Christ and promote sexual promiscuity. We who are Christian must have the courage to reject the "tired old sins" of the past and walk in the light of the life-giving and love-giving principles of Jesus Christ.

Love and Life in Marriage

Part of living a holy life is living a chaste life. The Catholic Church teaches that sex before marriage is a grave sin (CCC 2353). The Catholic Church actively teaches its teenagers and adults to abstain from sex until marriage. While society is handing out condoms and teaching "safe sex," the Catholic Church is teaching its young people abstinence.

The Church teaches that children should be brought into the world in the context of a loving family with a mother and a father who love each other and are devoted to one another. The mother and father love each other unconditionally, the same way that God loves them. The two of them create this child out of the love they have for one another. Therefore, the child is loved into existence. God's plan is for married couples, united in love and lifelong commitment, to lovingly bring children into the world.

Yet society ridicules the Catholic Church for teaching our teenagers and adults to save sex for marriage; to save sex for the person we commit ourselves to for the rest of our lives. Society doesn't understand that the Church simply wants to guide its members in the ways of God; that the Church simply wants us to understand God's plan for our lives.

The truth of our society is that sex is everywhere; absolutely everywhere. It is in much of the commercials we see on TV no matter what channel we are watching. It is in much of the shows we watch on TV and most of the movies we see at the movie theater. I'm sure you've noticed that it is even in the books you are reading and all over the Internet. Media sends the message that you should be having sex often and with many different people. When parents teach that this is wrong, teens tend to roll their eyes and say that their parents just don't understand their current generation. When adults do it, they are seen as exercising their right to behave "like an adult."

Yet we clearly have the words of the Bible telling us that sex outside of marriage is morally wrong. Why would God change His mind about what is morally right and wrong? If God commanded that an act was immoral, would He suddenly, thirty generations later, decide it was moral after all? Would God, who is all knowing and all powerful and all eternal, suddenly change His mind on morality?

No, He would not. Time exists for God as one. The present, the past, and the future are all one. He knows what has happened and what will happen. If a certain act was immoral

1,000 years ago and God condemned it then, we need to understand that He still condemns it today.

As was mentioned earlier, Marriage is a sacrament. It is a covenant between a husband and a wife. It is a bond that cannot be broken. Remember, a covenant isn't simply an agreement between two people. It is not a situation in which we promise, "I'll do this for you and you do this for me." Instead it is, "You belong to me and I belong to you." In marriage, we create a family bond. Just as we belong to God, when we enter into covenant with Him at our Baptism, the married couple belongs to each other when they enter the Marriage Covenant (CCC 2364). Until we create that lifelong commitment, that covenant bond, we do not belong to each other. Therefore the marriage act, the sexual act, belongs inside the boundaries of the covenant relationship.

God asks the married couple, who were created in His image and likeness, to love as He loves and to create out of love as He created out of love. Marriage is between two people who are completely devoted to each other the same way that God the Father is completely devoted to the Son and the Son completely devoted to the Father. The love between the Father and the Son is so strong that is exists as a Third Person—the Holy Spirit. The love between a man and a woman is so strong that it is capable of creating life; a child—a third person. In this, God rejoices!

Just as God loves, He asks the married couple to love. Just as God created life, He asks the married couple to create life. God's love is life producing. This love and this life cannot be separated. In other words, we cannot separate God's love from His creative act; from His creation of life. Life was created out of God's love! In the same way, the love between a man and a woman; a married couple, is life producing. This love between a married couple, and the life it is capable of producing, cannot be separated. When it is separated it is violated.

Let us apply this knowledge. Let's say that there is a married couple who love each other and are committed to one another, but they do not want to produce life. In other words, they do not want to have children. In fact, the couple wants to keep themselves from producing a baby, so they use an artificial means of birth control. What have they done? They have separated the <u>life</u> and the <u>love principals</u> that God joined. They love each other, but they do not want that love to be creative. Therefore, they are not living in the image and likeness of God as He has called them to live. They do love each other, but they refuse to allow that love to create as God created. This goes against God's will and it displeases Him. It goes against the very nature or purpose of sex.

Artificial Contraception

Before the year 1930, all Christian denominations agreed that the use of artificial birth control was gravely immoral. They all agreed that sexual intercourse has been given to us by God to express love and to bring new human life into existence. To place an artificial barrier between that act and its natural result is to prevent God's purposes and is therefore immoral. But in 1930 the Anglican Church approved the use of contraceptives for married couples. In the next thirty years, nearly every Protestant denomination came not only to accept contraception, but also to promote its use. Planned Parenthood won over the majority of the population by arguing that contraception held the key to happier marriages.

After Vatican II, many Catholics expected the Church to permit the use of artificial contraceptives. Pope Paul VI, however, in the encyclical letter *On Human Live* affirmed traditional Catholic teaching. The Catholic Church stood alone in keeping the teachings against artificial contraceptives alive.

Did contraception produce happier marriages as Planned Parenthood claimed it would? What exactly has happened since 1960? Adultery, divorce, premarital sex, sexually-transmitted diseases, out-of-wedlock births, and abortion have increased to astronomical proportions. It is true in the United States today that more children are born to couples who are not married than to couples who are married.

What is the connection between this and contraception? Well it has to do with temptation. Please understand that people are often tempted to do things they shouldn't. There are deterrents, however, that curb these temptations and help to maintain order. For example, many people like to drive well over the speed limit. Because police officers could be taking radar at any given time anywhere, people tend to drive more slowly than they otherwise would. The fear of getting a ticket curbs their temptation to drive well over the limit. Take all of the police officers away and our roads would be extremely hazardous with people driving excessive speeds causing very dangerous situations.

Apply this same logic to sex. What would happen if we could follow all of our sexual impulses without consequences? People throughout history have been tempted to commit adultery. One of the main deterrents has been the fear of pregnancy. What then would happen if the fear of pregnancy was taken away? The adultery rate would skyrocket. Contraception takes the fear of pregnancy away and as a result the adultery rate has skyrocketed. Apply this same logic to pre-marital sex. If the fear of pregnancy was taken away, premarital sex would also skyrocket. This has also been the case (Mitchell Study).

Because no method of contraception is one hundred percent effective, an increase in adultery and premarital sex will inevitably lead to an increase in "unwanted" pregnancies. Then the "need" for abortion would logically follow and it has followed. There is only one reason to have an abortion—men and women are having sex without being "open to life." When fertility is viewed as a disease, contraception is considered the preventative medicine, and abortion is considered the cure. This is exactly the mentality that many in our society hold.

Has contraception held the key to happier marriages? Today, half of all marriages end in divorce (McKinley/Irvin). More children are born to couples who are not married than to couples who are married (U.S Vital Statistics Report 2010). These children are more likely to grow up in poverty and have less opportunity for higher education (U.S Census Bureau). Crime, drugs and violence tend to follow. Children as young as thirteen are seen in hospital emergency rooms and diagnosed with sexually transmitted diseases. Many of these young teenagers do not know such diseases exist and have no idea they were at risk for contracting them.

There are also risks involved in using artificial methods of birth control. Intrauterine devices (IUDs) have caused death and sterility. Medical reports show a higher incidence of cancer among women who use contraceptive pills, especially those who begin as teens and use the pill for a long time. If chemicals in vegetables, fruits, and animals can be dangerous to human beings, if people are concerned about side effects of medications, we may well wonder about the side effects of powerful drugs and chemicals whose sole purpose is to reverse the human reproductive process or render it ineffective. We may well wonder why more research has not been done to help couples determine when they are fertile, so that artificial means would be unnecessary.

Another negative effect of artificial methods of birth control is that they have placed emphasis more on the frequency of sexual acts than on their meaning. More sexual activity does not necessarily mean more happiness or better marriages. A nationally syndicated columnist asked her women readers: "Would you be content to be held close and treated tenderly and forget about the *act*?" More than ninety thousand women responded; seventy-two percent said, "Yes." Obviously, for these women, intercourse did not convey the love and affection they were looking for.

It is also worth noting that some methods of artificial birth control actually cause abortions. The IUD and some forms of the pill are abortifacient. They do not prevent contraception, but keep the baby from implanting in the mother's uterine wall after conception. Avoiding the possibility of such early abortions is another reason for using natural methods of family planning.

Natural Family Planning

Catholics who do follow the Church's teaching find that it has been a great blessing for marriage and family. The Couple to Couple League, a nonprofit organization founded in 1971, helps couples learn and practice the Sympto-Thermal Method of family planning. Couples using this method report that natural family planning benefits their marriages: It helps them become aware of their bodies and their natural fertility patterns, is very effective, keeps their sexual relationship alive, improves communication, and helps them understand the different needs of men and women. Similar results are reported by couples using the Billings/Ovulation Method and the National Procreative (NaPro) Technology of the Pope Paul VI institute. It teaches the highly effective Creighton Model Natural Family Planning System. It offers resources and medical assistance to couples by monitoring reproductive health, correcting reproductive disorders with modern technology, and offering assistance in high-risk pregnancies. More information can be found on their website (www.popepaulvi.com).

Ceremony without Sacrament (CCC1629)

The Catholic Church believes that "what God has joined, no one may divide." But a man and woman can exchange vows and rings at a wedding without being joined by God. For a real marriage, husband and wife must intend what God intends: that marriage be permanent, faithful, and open to children. They must be emotionally capable of such a marriage, and they must be free to marry.

Some people do not have these intentions going into their marriages. Instead they have contrasting intentions such as: "I'll stay married if my spouse make me happy; if not, we'll divorce." "No one person can keep another happy; therefore, we retain the right to have sex with other partners." "We will not have children because they interfere with the lifestyle we enjoy." The Catholic Church teaches that attitudes such as these "invalidate" a marriage, that is, they make a real marriage impossible.

A marriage ceremony is invalid if a spouse is incapable of entering into a loving union because of immaturity, psychological problems, or similar reasons, or if forced to marry. A ceremony is also invalid if one of the spouses is not free to marry because of a previous marriage or because marriage is forbidden by Church law or by a just civil law.

In these cases the wedding ceremony, even if Catholic, does not result in a valid marriage. Often such apparent marriages end in civil divorce, and one or both of the spouses may wish to marry in the Catholic Church. The official statement by the Church that no valid marriage existed between the two parties is called a declaration of nullity, or an annulment. An annulment is given by a diocesan tribunal, an office of the bishop, after a thorough investigation. It does not have civil effects and does not affect the legitimate status of children.

The Church may, on the authority of Paul (1 Corinthians 7:12-15), dissolve a marriage of unbaptized persons when one wishes to be baptized and the other refuses to live with a baptized person. This is called a "Pauline Privilege." The marriage of a baptized and an unbaptized person can also be dissolved under similar circumstances by the "Petrine Privilege," or "Privilege of the Faith."

The Catholic Church recognizes as valid the marriages of non-Catholics. In the eyes of the Church, civil divorce does not dissolve the marriages of Catholics or non-Catholics, although either may be declared invalid if the conditions for an annulment are present. Further, civil divorce does not exclude a Catholic from the practice of the faith. At times civil divorce may even be necessary to protect a spouse or children from abuse or mistreatment.

Understand clearly, however, that if a marriage is deemed valid after a thorough investigation by a diocesan tribunal, the Church does not have the power to grant an annulment. The tribunal must conduct an honest investigation and provide honest results.

A person who wishes to inquire into the possibility of a declaration of nullity should contact a parish priest. Each diocese has its own procedures; the priest can explain these and help get the process started.

A Path to Holiness

Remember that marriage is a great path to holiness. It is one of the Sacraments of Service or Vocation. In marriage we serve others by giving of ourselves. This selfless giving is difficult, but also very rewarding. Our most important job here on earth is to get to Heaven. Our second most important job is to take as many people with us as we can. In the context of the family and marriage, our mission becomes clear. We should help our spouse to grow in holiness every day. Then as a couple, we gently guide our children to holiness as well. It is in Heaven that we will all be together again and behold each other for all eternity.

XVI. Heaven

A Soul Visits Heaven

All of us have heard about people who claim that they actually died for a few minutes and then came back to life. We might even know such people. Most describe the same type of experience. Their soul leaves their body and floats upward. They are able to see their bodies below; doctors and nurses frantically working to save their life. Then they are gone. The soul enters a tunnel of some sort. Up ahead they see a bright light and they are drawn to it. The feeling is indescribable. It is warm; it is perfect. Sometimes they are stopped at this point and told that they must go back into their bodies. Reluctantly, the soul does so. Other times the soul travels on closer to the light all the while knowing that the light up ahead is the fulfillment of all they could ever want.

Sondra Abrahams is a woman who has had an outer body experience such as this. Archbishop Philip Hannan of New Orleans interviewed Sondra and produced a video entitled, "Her Life After Death" from his organization "Focus Worldwide Network of New Orleans." In the video, Archbishop Hannan points out that, "Sondra's insights are private revelations that one can accept or reject. We always study such accounts, and as Scripture advises, take from them only what is good; discerning not only the root experience, but also aspects of the content. But if you're like us, you find such insights informative and even fascinating." And it is true. Sondra's story is both informative and fascinating.

Back in 1970 Sondra was given a medication that was brand new on the market. She experienced a reaction to it that nearly killed her. After being rushed to the emergency room of a nearby hospital, the doctors frantically worked to save her life as

Sondra's soul floated upward. She explains that the first sensation she felt was one of wonder and awe. Sondra remembers thinking, "This is really cool!" She could see the entire emergency room and understood everything that was going on. Below her she could see that the doctor, working on her body, was cursing and throwing things at the nurses who were present there to help him. He was frustrated that nothing seemed to be working to get Sondra's heart beating again. She saw a man in the next station who was having a heart attack and beyond him, a boy who had broken his arm, was crying. It was then that the ceiling disappeared and Sondra entered the tunnel. She too saw the light up ahead and began heading toward it. As she moved along, the light grew bigger. Sondra felt that warm wonderful indescribable feeling too.

What is different about Sondra Abraham's story is that she was allowed to go all the way to the light. Sondra literally reached the light and saw what it was. The light was Jesus. Sondra says that Jesus is literally the light of the world. And that indescribable warm feeling everyone gets… that is Jesus' love for us. His love literally penetrates your entire soul.

Jesus allowed Sondra to come all the way to Him, because He had a mission for her. Jesus was sending Sondra back to do some work for Him. Jesus' mission for Sondra was for her to pray much and to tell her story. This is what she does today.

Sondra explains that everyone comes before Jesus when they die. Jesus shows everyone a life review; a review of their own life in great detail. Jesus showed Sondra everything that happened in her life from the time that she was a very small child to the present. Jesus showed Sondra every minute and Sondra was able to remember everything. She understood the times that she pleased Jesus very much, because she could feel His happiness and joy. Sondra also understood the times when she did not please Him, because she could feel His sadness and sorrow for her sins. She saw all the lost opportunities that she was given to do something good, but did not do it. She was able to see all of the opportunities she was given to receive God's grace, but passed them up. Sondra says that this life is our greatest opportunity to do good and kind things. Once we die, the opportunities cease. We truly should do all the good we can while we are here.

Sondra was able to see how her Guardian Angel walked with her during her life. Today, Sondra is able to see the angels on the earth. She explains that we all have at least one angel. Some people have many angels. Sondra herself has seven angels. These angels are here to help us and to protect us. Sondra tells us that when we pray for a priest by name, a legion of angels is sent to protect him from the devil.

Jesus told Sondra that He was going to show her Heaven, Hell, and Purgatory and He did exactly that. Sondra was allowed to see the lowest level of Heaven in all its beauty. Jesus told her not to look any higher. Sondra was not allowed to see God the Father, though she heard His voice. Jesus explained that if Sondra saw The Father, she would have to stay. Sondra saw souls everywhere. They were singing and praising God. They were joyous! They were so unbelievably happy! The music was so different than the music here on earth. It was indescribably beautiful. Sondra explains that even the flowers sway! She saw colors that do not even exist here on earth. Everyone is young and their joy never ends. They are continuously filled with God's love. It is never ending and always changing. Truly Heaven is the place we all want to live in for all eternity. What a gift Jesus has given us!

Sondra was also shown Purgatory. She describes it as levels. In these levels are suffering souls. In the lowest level the souls suffer much and it is very dark. Each level gets brighter and the suffering is less. Sondra explains that the quickest way for souls to move upward and out of Purgatory is for those of us left on the earth to pray for them. They can't pray for themselves and rely heavily on us to pray for them and to have Masses said for them. Many have been forgotten, because their loved ones here on earth think they are in Heaven and do not pray for them. Sondra explains that souls from Purgatory visit her at night asking her to pray for them. God allows them to come in order to ask Sondra for help. Since their loved ones here on earth do not pray for them, they seek prayers from Sondra who is willing to help them. Sondra explains that she has not had a full night's sleep in years. Her husband doesn't even ask what is going on any more. When he is awakened by a soul in the middle of the night, he just turns over and goes back to sleep. It has become a very routine occurrence at their house.

Sondra was also shown Hell. She says that it is like a large volcano that boils up. As it boils up, souls come up in the flames. They look hideous. They are in torment beyond belief and they curse God as they bubble up. Sondra asked Jesus, "Lord, how can you send a soul to such an awful place?" Jesus answered, "I do not send them there. They choose to go there themselves." Sondra asked, "Why would anyone choose that?" Jesus then showed her the life review of a man who was in Hell. Sondra watched the man's life review with utter amazement. He was mean to everyone he came into contact with. One day during his life, he entered a building. An elderly woman was walking behind him also intending to enter the same building. The man purposely slammed the door in her face causing her to fall backward onto the concrete sidewalk. The man laughed at what he had done. He lived his life daily with this hatred in his soul. Then one day the man was killed unexpectedly in a car accident. Like everyone else, his soul came before Jesus. Jesus said to him, "I have two questions. Are you sorry? And do you love me?" The man's soul opened its mouth and began to curse Jesus. With that,

Jesus waved His sacred hand and the soul left His sight. It began moving toward Hell. The soul suddenly realized that it was going to Hell. At this, Sondra looked into the soul's face. To her amazement the soul was content with going to Hell. It was not upset in the least. Clearly that soul had chosen Hell.

Sitting with Jesus, Sondra could see her own soul. She could look at herself. She quickly realized that she did not belong in Heaven. She could see that her soul was dark gray in color. The souls in Heaven were not gray. Instead they were brilliantly white. Sondra explains that no one has to tell you that you do not belong in Heaven. You can see that for yourself. Sondra understood then, that Purgatory would help her dark gray soul to become brilliantly white. She would have to spend time in Purgatory before she could enter Heaven. This did not upset her. She was thankful that Purgatory existed for this reason. She wanted Heaven so badly! Purgatory was her only way into Heaven. It would be the means through which her soul could be purified; could become brilliantly white.

Sondra was also allowed to see the Blessed Virgin, Mary. Mary told Sondra that she had heard every single prayer that Sondra had ever prayed to her. Mary explained that every time Sondra asked her to, she prayed. Mary was absolutely beautiful. Her love for Sondra was immeasurable.

Jesus then told Sondra that He was going to show her a little more. He said to her, "This is what people will soon think of my Father's gift of life." At that Sondra was shown an abortion mill. She did not know what it was, as this took place in 1970. The court case that legalized abortion, Roe Versus Wade, was another three years away. But Sondra realized that this was the killing of unborn babies. She looked at Jesus and saw that He was crying. Sondra could feel His deep, deep sadness over this. She said, "If only people knew how sad abortion makes our Lord, they would never call it a *choice* again."

Jesus then showed Sondra something that she termed "duplication." Sondra did not know what else to call it, but she saw human baby girls being duplicated. Jesus had shown Sondra the cloning of human beings. This angered Jesus, because in cloning human beings, men think they are God. Sondra says that nothing will appease God's anger if human cloning becomes a reality. As Sondra looked into the eyes of these duplicated human baby girls, she could tell that there was nothing behind their eyes. There was no spiritual life. To make matters worse, Sondra claims that the first cloned baby is named "Eve." This is a further insult to God.

Sondra was then sent back. The doctor in the hospital emergency room finally got a heartbeat and Sondra began to breathe. Sondra's body was alive. The first thing Sondra did when she awoke was to reprimand the doctor for cursing and throwing things at the nurses. He could not understand how Sondra could have been aware of that. She had no heartbeat at the time.

As Archbishop Philip Hannan said, "Sondra's insights are private revelations that one can accept or reject. But if you are like us, you find such insights informative and even fascinating." I find Sondra's story to be fascinating and this is why I share it with you. Again, her story can be found in the video, "Her Life After Death."

What is Heaven Like?

Heaven is the place where all of us are looking forward to spending eternity. Christians plan to go to Heaven and be with God forever. We wonder, what is Heaven like? What does God look like? What will we be doing there? Does anyone really know? We only know from what Jesus told us; what the apostles taught; and what Catechism says.

Jesus left no doubt about the reality of eternal life. He said, "For this is the will of my Father, that everyone who sees the Son and believes in Him may have eternal life" (John 6:40). Jesus said to the criminal who was crucified with Him, "Today you will be with me in Paradise" (Luke 23:43).

We don't know exactly what Heaven will be like. Paul says that he was "caught up into Paradise and heard ineffable things which on one may utter" (2 Corinthians 12:4). John writes, "Beloved, we are God's children now; what we shall be has not yet been revealed. We do know that when it is revealed, we shall be like Him, for we shall see Him as He is" (1 John 3:2). Heaven will surely fulfill our life here on earth. We experience *goodness* here on earth. We see the beauty of creation. We find learning new things interesting and exciting. Surely we will find this and much, much more in Heaven. Perhaps there will be colors that do not even exist here on earth. We may hear music more beautiful than any music here on earth. Perhaps the animals and plants will be alive with the love of God. It is hard for us to imagine complete fulfillment and happiness; complete joy and love. A place where there are no worries or problems; a place where there is only love. Imagine that place. Imagine spending eternity, *forever*, in that place. That's where you and I are headed. That's where we're going.

Saint John further tell us, "Then I saw a new Heaven and a new earth. God Himself will always be with them as their God. He will wipe every tear from their eyes, and there shall be no more death or mourning, wailing or pain, for the old order has passed away" (Revelation 21:1-4). What joy it will bring us to be in the presence of God! It is hard to imagine such happiness and satisfaction, but it will be ours. There will be no more sorrow. As Saint John puts it, God will wipe every tear from our eyes.

The greatest joy of Heaven will be to see God "face to face." "Blessed are the clean of heart," Jesus promised, "for they will see God" (Matt 5:8). Catholic tradition calls this vision of God the "beatific vision" because of the happiness it will bring us. What an incredible experience it will be to stand in the presence of our Creator. To realize that what we have been longing for since the first moments of our existence is now ours forever, to feel completely loved and to love without limits.

The Catechism states "We can therefore hope in the glory of heaven promised by God to those who love him and do his will. In every circumstance, each one of us should hope, with the grace of God, to persevere "to the end" and to obtain the joy of heaven, as God's eternal reward for the good works accomplished with the grace of Christ. In hope, the Church prays for "all men to be saved." She longs to be united with Christ, her Bridegroom, in the glory of heaven (CCC 1821). Heaven is the ultimate end and fulfillment of the deepest human longings, the state of supreme, definitive happiness" (CCC 1024).

The End of Life

This life, as we well know, is a time of testing and trial; it is eternity's proving ground. The happiness of Heaven consists essentially in the fulfillment of love. Unless we enter eternity with love for God in our hearts, we would be absolutely incapable of experiencing the happiness of Heaven. Our life on this earth is the time that God has given us to acquire and to, in a sense, *prove* our love for Him. God wants us to love creation for He gave it to us as a gift, for us to enjoy. But we must not love what God has created more than we love God Himself. We must not love the pleasures of this world, wealth, and fame above God. Whether life is at its best or at its worst, we must be able to say, "My God I love you!"

When we die, we are able to see things as they really are. The veil is lifted. We will see the devil for what he truly is and we will know his lies. We will see God and His goodness and understand that He is the one we should have chosen. At the moment of our death, we enter eternity. At that point, we are who we are. We do not suddenly become what we are not or what we have not been. We will not suddenly be sorry for sins if we were not sorry for them in this life. We will not suddenly be capable of loving God when we die, if we were not capable of loving Him while we were alive. Our movements toward God in this life are a great benefit to us in the next. Our sorrow over our sins in this life, helps us to make great gains for eternity. There is much we can do to help our eternal life here on earth. Our ability to help ourselves, however, ends when this life is over. So let us do all we can to become holy now. Every person's goal should be to reach sainthood for there are only saints in Heaven. The most important goal of our lives must be to reach Heaven. Our second most important goal must be to take as many people with us as we can.

XVII. Purgatory and Indulgences

The Catholic Belief in Purgatory

The Catholic Church has always taught that Purgatory exists. We have writings from the early Church Fathers regarding Purgatory, which shows every Catholic that this has been a Catholic teaching from the very beginning. The writings of the early "Church Fathers" Lactantius, St. John Chrysostom, and St. Augustine, dating back to the year 250 A.D., prove to us that the Apostles taught extensively on Purgatory. The Mass is also proof that we have always believed in Purgatory. The words of the Eucharistic Prayer mention the souls in Purgatory as we openly pray for them. We offer the Mass each day for a deceased member of our parish or a family member of a fellow parishioner. The catacombs in Rome are littered with ancient writings that speak of the faithful's belief in Purgatory as they offered prayers for the dead. The Bible is of course our proof as well.

Some Doctrines are explicitly spelled out word for word in the Bible. Some Doctrines are only implied; nevertheless they are there. The doctrine of Purgatory is one of those implied doctrines that we must piece together. This is true because God's people have always believed in Purgatory. Therefore, no direct explanation was needed to be written in the Bible. It is only in recent times that people have doubted the existence of Purgatory.

The word Purgatory is not found in the Bible, but do not let that bother you. The word Trinity is also not found in the Bible, yet we believe that our God is a Triune, three distinct persons consisting of God the Father, God the Son, and God the Holy Spirit. The Bible teaches very well that God is Father, Creator of Heaven and earth; that He is also Jesus, God's Word incarnate (made flesh); and that He is the Holy Spirit, the

Sanctifier. The Bible teaches this all the while without using the word *Trinity* even once.

Similarly, the Bible teaches that there is a place for souls to be purified prior to entering Heaven. The Bible teaches this well, without using the word Purgatory. The Bible shows us that an intermediate state of <u>purification</u> exists. It explains that there is a place of purging; of being tried by fire; of being refined; of being made pure; before one can enter Heaven.

The Doctrine of Purgatory Implied in the Bible

The Bible gives us some specific requirements in order to reach Heaven. Matthew 5:48 states, "Be perfect, just as your heavenly Father is perfect." And in Hebrews 12:14 we read, "Strive for peace with everyone, and for that holiness without which no one will see the Lord." The Book of Revelation 21:27 goes on to say that, "Nothing unclean will enter Heaven." Yet the Book of James 3:2 tells us that, "We all fall short".

Clearly the Bible tells us that we must be perfect as God is perfect; we must be holy or we will not see God; that nothing unclean will enter Heaven; and yet the truth is…"We all fall short." Purgatory provides that place for us to become holy; perfect; and clean, so that we can enter Heaven if we do not already possess these qualities at the moment of our death.

A second important lesson that the Bible teaches regarding Purgatory is that there are different degrees or types of sin. Not all sin is equal. In First John 5:16-17, Saint John tells us that there is sin that is not deadly—we call it Venial Sin. There is also sin that **is** *deadly*—we call it Mortal Sin. "If anyone sees his brother sinning, if the sin is not deadly, he should pray to God and He will give him life. This is only for those whose sin is *not deadly*. There is such a thing as deadly sin, about which I do not say that you should pray. All wrongdoing is sin, but there is sin that is *not deadly*."

Besides telling us that there is sin that is *deadly* and sin that is *not deadly*, John points out that we should pray for someone who has died, "If their sin was not deadly." If we do, John declares, "God will give him life." Think about this for a moment. The person whose sins were not deadly must therefore be in Purgatory. We would have no need to pray for someone in Heaven. For if a person is in Heaven, he has reached full happiness. John is saying that if we pray for him, God will grant him Heaven. John then goes on to say that we should not pray for someone who has died "if his sin **was** deadly." Why not? The person is not in Purgatory. That person, whose sins were deadly, is in Hell. It will do no good to pray for him.

In the Book of James 1:14-15, Saint James tells us that, "When sin reaches maturity it gives birth to death." Listen to James: "Each person is tempted when he is lured and enticed by his own desire. Then desire conceives and brings forth sin, and when sin reaches maturity it gives birth to death." The kind of death that James refers to is a spiritual death.

A third thing that the Bible teaches in regard to Purgatory is that we should settle disputes and make up for our sins while we are here on earth. If we are in need of Purgatory, we will be there until we have 'paid the last penny' or in other words until we have been purged of all our sins and the debt we owe for them. An example of this is in Matthew chapter five. We are told to settle our disputes with our enemies or we will end up coming before the judge and being thrown into prison. The Judge is God. The prison is Purgatory. It goes on to tell us that we will not be released from this prison until we have paid the last penny that we owe.

In Matthew Chapter 12 we are told that sins can be forgiven in the next life. This explains something very important regarding Purgatory. "Whoever speaks a word against the Son of Man will be forgiven; but whoever speaks against the Holy Spirit will not be forgiven, either is this age or in the age to come." The words 'in this age or in the age to come' truly show that there is forgiveness of sins in this life **and also** in the life to come. Where in the next life can sin be forgiven? If we are in Heaven, there is no sin to forgive. If we are in Hell, no sin is forgiven. So there must be a third place where sin can be forgiven. That third place, of course, is Purgatory.

In Paul's letter to the Hebrews 12:22-23 we read, "But you have come to Mount Zion and to the city of the living God, the heavenly Jerusalem…and to a judge who is God of all, and to the spirits of just men made perfect." From this Scripture passage we can easily see that there is a way, a process, through which the spirits of the "just" are made perfect.

Moreover in 1Corinthians 3:13-15 Paul tells us that "each man's work will become manifest; for the Day (judgment day) will disclose it, because it will be revealed with fire, and the fire will test what sort of work each one has done. If the work which any man has built on the foundation survives, he will receive a reward. If any man's work is burned up, he will suffer loss, though he himself will be saved, but only as through fire." Where is this place that a man, after he dies, suffers loss, as through fire, but is still saved? Is it Hell? No, once you are in Hell, you don't get out. Is it in Heaven? No, you don't suffer loss in Heaven. This clearly shows that in Purgatory we suffer loss through fire, but are still saved.

At Mass we pray for the dead. We have always done this. We give alms for the poor souls in Purgatory. This can also be found in the Bible. In 2Maccabees 12:44-46 Judas Maccabees prays for the dead and makes atonement for them that they might be freed from sin. Again, someone in Heaven does not need our prayers. The souls in Hell cannot benefit from our prayers, because nothing will get them out of Hell. Judas Maccabees prays, and we pray, for those who have died, because they could be in Purgatory. Our prayers can release them so that they can enter Heaven. Judas Maccabees was a devout Jew. Here we see clearly that the Israelites believed in Purgatory. This was also part of the Jewish faith at the time of Jesus.

In addition, Saint Peter tells us in 1Peter 3:18-20 that after His death, Jesus visited the dead and preached to the Spirits in Prison. *Prison* is the Bible's word for Purgatory. "Christ, put to death in the flesh, was brought to life in the Spirit. In the spirit He went to preach to the spirits in prison who had once been disobedient, while God patiently waited in the days of Noah during the building of the ark." Combine this passage with what Peter then says in Chapter 4, "For this is why the Gospel was preached even to the dead, that though condemned in the flesh in human estimation, they might live in the spirit in the estimation of God." These souls, who were in prison, were not in Hell. Jesus was preaching to them to save them. There would be no need to preach to those in Hell since there is no way to save them. These were obviously the souls that were in Purgatory who could be saved by Jesus preaching to them.

We also learn from the Bible that Paul prayed for a friend of his named, Onesiphorus, who had died. This is found in 2Timothy 1:16-18. Again, the only reason to pray for someone who has died is to help them to reach Heaven because they are in Purgatory. Notice that Paul does not assume that his dear friend is in Heaven. On the contrary, Paul assumes that his dear friend is in Purgatory and is in great need of prayer.

Purgatory Defined

Purgatory is a state of final purification after death and before entrance into Heaven for those who have died in God's friendship, but were only imperfectly purified. Purgatory is a final cleansing place where all of our imperfections are burned away before we can enter into the joy of Heaven. Understand that Purgatory is a place where very good people go; people who loved God their whole life. If we make it to Purgatory, we've made it to Heaven! Purgatory is therefore temporary. It is a temporary state of purification for the imperfect soul (CCC 1030).

Let's face it, not many people die perfectly united to Christ. But in order to enter Heaven, our soul must be perfect. We must be holy. Sin stained souls cannot be in the presence of God. I can't stress this enough. Please understand the Bible's words and its message of salvation, "Nothing unclean will enter Heaven" (Rev. 21:27). Purgatory is therefore, the door to Heaven for many, many people. This is true because many people pass through this life and arrive at the end with only a commonplace love for God. Becoming a saint and reaching holiness in this life was not of great importance to them. Purgatory, therefore, gives us the time we need to become perfect after death, so that we can enter Heaven. Purgatory is for all those who did not reach holiness while they were here on earth and must become a saint after they die.

In Purgatory, the souls of those people who have died in a state of grace, but with Venial Sins or with reparation due for forgiven Mortal and Venial Sins, are fully cleansed so they might enter Heaven. Let me explain it this way. If we die in a state of grace, which means God's Life *is* found to be in our soul, but we have Venial Sins that have not been forgiven, we may go to Purgatory and be cleansed of these sins. Why? Because again, "Nothing unclean will enter Heaven." Our Venial Sins may not enter Heaven. If we die in a state of grace, but we have not made restitution for all of our sins, we may go to Purgatory and will be allowed to make up for these sins before we enter Heaven. In Purgatory all remaining self-love is purged and purified until only the love of God remains in our soul.

Guilt and Punishment

In order to understand Purgatory further, we have to understand the difference between Guilt and Punishment. In order to understand Purgatory, ask this important question: Does God forgive the guilt of sin, but still require reparation or atonement for our sins? In other words, does God forgive sin, but still require us to repair the damage that our sins caused? Yes! When we are sorry for a sin we have committed, God forgives the **guilt** of that sin. We are no longer guilty. He still requires us, however, to repair the damage that our sin caused. We owe a debt for every sin we commit. We must repair the damage that every sin we committed has caused. That is why, when we go to confession, the priest gives us a **Penance** to do. The priest gives us something to do that will help us make up for our sins or repair the damage that our sin has caused.

Let us be clear. When we sin, there are two consequences: First, we are guilty of that sin. So **GUILT**, or Eternal Punishment, is one consequence. Second, we do not live in a vacuum. Our sin never affects just us. When we sin it affects the whole universe. Therefore, we are required by God to repair the damage that our sin has caused. We are required by God to make up for our sins. This is called reparation, expiation, or atonement. Or you can simply say that we owe a debt for every sin which will repair the damage that sin caused. This debt that we owe is called **Temporal Punishment**. Therefore, when we sin there are

2 Consequences—**Guilt and Temporal Punishment**. We are *guilty* and we owe a *debt* (CCC 1472).

The Broken Window

This might help you to understand. Let's say there is a group of teenagers who are heading outside to play baseball in the backyard. One of the adults says, "Don't throw the ball on *this* side of the house. The neighbor's house has many glass windows on this side and you could throw the ball and break one of those windows." So the teenagers go out and play ball, but they *do* throw the ball on the side of the house where the neighbor's widows are located and they *do* break one of those windows.

They sinned. They sinned because they did not do as they were told. Their disobedience caused the window to get broken. So these teenagers go to the neighbor's house and knock on his door. They explain to him how sorry they are that the window was broken saying, "We are very, very sorry for breaking your window. Would you please forgive us?" The neighbor replies, "Yes, of course I will forgive you. BUT you'll have to pay to fix the window."

Yes, the teenagers are forgiven, but they are not "off the hook." They will have to repair the damage that they caused. They will have to make the window right again; the way it was before they sinned. Yes, the guilt of their sin is forgiven, but these kids must repair the damage their sin caused. They must make up for it. They owe a debt called, "Temporal Punishment."

This is exactly how it works with God. When we are truly sorry for our sins, God will forgive those sins. God will forgive the *guilt* of those sins. Yet He still requires reparation for those sins. He still requires that we repair the damage that our sins caused or that we make up for our sins. We must pay the debt we owe. Again, that is why we are given a penance when we go to confession. This penance simply must be carried out. Understand though, that the penance we are given by the priest in the Sacrament of Reconciliation cannot make up for all the sins we have committed. This is because the penance that a priest gives if relatively light. Moreover, it is very unlikely that we confessed every sin we have committed. Many times, we do not remember all of our sins. The priest cannot give us a penance for sins he has no knowledge of.

So we as Catholics willingly make sacrifices in order to make up for our sins. For example, Catholics sometimes deprive themselves of certain things in order to repair the damage that our sins cause. This helps to pay the debt that we owe. We can make little sacrifices even daily. Everyone suffers in this life. So the Church encourages us to offer our daily trials and life sufferings up to the Lord, uniting our suffering with His. When we do this, it is redemptive. It helps us to repair the damage that our sins caused, because by uniting our suffering to Christ, we share in His suffering. This gives us the hope of sharing in His Resurrection. Yes, our sins are forgiven if we are sorry, but that doesn't mean that they go unpunished. We owe Temporal Punishment for every sin we commit. We can either make up for our sins in this life, right here on earth, or we can wait and make up for our sins in the next life after we die. It is our choice. We can either pay the debt that we owe for our sins here or we can wait and pay the debt when we die.

Our Bishop, Robert Baker, teaches that if we wait until we die to repair the damage that our sins caused, we could spend quite a long time in Purgatory. This is why he recommends all Catholics to pray "The Morning Offering" each morning as we begin our day. In this prayer, we offer to Jesus our prayers, works, joys, and sufferings of the day for His intentions as well as reparation for our sins. In praying this prayer, everything we do throughout the day becomes a prayer we offer up to Christ. It also gets us into the habit of asking for Indulgences and helps us to meet some of the requirements in gaining them. The prayer "The Morning Offering" is written here for you:

Oh Jesus, through the Immaculate Heart of Mary, I offer you all of my prayers, works, joys, and sufferings of this day for all the intentions of Your most Sacred Heart; in union with the most Holy Sacrifice of the Mass throughout the world, in reparation for my sins, for the intentions of all, and in particular for the Holy Father's intentions. I wish to gain all the Indulgences attached to the prayers I shall say and the good works I shall perform this day. Amen.

David, Bathsheba, and the Prophet Nathan (2 Sam 11 and 12)

There is a story in the Old Testament that shows quite clearly that God requires reparation for our sin. It is found in 2 Samuel Chapters 11 and 12. And the story goes like this:

David was King of all of Israel. As king, he sent his men off to fight in battle, but David did not go with them. The King was supposed to go and fight with his men, but David stayed home instead. While all the men were off fighting, David had lots of time on his hands. One day, as he loafed around, he saw a beautiful woman bathing on the top of her house. He decided to have her brought to him and ordered this to be done. David then had sexual relations with her. The woman was Bathsheba, the wife of Uriah the Hittite, who was one of the men off fighting for David.

Bathsheba conceived in her womb David's child as a result of their union, but David did not want her Husband, Uriah, to find out about this. David did not want anyone to know that he impregnated Bathsheba, because he had committed adultery! So David devised a plan. He sent for Uriah on the battle field and had Uriah brought home from the war. David told Uriah to go and relax and *be* with his wife, Bathsheba. David hoped that Uriah would have sexual relations with his wife. Soon Uriah would know that Bathsheba was pregnant and if he had sexual relations with his wife, he would assume that the child was his. But David's plan failed. It failed because Uriah refused to go into the house and *be* with his wife. He felt guilty that all the men were off fighting while he was at home enjoying himself. Uriah did not have sexual relations with his wife.

David then devised a second plan. He sent Uriah back to fight and gave him a note to take to the commanding officer. The note ordered that Uriah be placed on the front line in the fighting. David told the commanding officer to suddenly pull back the forces and leave Uriah there to fight alone.

That is exactly what happened. The commanding officer put Uriah up front to fight and then suddenly pulled the army back, leaving Uriah to fight alone. As a result, Uriah was killed. This is the exact result that David wanted. With Uriah dead, David felt free to take Bathsheba to be his wife. It would now be fine that the child she carried was his.

God became so angry with David for what he had done that He sent a prophet by the name of Nathan to see David. The prophet Nathan said to David, "Listen to this story and be the judge of it. There were two men who lived in a town. One was rich and the other was very poor. The rich man had flocks and flocks of sheep, huge in number, but the poor man had only one little female lamb that he had bought with his own money. This poor man loved his little lamb. He fed her with scraps from his table and she slept with him at night. One day the rich man had a guest over for dinner and decided to cook a lamb for him. The rich man was so stingy that he didn't want to cook one of *his* lambs for the guest. Instead, he took the poor man's lamb away from him and cooked it."

As the prophet Nathan finished the story, David grew very angry and said, "The rich man you speak of, he deserves to die!" How could he do such a horrible thing to that poor man? The prophet Nathan looked David in the eye and said, "David, you are that man! And the Lord is very displeased with you!"

At once David understood. He had taken Uriah's wife just like the rich man had taken the poor man's lamb. David fell to his knees and repented saying, "I have sinned against the Lord." Understand clearly. David repented of his sin immediately. He saw the horrible things he had done and he was truly sorry. So the Prophet Nathan said to him, "The Lord on His part has forgiven your sin and you shall not die. *But since you have utterly spurned the Lord by this deed, the child that Bathsheba carries will surely die.*"

We can see from this story that God forgave the guilt of David's sin the moment he repented. However, God still required reparation for the sin in the form of suffering. Yes, David was forgiven, but God still required David to atone for his sin. David's punishment was that God did not permit the child to live.

God forgives the guilt of our sins and we are no longer guilty, but He also requires that we repair the damage our sin caused. He requires a punishment for our sins. This punishment is a debt that we owe and it must be paid. The Church calls this debt we owe "Temporal Punishment." This is not an eternal punishment. It is temporal. It lasts only for a time.

Nothing Unclean Will Enter Heaven

Why is it true that, "Nothing unclean will enter Heaven"? God is perfect holiness. Isaiah the prophet tells us, "Holy, holy, holy is the Lord God Almighty." (Isaiah 6:3) So God is perfectly holy and He cannot therefore be in the presence of sin that is completely unholy. Because God is perfectly holy, we, who were made in His image and likeness, are called to that same holiness. We have to strive to be holy as God is holy. Remember what it says in Matthew chapter 5:48 "Be perfect as your Heavenly Father is perfect." And in 1Peter 1:15-16 "As He who called you is holy, be holy yourselves in every aspect of your conduct for it is written, be holy because I am holy." And thirdly, scripture tells us that without perfect holiness, no man can see God. In Hebrews 12:14 it says, "Strive for peace with everyone and for that holiness without which no one will see the Lord." Realistically, we may never reach that kind of holiness in our life time. We are supposed to strive for that holiness, but most people will probably not reach it. They could. They are capable of it. But most people won't because it is simply not a priority in their lives. So there has to be a place for us to get cleaned up and finish becoming holy. There has to be a place where we can have sin and the stain of sin and the reparation due to sin purged out of our souls. Purgatory is that place for those who are going to Heaven, to stop and get rid of anything that is hanging on or anything they didn't get right before they died. Purgatory is a place where, thanks be to God, we can get cleaned up so that we can enter Heaven for all Eternity.

There are other ways in which to see the need for Purgatory. As Sondra Abrahams put it, "The souls in Heaven were brilliantly white, but my soul was dark gray. No one had to tell me that I needed Purgatory. I could see that for myself. We really do judge ourselves." Here we see that Sondra was convinced of the need for Purgatory in order for her soul to become brilliantly white like the souls in Heaven. Another way to see the need for Purgatory, is in the same way we need our eyes to adjust to the light first thing in the morning. When we wake up and it is still dark, we have the need to shield our eyes from a light that is suddenly turned on. Our eyes must adjust to the light or we cannot see. It even hurts to look at the light. We can also see the need for Purgatory in this way. If our souls are not holy enough to look upon the face of God in all its brilliance and glory, we need a time to adjust to that brilliance; to become holy enough to look upon the Beatific Vision. Purgatory provides that adjustment for us.

The Specifics of Purgatory

One of the best books that I have read on the subject of Purgatory is entitled, <u>An Unpublished Manuscript on Purgatory</u>. This book contains the words of the soul of a deceased religious sister who is in Purgatory. She has been allowed by God to make visits to one of her colleagues who is still living. The Catholic Church has declared that there is nothing contained in this book that is contrary to Catholic Teaching. It has been given the Imprimatur by His Eminence, Lawrence Cardinal Shehan, who was Archbishop of Baltimore when the book was published in 1967. Whether we believe what is contained in the book or not, is up to us.

According to "An Unpublished Manuscript on Purgatory," there are different stages or levels in Purgatory. The lower levels are where souls suffer the greatest. This is where the guiltiest find themselves. The lowest level is the most painful. It is like a temporary Hell. In this level "are sinners who have committed terrible crimes during life and whose death came as a surprise. It was almost a miracle that they were saved, and often by the prayers of holy parents." In the next level up "are the souls who, though they did not commit great crimes like the others, were indifferent toward God. They are in Purgatory for their long years of indifference." Often times they are abandoned without prayers or are not allowed to profit from the prayers said for them. You see, because God is just, He deals with us in the same way we acted toward Him in our life.

In the next level higher, one suffers a great deal, but less than in the lower levels. In this level "are the souls of those who died with Venial Sins not fully expiated before death, or with Mortal Sins that have been forgiven but for which they have not made entire satisfaction."

As one moves up through these levels, the suffering becomes less. It is in the lowest levels that there is fire, as it is very close to Hell. At the highest level is the "Purgatory of Desire" or the Threshold. In this level it is painful in that the soul is deprived of the sight of God. The soul longs greatly to be with God and yet it must wait. Very few souls escape this level.

Judgment by God is individual. He takes all things into consideration. He is infinitely merciful and just. In Purgatory there are different degrees according to the merits of each soul. Understand though, that it takes just as long to become holy in Purgatory as it does on earth. So some souls are there for many years and even decades. In Purgatory, however, we can do nothing to help ourselves. We must rely on the help of others who pray for us. On earth we can help ourselves a great deal. This is why the prayer, "The Morning Offering" is so important. In that prayer we offer every single thing we do each day to God. In that, everything we do becomes redemptive. As a result, we do everything for the love of God. This is a great benefit for us as it helps us to become holy.

Consider also the role of the sacraments. Every sacrament places the very Life of God, Sanctifying Grace, into our souls. The more we receive the sacraments, especially Reconciliation and Eucharist, the more of God's Life we possess. We gradually become holier and holier as we receive them. At the moment of our death, we want to have reached a high level of holiness so that we can be admitted into Heaven immediately, without the need for Purgatory. The Grace we have received in the sacraments can guarantee that kind of holiness as long as we desired it and cooperated with it. In short, we are very wise to avail of all of the help that the Catholic Church makes available to us in attaining holiness. These Graces can help us to avoid Purgatory (CCC 1436).

Indulgences Explained

It is the job of Holy Mother Church to guide you to Heaven and to help you go straight there. So I say again that the Church can help you avoid even Purgatory and go straight to Heaven. A great help that the Church gives to us in this regard is in the gaining of Indulgences. Remember that even though our sins may be forgiven; even though God forgives the *guilt* of our sin; we still owe a *dept*. We still owe a debt for our sins, called Temporal Punishment. We are still required to repair the damage our sins have caused. We must pay this debt, but how can we do it? What should we do? Think about it. You could have a lot of debt to pay. Many times, we don't even remember half of the sins we commit! How can we possibly make up for them all? It can become very overwhelming.

God knows it's hard and God knows we need help. This is why, in His great mercy, He has given His Church on earth the authority and the power to help us. The Church would like to give us a gift, an absolutely wonderful gift that will allow us to make up for our past sins by doing a few simple things. This gift is called an Indulgence. An Indulgence is a pardon of the Temporal Punishment (or debt) that we owe for the sins we have committed. The definition from the Catechism states "An Indulgence is a remission before God of the Temporal Punishment due to sins whose guilt has already been forgiven." Bishop Robert Baker, who is bishop of the Diocese of Birmingham in Alabama, teaches that many people do not ask for God's mercy and therefore end up in Purgatory needlessly.

Bishop Baker urges all Catholics to tell Jesus that we are sorry for our sins and to ask for His mercy. Jesus died in order to give us His mercy and He is eager to give it to us. Frequent confession and the gaining of Indulgences are a means for seeking His mercy.

There are two types of Indulgences: There are **Plenary Indulgences** and there are **Partial Indulgences**. Plenary Indulgences are *full* Indulgences. If we simply meet the requirements to gain a **Plenary Indulgence** we will be able to atone for all of the temporal punishment we owe for the forgiven sins we have committed up to that point in our entire life. If we gain a **Partial Indulgence**, it will atone for *some* or a *portion* of the temporal punishment we owe for the forgiven sins we have committed. Partial means part. So part of the temporal punishment; part of the debt we owe will be atoned for (CCC 1471).

Indulgences have Five Requirements

To gain an Indulgence, we simply have to meet the requirements or conditions of the Indulgence. Once we have done that faithfully, we can rest assured that the Indulgence was granted to us. Indulgences are a gift; a pardon of the Temporal Punishment or debt that we owe for the sins we have committed. Keep in mind that first our sins must be forgiven. Indulgences help us pay the debt that we owe for forgiven sin.

By offering a Plenary Indulgence to us, the Church presents all Catholics with an opportunity to purify our soul right here on earth. We can purify our soul right here on earth, instead of waiting until we reach Purgatory. In fact, we can purify our soul right here and completely avoid Purgatory all together, as long as we are very serious about this. We can obtain a Plenary

Indulgence once each day. We can obtain a Partial Indulgence many, many times each day.

1) To gain an Indulgence the Catholic must first be in a state of grace. In other words, the Catholic must not be guilty of any Mortal Sin. This means that if we have committed any Mortal Sin, we must confess it before we can seek to gain an Indulgence.

2) Second, the person must have no attachment to sin, either Mortal or Venial. This means that the person has to profess in their hearts that they do not want to sin and that they are going to avoid all sin and try their best to not sin any more. Addictions to sinful things must be first given up.

3) Third, the person must make a good confession to a priest within 21 days before or after the day that the Indulgence is sought.

4) Fourth, the person must receive Holy Communion also within 21 days either before or after the day the Indulgence is sought. Each Indulgence requires that you receive the Eucharist.

5) Fifth, the person must pray for the intentions of the Holy Father usually by praying one Our Father, one Hail Mary, and one Glory Be. Other prayers may be substituted.

Lastly, the person does the task that grants the Indulgence and has the intention of gaining the Indulgence. This could be praying the Rosary in a church; making the Stations of the Cross; praying in the presence of the Blessed Sacrament; reading and meditating upon Scripture. A complete list of Plenary and Partial Indulgences is provided in the next section entitled: "A Handbook on Indulgences." There you can follow the directions and seek to gain an Indulgence on your own.

How Can the Church Grant Indulgences?

How can the Catholic Church simply tell Catholics that if they meet these requirements the debt they owe for their past sins will be paid? First we have to understand that when Jesus died for us on the cross; healed people; taught people; and all the other good works He performed; He built an inexhaustible "Treasury of Graces." What Jesus did for us is simply immeasurable! To a lesser degree, the good works of our Blessed Mother Mary and all the Saints are also part of this Treasury of Graces. We too can contribute to this Treasury by our prayers, works, sacrifices, and sufferings by offering them to God. The Church therefore possesses this Treasury of Graces.

The Pope is the Vicar of Christ here on earth. He has been given the 'Keys to the Kingdom' by Jesus. Our Lord granted him the power to "bind and loose." Our Holy Father the Pope can therefore draw upon this Treasury of Merit and grant the tremendous privilege of a Plenary Indulgence to us. When our Holy Father grants an Indulgence to us, he is acting on his spiritual authority to do it. He certainly has the authority to grant these Indulgences to us. When the Holy Father does grant an Indulgence, it is also an act of charity and compassion for us. Let us be grateful and accept this gift.

Pray for the Dead

The souls in Purgatory desperately need our prayers. It is very important that we do not forget our deceased loved ones who may be in Purgatory. It is better for us to assume that they are in Purgatory and continue to pray for them than to assume they are in Heaven and abandon them while they need us. They benefit mostly by having the Holy Sacrifice of the Mass offered for them. If they are already in Heaven, do not worry. The Mass being offered will benefit someone else. It never goes to waste (CCC 1079).

To have a Mass offered for a deceased loved one, simply go to any Catholic Church and tell them that you want to have a Mass offered for a deceased loved one. They have a calendar for this and can give you a list of Mass times and dates that are available. Choose a date and time that is good for you, because you will want to attend that Mass. It is customary to pay a sum of money, usually $10.00. However, the amount paid is really up to you. This money is simply a stipend paid to the priest who offers the Mass for your deceased loved one. The priest is therefore required to offer the Mass for the person scheduled and you have a guarantee that it will be done.

Souls in Purgatory also benefit when we gain a Plenary Indulgences for them. Simply gain a Plenary Indulgence as you normally would and offer it to God for one or all of your deceased loved ones. The Indulgence that helps them the most is the Stations of the Cross. I recommend a book entitled, "The Way of the Cross for the Holy Souls in Purgatory" by Susan Tassone. It is available from Our Sunday Visitor at www.osv.com. This book is a meditation on the Stations of the Cross that you can do on your own by simply walking from one station to the next in any Catholic Church. It is truly a beautiful devotion. Some mornings I set my alarm to awake one half hour before I actually need to. That way I can do this devotion and gain an Indulgence for my deceased relatives. I greatly benefit from this, because it brings me closer to Jesus every time I do it. At the same time I am helping those who were near and dear to me in life.

There is a prayer that we as Catholics say for our deceased loved ones. This is a great prayer to pray every day. Name your relatives that are deceased and pray: *"Eternal rest grant unto them, O Lord. And let perpetual light shine upon them.*

May their souls and the souls of all the faithfully departed,
through the mercy of God, rest in peace. Amen."

All the information contained in this book on the subject of Indulgences can be found in <u>The Handbook of Indulgences Norms and Grants</u> published by "Catholic Book Publishing Corp. New York.

A Word About "the Selling of Indulgences"

One of Martin Luther's biggest complaints with the Church involved what he termed as the "selling of Indulgences." I want to make it perfectly clear that one could never "buy" Indulgences. One of the choices in gaining an Indulgence at the time was the giving of alms. One had the option of gaining an Indulgence by making a charitable contribution. Many charitable contributions were made at the time for the building of Saint Peter's Basilica in Rome. There were no outright selling of Indulgences. To give money to God or to the poor is a praiseworthy act when it is done with the right motives. Most people at the time understood this.

In 1567 the Council of Trent instituted reforms in the practice of granting indulgences. Because of the confusion involving the granting of Indulgences for the giving of alms, Pope Pius V canceled all grants of indulgences involving any fees or other financial transactions.

The evangelical historian Karl August Meissinger said of Martin Luther: "If Luther returned today, he would find to his astonishment a Roman Catholic Church which he would never have attacked in her present aspect. Above all he would see that not one of the abuses which were the actual occasion of his break with Rome remains in existence."

Recommended Reading on Purgatory:

-<u>Hungry Souls</u> by Gerard J M Van Den AArdweg
-<u>An Unpublished Manuscript on Purgatory</u>
-<u>After Life</u> by Michael H. Brown
-<u>The Amazing Secret of the Souls in Purgatory</u> by Sister Emmanuel of Medjugorje

A Handbook for Gaining Indulgences

Full Definition of Indulgences

An Indulgence is the remission before God, of the **Temporal Punishment** due to sins whose guilt has already been forgiven, which the faithful Christian who is duly disposed gains under certain defined conditions through the Church's help when, as a minister of redemption, she dispenses and applies with authority the treasury of the satisfactions won by Christ and the saints.

An Explanation of Indulgences

There are two consequences for every sin we commit. One is **Guilt** and the other is **Temporal Punishment**. When we confess a sin and are sorry for committing it, God forgives the **guilt** of that sin. We are no longer guilty. However, we still owe a **debt** for that sin. We are still required to repair the damage that sin caused in the world. We are therefore required to make reparation for that sin. Another way of saying this is that we owe a debt for the sin. This debt that we owe is called **Temporal Punishment**.

Indulgences are gifts or pardons that the Church gives to us in order to lessen the Temporal Punishment that we owe to make up for the forgiven sins we have committed. The Church gives us a task to complete and some conditions to follow. If we follow the conditions and complete the task, we gain or obtain the Indulgence. This Indulgence either atones for all Temporal Punishment or part of it.

Two Types of Indulgences

There are two types of Indulgences, Plenary and Partial. **Plenary Indulgences** atone for from all of the Temporal Punishment or all of the debt that we owe for all of the forgiven sins we have ever committed up until that time. **Partial Indulgences** atone for some of the Temporal Punishment or some of the debt that we owe for the forgiven sins we have committed.

A person can gain or obtain one Plenary Indulgence per day. A person can gain many Partial Indulgences each day.

The Church as the Authority to Grant Indulgences

What Jesus has done for us is immeasurable. Jesus' work of redemption on the cross has built an infinite 'Treasury of Graces,' because His work of redemption is infinite in itself. To a lesser degree, the Blessed Virgin Mary has contributed to this Treasury of Graces by her good works throughout her life and the way she cooperated with God's plan of salvation. The Saints (to an even lesser degree) helped to contribute to this Treasury of Graces by their good works. We too can contribute to this Treasury by our prayers, works, sacrifices, and sufferings by offering them to God.

So the Church possesses this infinite Treasury of Graces filled with the works of Christ, filled with the works of Our Lady, filled with the works of the saints, and filled with our good works. Our Holy Father, the Pope, who is vicar of Christ here on earth, who has been given the 'Keys to the Kingdom' and the power to 'Bind and Loose,' can draw upon this Treasury of Graces and grant the tremendous privilege of a Plenary Indulgence to us.

When our Holy Father grants an Indulgence to us, he is acting on his spiritual authority to do it. He has the authority to grant these Indulgences to us. When the Holy Father, the Pope, grants an Indulgence, it is also an act of charity and compassion toward us. He grants it to us because he loves us and he wants to encourage us to continue on our path toward Heaven. An Indulgence is truly a gift that is given to us.

Five Conditions that Must be Met to Obtain an Indulgence

In order to receive an Indulgence, the following five conditions must be fulfilled:

1) The Catholic must be in a state of Grace—in other words, not guilty of any Mortal Sin. *(If the Catholic is guilty of a Mortal Sin, he or she must confess the sin and receive absolution by a priest.)*

2) The Catholic must have no attachment to sin—the person feels in their heart that they do not want to sin anymore. *(If the Catholic is attached to a sin, he or she must first break this habit. Examples may include a drug or alcohol dependency or an addiction to pornography.)*

3) The Catholic must make a good confession to a priest within 21 days before the Indulgence is sought or within 21 days after the Indulgence is sought.

4) The Catholic must receive Holy Communion within 21 days before the Indulgence is sought or within 21 days after the Indulgence is sought. *(The Catholic must receive the Eucharist for each Plenary Indulgence sought.)*

5) The Catholic must pray for the intentions of the Holy Father (*usually by praying one Our Father, one Hail Mary, and one Glory Be*).

Plenary Indulgences Available Each Day

A Plenary Indulgence is granted each day to Catholics who complete one the following tasks and meet the above requirements.

- ❖ Visit the Blessed Sacrament for at least a half an hour.
- ❖ Pray the Stations of the Cross in a Catholic Church.
- ❖ Pray the Rosary in a Catholic Church, as a family, or in a prayer group.

❖ Read the Sacred Scriptures as spiritual reading from an approved Holy Bible with reverence for at least a half an hour.

Plenary Indulgences Available at Special Times of the Year

These Plenary Indulgences are available at only special times of the year and are granted to Catholics who complete any of the following tasks and meet the above requirements:

❖ Devoutly participate in a solemn Eucharistic Procession, held inside or outside the parish church, especially on the Solemnity of the Body and Blood of Christ (Feast of Corpus Christi).

❖ Receive Holy Communion for the very first time as a First Communicant or devoutly attend the First Holy Communion Mass of others.

❖ Spend at least three entire days in the spiritual exercises of a retreat.

❖ Devoutly participate in the Adoration of the Cross in the solemn liturgical action of Good Friday. (Good Friday evening service)

❖ Renew your baptismal vows in any legitimately approved formula at the celebration of the Easter Vigil or on the anniversary of your own Baptism.

Plenary Indulgence Available at the Point of Death

This Plenary Indulgence is granted at the point of death to any Catholic. If the person cannot fulfill the usual conditions personally, the Church dispenses the person from those requirements.

❖ Receive the Apostolic Pardon from a priest near the point of death.

If a priest is unavailable, Holy Mother Church generously grants this plenary Indulgence at the point of death provided the person has been in the habit of reciting some prayers during their lifetime and is in a state of grace.

Partial Indulgences Available Throughout the Year

A Partial Indulgence is granted to Catholics each day who complete any of the following tasks and meet the 5 Conditions. *Keep in mind that if one seeks to obtain a Plenary Indulgence but does not completely fulfill all of the conditions, he will still receive a Partial Indulgence.*

❖ While carrying out your duties and enduring the hardships of life, raise your mind in humble trust to God and make some sort of pious prayer such as "Jesus, I trust in you"; "Lord, have mercy on me, a sinner"; "Jesus, Mary, Joseph"; or "All for Jesus".

❖ Led by the spirit of faith, give compassionately of yourself or of your goods to serve others in need.

❖ In a spirit of penance, voluntarily abstain from something that is pleasurable. (Give up something)

❖ Give clear and open witness of your faith before others.

❖ Teach or study Christian doctrine.

❖ Visit the Blessed Sacrament for adoration.

❖ Make an act of thanksgiving after communion using an approved Church prayer such as the "Anima Christi".

❖ Examine your conscience with the purpose of amendment—a purpose of changing your ways and trying hard to sin no more.

❖ Recite the 'Act of Contrition' before going to Confession.

❖ Devoutly use articles of devotion that have been properly blessed by either a priest or deacon such as a Rosary, medals, and scapulars.

- For personal learning, devoutly spend time in mental prayer.
- Either at dawn, noon, or evening devoutly recite the "angelus" with its accompanying prayer.
- Devoutly address the Blessed Virgin Mary with some approved prayer such as the "Hail Mary," "Memorare," or "Hail Holy Queen."
- Devoutly invoke the care of your guardian angel with a duly approved prayer such as "The Prayer to the Guardian Angel"—Angel of God, my guardian dear…
- Devoutly recite approved litanies such as "The Litany of the Most Holy Name of Jesus," "The Most Sacred Heart of Jesus," or "The Blessed Virgin Mary."
- Devoutly offer grace before and after meals with prayers such as "Bless us, O Lord" prayer before meals and the "We give you thanks, Almighty God" prayer after meals.
- Devoutly sign yourself with the Sign of the Cross using the customary words, "In the name of the Father, and of the Son, and of the Holy Spirit."
- Recite an Act of Faith, Hope, and Love in any legitimate formula.
- Recite the Apostles' Creed or the Nicene Creed.

Indulgences Granted to Those in Purgatory

Indulgences can be obtained for yourself or you can obtain them for someone who is in Purgatory. Any Indulgence can be given to those in Purgatory, but there is a Plenary and Partial Indulgence that can only be applied to those in Purgatory:

Plenary Indulgence only for those in Purgatory: On any or each day from November 1st to the 8th devoutly visit a cemetery and pray for the departed.

Partial Indulgence: Visit a cemetery and pray for the deceased any day of the year.

XVIII.   Hell

Why Do We Believe in Hell?

Why do we as Catholics believe in the existence of Hell? "We believe in the existence of Hell because the Church teaches that Hell truly exists. Jesus taught the existence of Hell. The Apostles continued to teach the existence of Hell. And the Bible, the inspired Word of God, teaches the existence of Hell. There is more on the subject of Hell in the Gospels than anywhere else in the Bible. Jesus spoke more about Hell than He did Heaven. So first and foremost, we believe in the existence of Hell because it was taught by Christ and transmitted down through the centuries by the Apostles in the New Testament and by their successors.

If you read all four gospels, you see that Jesus really tried to instill fear in people concerning Hell. He wanted them to be afraid of it so they would not end up there. Jesus compared Hell to Gehenna. Gehenna was a garbage dump outside of Jerusalem that burned 24 hours a day seven days a week. Jesus said that Hell was like Gehenna—always on fire (CCC 1034).

Jesus spends much time in the Gospels warning people what will cause them to go to Hell. He teaches us well how to avoid Hell. In fact Jesus uses the word Hell 28 times in the Gospels and He speaks of eternal punishment 90 times!

Think about it. If our Lord spoke that much about Hell, not only do we have to believe that Hell exists; we have to realize that God is trying to warn us about it. He is trying to keep us from ending up there. We simply can't ignore this warning!

Scripture Passages Concerning Hell

Let's take a look at some Scripture passages concerning Hell. In Matthew Chapter 3: 7-10, John the Baptist said, "Produce good fruit. Even now the ax lies at the root of the trees. Every tree that does not bear good fruit will be cut down and thrown into the fire." Do you suppose John was speaking literally about trees? No. He is talking about people who do not produce good fruit; people who do not do good works. What is this fire they will be thrown into? Isn't it Hell?

There is also the Parable of the "Wheat and Weeds" in the 13th chapter of Matthew's Gospel verses 24-30. Jesus says, "The Kingdom of God is like a man who planted good seeds in his fields, but his enemy came and planted weeds all through the wheat. In this way, both the wheat and the weeds grew up together. His workers came and asked, 'Should we pull the weeds up?' But the man said, 'No, do not pull the weeds up, because you might also pull up the wheat. Let's wait until the harvest.' At harvest time the man gave the instructions to bind the weeds together for burning and to place the wheat into his barn."

When the disciples of Jesus were alone with Him, they asked Him to explain this parable saying, "What does this mean?" Jesus answered them saying that the **man who plants** the seeds is the Son of Man—or in other words Jesus, Himself. The **good seeds** are the children of God—those who love and obey God. The **weeds** are the children of the evil one—Satan. The **enemy** who plants the weeds is Satan, himself. The **harvest** is the end of the world. The **workers** are the angels. All those who cause others to sin and all evil doers will be collected and thrown into Hell. The righteous will be welcomed into Heaven (Matt 13:36-43).

There is also Matthew Chapter 10:28 where we read: "Do not be afraid of those who kill the body but cannot kill the soul.

Rather, be afraid of the one who can destroy both soul and body in Gehenna." Who can do that? Who can destroy both body and soul in Gehenna? Only God can do that. Jesus is saying that we should have a healthy "Fear of the Lord" or a feeling of "wonder and awe" toward our God. This is true, but many people show very little respect for God and His authority. They speak His name in vain; they curse God. They blame Him for every bad thing that happens in their lives. They sin against Him and live any kind of lifestyle they please. They think that no matter what they do God will welcome them into Heaven, because He is all merciful. God is all merciful, but He is also completely just. In order to receive His mercy, we must repent of our sins and desire His mercy. If we repent, we will be forgiven, but if we persist in our sin, in a state of impenitence, we will receive justice. We cannot be forgiven if we are not sorry.

In Matthew Chapter five starting with verse 30 Jesus says, "If your right eye causes you to sin, tear it out and throw it away. It is better for you to lose your eye than have your whole body thrown into Gehenna. And if your right hand causes you to sin, cut it off and throw it away. It is better for you to lose your hand than to have your whole body go into Gehenna."

There are many, many more examples Jesus gave of Hell and eternal punishment, but we cannot possibly list them all here. Simply understand this: If we were to deny and reject the Church's teaching on Hell; If we were to say, "I just don't believe Hell really exists;" or "I believe everyone goes to Heaven;" we would be denying and rejecting an essential part of the Bible's message and we would make a liar out of God. After all it is Jesus who declares, "Depart from me you accursed into everlasting fire which was prepared for the devil and his angels" (Matt 25:41).

No One Wants to Hear about "Hell"

It is true that our soul is going to live forever, long after our body dies. This knowledge should cause us to focus on the state of our spirituality. We are always concerned with our bodies and what our bodies want. We do need to take care of our bodies, this is true. But we must give priority to our spiritual growth. We must cease to live solely by our physical lives and begin to live by our spiritual lives. Saint Paul called us to live by the 'Spirit' instead of by the flesh (Gal 5:16-17). After all, who is going to make sure that our soul reaches Heaven? That is our own responsibility. *We* have to make sure that *we* get to Heaven by choosing the *good* and avoiding the *bad*. We have to feed our souls the way we feed our bodies. Understand clearly, you are not a body that has a soul. You are a soul that has a body (CCC 363-364).

What we do today determines where we will spend eternity. Our choices for eternity are either Heaven or Hell. Most people don't like to talk about Hell. The Church used to talk about Hell a lot more often, but because nobody likes to talk about it, we tend to avoid it. The fact is we avoid it way too much. We avoid it to the point where people have begun to think that Hell does not exist and that Satan is not real. Nothing could be further from the truth. Most Christians, however, still believe that Hell exists. It's just that they believe very few people actually go there. They believe that only those who commit murder and such, go to Hell. Well, let us examine the words of Jesus. In Matthew 7:13-14 Jesus says, "Enter through the narrow gate, for the gate is wide and the road broad that leads to destruction and those who enter it are many. How narrow the gate and constricted the road that leads to life. And those who find it are few." Our society acts as though the opposite were true. We seem to proceed as if the road to Heaven is broad and the gate wide, while the road to Hell is constricted and the gate narrow. This is not what Jesus taught.

It's not easy to hear the truth about Hell, but be glad that at least someone told you the truth. It is far better to know the truth now, rather than to learn about it when it is too late.

Satan

Satan's greatest accomplishment has been to convince people that he doesn't exist. This is a lie. Satan does exist and it is his mission to ruin each and every soul created by God (CCC 414). Before God created man, He created Angels. Angels are pure spirits. In other words, they have no bodies. It is true that people have seen angels and they have appeared in bodily form and looked like men. That is because God wanted them to take on a human form. The truth is, angels are spirit only, whereas we are spirit and body (CCC 350).

The second thing that is true about angels is that they are higher beings than we are. They are actually more like God than they are like us. They are of a higher intelligence, beauty, and power. Angels are brilliant in mind and have a *Free Will*. They live face to face with God. However, they rank far below God in power and dignity (CCC 329).

They, like us, were created to know God, to love God, and to serve God. They are grouped into nine choirs. The highest among them are the Seraphim and Cherubim. Every one of us has a guardian angel; an angel assigned to us to watch over us and to guide us (CCC 336).

After God created the angels, not all of them remained faithful to Him. Satan, or Lucifer, was a Seraphim, which means, "burning angel." He was one of the highest angels created. Satan, or Lucifer, became what we call a "Fallen Angel." How?

The common consensus of the theologians, and therefore the common consensus of Catholic theology, states that after the angels were created, but before they saw the Beatific Vision (before they saw God), the angels were tested. How did God test them? God the Father revealed to the angels that at some time in the future, God the Son would become a man. With this revelation, Lucifer declared, "I will not serve." As a high angel, Lucifer refused to lower himself to be the servant of a 'God-man'. Man was lower than Lucifer in the order of creation and he refused to serve someone lower than himself. Lucifer thought of himself as equal to God. This pride caused him to fall.

The majority of the angels were victorious in their moral test. They accepted the incarnation; the Second Person of the Trinity becoming man, and they received the Beatific Vision. However, some angels, out of pride, followed Lucifer.

Lucifer became so infatuated with himself that he forgot that he was dependent on God for his very life. Lucifer has not life in himself; he was created. He gets life from the same place we do, God. Just the same he rebelled against God with the words, "I will not serve!" At this, an angel of the eighth choir, the choir of Archangels, cried out, "Who is like unto God?" meaning, "Who is equal to God?" And that is the exact meaning of the Hebrew word "Mikha'el" where this angel got his name "Michael." God then brought Michael forward and made of him the commander of the heavenly hosts. A great battle was then fought between Michael and his angels and the Great Dragon, Lucifer and his angels. This can be found in the Book of Revelation chapter 12.

Lucifer did not prevail. He did not win the battle that took place in Heaven and he was cast down to the earth and his angels were cast down with him. With these angels we have the beginning of Hell, an eternal separation from God. These fallen angels have the desire to bring down as many human beings as they can into the state of perpetual separation from God. There is a saying that goes like this: "The corruption of the best is the worst." It is only when the very best is corrupted that you have the potential for the very worst. It is only when the highest angel rebels against God that you create the possibility for Satan, the worst creature, and Hell, the worst creaturely condition. If Lucifer could not be like God, then he desires other creatures to experience this same distance from God.

Lucifer again, was a Seraphim, a burning angel. In his rebellion against God, he lost all of his glory, but none of his nature. He is disgraced and fallen, but he never ceases to be what God created him to be, "a burning one." So he possesses no glory, but he continues to burn. He is the lowest of all creatures.

Sin unites us to Lucifer

Lucifer sinned against the infinite dignity and glory of the living God. When we commit Mortal Sin, we do the exact same. All sin turns us from God and unites us to Satan. That is why Hell is the logical result of turning away from God. It is the result of following the example of Satan and uniting ourselves with the misdeeds of the demons. That is why we call it Mortal Sin, because of its mortal consequences. It kills God's Life in us and deprives us of God's presence. When we persist in that sin in a state of impenitence, it is a rejection of God's law and more importantly a rejection of His mercy. This is a mercy that we do not deserve. It is a mercy that God poured out upon us by sending us Jesus Christ. God, in Jesus, paid a debt He didn't owe, because we owed a debt we couldn't pay. To turn away from mercy with final impenitence and hardness of heart is to sin against the infinite majesty, glory, and justice of God. Even more so, we sin against the merciful love of God. Rejecting God and wanting our own will to be done and not God's will to be done, unites us to Lucifer. We never want to unite ourselves to him.

Is Hell a Physical Place or a State of Being?

Does Hell exist as a physical place of punishment? Or, is it simply a state of being; a separation from God? The Church teaches that Hell is a state where the souls of the damned suffer with the devils. All the souls in Hell suffer. How badly they suffer depends on how bad their behavior was while they were on earth (CCC 1035).

All those in Hell suffer the misery of being in the company of the devils and also in the company of all the evil people who lived on the earth. In 1 John 2:11 we read, "He who hates his brother walks in darkness." Hell is that *place* where there is only darkness. This is because Hell is the absence of love and the absence of Jesus who is the 'Light of the World.' It is the absence of God.

People often ask, "Where is Hell?" We must really think of Hell as a state of being rather than a place. This is hard for us because we have bodies and our bodies are always 'somewhere.' Theologians and Scripture scholars have sometimes theorized that Hell may possibly exist inside the earth. They get this idea because of the story found in the Book of Numbers chapter 16. When the Israelites were wandering in the desert and getting their instruction from Moses, two men by the names of Dathan and Abiram rebelled against Moses. They told Moses that they were not going to listen to him anymore and that he had no right to tell any of them what to do. This was wrong of them. Moses did have the right to tell them what to do, because God had chosen Moses to lead His people. God spoke to Moses and God told Moses what to tell the people. Moses' authority was real. Similarly, people today refuse to listen to our Holy Father, the Pope. Yet, his authority is every bit as real; given to him by Jesus after His Resurrection. Moses' authority is a foreshadowing of the Pope's authority today. This is another example of how the Old Testament foreshadows the New Testament which fulfills it. So obviously, God was very angry with Dathan and Abiram for rebelling against Moses. For in rejecting Moses, they were rejecting God. Because of their rebellion, God made the earth open up and swallow Dathan, Abiram and all their descendants and possessions. They went down to Hell alive. Here is the passage from the Book of Numbers: "The ground beneath them split open, and the earth opened its mouth and swallowed them and their families and all their possessions. They went down alive to the netherworld with all belonging to them. The earth closed over them and they perished from the community. All the Israelites near them fled shrieking, 'The earth might swallow us too!'"

Does this mean that Hell exists inside of the earth? Certainly not. It is mere speculation. And as I mentioned earlier, we should think of Hell as a state of being rather than a place. A wise saint by the name of Saint John Chrysostom once said, "We must not ask where Hell is, but instead we must ask how we are to avoid going there." How true! Each of us should be more concerned with avoiding Hell and doing what is good.

What is Hell?

The Catechism of the Catholic Church defines Hell as: "The state of definitive self-exclusion from communion with God and the blessed reserved for those who refuse by their own free choice to believe and be converted from sin, even to the end of their lives" (CCC Glossary p.881). Hell is the eternal separation from God. Hell is a state of being to which those who are wicked are condemned. These wicked souls are not allowed to ever lay eyes on God and they are in dreadful torments for all eternity. The chief punishment of Hell is that the person is separated from God forever. We call this "the Pain of Loss." This separation from God causes the soul to suffer the most, because human beings are created for God alone. We were truly created for God and to be with God. When we finally reach Him, we will have found complete happiness (CCC 1035). This is not some extrinsic pain that God inflicts and maintains. It is the natural and logical consequence of what happens to people who continuously reject God. God simply gives the person what they want: a life without Him.

Imagine a soul that cannot reach God and is completely separated from Him forever. Instead of finding complete happiness, that soul finds complete misery. God is love; pure love. So imagine a place where there is no love. There is nothing worse than this "pain of loss." Physical pain doesn't even compare to how it feels to lose God completely. There is no hope, because nothing can get a person out of Hell once they choose it. The person remains there literally for eternity.

Besides this, "Pain of Loss," the souls in Hell suffer in various other ways too. These souls can see the devil as he really is: more horrible than we can imagine, and yet they must remain with him. They also suffer from shame, regret, despair and also the pain of the senses or what we call "the Pain of Sense". With the pain of the senses, the lost souls are continually tormented in all of their five senses. Whereas the "Pain of Loss" is felt on the inside, the "Pain of Sense" is felt on the outside. This is the fire. Understand though that the fire of Hell is totally different than fire as we know it. The fire of Hell does not give off any light. Therefore the person remains in darkness. Also the fire of Hell does not consume anything it burns. It causes greater pain than the fire of this earth because it affects both the body and the soul.

In this life all of the knowledge of God and truth are significantly veiled. After our death, the veil is removed and we can see God and truth as they really are. By turning to Christ in this life, we gradually become more like Him in His great beauty. However, if we turn to sin and the devil we will likewise become more like him in his extreme horror and ugliness. What we become through our beliefs and actions in this life is revealed with utter clarity after death.

Our Lady of Fatima

The Blessed Virgin Mary appeared to three children in Fatima Portugal in 1917. You may have heard of, "Our Lady of Fatima." In this apparition, the Blessed Virgin Mary showed three children visions. One vision that she showed to the children was a vision of Hell. The oldest child, Lucia Santos, became a religious sister and later recorded what she saw in this vision of Hell. Sister Lucia said this: "Our Lady showed us a great sea of fire which seemed to be under the earth. Plunged in this fire were demons and souls in human form, like transparent burning embers, all blackened or burnished bronze. They were floating about and were raised into the air by the flames that issued from within themselves together with great clouds of smoke. They would fall back on every side like sparks in a huge fire, without weight or equilibrium. We could hear shrieks and groans of pain and despair, which horrified us and made us tremble with fear. The demons could be distinguished by their terrifying and repulsive likeness to frightful and unknown animals, all black and transparent. This vision lasted but an instant. How can we ever be grateful enough to our kind heavenly Mother, who had already prepared us by promising, in the first apparition, to take us to Heaven? Otherwise, I think we would have died of fear and terror" (Congregation for the Doctrine of the Faith, "The Message of Fatima" www.vatican.va).

Which Souls go to Hell?

Which souls go to Hell? The Catholic Church does not judge. God alone judges. However, the Church teaches that those who choose to live apart from God while on earth <u>and</u> die in a state of unrepentant Mortal Sin will go to Hell. Understand though, God does not send a person to Hell. They send themselves (CCC 1861).

Pope John Paul II said, "Hell is not a punishment imposed externally by God, but instead, it is the natural consequence of an unrepentant sinners choice to live apart from God." Those who go to Hell have clearly chosen Hell. God does not impose it. A person goes to Hell because he has chosen to live apart from God; he is not sorry for his sins; he does not want to live in God's light. He has completely and utterly rejected God and His mercy. CS Lewis wrote, "The door to Hell is locked from the inside." Though they despise the torments of Hell, they would despise the presence of God in Heaven even more.

As each person dies he or she actually rushes to where they *want* to be. In a very real way each person chooses their own destiny over the course of their lifetime and, at the moment of death, embraces what has truly become their choice. The person simply keeps on living the same life for eternity that he had lived here on earth. If God is not the most important part of our lives now, how will He suddenly become the most important part of our lives when we die? Now is the time of mercy, but with death the time of mercy, the time to freely respond to the offer of salvation in Jesus, comes to an end.

St. Thomas Aquinas said that the sinner in Hell regrets his sin, but not because of guilt, but because of its terrifying consequences. That is why a sinner in Hell resents God, but he won't repent to God. If there was a moment of contrition (sorrow for sin) in a sinner in Hell, it would instantly set him loose to fly upward into God's presence. As Saint Catherine of Siena has said, "One drop of contrition could empty Hell."

What about the person who commits Mortal Sin up until his death bed and then at the last moment repents? At the last moment of a person's life, God's mercy will hear the faintest cry; the weakest whisper of repentance that comes from the hardest sinner. That's how great God's mercy is. We must remember though, once we die, we pass into a spiritual condition like that of the angels. We have sealed our fate. We have finalized our everlasting existence. Why? Because the ability to change and to help ourselves has come to an end. It is then that the veil is lifted and our Free Will is gone. We have no choice but to believe in God for we can see Him as He truly is.

God Could Never Send Anyone to an Eternity of Punishment; Right?

People say, "God is so good and He is so merciful. He could never send anyone to an eternity of punishment. God made all of us for Him. He made all of us for Heaven. Why would He let any of us spend eternity in Hell?"

The problem is that people who say these things are simply confused. They think that God sends people to Hell and that is simply not true. As I said before, God doesn't send anyone to Hell. Sinners send themselves. They literally choose Hell.

We have the freedom to choose God, but we also have the freedom to refuse God. Since God is pure love, to refuse God is to cut ourselves off from that love; that life; that God alone is. God is infinitely holy and He is infinitely just. He is perfect love. Sinning against God is not like sinning against your brother or your sister. One Mortal Sin against God is infinitely serious! It deserves a punishment immeasurably worse than life in prison; immeasurably worse than anything you or I can think of.

God created men and women with a Free Will and God takes Free Will very seriously. So seriously, that He does not force anyone to be saved, but leaves every person the option of saying, "No" to Him (CCC 1743).

If you turn your back on God, He will not stop you. He will allow you to walk away from Him; walk away from Him all the way to Hell. He hates it. He wishes you would choose Him, but He will not stop you. God is not going to drag anyone kicking and screaming into Heaven. We have a Free Will. If we want Heaven, then we have to choose Heaven.

We must take God seriously when He warns us of the possibility of rejecting by Him for all Eternity. God doesn't trick people into Hell. They don't go blindfolded into Hell. They go to Hell with both eyes open. God doesn't send people to Hell. Our sins; our impenitence; and our rejection of God, send us to Hell. To avoid Hell, we have to choose to be pure; pure in mind, heart, and body.

Resurrection of the Body

Someday your body will join your soul wherever it has been sent for all eternity. In the Apostles Creed, we recite, "I believe in the resurrection of the body and life everlasting." This means that at the end of the world, the human body is united with the soul. The body will share, either in the rewards or the punishment of the soul, just as it shared in our good or evil deeds on earth. So the Church teaches that there is a particular judgment when we die and that is individual—we will either go to Heaven; Purgatory first and then Heaven; or Hell. Then a final judgment will take place at the end of the world and that is either Heaven or Hell. Don't think that this is a second chance. This final judgment will not change the judgment that takes place at the moment of our death (CCC 997-998).

We Must Take God at His Word

The idea of an Eternal Hell and everlasting punishment is not a popular concept in this modern world. But just because people don't like the idea does not mean they can dismiss it and say it is not so. God Himself has told us that Hell exists and He has told us that Hell exists for our own benefit. We would be smart to not forget it exists and do all we can to avoid it.

The Church wants to guide us to Heaven and help us to think often about the four last things: Death; Judgment; Heaven; and Hell. It is not merciful to tell someone that they are doing just fine when all the while they continue to persist in Mortal Sin. This is why the Church constantly warns us to be careful not to sin. What if our friend was committing adultery and we found out about it. Instead of telling him not to do this, we encourage our friend to continue to be unfaithful. What if we said, "Good for you! Do whatever makes you happy."? We would be allowing our friend; a person whom we care about and even love; to lead a life toward Hell. That's not merciful. That is merci—less! If you love someone, you should want what is best for him. Isn't eternal happiness best for him? Do you want your friends to end up in Hell? Is that what is best for them? Give good advice to your friends and loved ones. Lead them toward Heaven. And choose the kind of friends that will lead you to Heaven.

The Truth from the Catechism

"We cannot be united with God unless we freely choose to love Him. We cannot love God if we sin gravely against Him; against our neighbor; or against ourselves. As Saint John said, He who does not love remains in death. Our Lord warns us that we will be separated from Him if we fail to meet the serious needs of the poor. If we die in a state of Mortal Sin without repenting and accepting God's merciful love, we will remain separated from Him forever. This is not because God chooses it, but because we choose it" (CCC 1033).

Let us set our sights on Heaven and keep a constant course in that direction.

XIX. The Communion of Saints

What is the Communion of Saints?

The word "communion" means "union with." We believe that there exists a union, a fellowship among all souls in whom dwells the Holy Spirit, the Spirit of Christ. We believe that a union exists in all those who have the Life of God, Sanctifying Grace, in their souls. We are in union with all those who belong to the Church no matter where they may be. This union or fellowship therefore, includes ourselves, members of the Church here upon earth, those souls in Purgatory, and the saints in Heaven.

Our branch of the communion of saints is called the "Church Militant." Those of us who are members of the Church on earth are called the Church Militant, because we are part of the Church that is still struggling; still fighting against sin and evil. We must continue to "fight the good fight."

The souls in Purgatory are also members of the communion of saints. They are established in grace forever, even though their minor sins and debts of penance still have to be purged away. They cannot see God, but the Holy Spirit is in them and with them, never again to be lost. We refer to this branch of the Church as the "Church Suffering."

Finally there is the "Church Triumphant." It is made up of all the souls of the blessed in Heaven. This is the everlasting Church; the eternal Church. They have finished the good fight and have arrived triumphantly into bliss of Heaven.

What Does the Communion of Saints Mean in Practice?

The communion of saints means that all of us who are united in Christ—the saints in Heaven, the souls in Purgatory, and we upon the earth—must be mindful of the needs of one another. The saints in Heaven are not so rapt in their own bliss that they forget the souls they have left behind. In fact, they could never forget. Their perfect love for God includes a love for all the souls whom God has made; all the souls in whom God Himself dwells; all the souls for whom Jesus died. The saints love those whom God loves. The love that the blessed in Heaven have for the souls in Purgatory and the souls on earth is not a passive love. Instead it is an active love. This is easy to understand. Those of us who know God and love God with all our hearts and are becoming holy, find it hard to hold back that knowledge and love. Even though we are imperfect, we want to share our faith with others and lead them to that same knowledge and love. How much more would the souls in Heaven feel this way in their perfect union with Christ! The saints long to help souls reach Heaven. And if the prayer of a good man on earth has power with God, there is no estimating the power of the prayers which the saints offer for us.

The saints in Heaven pray for the souls in Purgatory and for us. We in return ask for their prayers and are grateful for them. We give them honor and reverence and this pleases God. You see, the saints are masterpieces of God's grace. When we honor them, we are honoring their maker, their sanctifier, and their redeemer. Just as an artist is honored when his painting is praised, God is honored when His saints are praised. For we do not reach Heaven on our own, but only by the grace of God. He accomplishes every good thing we do.

It is worth remembering that when we honor the saints, we are undoubtedly honoring many of our own loved ones who are now with God in Heaven. Every soul in Heaven is a saint, not just the canonized ones. That is why the Church dedicates one day to the honor of the whole Church Triumphant, the Feast of All Saints on November 1.

As members of the communion of saints, we upon the earth also pray for the suffering souls in Purgatory. They cannot help themselves now; their time for receiving the grace and mercy of God is over. But we can relieve their sufferings and speed them on to Heaven by our prayers for them, by the Masses we offer for them, and by the Indulgences we gain for them. God is concerned about these souls. It is His *will* that we be concerned for them and help them as much as we are able.

The souls in Purgatory can pray for us as well. Some theologians say that their prayers are especially heard by God because they are so fervently made. Moreover, those whom we pray for in Purgatory, will remember us greatly as they reach Heaven. They will not forget those whose prayers helped them to gain entrance into the Kingdom of God.

It is obvious that we upon the earth must also pray for and help one another if we are to be faithful to our obligations as members of the communion of saints. Love of neighbor is love of God. Performing the Corporal and Spiritual Works of Mercy help us to grow in this virtue of love.

Remembering and Honoring the Saints is Biblical

Some people criticize Catholics for honoring the saints, but it is biblical to do so. The eleventh chapter of Hebrews is a "verbal memorial" in honor of the holy men and women of the Old Testament. It honors the faith of Abel, Enoch, Noah, Abraham, Isaac, Jacob, Joseph, Moses, Rahab, Gideon, Barak, Samson, Jephthah, David, Samuel and the prophets. Hebrews 13:7 advises: "Remember your leaders who spoke the word of God to you. Consider the outcome of their way of life and imitate their faith."

As a country we honor great people of the past. In our nation's capital the Washington Monument, the Lincoln

Memorial, and many other shrines and statues have been build honoring government and military leaders. Catholics name churches after saints and erect statues to honor spiritual leaders. God is not against statues and even commanded the Jews to make them (Exodus 25:18-21; 1 Kings 6:23-35).

Asking the saints to pray for us is also biblical. In the Book of Revelation, the saints in Heaven offer our prayers to God: "Each of the elders held a harp and gold bowls filled with incense, which are the prayers of the holy ones" (5:8). 2Maccabees 15:12-15 reports a vision in which the martyred high priest Onias and the prophet Jeremiah pray for the Jewish nation; the Jews believed that saints are aware of earthly events and pray for us. Moses and Elijah appear with Jesus at the Transfiguration and talk with Him about His coming Passion and death (Luke 9:28-36). Jesus speaks of the "joy in Heaven over one sinner who repents" (Luke 15:7). After the Resurrection of Jesus, saints appeared to people on earth (Matt 27:52-53). The Letter to the Hebrews compares life to a race we run while the great heroes of the past are in the stands cheering us on. "Therefore, since we are surrounded by so great a cloud of witnesses, let us persevere in running the race that lies before us" (Hebrews 12:1).

These passages illustrate the interaction between those in Heaven and those on earth. We should be aware of the presence and loving care of the saints. Those who are in Heaven are close to the knowledge and love of God and, therefore, are more aware of our needs and more devoted to us than they were on earth. We are never alone, for we live "in communion" with the saints.

Praying to the Saints

Sometimes Catholics are asked, "Why do you pray to the saints? Why don't you just pray directly to God?" It is important to make it clear that Catholic do pray directly to God. It is only on occasion that we pray to saints. Having said that, we should first note that the word "pray" is used in two different ways by Catholics. We "pray" to God as the source of all blessings. We "pray" to the saints in the sense that we ask them to pray with us and for us. This is illustrated in two prayers frequently said by Catholics. In the *Lord's Prayer*, we ask God to "give us this day our daily bread" and to "forgive us our trespasses." In the *Hail Mary*, we ask Mary to "pray for us sinners."

Catholics are sometimes criticized for "worshiping" the saints, especially Mary. We do not worship the saints. *Worship* and *adoration* are terms that refer to the act of acknowledging God as the Supreme Being. We as Catholics worship and adore God alone.

Why pray to the saints at all? The answer lies in the importance of prayer with others and for others. Jesus places a special importance in common prayer: "For where two or three are gathered together in my name, there am I in the midst of them" (Matt 18:20). Since there is a particular value in praying with others, and since the Bible shows that those in Heaven pray for us, it certainly makes sense for us to pray *with* the saints.

It also makes sense for us to ask them to pray *for* us. Paul wrote to the Colossians: "Persevere in prayer, being watchful in it with thanksgiving; at the same time, pray for us too" (4:2-3). Paul prayed directly to God, but he felt it was important to have others intercede for him. It is worth saying here that, just because someone is in Heaven does not mean they no longer have contact with us and cannot pray for us. Why would they suddenly be out of reach just because they have entered Heaven? If the prayers of those on earth have value, then how much more so the prayers of the saints who stand at the throne of God in Heaven!

It is very important to note that the prayers of others are needed, not to convince God to bless us, but to open us up to the blessings God wants us to receive. Since that is the case, the more intercessors we have on earth and in Heaven, the more we can be freed of the hindrances of sin and unbelief which keep us from receiving God's assistance.

We do pray directly to God and often. But that is not to say that we cannot ask the saints to pray for us. Our prayers to God take on new life and power when we join them to the prayers of the saints. Prayer to the saints "keeps us in touch" with them until we join them in Heaven.

The Canonization of Saints (CCC 828)

Canonization, the process the Church uses to name a saint, has been used since the tenth century. Starting with the first martyrs of the early Church around the year 100 A.D., saints were chosen by public acclaim. Though this was a more democratic way to recognize saints, some saints' stories were distorted by legend and some never existed. Gradually, the bishops and finally the Vatican took over authority for approving saints.

In 1983, Pope John Paul II made sweeping changes in the canonization procedure. The process begins after the death of a Catholic whom people regard as holy. Often, the process starts many years after death in order give perspective on the candidate. The local bishop investigates the candidate's life and writings for heroic virtue (or martyrdom) and orthodoxy of doctrine. Then a panel of theologians at the Vatican evaluates the candidate. After approval by the panel and cardinals of the Congregation for the Causes of Saints, the pope proclaims the candidate "venerable."

The next step, beatification, requires evidence of one miracle (except in the case of martyrs). Since miracles are considered proof that the person is in Heaven and can intercede for u. The miracle must take place after the candidate's death and as a result of a specific petition to the candidate. When the pope proclaims the candidate beatified or "blessed," the person can be venerated by a particular region or group of people with whom the person holds special importance. Only after a second miracle will the pope canonize the saint (this includes martyrs as well). The title of saint tells us that the person lived a holy life, is in Heaven, and is to be honored by the universal Church. Canonization does not "make" a person a saint; it recognizes what God has already done.

XX. Catholic Morality

The Authority of the Catholic Church

How do you and I know for sure what is morally right and what is morally wrong? Where does our sense of morality come from? Is this something that we as individuals decide for ourselves or is there something deeper behind it? I think that all of us know deep down that some actions are wrong. We know it to the very core of our being. It is somehow written in our DNA. We have all been given a conscience; an ability to judge right from wrong. Our parents have helped to fine tune our sense of morality and conscience. They began teaching us right from wrong when we were young children. Then, at the age of five or six we went off to school and we learned a little more about what is right and what is wrong, especially when dealing with others our own age. But let's admit it, there's an awful lot of confusion out there in the world isn't there? People just don't agree about what is morally right and what is morally wrong when it comes to a lot of issues that face us today. Many people just don't know who to believe, so they try to make up their own minds. In many cases they tend to change their minds depending on the circumstances. The truth is there doesn't seem to be a clear right and wrong to anything anymore. We are immersed in a society of relativism. We are even taught by society not to impose our views on others. What is wrong for one person may not be wrong for someone else, society teaches. Yet we have laws that prohibit certain kinds of behaviors, which tend to contradict that ideal altogether.

What society teaches and what churches teach seem to be opposites. We live in a society that makes fun of churches who tell us that a certain act is immoral. If we follow what our church teaches and avoid what our church says is wrong, people will literally make fun of that. Many people, therefore, tend to ignore what the Church teaches because they don't want to be laughed at or made fun of. Unfortunately, this is the kind of world we live in today.

Is it possible that there really is a clear cut morality in this world? Is it possible that we really don't have to fend for ourselves and try to figure everything out on our own? Yes, there is a clear cut morality. There is a clear cut morality, because we are not the ones who determine what is morally right and wrong. That job belongs to God and God alone. You and I really don't have to come up with our own set of morality. All we have to do is follow the moral law set for us by God (CCC 2420).

So how do you and I learn God's moral law? We learn it from the Church that God left in charge on this earth; The Catholic Church. The Catholic Church is the one place that we can come to hear the Truth. What is morally right and wrong is always clear; always consistent; and always rock solid. The Catholic Church has always been our sure guide down through the ages, because it is the Church started by Jesus. Jesus is the Way, the Truth, and the Life (John 14:6).

When Jesus ascended into Heaven, He did not leave us alone to fend for ourselves. Instead, Jesus left a Church in charge and He promised that the Holy Spirit would guide this Church and that the gates of Hell would never prevail against it (Matt 16:18). Jesus promised that the Church, He was leaving in charge, would guide all mankind until He comes again. The Catholic Church is that Church that Jesus promised.

What is the most important job of the Catholic Church? The job of the Church is to guide you and me to Heaven so that we can spend eternity with God and be completely happy forever. That is exactly what the Church does for us. The Church teaches us what we need to know to get to Heaven. The Church provides us with opportunities to grow in holiness by offering the sacraments to us so that we can fill our souls with God's Life— His Grace. The Church guides us morally so that we do not make the kind of wrong decisions that will cost us our eternal life. Jesus left a Church in charge so that this Church could and would guide us to Heaven; to all truth. This is a plain and simple straight forward fact. Why else would we need the Church and what could be more important for Jesus to leave behind? Nothing is more important than guiding us safely back to God from whom we came (CCC 851).

The problem today is that people do not understand that the Catholic Church has real authority on earth. Because of this, many people tend to make fun of and question the guidance that the Church gives to all of us here on earth. It is important for us to understand the words of the Bible clearly and to realize that these are God's words. Jesus said to His Apostles, the leaders of His Church, "Whoever hears you, hears me!" (Luke 10:16). The words, "Whoever hears you, hears me" are very strong words. The Apostles were given real authority; the authority to speak for Jesus! He knew that He would guide His Church so closely that literally when we hear the words of the Apostles, we hear the words of Jesus!

Jesus also said to His Apostles, "I give you the keys to the kingdom of Heaven" (Matt 16:19). These words have a meaning that makes reference to Old Testament Scripture. You see Jesus was referring to the Kingdom of David. In the Kingdom of David, the Chief Steward of the Kingdom was given the 'Keys to the Kingdom'. When a person is given the 'Keys,' he has been given great authority. If you have the keys, you are the one who is in charge! If you have the keys, you are the one who can unlock all the doors and run the place! In short, the one who holds the keys is the one who makes the decisions!

Jesus had truly given His Apostles the 'Keys to the Kingdom.' The original twelve Apostles handed those keys down to the next generation of Apostles. That generation handed the keys down to the next generation of Apostles and so on. For two thousand years those keys have been handed down. Our Bishops hold the keys! They have the authority. Therefore, we have the guarantee from Jesus that whoever hears the Apostles, hears Him. We have to understand that this authority had to be passed down and it was passed down. If Jesus did not want this authority passed down, we would have come to end the world by now. You and I are entitled to the same guarantee given to the early Christians; the guarantee that Christ is still leading His Church and will continue to lead His Church until He comes again in glory.

Jesus also said to His Apostles, "Whatever you bind on earth will be bound in Heaven and whatever you loosen on earth will stay loose in Heaven" (Matt 16:19). What did Jesus mean by this? Again this is Old Testament language. Basically it means that the Apostles have been given the authority to make binding and lasting decisions and those decisions are honored in Heaven!

Remember that Jesus also gave the Apostles the power to forgive sin, "If you forgive the sins of any, they are forgiven; if you retain the sins of any, they are retained" (John 20:23). Moreover, Jesus gave the apostles the power to offer sacrifice; the Eucharist. In 1 Corinthians 11:23-24 Paul says, "For I received from the Lord what I also delivered to you that the Lord Jesus on the night when He was betrayed took bread, and when He had given thanks, He broke it, and said, 'This is my body which is given up for you. Do this in remembrance of me.'" Jesus even gave the Apostles the power to discipline. In Matthew chapter 18 starting with verse 15 we read, "If your brother sins against you, go and tell him his fault, between you and him alone. If he listens to you, you have gained your brother. But if he does not listen, take one or two others along with you, that every word may be confirmed by the evidence of two or three witnesses. If he refuses to listen to them, <u>tell it to the Church, and if he refuses to listen even to the Church, let him be to you as a Gentile and a tax collector</u>."

Then Jesus did one other thing. He put one of the Apostles in charge of the others. Jesus put Peter in charge. Peter became the "Rock" that Jesus built the Church upon and Peter was made the official keeper of the keys. Peter is the one who actually holds the keys in his hands. Peter passed the keys down to Linus; Linus passed the keys to Cletus; Cletus passed the keys to Clement; Clement passed the keys to Avaristus and so on all the way to Pope Francis, our Pope today. Pope Francis is Peter.

Put all of this together and you will understand the authority of the Church well. "I say to you, Simon, son of Jonah, you are rock, and upon this rock I will build my Church, and the gates of hell shall not prevail against it. I will give you the keys to the Kingdom of Heaven, and whatever you bind on earth shall be bound in Heaven, and whatever you loose on earth shall be loosed in Heaven" (Matthew 16:17-19). "Whoever hears you, hears me" (Luke 10:16).

You will find it very comforting to know that in 2,000 years not one Pope has changed a single doctrine of our faith or a doctrine of our morality. They have simply preserved the teachings that were entrusted to them and they have passed them down safely to us. Understand clearly what this means. This means that what our Pope teaches today is the same as what Peter taught! Our faith is pure! It has been preserved! And the purity of it has been passed down. This is what Jesus meant when He said, "The Gates of Hell shall not prevail against it"; against the Church (CCC 85-86).

Think about it. What would happen if the Pope could change what we believe? It would be mass chaos wouldn't it? Our beliefs would change every time the College of Cardinals elected a new Pope! And how could that be? How could it be Jesus' Church if the doctrine and morals constantly changed? Instead, if it is truly Jesus' Church, the doctrines and morals cannot change; unless Christ Himself changes them. So you see, our Holy Father, the Pope, and our holy bishops in union with him, simply *safe guard* the deposit of Faith; the teachings that were given to us by Jesus Himself! The popes and the bishops keep the faith pure; they keep it safe; and they don't allow anyone to change it. That way it will always be kept safe and sound for the next generation. That is why we can trust our Catholic Faith.

So the Catholic Church, with the preserved teachings of Jesus, is here and available to you. The Catholic Church wants to guide your moral life so that it can help you to reach Heaven. If you think about it, this is a real gift from God. None of us has to wonder what is morally right or wrong. None of us has to wonder what real Truth is. None of us has to decide what is right and wrong for ourselves. We live in a crazy mixed up world that can't seem to agree upon morality. The Church has the answer to this moral dilemma. You and I can simply come to the Church and allow it to guide us. What a blessing to have the Truth!

The Acceptance of this Authority

Sadly, many people do not accept the authority of the Catholic Church. Even sadder is the fact that when you accept the authority of the Catholic Church and follow it, people will ridicule you. Nevertheless, I am asking you to accept the authority of the Catholic Church anyway; even if others deride you. I am asking you to believe that your Pope possesses the

'Keys to the Kingdom' and that those keys were given to him by Jesus Himself. I am asking you to believe this, because it is the Truth. It is absolutely the Truth.

Because the Pope holds the 'Keys to the Kingdom'; because Jesus promised that the 'Gates of Hell' would not prevail against His Church; we understand that when our Holy Father, the Pope, teaches on matters of faith and on matters of morals, he is infallible. This means that he cannot teach falsely concerning these matters. We can completely trust the Pope's teachings on matters of faith and morals. He is prevented, by the Holy Spirit, from teaching falsely from the Chair of Peter (CCC 891). Jesus gave us this guarantee and that makes perfect sense doesn't it? If the Pope was allowed to lead us astray, how would any of us be able to reach Heaven? What good would Christ's Church be if it was unable to lead us to Heaven? Jesus gave the guarantee that the Church's teachings on matters of faith and morals would be preserved. These are absolutely necessary to reach Heaven.

So I say again, our popes have not changed one truth of our faith. Our popes have not changed one teaching on morality. They have simply safeguarded the Deposit of Faith for 2,000 years. So when our Pope stands before us and he says that some act is immoral, he's right! He is absolutely right. It is immoral and we should not do it. Our Church is trying to lead us to Heaven. Our Church is trying to keep us from ending up in Hell. So the Church tells us, "Don't do that! It's immoral; it's wrong; please let me guide you. Let me help you reach Heaven." Our Pope is the Vicar of Christ here on earth. He speaks for Jesus. He truly does. Every one of us has the responsibility to learn the Moral Law of God. If we refuse to listen to the Church, and we act immorally, we will be held accountable for our actions (CCC 882).

There is Much Confusion

A lot of people in today's world simply do not understand this. They think the Pope invents the moral law and expects us to follow it. They even go as far as to ridicule the teachings of the Church or call them "old fashioned". They believe that the Church is wrong and needs to get with the times. They feel that they know better than 2,000 years of the best Catholic minds. What's worse is that these conclusions are often reached with little more than a surface understanding of what the Church teaches and why. As I said, our Holy Father simply keeps the teachings of Jesus Christ safe and passes them on to us. When we reject the teachings of the Church, we reject the teachings of Jesus. It is really that simple.

The problem with morality today is that many people think that we should determine what is right and wrong. They think that it should be people like you and me who decide what is right and what is wrong. All of us need to understand that people like you and me cannot decide what is right and wrong. We are fallen individuals possessing character and integrity far below that of God. When we determine what is morally right and wrong, we turn ourselves into God. We seize His power for ourselves. God has always been the one who has determined right from wrong; not us. It has always been God's decision, because He created us and He created the moral law (CCC 1951).

Remember the teaching in Genesis? God told Adam and Eve that they could eat of any tree in the Garden except the Tree of Knowledge of Good and Evil. God said do not eat the fruit of that tree, didn't He? God, from the very beginning, placed boundaries on us. From the very beginning God told us what we could do and what we could not do.

Who wrote the Ten Commandments? Did Moses write them... or did God? Of course it was God. In fact, the first five books of the Bible are called the Torah or Law. This was the written law for God's people; five books of law. Do you see? The Bible is God's Word and in it God gives us the law. Understand clearly that God is the one who has always determined what was right and wrong? It's always been God from the very beginning. The Bible is proof of that.

When Adam and Eve ate of "the Tree of Knowledge of Good and Evil" they were trying to seize for themselves the ability to know good from evil; hence the name of the tree. Satan even tempted them with the words, "You will not die. Instead you will become like gods knowing what is good and what is evil" (Gen 3:4-5). Adam and Eve did not possess the ability to determine morality. Only God possessed that ability. That is why the tree was so tempting. They could become like God and possess that ability for themselves by eating its fruit.

The Preserved Teaching

The Bible is our greatest source of teaching on morality. The Bible is our morality guidebook. The Bible *is* God's Word. God wrote the Bible. He inspired people to do the actual writing, but every word of it is God's. The Catholic Church gave the Bible to the world. The Bible is a product of the Church. And remember, it is through 'Sacred Tradition' that we interpret the Bible. The Catholic Church has the teachings of the Apostles; the example of their lives; the institutions that they created; and we have the Bible. This is all that is needed in order to determine right from wrong. The Church uses this to guide you to Heaven.

So what does the Church teach specifically about morality? After all, this is something that you and I really need to understand. We are Christians. We are Christians because we follow the teachings of Christ and believe that He is the only begotten Son of God; one in being with God the Father and the

Holy Spirit. We have been baptized into the Christian Faith. This means that you and I belong to Christ. We are His. We entered into a Covenant with God when we were baptized. You, as an individual, make this Covenant between you and God complete the day you get confirmed. Remember, a Covenant is a family relationship. God becomes your Father and you become His very own child. A Covenant is a family bond and therefore cannot be broken. You must abide by the rules of the Covenant and God must abide by the rules of the Covenant. You promise to worship only God and to follow His ways. God promises to be your very own Father and take care of you completely (CCC 2061-2063).

We are Christians, therefore, we can't just live any old way. We have to live in a whole new way. We must strive to become the people we were created to become. You and I were made in the image and likeness of God. When we are baptized and confirmed, we are called to live in that image and be of that likeness that is God. We're called to be of a higher nature; more holy; more loving; more like God (CCC 1265-1266).

The sacraments completely transform us. They make us holy. Therefore, we are gradually made holy and we act as though we are holy. That means that there are certain things we are not going to do. There are certain things that we are going to do. For example, we are going to worship God. We are going to attend Mass on the Sabbath. We are going to treat others with love and respect. We aren't going to steal. We aren't going to lie. We aren't going to cheat. We have higher standards; a higher integrity. We have a higher spirituality than much of society and the way we live shows it!

Our God has always existed. He was perfectly happy in His own existence, but He chose to create. He chose to create out of love. You could say then that God's love is creative. God's love created life. His love created the universe. His love created the earth. His love created the plants and the animals. And in His creative love, God chose to create you and me. God created you and me in His image and likeness. This means that He created us to <u>be</u> like Him; to love as He loves; and to create as He created.

Here is an important spiritual truth: God does not *need* you. God does not *need* me. That is the key to understanding your worth. God does not need you or me. God is God. He is perfect. He is absolute. God does not need you. Yet, you are here… What this means is that you have been loved into existence. This means that you were created just because God loves you. You are here, not because you can <u>do something</u> for God and therefore make His life better or more meaningful. He doesn't need you. You are here, because of His love. You have been loved into existence. This love gives you your worth. This is why human life is so precious; why it is worth so much! Because we were loved into existence, it is God's love that gives us our worth! Our worth is not based on our abilities; our talents; or our intelligence. Our worth is based only in the love we were created in (CCC 293).

God, who created us in His own image and likeness, asks us to love the way He loves… unconditionally. He asks us to completely love Him and to completely love the others that He has created. Therefore, we should not love others for what they can do for us, but just love them unconditionally; as He loves. This teaching is the basis for all morality. When we finally understand this, we begin to understand what is right and wrong. This is true because everything stems from this teaching. God loves each and every one of us unconditionally. This means that He does not love you more than me and he does not love me more than you. He loves a bank robber or a murderer just as much as he loves a saint. God loves an old person just as much as a new born baby. God does not love someone who accomplishes great things more than someone who accomplishes nothing. He does not love us any less if we suddenly went into a comma and could do nothing but lay there.

What we do and who we are does not give us our worth in the eyes of God. No one is worth more than another. Our lives are precious just because we are loved by God. God's love for us gives us our worth!

And what is our worth? We are precious simply because we are loved by God. So someone who is brilliant is not worth more than someone who is mentally handicapped. Both lives are equal! God loves both the same. Therefore both are worth the same! This is why Human Life is Sacred. Sacred means belonging to God! Therefore, human life belongs to God!

A Specific Story

I want you to understand society's morality and how it differs from God's morality. Today we have made such great medical advances that our doctors are able to tell a pregnant woman whether her baby is developing normally or whether it has some sort of defect. A friend of mine, named Elizabeth, gave birth to a baby boy a while back. Elizabeth had an older daughter who was high school age. She and her husband had been trying to have another child for years. Finally after several miscarriages, Elizabeth was pregnant again at the age of forty. She and her husband were very excited and prayed that this baby would live. An ultrasound showed that the baby was a boy, so they chose the name, Matthew, for him. As part of Elizabeth's prenatal care, a routine test was done on the baby. The test results showed that Matthew had 'Down Syndrome.' Immediately Elizabeth and her husband were advised by their doctor and nurses to have an abortion. Why? Well, the baby was not 'normal'. He had 'Down Syndrome.' Surely Elizabeth and her husband would not want to keep this child who was obviously less than perfect.

This happens every day in our hospitals and doctors' offices. Women are advised to have an abortion if there is any kind of abnormality with their babies. What is society saying when they advise us to terminate the life of an unborn baby, because it is not considered perfect? Society is saying that this child's life is not worth as much as the life of a "normal" baby. Because Matthew tested to have 'Down Syndrome,' his life was suddenly not worth as much as a perfectly normal child. Do you see how contrary this teaching is to God's teaching? God says, "You are precious! You are Sacred! Not because of what you can do for me, but simply because I love you!" Society says, "If you are mentally or physically handicapped, your life is worth nothing and should be ended before you are born. You will be an unwanted burden to your parents. We should save your parents the inconvenience you will cause."

Elizabeth and her husband refused to take the advice of the doctors and nurses who advised them to abort Matthew. Instead, they began to look into the kind of help they might need to care for a child with 'Down Syndrome.' Elizabeth even asked the doctors and nurses why they did not offer families, in this situation, help to care for children with special needs, rather than to advise them to terminate the pregnancy. Matthew was born a few months later. He was born a perfectly normal bouncing baby boy. The test results had been incorrect. Matthew did not have 'Down Syndrome' after all. If Elizabeth had terminated the pregnancy, she would have terminated a perfectly healthy and normal baby boy.

God created us and we are therefore His property. We exist because of Him. We belong to Him and we are hoping to go back to Him where we belong. This is basic Christian teaching. Human life is a gift from God. God gives us this gift of life and what we do with this life is our gift back to God. God gives us the gift of life and we try our best to do great things with it; great things that will glorify Him. Those great things that we do are our gifts back to God. We don't own ourselves. We never have and we never will. We are Christians! We are God's property. We belong to Him. Human life is Sacred. We are Sacred.

Apply the Knowledge:

When you and I begin to understand that we were made in the image and likeness of God and that we are called to be like Him; to love like Him; to create as He created, we are able to understand morality much better. We finally begin to understand that we are called to higher heights; to live by the spirit and not by the flesh. So, I'm going to give you another example of how to apply this knowledge.

As in the case of Elizabeth's Matthew, it is common for society to tell us that one person's life is worth more than another person's life. Remember, this can't be true. God loves every single one of us the same. None of us is more important or worth more than anyone else in the eyes of God. God is calling us to love as He loves, unconditionally. So we should see everyone as God sees them; as equals. You see, when society tells us that one person's life is worth more than another person's life, there is bound to be trouble. This is the case with Euthanasia or assisted suicide. Society begins to see the elderly as possessing a life that is no longer valuable. The elderly are seen many times as a burden upon society or a burden upon their families.

Life has even become disposable as in embryonic stem cell research. Human embryos are used and disposed of at will. One would think that we would have learned from the Holocaust during World War II, in which six million Jews were systematically killed. Jews were considered "non-persons" to the Nazi's. Similarly, a pre-born child, a human embryo, and sometimes the elderly are considered non-persons today.

Abortion

Consider this: A young woman conceives a child, but she didn't mean to, because she is not married. She is still in school or possibly she is trying to get her career started. She is not ready or capable of caring for a child at this time in her life. Now she finds herself in a predicament. This is an unwanted pregnancy. This child is going to 'complicate' her life. Even being pregnant is going to complicate her life. So she begins to consider having an abortion.

The Church teaches plainly, "Abortion is the killing of an unborn baby. It is immoral. It is a deadly Mortal Sin." But Society rushes to council the girl saying, "You have the right to do whatever you want with your own body. It's your body. No one can tell you what you can and cannot do with it. Besides, it's not really a baby. It's just a clump of cells. If you don't want the baby you don't have to keep it. Simply have it aborted. All of your problems will be solved and you can get on with your life."

Well, who is this girl to believe? The Church, or society? Let us apply the knowledge. I explained previously that the Church speaks for Jesus. I explained that the Church possesses real authority given to it by Jesus to speak in His name. Jesus said to the Apostles, "Whoever hears you, hears me." Jesus said, "I give you the keys to the Kingdom. Whatever you bind on earth shall be bound in Heaven. Whatever you loose on earth shall be loosed in Heaven." This means that in order to do the will of God, this girl needs to listen to the Church. When the Church says, "It is a grave Mortal Sin to have an abortion"; it is really and truly speaking for God (CCC 2271-2272).

I also explained that the Church teachings on morality are not new. These teachings have simply been preserved and passed down to us for 2,000 years by our popes and bishops.

I also explained that one person is not worth more than another. God loves each of us equally. We have worth not because of what we can do, but because we are loved by God. Remember that I also explained that human life is sacred. Human life belongs to God. We don't own ourselves let alone another person.

When we apply this knowledge, we see that we cannot possibly have the right to terminate another person's life? It doesn't matter whether that person is growing inside of us or not. The unborn child is worth just as much to God as any child who is born! We don't suddenly become worth more just because we are born! God loves us just as much while we are developing inside of our mother waiting to be born as He does at the moment of our birth. This is true because God gives us our soul at the moment of conception.

Society tells us, "It's just a clump of cells." No, it is not a clump of cells. It is a human life and that human life was made in the image and likeness of God. There is no excuse anymore for someone to be fooled into thinking that this child is merely a clump of cells. With the use of ultrasound equipment, we can now see into the womb. We can see that what is there is simply a tiny human being; a human being that belongs to God. The child does not belong to the mother. The child is God's property and we cannot destroy what belongs to God. We have no right. And if the mother was given the opportunity to see the child growing within her, via an ultrasound, she would not see a clump of cells. She would instead see a child with a beating heart; active brain cells; DNA; a Circulatory and Nervous System; ten fingers; ten toes; and a pair of pleading eyes staring back at her. She would see another human being completely distinct from herself.

Society says, "You have the right to do whatever you want with your own body." No, you don't. Think about it. We can't do whatever we want. That is a ridiculous statement. We might have the ability to do whatever we want, but that doesn't mean we have the right to do whatever we want. If you are a Christian, you have to live by the rules of Christian life. Those rules are given to us by God through the Bible; through Sacred Tradition; and through the Church. If you are a Christian, you are called to higher heights; to live in the image and likeness of God; to be like Him; to live as He lives; to love as He loves; to imitate Christ. You can't do anything you want. Don't let society tell you that you can. That is a lie.

Can this girl really solve all of her problems by aborting this child? Can she simply "get on with her life"? No! Her soul will be in grave Mortal Sin! Studies show that women who have had abortions become greatly depressed and battle depression for years to come (Fergusson Study, New Zealand). No, this girl will not simply get on with her life. We are both body and soul. When we mortally wound our souls, we mortally wound ourselves.

Keep in mind, however, that if this girl decides to have the abortion and later realizes that it was a terrible mistake, as most women do, the Church will be there for her with open arms. The Sacrament of Reconciliation will be there to forgive her sin and to restore Sanctifying Grace to her soul. She will find great comfort and peace in the words said by the priest, "Your sins are forgiven. Go in peace." That is when the healing process will finally begin for her.

You see, the Church knows and understands the principals that Jesus taught. The Church has preserved them for 2,000 years. When the Church teaches that abortion is wrong, the Church is speaking for God. These are His truths that are being upheld. It is just as important to understand that the Church is equally there for us when we fall, ready to extend to us the mercy of Christ. In short, the Church is here to guide us and the Church is here to pick us up when we fall.

Abortion is an obvious example of something that the Church teaches against, but that society tries to convince people is all right for them to do. This puts the Catholic Church into the media spotlight. People laugh at the Church for being so backward; for not growing with the times. But the Catholic Church will not apologize for upholding the teachings of Jesus. She will not back down. The Church refuses to assimilate into society. How could we have confidence in a Church that abandoned the teachings of Jesus just because our society doesn't agree with them? We could not trust the Church if it backed down on these key issues. We are the ones who must make a choice. Are we going to stand with society or are we going to stand with Jesus?

Homosexuality

Practicing homosexuality is another issue that faces us today that the Catholic Church speaks against as morally wrong, yet society ignores or defends. This is a delicate subject which calls for compassion and understanding. First let's understand that some people do have same sex attraction. This is something that they deal with or struggle with on a daily basis. Let's also understand that same sex attraction is not a sin. The sin lies in having sex with a person of the same gender and not in the attraction itself. It is also important to understand that all of us deal with attractions that can lead to sin. Every one of us struggles. We all struggle to be good human beings. Some people are attracted to alcohol and if abused it becomes sinful. Some are attracted to pornography, which is sinful if the attraction is indulged. Some are prone to adultery, but must practice self-control. The point is that every single one of us struggles with something. It takes a lot of prayer and courage to overcome our struggles and lead a life that is devoid of sin and a life that is holy.

Saint Paul gives us a list of sins that can keep a person from entering Heaven. In 1Corinthians 6:9-10 Saint Paul says, "Do you not know that the unjust will not inherit the kingdom of God? Do not be deceived; neither fornicators, nor idolaters, nor adulterers, nor boy prostitutes, nor practicing homosexuals, nor thieves, nor the greedy, nor drunkards, nor slanderers, nor robbers will inherit the kingdom of God." You see, Saint Paul is listing many sins that we could be attracted to and should therefore avoid. Practicing homosexuality is not at the top of the list and it is not at the bottom of the list. It is simply on the list. All of these listed things are sinful. The way we make everything else in life more important than God is the sin of idolatry. The way we are greedy and only think of ourselves, is the sin of greed. The way we speak of others behind their backs, is the sin of slander. Again, we all struggle to be good people.

Homosexuality is a hot topic in today's society simply because we are all being asked to accept the practice of it as simply another lifestyle. States are granting marriages to homosexual couples. We constantly hear of 'Gay Rights' in the media as if Gays and Lesbians were a race of people. I would put forth to you that no one should be allowed to define another person neither by their sins nor by their sexual orientation. And in today's society the Catholic Church is literally laughed at for speaking of the practice of homosexuality as a sin. Society tells us that it is not a sin. So how does society explain Saint Paul's words in 1Corinthians?

Again, let's apply the knowledge. The Catholic Church speaks for God. Jesus said to the first Pope and the Apostles of the Catholic Church, "Whoever hears you, hears me. I give you the Keys to the Kingdom. What you bind on earth will be bound in Heaven. What you loose on earth will be loose in Heaven." I explained that the Church has not changed Christ's teachings, but only upholds them. So let us turn to the Bible. Does God speak against homosexual relationships in the Bible? Yes, He does. 1Corinthians 6:9-10 has already been mentioned. If we start at the beginning of the Bible, we find the first mention of it in Genesis chapter 19 and then in Leviticus chapters 18 and 20. Because they are relatively short, let us first look at some specific verses in Leviticus. In chapter 18 verse 22 we read, "You shall not lie with a male as with a woman; it is an abomination." In Leviticus chapter 20 verse 13 we read, "If a man lies with a male as with a woman, both of them shall be put to death for their abominable deed; they have forfeited their lives." These are very strong words. The Book of Leviticus was written in the time of Moses. This is part of the Torah or 'Law' given to the Israelites by God, through Moses.

In the nineteenth chapter of Genesis we read the story of the destruction of the city of Sodom. The city of Sodom was destroyed because of the wicked deeds of the men living there. When we read the entire story, we see clearly what aroused God's anger. The wicked deeds of the men in that city were homosexual acts and God destroyed the city because of these acts. This is where the word sodomy comes from today.

The following is a list of Bible verses referring to homosexuality for further study: Genesis 1:27: Complementarity of sexes reflects God's inner unity; Genesis 2:21-24: The transmission of life through total self-donation, becoming one flesh; Genesis 19: Original Sin deteriorates to Sodom's sin, and is therefore destroyed; Leviticus 18:22, 29: It is called an abomination, cut off from people; Leviticus 20:13: Both shall be put to death for abominable deed; Romans 1:27: Called unnatural, shameful, and perversity; 1Corinthians 6:9: Active homosexuals won't inherit the Kingdom of God; 1Timothy 1:9-10: Those who engage in such acts are called "sinners."

There in the Bible are God's strong words against practicing homosexuality. The Catholic Church simply preserves and defends these teachings handing them down from one generation to the next. Yet, the Church is criticized and even ridiculed for doing so. What would people have Jesus' Church do if not to stand up for His teachings and defend them? Could you trust a church that abandoned the teachings of Christ just because society didn't agree with them? The Catholic Church will not and should not apologize for teaching the truths of Jesus Christ. As people of God, we have to decide whether we are going to stand with society or stand with Jesus.

"I Don't See Anything Wrong With It"

In my job, I have had several teenagers say to me, "I don't see anything wrong with practicing homosexuality." When they say this to me, they are being completely sincere. They honestly do not see anything wrong with it and are looking for me to explain why it is wrong.

Let me start out by saying that we don't have to 'see' what is wrong with stealing. We don't have to 'see' what is wrong with adultery. We don't have to 'see' what is wrong with cheating. We don't have to 'see' what is wrong with anything in order for it to be wrong. Who are we that we have to 'see' what is wrong with something in order for it to be wrong? God says it is wrong. Why isn't that good enough for us? Why do we expect God to explain Himself? Again, God determines what is right and wrong, not us. He always has and He always will. It is our responsibility to discover what God has determined to be immoral and follow His Moral Law.

We have to stop making God into what we want Him to be and instead, discover who He really is. What will be our defense when we stand before Him in judgment? "Oh, I'm sorry, God. I didn't 'see' anything wrong with it." Believe me, it won't fly. We simply must swallow our pride and accept God's authority over us. He created us; not the other way around. We exist because of Him. Our loving Father wants us to be with Him for all eternity. That means that we have to accept that certain behaviors can keep that from happening. Ignorance or rejection of His teachings is not a defense.

Now having said that, let's discuss why it is wrong. The reason it is wrong to have sex with someone of your same gender is because the very act violates the nature of sex. It is the very same reason that it is wrong for a married couple to use artificial means of birth control. I am going to explain this again, but with different words this time (CCC2357-2359).

Everything and every person has a purpose; a nature; a reason they exist. When we violate that purpose, we violate the very person or thing. Sex has two purposes. First, its purpose is to unify the couple, both emotionally and physiologically. Its second purpose is procreation (creation of life).

I'm going to compare the two purposes of sex with the two purposes for eating. We also eat for two purposes. We eat for pleasure and to nourish our bodies. Is it possible for me to eat for pleasure and still nourish my body? Yes. The reason I ate might be because it tasted good and I wanted it. It still nourished my body; even though that wasn't the reason I chose to eat.

Is it possible for me to nourish my body and still enjoy eating? Yes. The reason I ate was to be healthy, so I carefully chose my food. At the same time, I enjoyed the food. It gave me pleasure.

Is it possible to separate those two purposes for eating? Yes, it is. Some people eat for pleasure, but do not want the calories. So what do they do? They chew and then spit out the food. Or they eat and then make themselves vomit. When this is done, the purposes for eating are violated. Therefore, the very nature of eating is violated.

You would never tell someone who was struggling with self-image that this act was all right to do. Instead, you would say to them, "Don't do that. You will harm your body."

The same is true when it comes to the nature of sex. A husband and a wife may engage in sexual relations because they want that intimacy; that close union and love with one another. Does that mean they are stopping a child from being conceived? No. It's just that getting pregnant wasn't the reason they engaged in sex that particular time.

A husband and a wife may engage in sexual relations because they want to become pregnant; they want to conceive a child. Does that mean that they cannot experience the unity, love and closeness of sex? No. It's just that the reason they engaged in sex that particular time, was to conceive a child.

Is it possible for a couple to violate the nature or purpose of sex by removing one of those two purposes? Absolutely! If they remove the unitive purpose of sex, one or both of them feels violated or used. This is what happens in the case of rape. When we purposefully remove the procreative purpose of sex, we have abandoned our call from God to create as He creates; our call to live in His image and likeness. We reduce sex to pleasure only; to using one person for our own personal pleasure. We violate our very own human nature.

Homosexual relations, by their very nature, can never contain the procreative purpose of sex. It therefore separates and violates the nature or purpose of sexual relations as it only has the unitive purpose and never the procreative purpose of sex.

If you tell someone that this is perfectly all right to do, then you are leading them on a path away from God who gave all things its purpose.

Love

Catholics have an advantage over people of all other religions. That is because the Church possesses the fullness of faith. We actually receive God's Sanctifying grace; His very Life into our souls. Every sacrament places the Life of God into our souls and helps to make us holy. As Catholics we don't just want to live a good and moral life, we want to strive for holiness. We want to live a holy life. Our goal is to become holy. God loved us into existence. He made us in His image and likeness. He wants us to love others the way He loves us.

That is really hard to do. Let's be honest. Some people are really hard to love. St. Thomas Aquinas said that "love is willing the good of the other as other." He said that love is willing the good of the other as other and then doing something about it. This means that we truly want good things to happen to everyone; not because if good things happen to them, we'll get some benefit. But instead, we want good things to happen to others just for them.

A lot of times, however, we love ourselves through other people. I'm nice to other people so that they will be nice to me. I'll treat you fairly so that you will treat me fairly in return. And we get mad when it doesn't work that way. We say, "I was nice to her and she was not nice to me in return!" That's just wrong isn't it? When we're nice to people, we expect them to be nice back!

That's not real love. Love is wanting good for the other person even if we get nothing in return. The love that you give away has been given to you by God. So when you love other people, you are giving God's love away. The more you give God's love away, the more love you get back from God in return. You can't out-give God! Give God's love away to everyone;

every single person; and you get more love in return. That is the truth.

Vices

Catholics memorize the "Seven Deadly Sins" as part of their religious upbringing. The Seven Deadly Sins are: Pride, Greed, Lust, Anger, Gluttony, Envy, and Sloth. These seven things can quickly lead us into committing Mortal or Deadly Sin. These deadly sins cause us to fail to love other people the way we should. They are vices.

Instead of remembering that it is God that truly makes us happy, we begin to search for things that make us happy. We begin to accumulate money and possessions, thinking that if we get enough money and we get enough possessions then we will be happy. We begin to search for pleasure thinking that if we get enough pleasure, then we will be happy. We search for praise thinking that if others praise us and tell us how great we are, then we will be happy. But none of that is true. We may find momentary pleasure in money, possessions, or the praise and compliments of others, but this does not last. Soon we are hot on the pursuit of more money, possessions, pleasure, or praise.

This need for money, possessions, or praise can drive us and cause us to treat others as if they are a threat to our wellbeing. We can quickly become jealous and even envious of others for the things they have. For example, if our coworkers are praised and we are not, we become jealous because it was praise that we didn't get. We become envious of them and perhaps we even talk about them behind their backs and say how they didn't deserve the praise that they received. If our neighbor buys a new car, we may become jealous or envious because we cannot afford to do that right now. We may even criticize them for always needing the latest thing.

But we are meant to relax and know that God loves us and understand that it is in Him that we find true happiness; happiness that is lasting and not fleeting. It is in God's love that we should find pleasure and rejoice. Then we are free to give God's love away to everyone.

Pride

Pride is the deadliest of the Deadly Sins. Pride is turning oneself into God. I stated in a previous chapter that pride was the great sin of Lucifer. Lucifer began to see himself as the center of all things. He was the center of it all, not God. He announced, "I will not serve! I will become the basis for what is good and what is evil, not God." Who rose up to fight Lucifer? It was Saint Michael! His name in Hebrew means, "Who is like God?" Lucifer said, "I will not serve! I am God!" and Michael said, "Who is like God?"

The opposite of pride is humility. Humility is seeing yourself in truth; seeing yourself as you truly are. So practice humility and you will fight against pride. Humility is a willingness to serve and being happy to do it. Humility is knowing who we are and understanding the purpose of the gifts and talents that God has given to us. Humility is taking those gifts and talents and using them to serve God with the best of our abilities. Humility is allowing God's Life and God's Love to surge through us. We should want to give God's love away every chance we get.

Envy

Envy is another deadly sin that we seem to have a constant struggle with. It goes beyond jealousy. Saint Thomas Aquinas said that "Envy is sorrow at another person's good."

This means that when someone else does well, it makes us sad because it wasn't us that did well.

Think about it. Sometimes when someone else does well, we don't even want to hear about it. We say rather half-heartedly, "Oh, that's great. I'm really happy for him." But turn this around and envy can get even worse! We can actually take pleasure at someone else's failure. If someone does poorly, deep down we rejoice. We are actually happy about it! We want to hear all about it. "You mean she messed up...tell me more!"

Where do these feelings come from? They come from fear. God has given every one of us certain talents. We should all take our talents and do great things to glorify God. We should be really happy when other people take their talents and do great things to glorify God. We should not become envious of them. Instead, we should cheer them on. God does not love us any less when someone else does something good. He loves us as much as He possibly can every single day; never any less; no matter what. Trust that you are being loved by God. Trust that God has given you a mission to fulfill. Trust that you are valuable, not because of any praise you are getting or the things that you own. Instead, you are valuable because you are loved by God.

Envy is the cause of most of the bullying that goes on in schools. It is what causes much of the gossip that goes on among adults. When someone posts unkind comments about someone else online, it is caused many times by the deadly sin of envy. And it is fed by the deadly sin of pride. Stay away from the bullying. Stay away from the gossiping. Never post something unkind online about another person. Never say in an email, on Twitter, on Facebook, or on any other social media, anything that you would not want someone to say to you or about you. The "Golden Rule" is still very relevant today.

The Ten Commandments

Following the Ten Commandments helps each of us to live a life in which we love God and love others. In the Ten Commandments God asks us to love Him the most and to take time to worship Him. He asks us to speak His name with respect and to put Him first in our lives. He then gives us guidelines on how we should treat others. We owe those in authority over us respect. We cannot harm others physically, mentally, or emotionally. We may not take things that do not belong to us nor can we destroy another's property. We have to be honest in our dealings with others; honest in our speech, and honest in our conduct. We simply must be faithful in our marriages and be pleased with what we have. Following the Ten Commandments helps us to live good and moral lives. It helps us to be truly happy for sin causes all of our problems.

Love and Holiness—The Purpose of Catholic Morality

"Actions speak louder than words." The study of our faith is meaningful only if it motivates us to act in a manner consistent with the teachings of Jesus. "What good is it, my brothers, if someone says he has faith but does not have works? Can that faith save him? If a brother or sister has nothing to wear and has no food for the day, and one of you says to them, 'Go in peace, keep warm, and eat well,' but you do not give them the necessities of the body, what good is it? So also faith of itself, if it does not have works, is dead" (James 2:14-17).

If we believe in Jesus Christ and accept the teaching of the Bible, we must translate our beliefs into action. We are brought to salvation by faith in Jesus Christ, but faith is more than emotion or thought. Faith involves decisions and actions modeled on those of Jesus. Without faith in Christ we can do nothing good, but if we do nothing good, we cannot have faith in Christ!

The teaching of Jesus demonstrates that we are free to make choices, that our choices should be in conformity with God's will, and that we are accountable for them. It is reassuring to know, that in matters this essential to our eternal life, we have the Church to guide us.

Life and freedom are God's gifts to us; what we become through our use of freedom is our gift to God. God places us on this earth and invites us to love and serve Him, opening ourselves to God's love for all eternity. Each day we are given life and freedom. Each day we determine the kind of person we will become. On one hand we have the grace of God assisting us to make the right decisions. On the other hand we are tempted by the devil, by people who sin, and by our own inborn weaknesses. When we make good and morally correct decisions, we lead a morally good life. When we go against the moral guidelines given by God, we sin.

The more we choose a certain course or way of acting, whether good or bad, the easier it becomes to perform that action. We get very good at whatever we practice. Thus we form either good habits, called virtues, or bad habits, called vices. The more we speak with kindness and gentleness, the more readily kind and gentle words come to our lips. The more we curse or gossip, the more these vices become ingrained in us.

The virtues of *Faith*, *Hope*, and *Love* are called the "Theological Virtues" because they are gifts of God and direct our relationship to God. By *faith* we acknowledge the reality of God in our lives and are able to believe in the truths that God reveals to us. By *hope* we have confident assurance of achieving eternal life in Heaven with the help of God's grace. By *love* we make the decision to put God first with all our heart, soul, mind, and strength, and to love our neighbor as ourselves. While these virtues are gifts of God, we must be willing to accept them from God and to live in such a way that they can grow stronger in us.

Other virtues which have a special place in Catholic tradition are the four *cardinal virtues*. *Prudence* helps us to do the right thing in any circumstance. *Justice* enables us to give others their due. *Fortitude* strengthens us to weather the difficulties and temptations of life. *Temperance* helps us to control our desires and to use the good things of life in a Christ-like way.

Part of becoming holy entails that we possess great virtue and integrity. Who are we when no one else is looking? What kind of a person are we, when no one else can see what we are doing? Our lives change when our habits change. When we practice virtue and holiness we become virtuous and holy people.

The purpose of each one of our lives is to reach the state of holiness in which we become saints. In Heaven there are only saints. We either become saints and reach Heaven, or we become conformed to the image of the demons, in Hell. Rest assured however, that it is not by our own merits and strength that we become saints, but by our complete trust in God alone. When we cooperate with the grace that God gives to us, we allow Him to work in our lives. He accomplishes every good thing we do. Relying on our own ability, strength, and merit will end in our detriment.

Enter by the Narrow Gate

Recall Jesus' words in Matthew 7:13-14, "Enter through the narrow gate; for the gate is wide and the road broad that leads to destruction, and those who enter it are many. How narrow the gate and constricted the road that leads to life. And those who find it are few." Jesus makes clear that drifting along with contemporary culture will not lead us to Heaven. He clearly teaches that if we want to arrive at complete happiness—eternal life with Him—we need to take the road and enter through that gate that leads to Heaven.

The purpose of our life is the glory of Heaven, and the only way to reach that goal is by absolute confidence in God. If we desire a close relationship with God, we shall have it. "For everyone who asks, receives; and the one who seeks, finds; and the one who knocks, the door will be opened (Matt 7:8). If we give our life to God, He will accept it. If we live our life for Him, He will glory in it. If we cooperate with His grace, He will accomplish all of our good works. If we seek to be holy, He will make us saints. Therefore, Catholic morality is simply that constricted path that will help lead you through the narrow gate (Matt 7:13-14).

XXI. We are Simply Stewards

Stewardship

When our parish priest lights the Paschal Candle before entering church for the Easter Vigil ceremony, he traces symbols on the candle and says the words: "Christ yesterday and today, the beginning and the end, Alpha and Omega; all time belongs to Him, and all the ages. To Him be the glory and power through every age for ever Amen." Christ is Risen! He is Truly Risen!

Everything in the universe belongs to Jesus Christ; everything and everyone. All of my time, all of my talent; everything that I have belongs to Jesus. But what does it mean to live as though we believe that everything we have and all that we are belongs to Jesus Christ? It means sharing it freely as disciples of Jesus Christ by living out the Gospel value of stewardship. It means walking a mile in the other person's shoes.

Living out the Gospel value of stewardship as a disciple means sharing your time, talent, and treasure. Why? Because everything you have to share is from God, and it is all meant for sharing. Being a disciple means sharing without counting the cost. Being a disciple means sharing even when we least feel like it, when we least can afford to do it, and when the person in need of our gift is the last person we wish to serve!

The Parable of the Talents

When we read the Gospels we find that Jesus often taught the crowds using parables. The "Parable of the Talents" is the parable that Jesus used to teach us about the call to and the meaning of Stewardship. The "Parable of the Talents" is found in Matthew 25:14-30. Jesus said, "The Kingdom of Heaven will be as when a **man,** who was going on a journey, called in his

servants and entrusted <u>his</u> possessions to them. To one he gave five talents; to another, two; to a third, one; each according to his ability. Then he went away.

Immediately the one who received five talents went and traded with them, and made another five. Likewise, the one who received two made another two. But the man, who received one, went off and dug a hole in the ground and buried his master's money.

After a long time the master of those servants came back and settled accounts with them. The one who had received five talents came forward bringing the additional five. He said, 'Master, you gave me five talents. See, I have made five more.' His master said to him, 'Well done, my good and faithful servant. Since you were faithful in small matters, I will give you great responsibilities. Come share your master's joy.'

Then the one who had received two talents also came forward and said, 'Master, you gave me two talents. See, I have made two more.' His master said to him, 'Well done, my good and faithful servant. Since you were faithful in small matters, I will give you great responsibilities. Come share your master's joy.'

Then the one who had received the one talent came forward and said, 'Master, I knew you were a demanding person, harvesting where you did not plant and gathering where you did not scatter; so out of fear I went off and buried your talent in the ground. Here it is back.' His master said to him in reply, 'You wicked, lazy servant! So you knew that I harvested where I did not plant and gathered where I did not scatter? Should you not then have put my money in the bank so that I could have gotten it back with interest on my return? Now then! Take the talent from him and give it to the one with ten. For to everyone who has, more will be given and he will grow rich; but from the one who has not, even what he has will be taken away. And throw this useless servant into the darkness outside, where there will be wailing and grinding of teeth.'"

Who do the people in this parable represent? The "**Master**" in this parable represents God. The **3 servants** represent ordinary people like you and me. This is true because you and I are servants of the Lord.

The Master of these servants gave to each **his money**. He gave each of them different amounts of coins depending on their abilities. This money represents God's gifts to us. God's gifts come to us in 4 forms: God gives each of us **Talents**. Some people are given many talents; some are given a few talents; and some are given less talents, yet all of us are given talents by God. God also gives us: **Time**. Time is a gift from God and it is a very precious gift that must not be wasted. God also gives us **Treasure** or in other words money. To some He gives a lot of money; to others He gives a fair amount of money; and still to others He gives less money. The last gift that God gives to us is **Tradition.** Tradition is our Faith—and that is one of our greatest gifts.

In the parable, the five, two, or one talent represents all of the gifts that God's gives to us: **Time, Talent, Treasure and Tradition.** Notice that the Master gives to the servants 'his possessions'. Our gifts of Time, Talent, Treasure, and Tradition do not belong to us. They are God's possessions. He simply loans them to us while we are on this earth. We are simply 'stewards' or care-takers of God's gifts.

Notice also that the Master of these servants told them to go and use these gifts to the best of their ability and to make them grow into something big. So we must understand what God is asking each of us to do. God gives each of us the gifts of Time, Talent, Treasure, and Tradition. He wants us to take these gifts and use them to the best of our ability. He wants us to use these gifts for the Kingdom of God. He wants us to use them to make the world a better place and to be the best person we can be. God wants us to do our best. He wants us to follow His plan for our lives and to grow closer to Him. God gives us a little time; a bit of money; a few talents; and our faith and He asks us to do great things with these gifts. In other words, we are to use these gifts throughout our lives in order to reach holiness. We are to use these gifts from God as our means of attaining holiness and becoming a saint so that we can come back to God and spend eternity with Him. Remember that what we do with these gifts throughout our lives is our gift back to God at the end.

So the Master came back and asked each of the Servants, "What have you done with the gifts that I have given you?" "What have you done with the Time, Talent, Treasure and Tradition that I have given to you? Did you use them to become holy?"

The First Servant doubled the five coins that the Master gave to him and now had ten coins. He took the gifts that God gave him and he did his best to love God back. By his actions, his words, and the way he lived his life, the First Servant did the will of God and doubled the gifts that God gave to him. He reached the kind of holiness needed to enter Heaven. The money that he made, 10 coins, was his gift back to God on judgment day. This servant was thus welcomed into the Heavenly Kingdom with the words, "Well done my good and faithful servant. Come share your master's joy."

The Second Servant likewise took his Time, Talent, Treasure, and Tradition and did the will of God. He doubled the two coins that the Master gave to him and ended up with four. He too took God's gifts and lived his life in service to God and doubled the gifts that God had given to him. He too reached the kind of holiness needed to enter Heaven. The money that he made, four coins, was his gift to God on judgment day. The Second Servant did just as well as the first servant. Even though he presented only four coins and not ten coins to the master, he did his very best. This servant was likewise welcomed into the Heavenly Kingdom with the words, "Well done my good and faithful servant. Come share your master's joy."

The Third Servant was given one coin. He gave back to God one coin. He took the gift that God had given to him and he did nothing with it. He took the gifts of Time, Talent, Treasure and Tradition and did not use them to do the will of God. He did not serve the Lord with his life. He did not use this gift to grow in holiness. He took his life and served only himself. This servant was, therefore, not welcomed into the Heavenly Kingdom. In fact, he was thrown into "the darkness where there is wailing and grinding of teeth!"

God has given each of us these gifts as well. God gives us the gift of Time. What we do with your time is our gift back to God. Therefore, we should use our time to serve the Lord and grow in holiness. God has given us many talents. There are many things that we are good at. What we do with our talents is our gift back to God. Therefore, we should use our talents to serve the Lord; to make the world a better place and to grow in holiness. God has given us Treasure or money. What we do with our money is our gift back to God. Therefore, we should use our money to serve the Lord and grow in holiness. Finally, God has given us a Tradition—A Faith—The Catholic Church. What we do with your faith is our gift back to God. Therefore, we should use our faith to serve the Lord. Seek a deep and close relationship with Him. Spend quality time in prayer. Seek to know His will for your life and continually grow in holiness.

God Has a Plan for Your Life

God has a plan for each of our lives. It is important that we ask for His guidance so that we follow the path that He has laid out for us. No matter what vocation we choose, whether we choose to get married; become a priest or Religious; or stay single, we can serve the Lord. No matter what career we choose, we can serve the Lord.

We have life because God has chosen to give us life. We are Christians and we, therefore, belong to God. We are His property. We are His very own children. We were made in His image and likeness and we are absolutely precious to God.

We are therefore called to be like Him. If we were made in His image and likeness, we are therefore called to be like God. We cannot act and be like the rest of the world. Christians are called to higher heights. We are called to serve the Lord. We are called to follow Jesus and imitate Him. We have to know what Jesus taught and do our best to live as He instructed. What we do with our lives is our gift to God, who has given us everything we have. We are called to live by the Spirit, and not by the flesh. We are called to stand with Jesus and to carefully filter the world through Him.

What does it mean to filter the world through Jesus? Well, it means to think critically about what the world teaches or what society teaches. These sources for morality cannot be trusted. As we think critically about what the world values and what the world teaches, we must compare that to what Jesus teaches and continues to teach through His Church. Often times the two do not match. When they do not match, we must understand that Jesus is the guide we must follow.

What exactly are we supposed to do then with our Time, our Talent, our Treasure, and our Tradition? Well, first we are called to give to others and not just to ourselves. We must take some of our time and use it to serve other people; to do good things for them. We must take our Talents and use them to make the world a better place. We must find out what God's plan is for each of our lives and follow it. If we do, we will find great happiness. This is true because happiness comes from doing the will of God. Doing the will of God makes us happy, because that is exactly what we were created to do.

Each of us must take our Treasure—our money—and use some of it to help those who don't have enough food or clothing or shelter. We can't spend *all* of our money on ourselves. We just can't. Not when people are starving. We also cannot take and take and take from our parish church and not help support it. We must give some of our money to the Church, because the things that our parish church does for us, cost money. We are called to support it.

Likewise we are called to take our Tradition—Our Catholic Faith—and live it. We must live our faith and grow closer to God each day always seeking a deeper and closer relationship with God on our journey toward Heaven. We have to continue to learn. The more we learn, the more excited we become about our faith. Jesus draws us to Him as we seek to know and understand. We must also pass our faith down to the next generation. We must teach our children what it means to follow Christ in word and in action. We have two important jobs in this world. Our first and most important job is to seek and obtain Heaven. Our second job is to take as many people with us as we can. We are responsible for passing the faith down to our children. We should be the kind of person who helps lead others closer to God by our words, actions and also our instruction.

Living in this way can be as simple as buying food for the poor when we do our own grocery shopping. It can be as simple as helping people when they ask you to help them. It can be as simple as doing the best job you can possibly do at your job or in school. It can be as simple as helping out around your house; something a small child can do. We are not here to be served. Jesus taught us that we are here to serve. We are all servants of the Lord.

Some people are called to a more complex form of Stewardship. Perhaps they travel to Haiti, for example, every few months to actually build homes for the poor people there. Perhaps they are called to be a priest, deacon, brother, or a sister. No matter what, we have all been called to do the very best we can in our ordinary lives every single day.

A Piece of the Puzzle

Have you ever looked at puzzle piece? Each piece is unique. No two puzzle pieces are exactly alike. You, like a puzzle piece, are a unique creation. No other person on this earth is like you. No one else could be you. You belong to God. He created you. He loves you. And He wants you to make it safely back to Him.

God gave you special talents and gifts that are unique to just you. No one else can do exactly what you can do. God has a plan for your life. A plan that is unique just to you. There is something that you can do for God that no one else can do.

Each piece of a puzzle fits perfectly in the place that was meant to receive it. There is nowhere else that puzzle piece would fit. You can try to force it into another place, but it just won't go. It just isn't right. No matter how you would try to make it fit, it's no use. There is no way that it can complete the picture.

Just as a puzzle piece only fits in one place in a puzzle, so too God has just one plan for your life. God has chosen a place in the Kingdom of God that, if you will simply follow His will for your life, you will fit perfectly. You can try to choose a different plan for your life; a plan that is different than what God has planned. And you can try to force it and make it fit, but it's of no use.

You see, when you follow God's plan for your life, there is no forcing trying to make things fit. Everything just fits perfectly and as a result you are happy. This is true because, happiness comes from doing the will of God. Doing the will of God makes us happy, because that is exactly what we were created to do. Would you be happy with a puzzle that all the pieces were placed where they do not belong? No, you would not be happy with the puzzle, because it would not create the picture it was meant to create. It would be a jumbled up mess. The same is true for you. You can never be happy if you are not in the correct place made for you in the Kingdom of God.

Have you ever built a puzzle only to find that a piece was missing? That missing piece ruins the whole puzzle, doesn't it? Each of us helps to build the Kingdom of God by the way we live our life; by doing the will of God. But what happens when someone refuses to follow God's plan for their life? Can someone else simply fill in their empty space in the Kingdom of God? Can another puzzle piece fill in the empty spot made by the missing piece? No. That piece won't fit. That piece can't complete the puzzle, because it has its own place.

Likewise someone else cannot do for God what He has planned for you. Someone else can't take your place and serve God the way that you can. He needs each of us to do His will in order to completely build the Kingdom of God. If we refuse to do His will and we go our own way, there is an empty space in the Kingdom; a space that is forever empty.

Each of us must find out what God has planned for our lives and if we follow His plan, we will be truly happy and we will help to build the Kingdom of God.

How do we find out what God has planned for our lives? All we have to do is pray. Simply pray and ask God to lead you down the path that He has chosen for you. Tell Him that you want to do His will and ask God to place His will before you. Don't worry. He will lead you. Some people are called to be priests. If God does not want a person to become a priest, He will not call that person. If He does call you, follow, and you will be happy. Some people are called to get married, but not everyone. For some, God does not plan marriage in their futures. He has the single life planned for them.

Give Until There's Nothing Left to Give

Stewardship is taking our **time, talent, treasure and tradition** that has been given to us by God and giving it back to Him in ways that will serve Him and others.

Stewardship is seeking God's plan for your life and living that plan. Stewardship is giving to others; serving others and not seeking to serve only ourselves. Jesus is our model.

Why do we serve and give and then give some more? Because every single thing we have is a gift from God. There is nothing we have that we obtained by ourselves. Everything we have is a gift from God. How much of our gifts did God give to us? He gave all of them to us. Then how much of these gifts do we give back to God? We give back all of them…100% of them. From this we understand that we are simply "stewards" or care-takers of the gifts that God has given to us.

How much is too much to give to God? Give until there is nothing left to give. Jesus gave until there was nothing left to give. Blood and water poured forth from His side when the soldier pierced Him. There was nothing left for Jesus to give. He gave until there was nothing left to give. So should we if we are to imitate Him; to live as He taught us to live.

No one can tell you how badly you need God. You can only figure that out by yourself. But you are only going to have that close deep relationship with Him; that full union with Him, if you offer yourself to Him and give until there's nothing left to give. God wants you to be holy. God wants you to be a saint. That's His biggest plan for your life. Second, God wants to use you to make others holy. Use the gifts that God has given you to reach this goal. Nothing will make you happier.

Remember, a steward is only a care-taker. Everything we have belongs to God. They are His possessions that He gives to us during our life. We are simply the care-takers or stewards of the gifts that God has given to us. What we do with these gifts is our gift back to God. At the end of our lives we too want to hear Jesus say to us, "Well done my good and faithful servant. Come share your master's joy."

XXII. Mary, Mother of God; Our Mother; And Advocate

The Catholic Church honors all those who have been named saints. They serve as great role models for us. In them we find great examples of holy lives that encourage us and give us hope. The Blessed Virgin, Mary is the saint that we as Catholics venerate the most. Catholics give special honor to Mary, the Mother of Jesus Christ. She was chosen by God to be the Mother of God's only Son. Without doubt, this was the greatest privilege and the most significant of all human accomplishments, after those of Jesus. The Bible states that "all ages" will call Mary blessed (Luke 1:48) and, in obedience to this passage, generations of Catholics have been proud to call Mary their "Blessed Mother."

The Church encourages us to seek a relationship with Mary and to practice devotions to her and rightly so. Mary's purpose is to leads us closer and closer to her Son, our Lord.

A New Adam and a New Eve

Adam and Eve were created with the very Life of God inside of their souls. They possessed Sanctifying Grace. God had the plan that Adam and Eve and their descendants would live for a period of time and then they would be taken into Heaven body and soul.

God placed them in a beautiful garden and gave them the fruit of the trees to eat. But Adam and Eve disobeyed God and His plan to bring them body and soul into Heaven was lost; for sinful souls cannot enter Heaven.

Adam and Eve's sin had brought death into the world. God had a choice. He could simply leave the human race to die in the death their sins had created or He could bring forth a 'New Adam' and a 'New Eve.' If He left the human race to die in death; that would mean that there would be nothing after death; nothing for any of us. But if God brought forth a 'New Adam' and a 'New Eve,' they would redeem the human race and God's original plan to give us Eternal Life could be realized. Instead of death and nothingness, there would be Eternal Life for all those who believed. So that is exactly what God did. He brought forth a 'New Adam' and a 'New Eve'. Jesus is the 'New Adam'. Mary is the 'New Eve' (CCC 411). This was the promise that God gave in the garden; to bring forth a woman whose offspring would crush the head of the serpent, "I will put enmity between you and the woman, and between your offspring and hers; He will strike at your head, while you strike at his heel" (Genesis 3:15).

St. Irenaeus of Lyons wrote in his apology "Against the Heresies," in the year 180 A.D. "Eve, having become disobedient, was made the cause of death, both to herself and to the entire human race; so also did Mary, yielding obedience, become the cause of salvation, both to herself and the whole human race. So also the knot of Eve's disobedience was loosed by the obedience of Mary. For what the virgin Eve had bound fast through unbelief, this did the virgin Mary set free through faith."

The Immaculate Conception of Mary—"Hail, Full of Grace"

The Catholic Church teaches us that Mary was conceived without sin. We believe in the "Immaculate Conception of Mary" and even celebrate it as a Holy Day of Obligation every year on December 8th. The doctrine of the Immaculate Conception teaches that Mary, by God's grace, was preserved from all stain of original sin and that she herself never sinned. When the doctrine was proclaimed by Pope Pius IX, he explained that Mary shared in the redemptive act of Christ in that she was saved by the foreseen merits of Christ.

The Immaculate Conception is rooted in Scripture. It was taught through sacred Tradition and believed universally by Catholics from every century dating back to the first. Mary was born without original sin and instead possessed the very Life of God in her soul just as Adam and Eve did, before the Fall; before they sinned. Mary remained sinless her entire life (CCC 411; 490-493).

In the Gospel of Luke chapter 1:26-38, Mary was visited by the Angel Gabriel who appeared to her. The Angel Gabriel addressed Mary with a name that described her, "Full of Grace" and proclaimed, "The Lord is with you." To be full of Grace means to be full of the Life of God; full of the Trinity; full of holiness. If one is full of grace, there is no room left for sin. In short, it means that Mary possessed Sanctifying Grace (CCC2676).

Since the Savior had not yet come and had not yet suffered and died for our sins, Mary was saved by the foreseen merits of Christ. Obviously, God willed this to be so in Mary; in the woman who was chosen to be the Mother of His only begotten Son; of His Word Incarnate.

If we think about it, this was the goal for all of us. This was the goal for Adam and Eve and for all men. We were all supposed to be without sin and we are all supposed to do our best not to sin. Each of us is called to be like Mary; sinless. Jesus accomplished in Mary what He desires to accomplish in all of us…holiness. Mary understood that God saved her. In her canticle (magnificat) she proclaims: "My soul proclaims the greatness of the Lord; my spirit rejoices in God my savior" (Luke

1:46-47). She was preserved from sin at her conception. She was saved ahead of time, before her conception. For there are two ways to be saved. If we fall into a deep pit and someone pulls us out and cleans us up, you have been saved. That's how it is with us. We all fall into the pit of sin and Jesus, by taking our sins upon Himself and dying on the cross, pulls us out of the pit and cleans us up. But there is another way to be saved. What if someone prevents us from falling into the pit in the first place? Aren't we also saved? Mary was prevented from falling into the pit of sin. She was saved from falling into sin by Jesus. Rather than waiting until after she sinned to save her, as it is with us, she was saved from sin before she sinned in the first place. She was even saved from Original Sin.

Faith and reason go hand in hand. There are some common sense reasons to believe this doctrine. First, sin separates us from God. God cannot be where there is sin. He cannot be in the presence of it. Therefore, someone sinful could not bear in her womb, Jesus, who is God. God prepared a special woman to be the Mother of His Son. How appropriate then, that the mother of the one who is "God Made Flesh" would be a pure and spotless virgin.

The doctrine of the Immaculate Conception of Mary has been passed down to us from the very Apostles who walked and talked with Jesus; walked and talked with Mary. It has been passed down to us in an unbroken line from one bishop to the next; one apostle to the next.

Theotokos—God Bearer—Mary, Mother of God

The Catholic Church firmly proclaims Mary to be "the Mother of God." We celebrate this doctrine every year on January first, "The Solemnity of the Blessed Virgin Mary, Mother of God" (CCC 495).

Some people have trouble understanding this and have been taught in their faiths that Mary is not the mother of God, she simply provided a body for Jesus. When we as Catholics say that Mary is the "Mother of God," this does not mean that Mary was the source of the divine nature of Jesus, but that she was the Mother of His human nature and that there was no time when the human Jesus was not God. The second Person of the Trinity existed from all eternity, but when the "Word became flesh," Jesus was both human and divine from the first moment of His conception. Mary is not the Mother of a human being who was adopted as God's Son. She is the Mother of Jesus Christ, both God and human.

Back in the year 431 A.D. there was a heretic by the name of Nestorius. Nestorius denied Mary the title of **Theotokos** or "God-bearer" or "Mother of God". Nestorius claimed that Mary only bore Christ's human nature in her womb, and proposed the alternative title **Christotokos** or "Christ-bearer" or "Mother of Christ".

Orthodox Catholic theologians recognized that Nestorius's theory would fracture Christ into two separate persons; one human and one divine, joined in a sort of loose unity, only one of whom was in her womb. The Church reacted in 431 with the Council of Ephesus, defining that Mary can be properly referred to as the "Mother of God," not in the sense that she is the source of the divine nature of Jesus, but in the sense that the person she carried in her womb was, in fact, God incarnate.

Those teaching this same theology today have fallen into the same heresy as Nestorius. This was dealt with by the Church over 1,582 years ago and unfortunately, we are still battling it today. Jesus was conceived by the power of the Holy Spirit. The Angel Gabriel said, "You will conceive and bear a Son and He will be the Son of the Most High." The baby in Mary's womb was Jesus and Jesus was both human and divine at the moment of His conception. He remains both human and divine today.

Moreover, when Mary went to visit her cousin Elizabeth, Elizabeth exclaimed in a loud voice, "How does this happen to me that the **Mother of my Lord** should come to me?" Notice that Elizabeth calls Mary "The Mother of my Lord". Clearly Elizabeth is referring to Mary as the "Mother of God," for the words *Lord* and *God* are used interchangeably.

The Blessed Mary, Ever-Virgin (CCC 499-507)

The Bible teaches that Mary was a virgin when she gave birth to Christ. The Catholic Church has always taught and believed that Mary remained a virgin her whole life. Early Christian writers agreed that Jesus had no blood brothers and sisters and that Mary remained a virgin. Saint Jerome (345-420) wrote that "learned men going back to apostolic times testified to the perpetual virginity of Mary." Early Protestants, like Luther and Calvin, also believed in Mary's perpetual virginity. More recently, however, their belief has been questioned.

The New Testament speaks of "brothers" and "sisters" of Jesus. But it never refers to other children of Mary or Joseph. There are many passages which indicate that Jesus did not have blood brothers or sisters. For example, two of those who are called brothers of Jesus, namely James and Joseph (Matthew 13:55), are later identified as sons of a woman other than Mary (Matt 27:56). If Mary had other children, it is difficult to explain why Jesus, as He hung on the cross, would have given Mary into the care of the "Beloved Disciple" (John 19:26-27). The word *brothers* is frequently used in the New Testament for the followers of Jesus (John 20:17-18, Luke 8:21). We also know that in Jesus' language of Aramaic, there was no specific word for "cousin" or "relative." The word *brother* was used interchangeably to refer to a relative or cousin.

The Church has been guided by the same Holy Spirit who inspired the Bible, and the Church teaches that the brothers and sisters of Jesus were actually relatives and followers. The Church believes that Mary remained ever a virgin and teaches the faithful to hold this believe to be true.

Suffering Along with Jesus

As Catholics we believe that Mary helped in the redemption of the human race. This means that she had a part in redeeming us. We do not say that she is "the Redeemer" or that she did as much as Jesus. We only say that she helped in our redemption and she did so by her obedience to the will of God.

We also say that Mary shared in the sufferings of Christ. How the events would unfold was not crystal clear to Mary when the Angel Gabriel appeared to her. She had questions such as, "How can this be since I have no relations with a man?" (Luke 1:34). The angel told her that the Holy Spirit would come upon her and that God's power would overshadow her; that the child would be called holy, the Son of God (Luke 1:35).

How would she explain to Joseph that she was suddenly pregnant with the Messiah? In those days they stoned women who were found pregnant outside of marriage. Possibly she worried that she could be stoned to death or that people would talk about her behind her back; about this scandal of how she was found to be with child before she and Joseph lived together. Even though Mary was not sure how these events would unfold, she trusted God. She said, "Behold, I am the handmaid of the Lord. May it be done to me according to your word" (Luke 1:38).

Near the end of her nine month term, Mary learns that she and Joseph must travel all the way to Bethlehem (on a donkey) to be counted in the census. She and Joseph arrive in Bethlehem only to find that there is no place for them to stay and she is about to give birth. Mary gives birth to the Savior of the world in a stable for animals. Still she trusted that this was God's plan.

The Holy Family then traveled to Jerusalem to present Jesus to God, in the temple. Jesus had entered the Covenant of His Father Abraham when He was circumcised. Now as part of the precepts of the law, He was presented in the temple. There was an old man at the Temple, named Simeon, who had been watching for the Messiah of Israel to be born. The prophet Daniel was told by the angel Gabriel that the exile of God's people would last 490 years (Daniel 9:24). At the end of the 490 years, the Messiah would come. At this point it had been 490 years and many in Israel were waiting for the Messiah. Simeon was told by God that he would not die until he saw the face of God's *Anointed One*; the Messiah. When Mary and Joseph brought Jesus to the temple, Simeon took one look at Jesus and knew He was God's *Anointed One*. Simeon took Jesus into his arms and said to Mary, "Behold, this child is appointed for the fall and rise of many in Israel. And you yourself, a sword will pierce" (Luke 2:34-35). Simeon thus predicted that Mary was going to suffer along with her Son.

Mary and Joseph returned to Bethlehem until Joseph had a dream that King Herod wanted to kill Jesus. The Holy Family had to flee in the middle of the night to Egypt and stay there until the death of King Herod. This family suddenly found themselves refugees. They had to go into hiding. They were forced to start a new life in a strange country.

When Jesus was twelve years old, the Holy Family traveled to Jerusalem for the Passover Feast. As the family returned to Nazareth, Mary realized that Jesus was not among them or their relatives. Mary and Joseph returned to Jerusalem in search of Jesus. It took three days to find Him. Mary was deeply worried (Luke 2:41-52).

At age 30, Jesus left her to begin His mission. Mary knew that Jesus' mission would end with His suffering and death. This is because she knew the Scriptures and how the prophets foretold of the suffering servant. She met Jesus on the way to the cross, full of tears, wishing she could take His pain away. She saw her beloved Son hanging on a cross. Mary saw Him die. Jesus was taken down from the cross and laid in her arms as complete sorrow engulfed her being.

As Catholics we see the sufferings of Mary. A sword certainly did pierce her heart, just as Simeon predicted. This is why Mary is sometimes referred to as, "Our Lady of Sorrows." Each year on September 15th, we celebrate the Feast of "Our Lady of Sorrows" and the remembrance of the seven ways Mary's heart was pierced:

- The Prophecy of Simeon
- The Flight into Egypt
- The Loss of the Child Jesus in the Temple
- The Meeting of Jesus and Mary on the Way of the Cross
- The Crucifixion and Death of Jesus
- The Taking down of the Body of Jesus from the Cross.
- The Burial of Jesus

The Assumption Body and Soul of Mary into Heaven

As Catholics we joyfully celebrate the fact that Mary was assumed into Heaven, body and soul. We maintain that Mary died as any of us die. However, we believe that shortly after her death, Mary's body was assumed into Heaven by Jesus to be united with her soul. This is called "the Assumption of Mary" and this feast day is celebrated on August 15th each year (CCC 966).

The doctrine of the Assumption is an important aspect of Catholic belief, infallibly taught by the Church. It was defined in 1950 by Pope Pius XII, not on his own initiative, but in answer to millions of petitions from all over the world. Its scriptural basis is John's vision in Revelation chapter 12 of Christ's Mother, wearing a crown of twelve stars, clothed with the sun, with the moon under her feet. It proclaims that at the end of Mary's life on earth, Jesus gave her victory over death, and her body shared fully in His Resurrection, as ours will only at the end of time. Because Mary never sinned, she was able to experience complete union with her Son, Jesus. This doctrine is a sign of hope because it points the way to Heaven for us, who are like Mary, members of the Church.

Let's look at this Scripture passage from the twelfth chapter of the Book of Revelation in detail: "A great sign appeared in the sky, a woman clothed with the sun, with the moon under her feet, and on her head a crown of twelve stars. She was with child and wailed aloud in pain as she labored to give birth. Then another sign appeared in the sky; it was a huge red dragon, with seven heads and ten horns, and on its heads were seven diadems. Its tail swept away a third of the stars in the sky and hurled them down to the earth. Then the dragon stood before the woman about to give birth, to devour her child when she gave birth. She gave birth to a son, a male child, destined to rule all the nations with an iron rod. Her child was caught up to God and His throne. The woman herself fled into the desert where she had a place prepared by God, that there she might be taken care of for twelve hundred and sixty days" (Revelation 12: 1-6). This is a long passage, but in reading it in its entirety, it becomes quite obvious that it refers to Mary. For the woman in the passage gives "birth to a Son, a male child, destined to rule all the nations with an iron rod." Who other than Mary has given birth to a Son destined to rule all nations? This reference is clearly about Jesus and His mother. Again, this vision shows Christ's Mother, wearing a crown of twelve stars, clothed with the sun, with the moon under her feet. It proclaims that at the end of Mary's life on earth, Jesus gave her victory over death, and her body shared fully in His Resurrection, as ours will only at the end of time.

We don't have any record of how the Assumption of Mary took place, however, it can be read in detail from the Visions of Venerable Anne Catherine Emmerich in the book, The Life of Jesus Christ and Biblical Revelations. This four volume set of books contains the day by day account of the three-year Public Life of Christ, actually witnessed in *vision* by one of the greatest mystics in the history of the Church, Venerable Anne Catherine Emmerich. Venerable Anne Catherine Emmerich explains that in the vision of the Assumption, Mary was living with the Apostle John, who had gone to Ephesus to spread the gospel. In her sixty-third year, Mary called all the Apostles to her in prayer. One by one they arrived in Ephesus. While they were there, Mary died. The apostles celebrated Mass at the house where Mary lived, while she lay on a small couch. They gave her communion; the Eucharist—the Body and Blood of Jesus. She lay back down and died a few moments later. The women prepared her body for burial anointing it and wrapping it in burial cloths, while Andrew and Matthias were busy preparing the place of burial. The apostles took her body to the tomb carrying her the entire way in a little coffin. They laid the coffin inside the tomb on a raised stone and sealed the coffin with leather straps in three places. Then they prayed and closed the tomb. In front of this place they planted berry bushes and flowers concealing its entrance. Then they knelt in prayer again outside the tomb. Soon they noticed a radiant cloud that seemed to come to the earth and to the tomb. Some of the Apostles were frightened and looked downward, while others were awestruck and looked upward.

Anne Catherine could see what was in the cloud, but the Apostles could not. Anne Catherine saw the soul of the Blessed Mother joyfully descending the cloud toward the tomb. Then she could see Jesus in the cloud bringing His Mother, body and soul, to Heaven with Him; surrounded by angels. The mood was a joyous one.

Once the radiant cloud departed, the Apostles made their way back to the little house. The following day, Thomas and a couple of other disciples arrived. Thomas was struck with grief that he had arrived late and was not among them when the Blessed Mother had died. The Apostles took Thomas and the other disciples to the tomb where Mary had been laid. When they arrived to the place, John opened the tomb and entered into it. With Thomas beside him, he loosened the three straps and raised the lid on the coffin laying it aside. There they saw with amazement the grave clothes still wrapped around but empty. The body of the Blessed Virgin was gone. John called to the others outside the cave, "Come see and wonder. She is no longer here." The others walked in two by two and saw for themselves. With uplifted arms they looked up to Heaven weeping and praising God, for they remembered the radiant cloud they had seen the night before. John took the Blessed Virgin's grave-clothes and the coffin with great reverence out of the tomb to keep as relics. They then closed the tomb and returned home.

The visions of Anne Catherine Emmerich have been approved by the Church. However, as members of the Church we are free to believe them or to discard them. The approval from the Church lets us know that there is nothing contained in them that is contrary to Church teaching. What is important to believe is not necessarily how it happened, but that it did happen. Mary was assumed into Heaven body and soul.

Another interesting thing to keep in mind when pondering the Assumption of the Blessed Virgin, Mary is that Christians have always venerated the bones of the saints. When a saint died, the bones were kept and treated with great reverence. They have become relics buried under and inside of the altars used in Catholic Churches. No one has ever claimed to have the bones of the Blessed Virgin Mary. Yet she was and always has been considered the greatest saint.

Another thing to keep in mind is that Jesus is "the New Adam" and Mary is "the New Eve". It was God's original plan for Adam and Eve that they would be taken to Heaven body and soul. Because they sinned, that did not happen, but what about Jesus and Mary? If they are the 'New Adam' and the 'New Eve' and they did all things according to God's plan, wouldn't He then take both of them body and soul into Heaven as He originally planned to do? Jesus, being God, ascended into Heaven. He went to Heaven by His own power. Mary, being only human and not divine, was taken into Heaven (assumed). She could not go on her own power.

Mary is Our Spiritual Mother

Mary is our 'Spiritual Mother' and the 'Mother of the Church' (CCC 501, 963). We believe that she was given to us by Jesus to be our 'Spiritual Mother' while He was hanging on the cross. Let's look at that Scripture for a moment. In the gospel of John chapter 19 verses 26 and 27, Jesus speaks while He is on the cross. Standing at the foot of the cross were His mother, Mary, the apostle John, Mary, His mother's sister-in-law; and Mary Magdalene. We have to pay particular attention to everything that Jesus said while He was on the cross, because it is so very difficult to speak while hanging on the cross. In fact, it was nearly impossible to speak. Yet, Jesus said several things. These things Jesus spoke must have been very important since He took the trouble to say them. At one point, Jesus looked down at His Mother and said, "Woman, behold your son." He then looked at John, His disciple, and said, "Son, behold your mother." At that moment, Jesus gave His mother to all of us as our 'Spiritual Mother'. We became Mary's spiritual children; her spiritual offspring. Jesus was not simply talking to Mary and John. He was talking to all of us. Jesus was giving His mother to the whole world. Who would have understood this teaching better than John himself? John the apostle explained and taught that Mary became our 'Spiritual Mother' that day and the Mother of the Church (CCC 964).

She is Called "Woman" in Scripture

Let us delve into the Bible, both the Old Testament and the New Testament for a little bit and consider the word, "*Woman*," used in the Bible to mean a specific person. First, let us go back to the beginning, the book of Genesis Chapter 3 verse 15. Right after Adam and Eve sinned against God by eating the fruit of the Tree of Knowledge of Good and Evil, God cursed the serpent who was Satan. In verse 15 we get the "Protoevangelium" or the first announcement of Good News. Think about this. Adam and Eve had everything! But still they rejected God. Our God is so good; so merciful; that immediately He promises something good to them. God said, "I will put enmity between you and *the woman*. I will put enmity between your offspring and the offspring of *the woman*. Her offspring shall crush your head, while your offspring strikes at His heal." Way back in the beginning; way back in Genesis; we have a *woman* identified as a key figure in our redemption. *The woman* of course is Mary. Her offspring, of course, is Jesus. But Jesus makes this clear to us. He wants us to understand that the "*Woman*," named in Genesis Chapter 3, is none other than His mother. So this theme of the "*Woman*" continues on into the New Testament.

In the Gospel of John chapter 2 we read about the wedding in Cana. Mary, Jesus, and the disciples are at a wedding feast of a family friend when suddenly they run out of wine. Mary is the one who is first made aware of the problem. To save the bride and groom embarrassment, Mary comes to Jesus and tells Him about the situation. Mary simply says to Jesus, "They have no wine." Notice how Jesus responds to Mary, His mother. He says to her, "Woman, how does your concern affect me? My hour has not yet come." Have you ever wondered why Jesus refers to His mother as "Woman"? His words almost seem to indicate disrespect. Yet I know in my heart that Jesus never sinned, so He would never show disrespect to His mother. I later learned that for Jewish people of Jesus' time, the term "*Woman*" was a sign of great respect; not disrespect. The Church teaches us that Jesus refers to His mother as "*Woman*" so that you and I will make the connection between Mary, His mother, and the "*Woman*" in Genesis whose offspring will crush the head of Satan.

Continuing into the New Testament and into the Gospel of John chapter 19, we are at the foot of the cross. It is here that Jesus calls His mother, '*Woman*' again. "*Woman*, behold your son." Again, Jesus is making sure we understand that Mary is the "*Woman*" in Genesis whose offspring will crush the head of Satan.

If we go even further into the New Testament to the Book of Revelation, Chapter 11, John sees the Ark of the Covenant and the Ark of the Covenant is a *Woman*. In Chapter 12 John begins describing the Ark, which again is a *woman*. John saw "a woman, clothed with the sun, with the moon under her feet, and on her head a crown of twelve stars." This *woman* that John is seeing;

this *woman* who is the Ark of the Covenant; is Mary. Mary is the Ark of the Covenant.

Mary, the Ark of the Covenant

John sees the Ark of the New Covenant in Heaven. Before we can discuss how Mary is the fulfilled Ark of the Covenant, an understanding of "Types" is needed. A *Type* is a person, a thing, or an event in the Old Testament that prefigures a reality in the New Testament. The New Testament realities are always more glorious, more effective, or more universal than their Old Testament *Type*. St. Augustine said, "The Old Testament is the New concealed, but the New Testament is the Old revealed." In other words, there are people, things or events in the Old Testament that become gloriously revealed in the New Testament. As I mentioned earlier, Jesus is the New Testament Adam and Mary is the New Testament Eve. Jesus and Mary are far more glorious and completely fulfill what Adam and Eve were meant to be! Adam therefore is the Old Testament *Type* of Jesus, while Eve is the Old Testament *Type* of Mary. Eve tied a knot of disobedience that Mary untied by her obedience. Jesus died in obedience to God; something that Adam was not willing to do.

How does this help us to understand Mary as the Ark of the Covenant? Well, 1,000 years before the birth of Mary there was a sacred chest of wood. This chest of wood was covered in Gold and made in the time of Moses. This chest of wood was called, "the Ark of the Covenant." The Israelites carried it wherever they went for it truly contained God Himself.

Yes, it was true. The Ark of the Covenant contained God. He was inside the Ark, but how? Well, contained inside the Ark was the stone tablets inscribed with the Ten Commandments written with the very hand of God. The Ark also contained

390

Aaron's rod; the rod that the High Priest, Aaron, used. This rod actually sprouted and budded as if it were still a live tree. In addition, the Ark contained an urn of Manna; Manna that fell from Heaven and sustained the children of Israel while they wandered in the desert. This precious Ark of the Old Covenant prefigured the arrival of Mary; the Ark of the New Covenant.

Let's examine the similarities between the Old Testament Ark and Mary, the New Testament Ark. In the Old Testament, we are told that David rose and went up to the Hill country of Judea. In the New Testament, we are told that Mary, pregnant with Jesus, rose and went up to the hill country of Judea to visit her cousin Elizabeth.

In the Old Testament, we are told that David asked, "Who am I that the Ark of the Lord should come to me?" In the New Testament, we are told that Elizabeth asked, "Who am I that the Mother of my Lord should come to me?"

In the Old Testament we are told that the Ark stayed in the house of Obed-Edom for 3 months. In the New Testament we are told that Mary stayed in the house of Elizabeth for 3 months.

In the Old Testament, we are told that David leaped and danced before the Ark. In the New Testament, we are told that John the Baptist leaped in the womb of his mother Elizabeth at the sound of Mary's voice.

In the Old Testament we are told that the Tabernacle, which housed the Ark, was covered or overshadowed by the Glory Cloud and that the Glory of the Lord filled the Tabernacle. In the New Testament, we are told by the Angel Gabriel that the Holy Spirit would come upon Mary and the power of the Most High would overshadow her.

More important than anything else is what is contained inside of the Old Testament and the New Testament Arks:
1) Inside the Old Testament Ark was the Law of God inscribed on stone tablets; God's actual words inscribed in stone. In the

womb of Mary is Jesus, the Word of God made Flesh. 2) Inside the Old Testament Ark was an urn containing Manna; bread that fell from the sky to feed the Israelites as they wandered through the dessert. They called this the "bread from Heaven." Inside of Mary's womb is Jesus, the Bread of Life, who has come down from Heaven. Jesus is the bread that we as Catholics eat at every Mass. 3) Inside the Old Testament Ark was found the budding Rod of Aaron, the High Priest of the Israelites. Inside the womb of Mary is Jesus, the true and Eternal High Priest, Himself. What amazing parallels there are between these two arks! Both Arks contained God, but Mary is the new and eternal Ark of the New and Eternal Covenant revealing the Son of God to us.

Mary's Role in the Church

What exactly is Mary's role? What does she do for the Church today? First of all it is important to understand that the Church is "The Kingdom of God". The Church is God's Kingdom. It exists here on earth and it also exists in Heaven and in Purgatory. So the question we are actually asking is: What is Mary's role in the Kingdom of God? The answer is simple: Mary is the Queen Mother. She is the Queen of Heaven.

When the angel Gabriel appeared to Mary to tell her that God wanted her to be the Mother of His Son, the angel said, "Behold, you will conceive in your womb and bear a son, and you shall name Him Jesus. He will be great and will be called Son of the Most High, *and the Lord God will give Him the throne of David His Father, and He will rule over the house of Jacob forever, and of His kingdom, there will be no end*" (Luke chapter 1 starting with verse 30). Now these words are very important. The angel mentions King David; that Jesus will have the throne of King David; and that He will rule this Kingdom, called the house of Jacob, forever without end. Jacob of course is the son of Isaac. Isaac was, of course, the son of Abraham. Jacob, whose name was changed by God to *Israel*, had twelve sons and from these twelve sons came the "Twelve Tribes of Israel." David became the second king to rule over the house of Jacob. He was the beloved King of Israel who united God's people, the Israelites. All Jews, including Mary, would have understood the Kingdom of David. They would have understood exactly how that Kingdom was run. These words spoken by the angel Gabriel seem a bit confusing to us, but to Mary they had great meaning. Gabriel is explaining that the "Kingdom of God" is going to be the fulfillment of the "Kingdom of David" that took place here on earth. Jesus is to be the new king of this new kingdom, the Kingdom of God.

Since Jesus will sit on the "throne of His Father David," the structure for the Kingdom of David will also be the structure for the Kingdom of God. The Kingdom of God will be more glorious, however, because it will fulfill the Kingdom of David. This is another example of a *Type*. The "Kingdom of David" is the Old Testament *Type* for the "Kingdom of God." This means that if we understand the Kingdom of David, then we will understand the Kingdom of God. So let us examine the structure of the Kingdom of David so that we can understand the structure of the Kingdom of God—the Church.

In the Kingdom of David there were three very important positions of authority. The three positions of authority that we find in the Old Testament book, First Kings, are: King, Queen Mother, and Chief Steward. Let us examine each of these. First, there was the position of the *King*. In First Kings, Solomon was made King by David on his death bed. The King was the *anointed one* of God. David had been anointed king and now Solomon was anointed king.

Second, there was the position of the *Queen Mother*. The Queen Mother was exactly what the title suggests. She was the mother of the King. Since Solomon was King in the example found in the First Book of Kings, the Queen Mother, then, was Solomon's mother, Bathsheba.

Third, there was the position of the Chief Steward, who was appointed by the King. The Chief Steward was the main steward of the kingdom. It was his job to rule in the king's absence until his return. The Chief Steward was given the "Keys to the Kingdom," which was a symbol of his authority to rule in the king's absence. The one with the keys is the one who is in charge.

This is the pattern then for the Kingdom of God—the Church. If the Kingdom of David had a King, who was Solomon—David's son, then the Kingdom of God must also have a King who is God's Son—Jesus. If the Kingdom of David had a Queen Mother, who was the King's mother; Solomon's Mother—Bathsheba, then the Kingdom of God must also have a Queen Mother who is the King's Mother; Jesus' mother—Mary. If the Kingdom of David had a Chief Steward, who was given the keys to the Kingdom; the authority to rule in the king's absence, then the Kingdom of God must also have a Chief Steward who has been given the keys to the kingdom and the authority to rule in the King's absence. To whom did Jesus give the keys to the Kingdom? Please recall the words of Jesus from Matthew's Gospel chapter 16: "I say to you, you are Peter and upon this Rock I will build my Church and the gates of Hell shall not prevail against it. *I give you the Keys to the Kingdom*. Whatever you bind on earth shall be bound in Heaven and whatever you loose on earth shall be loosed in Heaven." Jesus gave the keys to the Kingdom to Peter, the first Pope of the Church. Subsequently, these keys have been passed down to each pope all the way to Pope Francis.

Let us focus then on the position of the Queen Mother who is the King's mother. If Jesus is to be the King, and Mary is

His mother, then Mary is destined to be the 'Queen Mother.' Mary, fully understanding the angel's words, goes off to visit her cousin Elizabeth. Elizabeth knows by the grace of the Holy Spirit that Mary bears in her womb the Christ child; that she is to be the Mother of the Savior. The Gospel of Luke tells us that "When Elizabeth heard Mary's greeting, the infant leaped in her womb, and Elizabeth, filled with the Holy Spirit, cried out in a loud voice and said, "Most blessed are you among women, and blessed is the fruit of your womb. And how does this happen to me that the mother of my Lord should come to me?" Here Elizabeth fully recognizes Mary as the Queen Mother. She is astonished that the Mother of her Lord; the mother of the King; the mother of God; *the Queen Mother;* has come to visit her. Knowing that she is to become the *Queen Mother*, Mary cries out in complete humility, "My soul proclaims the greatness of the Lord. My spirit rejoices in God my savior, for He has looked upon His handmaid's lowliness. Behold, from now on all ages will call me blessed. The Almighty has done great things for me and holy is His name."

The Role of the Queen Mother

Learning what the Queen Mother's role entailed in the Davidic Kingdom, will help us to then understand what Mary's role entails as *Queen Mother* in God's Kingdom. In First Kings chapter two we have a great example of what the job of the Queen Mother entailed. On his death bed, David makes his son Solomon the new King. Solomon then takes over as King as soon as David dies. If Solomon is King, then Solomon's mother would be the Queen Mother. Bathsheba was Solomon's mother so she immediately becomes the Queen Mother. A man by the name of Adonijah comes to make a request of the new King, but he does not go directly to King Solomon. Instead he goes to the Queen Mother, Bathsheba. Adonijah wants to make a request of King

Solomon. Adonijah wants a girl, named Abishag, to be his wife. So he comes to Bathsheba, the Queen Mother, and asks Bathsheba to go and ask King Solomon on his behalf, if he may take Abishag to be his wife. Adonijah says in essence to Bathsheba: "Please ask the king for me. He will not refuse you. Make this request on my behalf, because the King will not refuse if you do the asking."

Let us analyze this a bit. Adonijah, wants Abishag to be his wife. Adonijah goes to Bathsheba, the Queen Mother, to make this request. He does not go to the Queen Mother because she can grant this request. He simply wants the Queen Mother to go to the King on his behalf and ask the king for him. Why? Adonijah wants the Queen Mother to ask King Solomon because the King will not refuse to grant his mother, the Queen Mother, whatever she wishes. Going through the Queen Mother, the King is more likely to grant Adonijah's request. Adonijah goes to the Queen Mother and asks the Queen Mother to go to the King *for him*. Why? That was the job of the Queen Mother. The Queen Mother was the advocate for the people. The people could go to the Queen Mother and make a request and the Queen Mother would ask the King for them. The King was more likely to answer the request favorably if his mother made the request. The Queen Mother was the intercessor to the King.

In the Catholic Church, which is the Kingdom of God here on earth and Jesus' Kingdom, this is still the role of the *Queen Mother*. Just as it was in the Kingdom of David, it is done in the Kingdom of God. We can go to Mary and ask her to go to Jesus, the King, on our behalf. Mary is our advocate; our intercessor. We talk to Mary and ask her to pray for us and in doing so we are asking Mary to go to Jesus for us (CCC 969). We do this especially when what we are praying for is of great importance, because the King is more likely to answer favorably if His mother is the one who makes the request. Just as it was in the Kingdom of David it is in the Kingdom of God.

We can easily see from this Old Testament example that Mary, our Mother; our advocate; our intercessor; is a teaching that is deeply rooted in the history of Israel and completely established by God. Mary is the *Queen Mother* of the Kingdom that now exists in Heaven and on earth as the Church.

In the New Testament story of the Wedding Feast in Cana, we have a great example of Mary's role as intercessor. The bride and groom run out of wine at the wedding in Cana. This is a great embarrassment. Mary is informed of this great problem first. The people turn to Mary and ask her to help with the problem. She is the first to know. Mary cannot create new wine. She cannot answer the prayer herself, so what does she do? She goes to Jesus. The people went to Mary for help and Mary in turn goes to Jesus for them.

We Do Not Worship Mary; We Honor Her

Catholics are sometimes accused of worshipping Mary. The truth is that Catholics do not worship Mary. However, we proudly honor her. Again, this is biblical. In the Gospel of Luke Mary says of herself, "Behold, from now on all ages will call me blessed." (Luke 1:48) In obedience to this passage, generations of Catholics have been proud to call Mary their "Blessed Mother."

Today our society honors many people; people who have done great things. We honor our parents as the Fourth Commandment instructs us to do. We have pictures of our grandparents in our homes, because we love and honor them. Our society even honors football players; baseball players; musicians; actors and all kinds of people who have done extraordinary things as part of their careers or jobs. We honor the military and fire fighters who put their lives on the line. Our society honors rescue workers and police officers who do extraordinary things. We honor George Washington, Abraham Lincoln, and Martin Luther King by giving everyone a day off of school and work to recognize the accomplishments of these great men! Many of us honor Mary because of the example she showed to us in how to be a perfect disciple of Jesus. Mary totally conformed to God's will. She did everything God asked her to do and she did it perfectly.

Think about what Eve caused to happen. Eve was created without sin. She possessed the very Life of God in her soul. Yet she chose to sin against God and Adam chose to sin against God; causing all of us to sin against God. Look at the mess sin has created in our world. It is literally the source of all our problems on this earth. Mary said, "Yes" to God. Her 'Yes' helped to bring about our redemption; our salvation. Think about what would have happened if Mary had said, "No" as Eve said "No". There would have been no savior; no redemption; no going to Heaven if Mary had said, "No." Mary's "Yes" opened up the way for God to send His only Son to die for us so that we could have eternal life with Him in Heaven.

If society can honor a football player who makes a spectacular touchdown; basketball players who seem to be able to fly through the air; baseball players who can hit hundreds of homeruns; racecar drivers who win upwards of 200 races; if we can honor George Washington, Abraham Lincoln, and Martin Luther King for their great acts in aiding our country, we as Catholics can certainly honor the Mother of Jesus who made it possible for God's Son to come into this world; suffer for us; die for us; and open the gates of Heaven. What is more important than being saved; than being allowed to live with God in Heaven for all Eternity? Nothing is more important than that!

We think so much about our heroes here in the United States. We want to be like all those sports figures or singers or actors who have done well. Mary is what we are all called to be. Mary was without sin. She was born without sin and she never sinned during her life. She is who we should want to be like. As Catholics, we give Mary the greatest honor. We venerate Mary the most, because she is our perfect example and her, "Yes" brought about our salvation.

The Apparitions of Mary

Mary is our Mother, and Catholics have experienced her intercession in many ways. Generations of believers have praised Mary as one who has led them to the grace of God. Many trustworthy and holy individuals have reported apparitions of Mary, often accompanied by messages that have been the source of countless blessings. Shrines at the sites of such appearances are visited by millions of people every year, most notably are: Our Lady of Guadalupe in Mexico, at Lourdes in France, and at Fatima in Portugal. All of these apparitions are similar in that Mary appears to the poorest and humblest among us rather than to the rich or learned. Her message is always the same. She calls us to repent of our disobedience to God; to return to a life of prayer and penance; a life of faith and love. To convince us of God's love and mercy, she brings His healing to many.

What does the Church do when a person reports an apparition of Mary? The Church employs a long process in reviewing the validity of the reported apparitions. Nothing new is ever revealed in these apparitions. The message can never be contrary to the teaching of the Church given to us by the Apostles. So a message given to us by Mary in an authentic apparition will never convey anything that is contrary to the teaching of the Church. The Church classifies apparitions into one of three categories: Either it is 1) Not worthy of belief. In other words, don't believe it. 2) Not contrary to faith. In other words, it is consistent with the teaching of the Church or 3) Worthy of belief. In other words, it is worth believing. The Catholic Church does not require that its members believe in such appearances, but there have been official declarations that some apparitions and the messages associated with them are not contrary to Catholic doctrine and are worthy of belief. We believe on the evidence of Scripture that God sends angels as messengers, and it is reasonable to believe that Jesus can send His Mother as an emissary.

Many miracles of healing have occurred at Marian shrines; hundreds of them have been carefully studied by medical bureaus and have been declared to be beyond any medical explanation. The shrine at Lourdes is especially noted for its miracles. Anyone who studies these miracles, as they have been described in numerous books and magazine articles, cannot help but be amazed at the evident presence of God's power and grace working through the intercession of Mary.

Jesus said that we can judge a tree by its fruit. We can certainly see the good fruit of God's blessings flowing from Guadalupe, Lourdes, and Fatima. They are evidence of God's loving care and of Mary's maternal affection for people of every race and nation.

Our Lady of Guadalupe

The Blessed Virgin Mary appeared to an Aztec Indian named Juan Diego in Mexico in the year 1531. This was a time of great difficulty for the Aztec Indians who had been recently conquered by Cortez. These Indians had been enslaved into forced labor and millions had died of smallpox. Christianity was being forced upon them by the Spaniards, because the Indian religion included the sacrifice of children and babies among other terrible acts.

One morning Juan Diego was on his way to Mass. As he walked up a hill called Tepeyac, just outside of Mexico City, he saw a beautiful lady. The lady spoke to him in his native language. She told Juan that she was the Virgin Mary, the Mother of God. She told Juan that she wanted him to take a message to the local bishop. She wanted a church built on that very hill in her honor.

Juan immediately went to see the local bishop, Bishop Zumarraga, and told him all that had happened. Bishop Zumarraga was very skeptical and didn't really believe Juan. He told Juan to come back some other time and speak to him about this matter. Juan returned to the hill Tepeyac and there he saw the lady again. He knelt before her and said, "My Lady, the bishop did not believe me. I am unworthy of your trust. Please send someone else." The Blessed Virgin Mary said to Juan, "My son, you are the one I have chosen. Return to the Bishop tomorrow and repeat my request for a church in this place." The next day was Sunday. After Mass, Juan went to Mexico City again to see the bishop. Again he told the bishop that the Virgin Mary, Mother of God, had told him that she wanted a church built on the hill Tepeyac. The Bishop told Juan that he wanted the lady to give him a sign as proof that she was really Mary, the Mother of God, who spoke to him.

Again, as he was returning home, Juan met the Virgin Mary on the hill Tepeyac and he told her that the bishop wanted a sign. Mary asked Juan to return at daybreak the next day and she would provide a sign. The next day, however, Juan did not come, because when he awoke his uncle, with whom he lived, was very sick with a fever. The next day, December 12th, Juan awoke to find that his uncle's condition had worsened. Fearing that his uncle would die, Juan hurried to get a priest. Again he met the Virgin Mary on the hill. Juan told Mary that he could not help her; that he was on his way to get a priest for his uncle who was dying. The Blessed Virgin Mary told Juan that his uncle was already cured by her intercession and not to worry any longer. She pointed up the hill and told Juan to cut the flowers growing there. Juan was amazed when he reached the top of the hill that there were roses growing everywhere, even though it was the middle of the winter. Juan cut the roses and returned to Mary. Mary took the roses and arranged them with her own hands into Juan's work apron, called a tilma. Then she told Juan to take the roses to the bishop as the sign that he wanted.

Juan did as the Virgin Mary told him. He took the roses in his work apron or tilma to the bishop. When Juan met the bishop, he opened his tilma to show him the roses. The bishop immediately fell to his knees. The roses were an amazing sign since they simply do not grow in the winter, but there was an even more amazing sign imprinted on Juan's tilma. The vision of the lady that Juan had seen was printed on the front of Juan's tilma, in all her beauty and in living color. The Virgin was with child. She wore European clothing with Indian designs on them. She had the face of an Aztec. The Blessed Mother seemed to be uniting the two cultures.

When Juan returned home that day, he found his uncle had been cured just as Mary had said. A church was built as the Virgin Mary requested. Today the tilma that Juan was wearing, bearing the image of the Blessed Virgin Mary, is hanging in a large modern church in Mexico. Thousands of people from all over the world come to see it each year. Even more amazing is the fact that the tilma looks exactly the same today as it did then, even though it has been nearly 500 years. The tilma, made of cactus, has not deteriorated one bit and the image of the Blessed Mother is as vibrant and colorful today as it was in 1531

This apparition has been declared authentic on the basis of the proof of Juan's tilma, which shows the vision of Our Lady of

Guadalupe. Nine million Aztecs converted to Catholicism as a result of this apparition.

Our Lady of Lourdes

The most popular shrine of Our Lady in Europe is located at Lourdes, France. It receives five million visitors each year and was the place of the apparition of Our Lady of Lourdes.

A girl from a poor family, named Bernadette Soubirous, saw 18 visions of the Blessed Virgin Mary between February 11th and March 25th 1858, in the garden of Massabielle. By the 18th vision, twenty thousand people had gathered to pray with Bernadette. On February 24th, the lady told Bernadette to bathe in and drink from a spring near the grotto. Bernadette did as she was instructed, but the spring did not begin to flow where it could be seen by others until the next day. Since then this spring has been the source of miraculous healings.

On March 24th, the lady told Bernadette that she wanted a chapel built in the honor of the Blessed Virgin. In her final apparition on March 25th, the lady told Bernadette her identity. She said, "I am the Immaculate Conception." These apparitions have been declared authentic on the basis that so many have been miraculously healed by the waters at Lourdes. Millions make the pilgrimage to Lourdes every year. Many who are sick are cured.

Our Lady of Fatima

In Fatima, a small town in Portugal, the Blessed Virgin Mary appeared six times to three children: Lucia dos Santos, age 8 and her cousins Francisco and Jacinta Martos ages 7 and 6. The first vision was the appearance of an angel who called himself the Angel of Peace. The angel told the children to dedicate themselves to prayer, especially praying to the sacred heart of

Jesus and the Immaculate Heart of Mary. On May 13th 1917, while shepherding a herd, the children saw a beautiful lady dressed in white and surrounded by rays of brilliant light. The lady told the children to return on the 13th of each month until October, when she would reveal her identity to them. She told the children to pray the Rosary every day.

When the family of these children found out about this, they severely interrogated them. The adults tried to get the children to admit they were lying, but the children insisted that they were telling the truth.

During the vision on June 13th, known as the "First Secret," the children were shown a vision of hell and told that souls could be saved if more people would pray the Rosary and devote themselves to the Immaculate Heart of Mary. In the visions that followed from July to October, the children were given two more secrets. The second secret told them that World War I would end, but it predicted that World War II would occur if Russia did not convert and be consecrated to the Immaculate Heart of Mary.

The third secret remained a secret until June of 2000 when the Vatican released it. It was a vision of the Martyrdom of a "Bishop dressed in white". Most think it was a vision of the attempted assassination of Pope John Paul II by a 23-year-old Turk named Mehmet Ali Agca. Mehmet Ali Agca shot Pope John Paul II four times with a 9-mm pistol from a distance of 15 feet as the Pope drove through a crowd of 20,000 in St. Peter's Square on May 13, 1981. This man shot our Holy Father at very close range, yet the bullet miraculously missed every vital organ in his body. Notice how the date of May 13th corresponds to the apparitions at Fatima.

During the final vision, the lady told the children that she was "Our Lady of the Rosary." At this final apparition, 7,000 people gathered. It was raining very, very hard and the people were soaking wet. Suddenly the rain stopped and the sun came out. Witnesses saw the sun dance in the sky and then plunge toward the earth. People fell to their knees crying out to God to save them. At this the sun returned to its place in the sky and the rain-drenched people were suddenly dry and comfortable. This report of the "dancing sun" was reported in the newspapers.

The Apparitions of Fatima were declared authentic on October 13, 1930. The message of Fatima is this: 1) Practice Penance—do kind acts and sacrifices to make up for your sins. 2) Pray the Rosary daily. 3) Practice devotion to the Immaculate Heart of Mary.

There have been other apparitions of Our Lady, though they are not as popular. One is the apparition of 'Our Lady of Akita' in Japan. This apparition is quite relevant today especially in light of the 2011 earthquake that took place there causing a huge tsunami.

The Case of Medjugorje (Katie's Story)

I have a niece whose name is Katie. Back in 2000 when she was sixteen years old, she began to have night sweats. This was happening quite often, but she didn't give it much thought and did not tell anyone. Then Katie began to notice a lump on her neck. She ignored this too for a couple of months and told no one. Finally, she talked to her mother about it, who immediately took her to see a doctor.

Katie was diagnosed with Hodgkin's Lymphoma, a type of cancer. The good news was that 97% of the people who get this type of cancer survive. It is supposed to be a very curable cancer or so we were told.

Katie was immediately treated. She underwent chemotherapy and radiation treatments. The doctors assured us that at the end of these treatments the cancer would be gone and Katie would be just fine. But after the treatments, the cancer was not gone. In fact, the cancer continued to grow even through the treatments. Clearly Katie was not part of the 97% who survive this cancer. She was part of the 3% who do not.

The doctors began to get more aggressive. They would now be using stronger treatments on Katie. The doctors would do their best to save Katie's life, but as a result of these stronger treatments, her body would lose its ability to conceive and bear children.

Katie underwent these stronger more aggressive cancer treatments. Her hair fell out and she received a bone marrow transplant. At the age of 19, she went through menopause just as a fifty year old woman would, thus ruining her chances to bear children. But the most important thing was to save her life.

Once the treatments were over, Katie was examined again. The doctors were hopeful that the cancer would be gone. To their surprise, however, the cancer was not gone. In fact, it had continued to grow despite these more aggressive treatments. At this point, the doctors threw their hands up. They had done all they knew to do. There was nothing more they could do to help Katie. Her parents were told to make her comfortable. Katie was given a few months to live. "Make a Wish Foundation" of Indianapolis was called to action. This is a group that takes terminally ill children to places like Disney World. They give children a last request fun thing to do before they die. Indianapolis Colts players came to see Katie handing her signed footballs. Even Jeff Gordon and Tony Stuart, the famous race car drivers, visited Katie in her hospital room. Soon afterward, Katie was sent home to the care of her parents.

A month later Katie had an appointment to see how much the cancer had progressed. Sadly, it was still growing. All hope was lost or so people thought.

My family is Catholic and Katie's mother's family is Catholic as well. So both families turned to the only one who could save Katie's life. We turned to Jesus. A friend of ours was getting ready to travel to Medjugorje. Medjugorje is another place where people claim that the Blessed Mother has appeared. The apparitions at Medjugorje took place in the early 1980's. These apparitions have not been approved as of yet by the Catholic Church, however Pope John Paul II did approve pilgrimages to Medjugorje by the faithful.

Upon hearing that a friend of the family was traveling there, each one of our family members began to write a prayer to the Blessed Virgin Mary. In our prayers we asked Mother Mary to ask Jesus to save Katie's life. These letters were bundled up and taken directly to Medjugorje by our friend.

A month later, Katie had another appointment to see how much the cancer had progressed. Upon seeing the results, the doctors could not explain it. They did not understand it. Katie's cancer was gone; completely gone; and she is still cancer free to this day.

Katie married in her early twenties. Three months after her wedding, Katie conceived a child. She gave birth to her first son the following April. Ten months later, Katie conceived her second child. Today, she has three beautiful sons.

Katie was not supposed to live. She wasn't supposed to be able to conceive and bear children. She is a living miracle and her three boys are miracles as well. When our Blessed Mother prays, Jesus listens especially well. He can refuse her nothing.

The Rosary

One of the prayers that I want to encourage you to pray daily is the Rosary. I know what you are thinking: The Rosary takes twenty minutes to pray! Who has time to pray the Rosary every day? Understand that if you pray to Mary and ask her to pray for you she will do it. Do you understand how powerful her prayers are? Do you understand that at the hour of your death, Mary will be right there at your judgment praying for you; interceding for you to her Son, Jesus, and He will not deny her request to save you?

The Rosary is a devotion to Mary. It is a wonderful meditation upon the Gospel. It is an attempt to look at the life of Christ through the eyes of His mother. The Rosary has been called "The Stairway to Heaven" by Saint Francis de Sales and it truly is. According to our Popes, the Rosary is the most highly recommended form of prayer, second only to the Mass. In other words, the Mass is our greatest prayer. The Rosary is our second greatest prayer. When prayed slowly and with reverence we allow the Holy Spirit of God to work the Gospel into our hearts for the Rosary focuses us on the entire life of Jesus and Mary from the cradle to the grave and into the Kingdom of God.

The Rosary calls on Mary to pray for us. It is the greatest devotion to her. Our Lady of Fatima said that if we would only pray the Rosary every day, more souls would be saved; more souls would go to Heaven. When I learned that fact, I began praying the Rosary every day. If I miss a day and don't pray the Rosary, I feel like something is wrong with my day. It is not quite right. Because I pray it every day, I feel a great closeness to the Virgin Mary. I can tell that she is always with me. I know that there is no way that I can convince all of you to pray the Rosary every day, but I sure hope that my words will convinced some of you to pray it every day. It is very important that you have an active relationship with Mary. Devotion to Mary is devotion to

Jesus. No one can lead us to Jesus as well as Mary. She brought Jesus into the world. Now she brings the world to Jesus.

Marian Consecration

Mary desires to bring all of us into the merciful Heart of Jesus. It is her purpose to lead all souls to her beloved Son. Marian Consecration is total Consecration to Jesus through Mary. This is the surest, easiest, shortest, and most perfect means to becoming a saint. I highly recommend that you consecrate yourself to Jesus through Mary. There is a book entitled, "33 Days to Morning Glory," which is a "Do-It-Yourself Retreat" in preparation for Marian Consecration. This could be one of the most important books you will ever read. That book takes you step by step into what Marian Consecration truly means. I recommend that you read it.

Devotional Sacramentals,

As a sign of your Consecration to Jesus through Mary, you may want to begin wearing a Scapular or a Miraculous Medal. These are available online through "The Catholic Company." There is a special procedure for blessing and investiture of the Brown Scapular, which is the Scapular of Our Lady of Mount Carmel. Any priest can help you with this.

Blessed Pope John Paul II was consecrated to Jesus through Mary. He is a great example to us of a very "Marian Pope." Pope Pius XII said, "Let the Brown Scapular be your sign of consecration to the Immaculate Heart of Mary, which we are particularly urging in these perilous times."

XXIII. Dynamic and Engaged Catholics

When it comes to revitalizing Catholicism, I feel that Matthew Kelly is the expert. So in this final chapter, I am going to give you a taste some of his words of wisdom. The following information can be found on his website: DynamicCatholic.com The name of the book is The Four Signs of a Dynamic Catholic. I recommend this book to anyone who is Catholic as well as the other books written by Matthew Kelly. He also has many CD's available for purchase.

The Four Signs of a Dynamic Catholic

"As human beings we are constantly engaging and disengaging in everything we do. We engage and disengage at work, in marriage, as parents, in our quest for health and well-being, in personal finances, environmentally, politically, and, of course, we engage or disengage spiritually.

If you walk into any Catholic church next Sunday and look around, you will discover that some people are highly engaged, others are massively disengaged, and the majority are somewhere in between. Why? What is the difference between highly engaged Catholics and disengaged Catholics?

Answering this question is essential to the future of the Catholic Church. If we truly want to engage Catholics and reinvigorate parish life, we must first discover what drives engagement among Catholics. Four things make the difference between highly engaged Catholics and disengaged Catholics: the Four Signs of a Dynamic Catholic.

The Four Signs of a Dynamic Catholic are:

- PRAYER

- STUDY

- GENEROSITY

- EVANGELIZATION

What percentage of Catholics are "Dynamic?" Only 7 percent.

Only 7 percent of Catholics are engaged and dynamic. At first I found these results very discouraging, but it turns out this might be the best news the Catholic Church has received in decades. Why is it good news that only seven percent of American Catholics are highly engaged? Well, think about the tremendous contribution that the Catholic Church makes every day in communities large and small across America and around the world. Every single day we serve Catholics and non-Catholics around the world by feeding more people, housing more people, clothing more people, caring for more sick people, visiting more prisoners, and educating more students than any other institution on the planet. Now remember that all this is less than 7 percent of our capability. That is good news.

If just 7 percent of Catholics are accomplishing more than 80 percent of what we are doing today, imagine what 14 percent could do. Not to mention what 21 percent or 35 percent could accomplish. Our potential is incredible. The Catholic Church is a sleeping giant. We literally have the power to change the world."

Prayer

Dynamic Catholics have a daily commitment to prayer.

"God is not a distant force to these people, but rather a personal friend and adviser. They are trying to listen to the voice of God in their lives, and believe doing God's will is the only path that leads to lasting happiness in this changing world (and beyond).

Am I saying the other 93 percent of Catholics don't pray? No. Their prayer tends to be spontaneous but inconsistent. The 7%have a daily commitment to prayer, a routine. Prayer is a priority for them. They also tend to have a structured way of praying. Many of them pray at the same time every day. For some it means going to Mass in the morning and for others it means sitting down in a big, comfortable chair in a corner of their home or taking a walk, but they tend to abide by a structure.

Some start by simply talking to God about their day. Others begin their prayer by reading from the Bible. Still others have a favorite devotional book that they begin with. When they arrive at the time and place in their day for prayer, they have a plan; it is not left to chance or mood. They have a habit of prayer, which they cling to with great discipline.

What is important to recognize is that Dynamic Catholics have a time to pray, a place to pray, and a structure to their prayer.

The 93% certainly pray, but it tends to be when the mood strikes them or when some crisis emerges. The 7% pray in this way also, but their spontaneous prayer is deeply rooted in their daily discipline and commitment to a prayer routine."

Study

Dynamic Catholics are continuous learners.

"On average Dynamic Catholics spend fourteen minutes each day learning more about the faith. They see themselves as students of Jesus and his Church, and proactively make an effort to allow his teachings to form them.

Jesus doesn't just want followers. He wants disciples. To be a Christian disciple begins by sitting at the feet of Christ to learn. We all sit at the feet of someone to learn. Whose feet do you sit at? For some it is a talk show host and for others it is a politician; for others still it is a musician, an artist, a pastor, or a business leader. But none of these are a substitute for Jesus. The 7% are keenly interested in learning from Jesus and about Jesus. More than just a historic figure, he is seen as a friend, coach, mentor, and Savior. They believe that Jesus teaches them through the Scriptures, Christian tradition, and the Church.

Highly engaged Catholics read Catholic books, listen to Catholic CDs, watch DVDs about the faith, and tune in to Catholic radio and television programs. They go on retreats more regularly than most Catholics and attend spiritual events and conferences. They are hungry to learn more about the faith. They are continuous learners.

It is also important to note that even though they tend to know much more about the faith than the 93%, they have a position of humility, which is a critical element of the second sign. If they disagree with a Church teaching, they approach the issue in this way: "Why does the Church teach what she teaches? It is unlikely that I know better than two thousand years of the best Catholic theologians and philosophers. What am I missing?" From this perspective they explore what the Church teaches to further understand God's way, eager to discover the truth."

Generosity

Dynamic Catholics are generous.

"The 7% are universally described as being generous, not just with money and time, but with their love, appreciation, praise, virtue, and encouragement. They see generosity as the heart of Christianity and the proof that the teachings of Christ have taken root in their lives.

The most fascinating thing that came out of the interviews in relation to the third sign is that Dynamic Catholics believe that it starts with financial generosity. They describe love of money and attachment to the things of this world as a primary impediment to spiritual growth, and see this as something that everyone struggles with regardless of how much or how little we have.

Financially, Dynamic Catholics give several times more to their parish and other nonprofit organizations (as a percentage of their annual income) than their counterparts in the 93 percent.

But it is how comprehensively generosity is woven into their lives and the spontaneity with which they dispense it that was so inspiring to me. They are generous lovers, they are generous parents, they are generous with their colleagues at work, and they are generous with strangers who cross their path. They are generous with their virtue—generous with patience, kindness, and compassion. Generosity is not a religious requirement for the 7%; it's a way of life, a way of bringing the love of God to the world."

Evangelization

Dynamic Catholics invite others to grow spiritually by sharing the love of God with them.

"Having seen how a vibrant spiritual life has transformed them and every aspect of their lives, highly engaged Catholics want others to experience the joy that flows from having a dynamic relationship with God.

Dynamic Catholics regularly do and say things to share a Catholic perspective with the people who cross their paths.

Though they don't consider themselves to be actively evangelizing, they are constantly trying to help people develop vibrant spiritual lives by discovering the genius and beauty of Catholicism."

Catholic Resources

Matthew Kelly's words are encouraging. I share them with you because I hope to motivate you to become part of the 7 percent of Catholics who are engaged and dynamic. I encourage you to learn all you can about the Catholic Faith. There are so many resources available that you cannot possibly ever run out of books to read, CD's to listen to, or DVD's to watch. Here at our parish, Holy Spirit in Huntsville, Alabama, we offer adult classes that will help you to understand Scripture well, grow in your prayer life, and live your faith to the best of your ability. Those who take these classes are experiencing the faith like they never have before. Matthew Kelly and (his website) is a great place to start. I would also recommend Lighthouse Catholic media at **www.lighthousecatholicmedia.org** for CD's and St. Joseph Communications **www.saintjoe.net** for CD's and books on the Catholic Faith. I would also recommend the "Catholic Answers" website at **www.catholic.com**. This website provides a wealth of information including books.

My greatest teachers have been men who were raised Protestant and later became Catholic. They have been men in Protestant universities who were studying Church History so that they could earn their doctorate degree. After learning the truth of the history, they felt they had no choice but to become Catholic. Others were pastors in Protestant churches who set to develop a worship service that was authentic; the same worship service as the early Christians. In their studies, they found out that the Catholic Church is still worshiping just as the early Christians did. What choice did these pastors have, but to become Catholic and try to take their congregations with them? Still others were

Scripture scholars who kept asking questions about the Word. What does the Bible mean when it speaks of suffering loss through fire? Catholics say Purgatory. Others could not ignore Christ's words in the gospel of John chapter 6, "The bread that I will give is my Flesh for the life of the world. Unless you eat the flesh of the Son of Man and drink his blood you do not have life within you. Whoever eats my flesh and drinks my blood has eternal life and I will raise him on the last day." These were strong words, how could it refer to a symbol?

Whatever it was that brought them to the Catholic Faith matters not. The point is that they have become great Catholic apologists and lead people every day to the truth. I encourage you to listen to them.

So, You Wanted a Deep and Close Relationship with Jesus?

I have attempted in this book to show you how to gain that deep and close relationship with Jesus that you wanted so badly. I hope that you have been helped along your journey toward Christ by the words contained here. Let's take a few minutes to take a look back and see the big picture.

I think that we can safely say that there are seven basic steps to reaching a very deep relationship with Jesus, our Lord and Savior. First, **prayer** is extremely important. You cannot expect to have a relationship with anyone unless you communicate with that person. The same is true for Christ. You simply must pray every single day. You simply must talk to Jesus at every possible moment; even continuously throughout the day. Give your inside life to Him. Share every thought and every move with Him. The more you talk to Jesus the closer you come to Him and the more you will love Him.

Second, **attend Mass** every single week and more often if you can. The more often you receive the Eucharist the holier you become; the closer to Jesus you become. Placing His very Life into your soul conforms you to Him.

Third, a strong relationship with Mary is a sure way to become closer to Jesus. The Blessed Mother will lead you right to her Son. **Devotion to Jesus through Mary** is the fastest way to gain holiness.

Fourth, you need a pure soul that is free from sin. You need to humble yourself and tell the Lord that you are sorry for your sins. You must realize that your sins hurt Jesus. It is important to tell the Lord that you are sorry often. **Frequent confession** is a key to growing closer to Jesus.

Fifth, **rid your life of unholy things**. When you grow to love Jesus deeply, you will want to rid your life of the things that displease Him. Accept the teachings of the Church on morality and abide by these teachings. Strive for holiness; to do holy things; and to rid your life of unholy habits.

Sixth, remember that everything you have comes from God. Nothing is yours, but instead has been given to you by God. We are simply "Stewards" of God's gifts to us. So share what you have with those who are in need. Give of your time, talent, treasure and tradition in order to make the world a better place. Care for the poor. Support your Church. Love Jesus through the love you give to others. Your call to **Stewardship** is very important.

Seventh, you should have a **deep longing for heaven**. You should desire at all times to be with the Lord eternally. Jesus should be the one you love the most. Let everything you do guide you on a path toward Him. Remember that you have two important jobs in this world. Your number one job is to get to Heaven. Your number two job is to take as many people with you as you can.

May God bless you and make you holy!

XXIV. Basic Apologetics for Confirmed Catholics

Catholic Apologetics:

The word Apologetics means to give a reason for or to defend one's faith. Remember that above everything, in Apologetics, is charity. Our goal is to teach the Faith with love. Our job is not to tell people what to believe, but to simply explain the Faith and give them the truth. It is certainly true that Catholics can win the argument, but lose a soul in the process. We can easily prove that the Catholic Church is the truth, hands down. Historically, Biblically and Scripturally the Catholic Church possesses the truth and this can easily be proven. However, we can lose the person, for the sake of the argument. So above all in Apologetics, we must be filled with love. Gently teach the truth and you may win a soul in the process.

Table of Contents:

I.   What Church did Jesus start?

The fact is, Jesus founded a Church. In Matthew 16:18 Jesus said, "And I say to you, you are Peter, and upon this rock I will build my Church and the gates of the netherworld will not prevail against it." The true Church founded by Christ must go back in history to the time of Christ. It must be able to trace its doctrines back to the time of the Apostolic Church. Its leaders must be able to trace their authority all the way back to the Apostles in what is called Apostolic Succession; an unbroken line. Only the Catholic Church meets these requirements. The Catholic Church was founded by Jesus Christ in 33AD.

There are over 35,000 separate and registered Protestant denominations and only one Catholic Church. The Catholic Church is not a Christian denomination. It **is** the Church. No Protestant denomination can be found in history prior to the year 1517.

Major Protestant Denominations; Founder; Year Founded; and Location:

-Lutheran Church; Martin Luther; 1517; Germany

-Anglican Church; King Henry VIII; 1534; England

-Calvinists; John Calvin; 1555; Switzerland

-Presbyterians; John Knox; 1560; Scotland

-Congregationalists; Robert Brown; 1582; Holland

-Episcopalians; Samuel Seaberry; 1789; American Colonies

-Baptist Church; John Smith; 1609; Amsterdam

-Methodist Episcopal Church; John and Charles Wesley;
   1739; England
-United Brethren; Philip Otterbean and Martin Boem; 1800;
   Maryland
-Disciples of Christ; Thomas and Alexander Campbell; 1827;
   Kentucky
-Mormon Church; Joseph Smith; 1830; New York
-Salvation Army; William Booth; 1865; London, England

- Jehovah's Witnesses; Charles Taze Russell; 1874;
   Pennsylvania
- Christian Science; Mary Baker Eddy; 1879; Boston,
   Massachusetts
- Four-Square Gospel; Amy Semple McPherson; 1917; Los
   Angeles
- Calvary Chapels; Chuck Smith; 1965; Costa Mesa,
   California
- Harvest Christian Group; Greg Laury; 1972; Riverside,
   California
- Purpose Driven Church; Rick Warren; 1982; California

The newest Christian denomination happened just last week
when someone in a church somewhere became angry with
someone else and went across town; began renting a building;
and started his own Church. What doctrine will he teach? It is up
to him. What doctrines will he reject? It is up to him.

The word Catholic means "universal". It comes from the
Greek word **Katholou** meaning "on the whole" "the same
everywhere and everywhere the same". If you are Catholic, then
it means that you believe the things that all Christians have
believed from the beginning of the Church.

II.   The Bible Alone (Sola Scriptura)

Protestant Sols Scriptura View: The Bible is the only source of Divine Revelation from God. Therefore, Sacred Tradition and Papal authority (Pope) are rejected.

Catholic Church View: Sacred Scripture (Bible) and Sacred Tradition are equal sources of Divine Revelation from God.

For the first 400 years of its existence, the Christian Church did not have what we know of today as the Bible. The Old Testament existed, but the New Testament was not yet assembled.

Our faith was passed down from generation to generation by what is called Sacred Tradition. By Sacred Tradition we mean the preaching of the Apostles; the example they gave by their very lives; and the institutions they established among us such as the Mass and the Sacraments.

Jesus said, "Go into the whole world and proclaim the Gospel to every creature." He did not say, "Hand every person a book for them to follow." If it is true that the Bible is truly the only means that God revealed Himself to us, how did the Christian Church exist for 400 years without it?

The Gospels were not completed until the year 90 to 100 AD. It was not until the year 393, at the Council of Hippo, that the Bishops of the Catholic Church determined which of the 250—350 separate writings would make up the canon of scripture that was to become the New Testament. It was therefore, the Catholic Church that gave the Bible, as we know it today, to the world.

Once the Canon of Scripture was determined and a book could be made, it had to be copied by hand. This was done by Monks and it took one full year to create a copy of the Bible. The cost of the Bible was therefore one year's wages making it a book that only the very, very rich could afford. This was not a problem for the average person, however. For the average person was uneducated and did not know how to read. This was the case for over a thousand years.

So to think that every person had their own copy of the Bible and used it as their sole source of knowledge of the Christian faith is absurd. It has only been since the invention of the printing press that Bibles could be produced more rapidly. The Faith had to be and was passed down by Sacred Tradition as the Church continued to read and preach the Sacred Scripture in the Holy Sacrifice of the Mass reading it aloud to the people.

Bible Verses to Reference on this Subject:

1 Cor 11:2—hold fast to traditions I handed on to you

2 Thess 2:15—hold fast to traditions, whether oral or by letter

2 Thess 3:6—shun those acting not according to tradition

John 21:25—not everything Jesus said is recorded in Scripture

Mark 13:31—Heaven and Earth shall pass away, but My Words will not

Acts 20:35—Paul records a saying of Jesus not found in gospels

2 Tim 1:13—folow My sound words; guard the truth

2 Tim 2:2—what you heard entrust to faithful men

2 Pet 1:20—no prophecy is a matter of private interpretation

2 Pet 3:15-16—Paul's letters can be difficult ot grasp and interpret

1 Pet 1:25—God's eternal Word=word preached to you

Rom 10:17—faith comes from what is heard

1 Cor 15:1-2—being saved if you hold fast to the word I preached

Mark 16:15—go to whole world, proclaim gospel to every creature

Matthew 23:2-3—chair of Moses; observe whatever they tell you

III.   Faith Alone (Sola Fidei) and Not by Works

Protestant Sola Fidei View: Sola Fidei doctrine states that God legally credits the very righteousness of Christ to all those who believe in Him. If a person will only believe in Christ and profess it, God will legally transfer all of Christ's own righteousness to that person. This guarantees the person a seat in Heaven. There is no need to be concerned about sin; there is no obligation to do good works. Faith is all that is needed.

Catholic Church View: We gain Heaven through the Church, through the Eternal Covenant that Jesus made at the Last Supper sealed with His blood on the cross. We become holy over time. The Church leads us to a holy life through the sacraments. We gain Heaven "by grace, through faith, working in love." By our works we show that our faith is alive. So it is not by faith alone that we are saved, but instead by faith working through love. It is not salvation by faith alone or even by works alone, but the grace of God who gives us both faith and the desire to work in love of Him.

The Apostle James said, "What good is it, my brothers, if someone says he has faith but does not have works? Can that faith save him? If a brother or a sister has nothing to wear and has not food for the day, and one of you says to them, 'Go in peace, keep warm, and eat well,' but you do not give them the necessities of the body, what good is it? So also faith of itself, if it does not have works is dead. Indeed someone might say, 'you have faith and I have works.' Demonstrate your faith to me without works, and I will demonstrate my faith to you from my works. You believe that God is the Holy One. If you believe this, you do well. But even the demons believe that and tremble. You see that a man is justified by works and not by faith alone."

The entire Bible from Genesis to Revelation teaches that it is not by faith alone that we are saved and it is not by works alone that we are saved, but it is by BOTH Faith and Works that we are saved.

The Parable that Jesus told in Matthew Chapter 7 of the "House Built on Rock" illustrates that it is by Faith and Works that we are justified. Jesus said, "Everyone who listens to these words of mine AND ACTS ON THEM will be like a wise man who built his house on rock. And everyone who listens to these words of mine BUT DOES NOT ACT ON THEM will be like a foolish man who built his house on Sand."

Also in the Gospel of Matthew Jesus tells how He will sit in judgment with all the nations in front of Him and He will separate the good people from the bad as a shepherd separates the sheep from the goats. To the good He will welcome them into Heaven saying, "When I was hungry, you fed me; thirsty, you gave me drink; a stranger and you welcomed me; naked and you clothed me; ill and you cared for me; in prison and you visited me." But to the bad people He will say, "Depart from me you accursed, into the fire prepared for the devil and his angels. For I was hungry and you gave me no food; thirsty and you gave me no drink; a stranger and you did not welcome me; naked and you did not clothe me; ill and you did not care for me; in prison and you did not visit me. When you do this for the least of my brothers, you do it for me."

There are countless scripture verses supporting the Catholic view. For when you are Catholic, Scripture does not contradict itself or the teaching of the Church. The whole of Scripture supports it.

Bible Verses to Reference on this Subject:

James 2:24—a man is justified by works and not by faith alone
James 2:26—faith without works is dead
Gal 5:6—only thing that counts is faith working in love
1 Cor 13:2—faith without love is nothing
John 14:15—if you love Me, keep My commandments

Matthew 19:16-17—if you wish to enter into life, keep commandments

IV.   Mary—Veneration or Worship?

Criticism: Some Protestant faiths are taught that the Catholic Church worships Mary. They pray to her. They even have devotionals to her such as the Rosary. They go to her instead of going directly to Jesus or God. They say this is not worship. Even so, she is highly praised and this is wrong. Praise for Mary takes away praise from Jesus who is the one who deserves all praise.

Catholic Church View: The Catholic Church never has nor never will worship Mary. Instead, we venerate Mary. In other words, we honor her greatly. This does not take anything away from Jesus. Mary and Jesus do not work against one another. Instead, they have always worked together to fulfill God's plan. Mary always leads us to her Son. When Mary is honored, Jesus is very happy for He honored her too. In fact God bestowed the greatest honor to Mary that was ever given to a human being. He chose her to be the mother of His Only Begotten Son, our Lord, Jesus Christ. When we pray and ask Mary to pray for us, she only leads us closer to Jesus.

We honor Mary because of the example she showed us in how to be a perfect disciple of Jesus. Mary totally conformed to God's will. She said 'yes' to all that He asked her to do. Her 'yes' helped to bring about our redemption and salvation. We strive to be like her, the perfect role model. Think about it… No Mary… No Jesus.

In a world where we honor athletes for their personal achievements; actors for their superb acting ability; fire fighters and rescue workers for saving lives, why can't we honor the Mother of Jesus for cooperating fully in God's plan of Salvation?

Even the Ten Commandments call us to "Honor your Father and your mother." Mary is our spiritual mother. Therefore we should honor her too.

Mary herself predicted that all generations would honor her when she said, "Behold, from now on will all ages call me blessed." (Luke 1:48) "All ages or generations will call me blessed." This begs the question, why are Catholics the only Christians who call Mary blessed when the very Word of God from the Bible says that we will do this?

Moreover, when Mary greets her cousin Elizabeth, Scripture tells us that Elizabeth cried out in a loud voice, "Blessed are you among women." Catholics agree, truly blessed among women is Mary.

Conceived Without Sin:

The Catholic Church maintains that Mary was conceived without sin and remained sinless her entire life. This Truth is based in Scripture. When the angel Gabriel appeared to Mary he greeted her by saying, "Hail, Full of Grace." To be "Full of Grace" means to be full of the life of God; to possess the very life of God in your soul. Because of Original Sin no one possessed the life of God in their soul at that time. Yet the Angel Gabriel greets Mary as if this is how she is known in Heaven... as if it is her name.

Mary was saved out of time and is the example of what each of us was meant to be. She was born without sin and remained sinless her whole life. She is the "New Eve;" what Eve was supposed to be. Jesus saved Mary from sinning. He saves us from our sins. There is a difference, but he saved us both. Jesus simply kept Mary from sinning in the first place, rather than saving her after she sinned. Why? Because God cannot be in the presence of sin. Mary had to be born sinless and remain sinless so God could conceive in her womb Jesus, who is God incarnate.

Bible Verses to Reference on this Subject:
Luke 1:28—hail full of Grace the Lord is with you
Luke 1:30—you have found favor with God
Luke 1:37—for with God nothing shall be impossible
Gen 3:15—complete enmity between woman and Satin, sin
Ex 25:11-21—ark made of purest gold for God's word
*Rom 3:23—all have sinned and are deprived of God's glory
(this is quoting Psalm 14 where "all" has explicit exceptions)
*Luke 1:47—my spirit rejoices in God my savior (Mary
experienced a preventive saving from sin, like being prevented
from falling into a pit, requires a savior)

Mother of God:

Mary is the mother of Jesus, who is God the Son. She
conceived Him in her womb by the power of the Holy Spirit.
Even Elizabeth, Mary's cousin, recognized her as the Mother of
God when she proclaimed, "And how does this happen to me,
that the mother of my **Lord** should come to me?" (Luke 1:43)
Here Elizabeth names Mary the Mother of God; the mother of her
Lord. For Jews never spoke the name of God directly, but used
"Lord" instead.

Jesus is both God and man. His human nature can never
be separated from His Divine nature. Mary conceived and bore
the whole of Jesus; His humanity as well as His Divinity. But
understand she is not the mother of God the Father. She is the
mother of God the Son, the second person of the Holy Trinity.

Bible Verses to Reference on this Subject:
Luke 1:43—Elizabeth calls Mary "mother of my Lord" = God
Matt 1:23—virgin will bear a son, Emmanuel = "God is with us"
Luke 1:35—child born will be called holy, the Son of God
Gal 4:4—God sent His Son, born of a woman

Queen Mother:

The Kingdom of God is the fulfillment of the Davidic Kingdom on earth. In the Davidic Kingdom, there were three positions of authority. There was the <u>King</u>, who was Solomon. There was the <u>Queen Mother</u>, who was the mother of the King, Solomon's mother, Bathsheba. And there was the <u>Chief Steward</u>, who ruled in the absence of the King. He was given the "Keys to the Kingdom" and had the power to "Bind and Loose."

Likewise in the Kingdom of God there are three positions of authority. There is the <u>King</u>, who is <u>Jesus</u>. There is the <u>Queen Mother</u>, who is the mother of the King; the mother of Jesus, <u>Mary</u>. And there is the <u>Chief Steward</u>, whom Jesus gave the "Keys to the Kingdom" and the power to "Bind and Loose", the <u>Pope</u>, Peter being the first.

Mary's role is the same in the Kingdom of God that the Queen Mother had in the Davidic Kingdom. The Queen Mother acted as the intercessor for the people to the King. People could come to the Queen Mother and make a request. She would in turn make their request to the King; on their behalf.

Likewise, we can go to Mary, the Queen Mother, and ask her to pray to Jesus for us, on our behalf. So you see Mary's role is rooted deeply in Scripture.

It is not uncommon that we, as Christians, ask others to pray for us. We even say to one another, "I'll pray for you." How could it be wrong then, to ask the Blessed Virgin Mary to pray for us? As Christians, we do not believe that death is the end. Those in Heaven can pray for us just as those on earth can pray for us. They are fully alive in God's Kingdom.

This does not take away from our relationship or diminish our relationship with Jesus in any way. Jesus and Mary have never been at odds with one another, but have always worked hand in hand. This is still true today.

The Assumption of Mary Body and Soul into Heaven:

The Assumption of Mary is the anticipation of the resurrection of all Christians when our souls will be united with our bodies at the end of time. It is what was meant for us all.

Mary is not the only creature to be taken into Heaven body and soul. Elijah was also taken into Heaven in this way on a flaming chariot. "As they walked on conversing, a flaming chariot and flaming horses came between them and Elijah went up to Heaven in a whirlwind." (2 Kings 2:11)

Although the Assumption of Mary is not found explicitly in Sacred Scripture, it is very much a part of Sacred Tradition. It was taught by the Apostles and handed down to us by this same tradition.

Bible Verses to Reference on this Subject:

Gen 5:24 (Heb 11:5)—Enoch taken to Heaven without dying
2 Kings 2:11—Elijah assumed into Heaven in fiery chariot
Matt 27:52—many Saints who had fallen asleep were raised
1 Thess 4:17—caught up to meet the Lord in the air
1 Cor 15:52—we shall be instantly changed at last trumpet
Rom 6:23—for the wages of sin is death
Rev 11:19-12:1—ark in Heaven = woman clothed with sun

The Rosary: (Vain Repetition)

Protestants might say that the Rosary is against the Bible. In Matthew's gospel it says, "When you pray do not use vain repetition." Another verse that may be quoted is, "In prayer, do not babble on like the pagans, who think that they will be heard because of their many words" (Matt 6:7).

It is true that Jesus was against "vain" or insincere repetition, but not all repetition. Even Jesus used repetition when He repeated the same prayer three times in the Garden of

Gethsemane: For it is written, "He prayed a third time, saying the same words" (Matt 26:44). In the Parable of the Tax Collector, Jesus states that the Tax Collector repeated the prayer, "O God be merciful to me, a sinner," and yet he was justified while the man who had the long prayer wasn't. Moreover, consider the angels in the book of Revelation who, "day and night do not stop exclaiming 'holy, holy, holy is the Lord God Almighty, who was and who is and who is to come'" (Rev. 4:8).

Jesus also tells us in Matthew's Gospel to 'pray in secret,' but that doesn't mean we can't pray together in church. These two admonitions are against superficial prayer not prayer that is heartfelt and sincere. We must be careful to read Scripture as a whole and not separate each line from another taking the meaning as strictly literal. For if we do, the words 'pray in secret' would mean that we could never pray with others around or where they could see us. It is certain that Jesus did not mean that.

When we pray the Rosary, we reflect on the entire life of Jesus through the eyes of Mary. It is heartfelt and beautiful, not vain at all. It is truly meditative prayer as we reflect on the key events in the life of Jesus and His mother focusing our attention of Jesus and what the Gospel means in our lives. The Rosary is Scriptural. It is not prayed in vain nor do those who pray it babble.

V.   Peter and The Papacy

Criticism: Jesus did not build the Church on a person. Peter was never meant to be the head of the Church. Instead, Jesus built the Church on the confession of Peter when he said, "You are the Christ, the Son of the Living God." Jesus meant that He would build the Church on Peter's words not on him personally.

Catholic Church View: Jesus did build the Church upon Peter and made him the very first Pope, giving him the "Keys to the

Kingdom" and the power to "Bind and Loose." Jesus did make Peter the head of the Church here on earth. Peter's authority has been passed down in an unbroken line from one pope to the next for 2,000 years. The point is that Jesus was establishing authority and a guarantee that His Church would safely pass down His teachings from one generation to the next. He sent the Holy Spirit to lead and guide the Church. As Catholics we have the guarantee through our Holy Father, that what the Church teaches is right and true. He is the shepherd who guides us protecting us from the wolf.

In Matthew 16:13-19 Jesus named Simon, brother of Andrew, as the first pope of the Church. Jesus gives to Simon a new name that no one had ever been named before. Jesus renames him, "Rock."

As Jesus and the Apostles enter the area of Caesarea Philippi, He asks the 12 apostles, "Who do the people say that I am?" The 12 give various responses including, "John the Baptist, Elijah, Jeremiah, or one of the prophets." Then Jesus asks them, "Who do you say that I am?"

Only Simon, brother of Andrew, son of Jonah, answered and said, "You are the Christ, the Son of the Living God." Jesus immediately proclaims, "Blessed are you Simon, son of Jonah, for flesh and blood has not revealed this to you, but my Heavenly Father." Clearly Simon had received a revelation from God.

Jesus continues and says, "And I say to you, you are 'Rock' and on this Rock I will build my Church." Jesus had just given Simon a new name, "Rock." He then told Simon that He was going to build His Church upon him, who is now to be called "Rock" or as we say in English Peter.

Those who reject this Catholic claim maintain that Jesus' words in Greek would have been, "And I say to you, you are **Petros** and on this **Petra** I will build my Church." They say that "Petros" means little pebble in Greek referring to the man Peter as a little pebble. But Jesus said He was going to build His Church on this "<u>Petra</u>," Greek for big rock. So what Jesus meant was that He was going to build His Church on the big words that Peter confessed when he said, "You are the Christ, the Son of the Living God."

The problem with this theory is that Jesus was not speaking Greek. Jesus was speaking Aramaic. All serious Scripture Scholars know this to be true. So what Jesus really said was, "And I say to you, you are Kepha and on this Kepha I will build my Church. Kepha is Aramaic for rock. Notice that Jesus' words for rock did not change meaning. He said the word rock; named Simon, brother of Andrew "Rock"; and said He would build His Church on this man now named "Rock."

In addition, Jesus had taken the 12 apostles to the area of Caesarea Philippi, which was pagan country. In this area there was a temple that the Romans used to worship their ruler, the Caesar. This temple sat upon a giant rock over 200 feet wide and 500 feet tall. As the apostles looked at a temple, (a church), sitting upon a huge rock, Jesus proclaimed that Peter would be the rock that He would build His Church on. What a visual aid. Jesus' meaning was clear.

So how do we get the name 'Peter' from the name 'Kepha'? Kepha was translated from Aramaic into Greek as 'Petra' or 'rock'. However 'petra' is a feminine noun and can't be used to refer to a man. Hence the masculine ending "os" would need to be substituted when referring to Simon Peter, giving us "Petros." In this case the distinction between petra and petros in the Greek is merely a question of gender, not of meaning. Petros was then translated into English as Peter.

Once Jesus named Peter the rock that He would build His Church upon, He gave to him the authority of one who would be in charge. Jesus said, "I will give you the keys to the Kingdom of Heaven. Whatever you bind on earth shall be bound in Heaven and whatever you loose on earth shall be loosed in Heaven."

Keys are a sign of authority as the person in charge holds the keys. Keys unlock and lock doors. Keys open and close places. Binding and loosing has to do with making decisions. Jesus says that the decisions Peter makes on earth will be held bound in Heaven. Jesus says simply, you are taking my place. I will give my authority to you.

This is reminiscent of the Davidic Kingdom with its three positions of authority: the <u>King</u>; the <u>Queen Mother</u>; and the <u>Chief Steward</u> who was given the keys to the Kingdom and the power to bind and loose. The Kingdom of God is the fulfillment of the Davidic Kingdom of the Old Testament.

<u>Furthermore, the Bible itself supports Peter's role as the Apostle in charge</u>:

-In John 21:17 Jesus says only to Peter three times, "Feed my sheep."

-In Mark 16:7 An angel is sent to announce the Resurrection of Jesus to Peter.

-In Luke 24:34 The Risen Christ appears first to Peter.

-In Acts 1:13-26 Peter headed the meeting that elected a new apostle, Matthias, who would take the place of Judas Iscariot.

-In Acts 2:14 Peter led the apostles in preaching at Pentecost. At his words over 3,000 were baptized.

-In Acts 2:41 Peter received the first converts into the Church.

-In Acts 3:6-7 Peter performed the first miracle after Pentecost.

-In Acts 5:1-11 Peter inflicted the punishment on Ananias and Sapphira.

-In Acts 8:21 Peter excommunicates the first heretic.

-In Acts 10:44-46 Peter has the revelation that gentiles can come into the Church. This revelation was given only to Peter.

-In Acts 15:7 Peter led the first council in Jerusalem.

-In Acts 15:19 Peter pronounces the first Dogmatic decision.

-In Matthew 16:18—upon this rock (Peter) I will build My Church.

In Matthew 16:19---I will give you the keys of the kingdom and the power to bind and loose.

In Luke 22:32—Peter's faith will strengthen his brethren.

In Galatians 1:18—after his conversion, Paul visits the chief Apostle who is Peter.

-In the New Testament, Peter's name is mentioned 195 more times than all of the other apostles. When the apostles are listed, Peter's name is always listed first.

A Living Continuing Authority:

When Christ established His Church, the New Israel, He set up a living continuing authority to teach, govern, and sanctify in His name. This living authority is called Apostolic because it began with the 12 Apostles and continued with their successors.

This apostolic authority preserved and interpreted the revelation of Jesus Christ to the world. This same apostolic authority determined the Canon of the Bible or in other words, which writings would make up the New Testament.

Even in the Old Testament through Moses there was a living continuing authority. This authority did not end when the New Testament was written. Rather it continued as the safeguard and authentic interpreter of Sacred Scripture.

Papal Infallibility:

The Pope, as Vicar of Christ on earth, is given protection from error when he teaches on matters of Faith and Morals. We do not say that the Holy Father is free from error, but only protected from teaching what is false on matters of Faith and Morals.

This protection is Scriptural. Jesus guaranteed this protection when he said, "And I say to you, you are Peter and on this Rock I will build my Church **and the gates of the netherworld shall not prevail against it.**" The gates of the netherworld would prevail against the Church if it was permitted to teach what is not the Truth of Jesus Christ. Also in John 16:13, Christ promised the Apostles that the Holy Spirit would "guide you into all truth."

VI.   Call No Man Father

Criticism: Catholics are unbiblical. The Bible plainly says, "Call no one on earth your father you have but one Father in Heaven." (Matt 23:9) Yet they call their priests "Father".

Catholic Church View: Jesus is not saying that we literally cannot call any person on earth "Father". He is simply saying that when it comes to salvation, we have only one Father in Heaven; only one teacher. Jesus is telling us not to attribute the Fatherhood of God to any man. He was trying to denounce the high minded Pharisees who love the best seats at feasts and liked to be honored. These Pharisees did many things to be noticed by men and that is not Godly. Instead, Jesus says, the one who is the greatest among you will become the servant to all the rest.

As with any Scripture verses, never take them out of context. Read the entire passage and you will fully understand the meaning. Protestants take this verse and use it in isolation to promote anti-Catholic doctrine. When this verse is left in context one can see that Jesus did not mean that we cannot call anyone "Father."

This Scripture also says not to call anyone "teacher" or "Master". Yet the Protestant Church does not object to calling a teacher by that name or a man using the salutation, Mister. Clearly there is a double standard here.

We introduce our own fathers by saying, "This is my father, Joseph Jordan." We call George Washington "the Father of our Country". We speak of our "Founding Fathers". Abraham Lincoln speaks the words, "Four score and seven years ago our **fathers** brought forth…" in the Gettysburg Address.

Jesus himself tells a parable in John 19:19-31 where He speaks of "Father Abraham" several times and also the "father of the rich man."

Even the Fourth Commandment requires us to honor our 'father' and our mother.

If what the Protestant church maintains is true, we could not even call our own father, "Father." Furthermore we could not speak of any teacher as "my teacher." We could not use the title, "Mr." to address a man. Common sense teaches that this is simply not what Jesus meant.

Clearly the apostles understood what Jesus was teaching, for Paul speaks of his parental care of his flock by calling them his "Beloved Children" in 1 Cor. 4:14. In verse 15 St. Paul says, "You do not have many fathers, for I became your father in Christ Jesus through the Gospel." And in the letter to Philemon, verse 10 St. Paul talks about his "child" Onesimus (remember St. Paul never married) saying, "whose father I have become in my imprisonment." In 1 John 2:12-13 St. John says, "I am writing to you, children, because your sins have been forgiven for His name sake. I am writing to you, fathers, because you know Him who is from the beginning." Clearly John refers to them as "fathers." Hebrews 12:9 refers to earthy "fathers".

Scripture clearly supports the Catholic use of the word 'Father' for our priests. Even Saint Paul speaks of himself as a spiritual father.

Bible Verses to Reference on this Subject:
Matt 19:19—Jesus confirms commandment: "honor father and
   mother"
Luke 16:24—Jesus refers to "Father Abraham"
Matt 5:29-30—Jesus uses hyperbole "pluck out eye; cut off
   hand"
Acts 7:2—St. Stephen calls Jewish leaders "fathers"
Acts 21:40, 22:1—St. Paul calls Jerusalem Jews "fathers"
Rom 4:16-17—Abraham is called "the father of us all"
1 Cor 4:14-15—I became your father in Christ through gospel
1 Tim 1:2— Paul calls Timothy "my true child in the faith"
Titus 1:4—Paul calls Titus "my true child in our common faith"
Heb 12:7-9—we have earthly father to discipline us
Luke 14:26—if anyone comes to Me without hating his father…
1 Thes 2:11—we treated you as a father treats his children
Philem 10—whose father I became in my imprisonment
1 John 2:13, 14—I write to you, fathers, because you know him

VII.   Canon of Scripture "Why do Catholics Have a Different Bible?"

The Misconception: The Catholic Church has 7 more books in the Old Testament of their Catholic Bibles than the Protestant Bible. They have added these books.

The Truth: There are 7 more books in the Old Testament of a Catholic Bible. That is true. However, it is not because the Catholic Church added these 7 books. It is because these 7 books have always been included in the Old Testament, even in the time of Jesus.

It is true that the New Testaments of Catholic and Protestant Bibles are the same, but the Old Testaments are different. The Catholic Bible includes the books of: Tobit, Judith, Baruch, Wisdom, Sirach, 1st and 2nd Maccabees, and parts of Daniel and Esther, while the Protestant Bible does not. Why?

There have been two approved Canons of Scripture used for the Old Testament. One was the Greek Translation called the "Alexandrian Cannon" or "Septuagint." The other accepted canon was the Hebrew Translation, called the "Palestinian Canon."

The Alexandrian Canon was completed between the year 250 and 125 BC. The Palestinian Canon was not adopted until around the year 100 AD, when these 7 books were removed.

This clearly shows that the Alexandrian Canon was the Canon of Scripture used by all Jews from 250 BC until the year 100 AD while Jesus was on the earth among us. The Christian Church adopted this Alexandrian Canon as the official Old Testament. It is the same Canon that is found in Catholic Bibles today.

In the year 100 A.D. the Jewish leaders met at Jamnia. The Jewish Rabbis of the time established a new Canon known as the Palestinian Canon. They rejected these 7 books on the basis that they could not find any original Hebrew counterparts to them.

The truth was that these 7 books were "pro-Roman". Since Rome had just destroyed the Temple in Jerusalem in 70 A.D., the Jewish Leaders did not want any "pro-Roman" books in their Bible.

Moreover, the Christians were using the Alexandrian Canon, so in reaction to this new Christian Church, the Jewish leaders of the time rejected these 7 books.

In the year 1948 the Dead Sea Scrolls were discovered. Among the scrolls were many of the Hebrew counterparts to these 7 books. This makes the Jewish argument at the Council of

Jamnia no longer valid. These books did indeed have Hebrew counterparts and should have never been rejected.

Here is the main point: The Old Testament that Jesus used is the same Old Testament that Catholics use and the same Old Testament that the Christian Church has always used. This was the Old Testament officially adopted by the Christian Church and was uncontested until Martin Luther made changes.

Martin Luther, in reaction to the Catholic Church, accepted the Palestinian Canon established by the Jewish Leaders at Jamnia and rejected the Alexandrian Canon, which had always been used. He did this largely because those 7 books contradicted his new teaching, Sola Fidei, stating that we are saved by faith alone.

Martin Luther also wanted to remove the books of James, Esther, and Revelation from the Bible. He also added the word "alone" to his German translation of the Bible in Romans 3:28, making it read, "The just shall live by faith (alone)." He was later made to remove this word.

It is possible that a Protestant friend would ask you where these 7 books are quoted by the writers of the New Testament. Being quoted in the New Testament is their criteria as to whether a book should be considered part of the Old Testament. They have been taught that these 7 books are not quoted in the New Testament and therefore should not be part of the Old Testament.

The answer to this question is a simple one. Using this criteria for determining if a book should be considered part of the Old Testament is wrong. The Old Testament Books: Song of Songs, Ecclesiastes, Esther, Obadiah, Zephaniah, Judges, 1st Chronicles, Ezra, Nehemiah, Lamentations, and Nahum are considered valid books of the Old Testament by Protestants, yet none are quoted from by the writers of the New Testament.

You should also tell this person that those 7 books were considered by all Christians everywhere to be part of the Bible ever since it was put together in the early centuries of the

Christianity. Then ask him by what authority Martin Luther had decided to throw out those 7 books of the Old Testament. He will not have an easy time answering this question.

It is also true that several of these 7 books are indeed quoted from by the writers of the New Testament. So it is very possible to answer his original question: 1) Hebrews chapter 11:35 refers to 2Maccabees chapter 7. 2) Matthew 6:14 comes straight from Sirach 28:2. 3) Matthew 7:12 refers to Tobit 4:15. 4) Matthew 7:16 directly relates to Judith 27:6. 6) Matthew 27:43 directly relates to Wisdom 2:18-19. 7) Romans 1:20 matches Wisdom 13:1. And 8) James 1:19 directly quotes Sirach 5:11-13.

VIII.   Catholics Don't Use the Bible

Criticism: Good Protestants take their Bible with them to church every Sunday, but you never see Catholics carrying a Bible into their churches. They don't even use the Bible! Good Christians should be Bible-Centered people!

Protestants are lacking the history of our faith. This is not their fault and the best thing we can do is to teach them the truth.

If one was to study ancient Christian worship, taught to the people by the apostles, one would see that it centered around the altar and a Eucharistic Sacrifice just as the Catholic Church worships today.

Christian worship has always involved the Sacrifice that takes place at every Mass. We offer to God the only Sacrifice that has ever pleased Him… We offer Him the Sacrifice of His very own Son on the cross; the sacrifice that saves each of us.

To receive Jesus' Body, Blood, Soul, and Divinity, where His very own Life is placed into our souls giving us the strength to go out and change the world… is what Catholic Christian worship has been about for over 2,000 years.

Our worship, unlike Protestant worship, is not centered around Scripture and preaching. It is again centered on the Eucharistic Sacrifice. But that does not mean that Scripture is not part of our worship. No. Far from it. The Mass is made up of two main parts: "The Liturgy of the Word" and "The Liturgy of the Eucharist." Catholics spend half of the Mass centered on Scripture so that we can hear the very Word of God in preparation for our participation in that once and for all redeeming sacrifice that Jesus offered for our sins.

As far as bringing Bibles to church with us, what Protestants don't know is that we have a Missalette in the pews. A Missalette is a "mini-Missal." Inside the Missalette is the Scripture readings for that day already written out for us. This allows us to follow along as they are proclaimed. We do not have to bring our Bibles since there is a Missalette for every person. Moreover, the Catholic Church reads through the entire Bible, Old and New Testament, every three years. In addition, over 90% of the words used at Mass come directly from Scripture. Our worship is truly Scripture based.

There are parts of the Bible that the Protestant Church never reads. Their preachers and ministers, in many denominations, can decide what Scripture verses to read each Sunday. The Catholic Church, on the other hand, must follow a three year plan in union with the entire Church worldwide. This is what is contained in the Roman Missal.

Catholics do not quote Scripture, chapter, and verse as Protestants do, but we know the Scriptures very well as they have been read to us our whole lives.

What Catholics need to do better, is read the Bible on their own and take approved Catholic Scripture Studies such as "The Great Adventure" from Ascension Press. Many devout Catholics do this, but all should.

IX.   Where did the Bible Come From?

Where did the Bible come from anyway? Well, the Old Testament was established before the time of Christ as we mentioned under "Why Do Catholics Have a Different Bible?" The Old Testament that Catholics use is the Alexandrian Canon established between 250 and 125 BC. Therefore, the early Christian Church simply adopted this as the Canon of Scripture for the Old Testament. If it was good enough for our Lord, it was good enough for us.

The Canon of Scripture for the New Testament was established at the Council of Hippo in 393 AD and at the Council of Carthage in 419 AD. Who determined which of the 250—350 writings were "Inspired" and would become part of the New Testament or "New Covenant" Canon? It was the Bishops of the Catholic Church in union with the Pope. These councils met in order to determine which of the 250—350 writings would be read (and were therefore inspired) at the Mass.

It is interesting that Protestants reject the Magisterium of the Catholic Church stating that Jesus never intended to put anyone in charge of His Church. Yet they accept and profess the very Bible that the Magisterium of the Catholic Church gave to them.

From this we can easily see that the Christian Church existed for over 400 years before the Canon of the Bible was complete. The Church passed its faith down from generation to generation by Sacred Tradition: 1) The preaching of the Apostles 2) The example of their very lives given to us by the Apostles 3) The institutions established by the Apostles: The Sacraments; The Mass. We also had the various writings of the Apostles that were read to the faithful at Mass and also available for them to read themselves. That is, if they knew how to read.

So help your Protestant friends to understand that the idea of "Sola Scriptura" the Bible Alone, could not possibly be correct when the Christian Church existed for 400 years before there was the Bible as we know it today.

X.   Crucifix or Cross

Criticism: Why do Catholics keep Jesus on the cross? Don't they know He has risen from the dead? This crucifix of theirs is obsolete.

To say that a crucifix, which shows Jesus hanging on the cross, is obsolete is to say that the scripture verse John 3:16 is obsolete: "For God so loved the world that He gave His only Son, so that everyone who believes in him might not perish but might have eternal life."

The Crucifix is simply a Word picture for the Scripture verse of John 3:16. No Protestant would ever say that John 3:16 is obsolete.

Catholics place the Crucifix in the Church; in their homes in several places; in their classrooms in Catholic Schools; in their meeting rooms and places of gatherings because we never want to forget the price that was paid so that we can have Eternal Life in Heaven.

We do not take this for granted but come to Mass weekly, even daily, to offer Eucharist "Thanksgiving" for this gift that has been given to us.

Catholics make the **Sign of the Cross** for several reasons. Here are a few: First, this reminds us who God is: He is our Father; He is the Son who redeemed us; He is the Holy Spirit who dwells inside of us and makes us holy...The Blessed Trinity.

Second, we make the Sign of the Cross to invoke God's protection upon us or as part of a prayer for others.

Third, we make the Sign of the Cross to remember that we are Baptized Christians and that we must live in a new way.

We make the Sign of the Cross using Holy Water as a way of blessing ourselves and recalling our Baptism.

XI.   Infant Baptism

Criticism: Baptism is just symbolic. It doesn't save a person. It is faith that saves a person. We must profess our belief in Jesus. A baby can't give his heart to Jesus.

Catholic Church View: Baptism is not just symbolic. It truly washes away Original Sin and places the very life of God inside of us. This is truly how one is born again and becomes a child of God. This is how we enter God's Covenant.

Catholic Parents profess the faith <u>for their children</u> just as Jewish parents of the Old Testament did when they brought their infants to the Temple to present them to the Lord and for circumcision. Circumcision was the exterior sign that the child had entered into God's Covenant. St. Paul refers to Baptism as a "circumcision not administered by hand." (Colossians 2:11) In other words it is God Himself who baptizes.

Just as the Great Flood washed away sin at the time of Noah, so baptism washes away sin and saves us. St. Peter wrote of the flood, "This prefigured baptism, which now saves you." (1Peter 3:21)

Jesus explained that Baptism is the way to be born again when He said, "Unless one is born again of water and the Spirit he cannot enter the kingdom of God." John 3:5.

These words of Jesus also teach us that baptism is not just symbolic. Otherwise we would not be "born again of the **Spirit**." God's Spirit enters us at baptism as Saint Paul tells us that "your body is a temple of the Holy Spirit." (1 Corinthians 6:19)

In Matthew 28 Jesus gives the great commission, "Go therefore, and make disciples of all nations, baptizing them in the name of the Father, and of the Son, and of the Holy Spirit." Did

Jesus intend for the Apostles to baptize only Adults? In the book of Acts, chapter 16, we see two instances of Paul baptizing entire households. And in 1 Corinthians 1:16, St. Paul recalls baptizing the household of Stephanas.

The First Christians were all Jewish converts to the faith. As Jews their infant children had been welcomed into the Old Covenant through circumcision. So of course their infant children would be welcomed as well into the New Covenant of Christianity through Baptism. It would have been unthinkable to believe otherwise. St. Paul tells us in Colossians that Baptism replaces circumcision. If the Church changed the Old Covenant practice and began to exclude children below some theoretical "age of reason," it would have created a controversy as large as that of circumcising Gentile converts. Yet the New Testament gives no hint that the subject was ever even brought up, much less debated.

Thus there was never any controversy in the early Church over the practice of infant baptism until the third century when the Council of Carthage (A.D. 252) condemned the novel proposition that baptism ought to be postponed until the eighth day after birth. The Church retained the ancient practice of baptizing infants even earlier than the eighth day.

<u>Bible Verses to Reference:</u>
John 3:5; Mark 16:16—Baptism is required for entering Heaven
1 Cor 15:21-22—in Adam all die, in Christ all made alive
Mark 10:14—let children come; to such belongs the kingdom
Luke 18:15—people were bring even infants to Him…
Col 2:11-12—Baptism has replaced circumcision
Joshua—24:15—as for me and my house, we will serve Lord
John 3:5, 22—born of water and Spirit; Apostles begin baptizing
Titus 3:5—saved us through bath of rebirth and renewal by Holy
 Spirit
Acts 2:37-38—repent, be baptized, receive gift of Holy Spirit

Acts 22:16—get selves baptized and sins washed away
1 Cor 6:11—you were washed, sanctified, justified
Rom 6:4—baptized into death; live in newness of life
1 Pet 3:21—Baptism…now saves you

XII. Thou Shall Not Make Graven Images

Criticism: Catholics have statues in their churches and they bow down and worship them.

Catholics do not worship statues. However, the Catholic Church has always had statues and stained glass windows depicting saints and Bible stories. This has been true for centuries. Why?

As was explained earlier, the Canon of Scripture was not complete until after 400 AD. The Church existed for over 400 years before there was a Bible as we know it today. So how did the people learn the Bible stories?

They learned them by hearing them read aloud at Mass.

How did the people learn about the Martyrs and Saints who led such great examples of the faith? They heard about them by oral tradition and the feast days of the saints at Mass.

Stained glass windows in the Churches have always depicted the stories of the Bible or the stories of the saints. They gave people a picture for the stories they were hearing. The statues likewise gave the people a picture for the person they learned so much about.

This is especially important since even after the Canon of Scripture was complete, most people could not read or write until the 1800's. Even if they had their own Bible, they didn't know how to read.

Today most people, Protestants and Catholics alike, have Nativity Scenes in their homes depicting the birth of Jesus. They put them out at Christmas. Most churches, Protestant and

Catholic alike, put up this scene at Christmas time inside or outside their churches. Here they are using statues to depict a specific story in the Gospel. Does it mean they are worshiping these statues? No, of course they are not.

A "graven image" is a carving that represents God. None of the statues that Catholics have represent God. We do not have a statue nor have we ever had a statue that represents God.

The statues we have represent real people whom we honor for their great example of how to serve God. They remind us to lead a holy life just as that person once did.

XIII. Burned Bibles; Chained Bibles; and Latin Bibles

Criticism: The Catholic Church chained Bibles down so the people could not take the Bibles to read on their own; they refused to translate the Bible from Latin it into the language of the common person so individuals could read it for themselves; and they even burned Bibles! The Catholic Church wanted to destroy the Bible!

If the Catholic Church wanted to destroy the Bible, why did Catholic monks work diligently through the centuries making copies of it? Before the printing press (1450), copies of the Bible were hand written with beauty and painstaking accuracy taking one year to complete.

Chained Bibles:

The Catholic Church did chain Bibles down inside the churches. This was because each copy was precious, both spiritually and materially. The chain kept it safe from loss or from theft, so that all the people of the church community could benefit from it. All books in libraries at that time were also chained down to keep them from being stolen, as libraries had only one copy of each book. This was a common practice with books.

Bible Translation:

The Catholic Church commissioned St. Jerome to translate the Bible into Latin in the 5th century because at that time, Latin <u>was</u> the language of the people. Even after a thousand years, Latin still remained the universal language in Europe.

Translating the Bible into other languages during the Middle Ages was simply impractical because most of the languages did not have an alphabet.

Also, very few people at that time could read. Only the very educated at that time could read, and if they could read, they read Latin. Therefore there was not a great need to translate the Bible into other languages at that time. However the Church did translate the Bible into old English during the Middle Ages.

Burned Bibles:

The Catholic Church did burn the Wycliffe and Tyndale Bibles. Why?

John Wycliffe translated the Bible into English, but his secretary added a prologue that included propaganda against the Church. Adding to or taking anything away from the Bible has never been allowed. The Bible is the Word of God. Men cannot add or take away from it.

William Tyndale's translation of the Bible was also burned. It contained upwards of 2,000 errors. St. Thomas More commented that, "searching for errors in the Tyndale Bible was similar to searching for water in the sea." Clearly Tyndale had corrupted the Scripture.

It is one matter to destroy the real thing and another to destroy a counterfeit. The Church prohibited these corrupt Bibles in order to preserve the truth of Christ's Gospel. As St. Peter warns us, "The ignorant and unstable can distort the Scriptures to their own destruction." (2 Peter 3:16)

XIV.   The Eucharist

Criticism: **The communion wafer is just a symbol of Jesus, but Catholics worship it as if it is really Jesus.**

It is true, the bread and wine become the Body, Blood, Soul, and Divinity of Jesus at every Mass. And Catholics do worship the Eucharist, for it is truly Christ.

What Protestants don't understand is that this was God's plan all along; starting in the Old Testament and coming into fulfillment into the New.

The Catholic Church has ALWAYS believed this to be true. We can trace this teaching all the way back to the first century.

The Eucharist is the Source and Summit of our faith. It is how God remains with us and sanctifies us (makes us holy). Jesus doesn't simply come to us spiritually. He comes to us physically as well as Jesus said it would be, "Whoever eats my flesh and drinks my blood remains in Me and I in him" (John 6:56).

Starting in the Old Testament the High Priest Melchizadek gave a blessing to Abraham using bread and wine. (Gen. 14:18-20) This foreshadowed Jesus, the Eternal High Priest, who gives us a blessing using bread and wine—which becomes His Body and Blood at Mass.

In the Book of Exodus God saved His people with the blood of the **Passover Lamb**. This Lamb was perfect, spotless. It had to be sacrificed and eaten so that God's people could be saved from death. This was the foreshadowing of Jesus, the **Lamb of God**, who was sacrificed for us in order to save us from eternal death—Hell. The **Lamb of God** would have to be sacrificed and eaten just as the Passover Lamb was sacrificed and eaten. The Eucharist is the **New Manna** the fulfillment of the manna that the Israelites ate in the desert while they waited to enter the Promised Land. Jesus is the **New Manna** that we now eat as we wait to enter the New Covenant (Testament) Promised Land of Heaven. The Eucharist is also the fulfillment of the "Bread of Presence" that was kept in the Tabernacle. This bread was truly the presence of God for the Israelites. Three times per year this bread was held up; elevated for the people to see and adore, while the priests of the temple proclaimed, "Behold God's love for you." The Hebrew word for the "Bread of the Presence" or "Shrew-Bread" can literally be rendered 'Bread of the face.' This bread was the presence of the face of God to the Israelites the symbol of their covenant with God. So to the Eucharist, which is Jesus present to us in body, is our covenant with Him.

John the Baptist, sent to pave the way for the Messiah, points out Jesus to the crowds by saying of Him, "Behold, the Lamb of God who takes away the sins of the world." Here John makes it clear that Jesus is truly the **Lamb of God** who will be sacrificed for our sins.

In John chapter 6 Jesus tells us that we must eat His Body and drink His Blood or we will not have life within us. How true! He continues by saying, "I am the living bread that came down from Heaven, whoever eats this bread will live forever… and the bread that I will give is my flesh for the life of the world."

This was difficult to believe! The Jews quarreled saying, "How can this man give us his flesh to eat?" They could not accept it. Even Jesus' disciples (not the apostles) turned and walked away, rejecting His teaching. They understood that Jesus was literally saying that they must eat His Flesh and drink His Blood. They just refused to accept it.

Most importantly, Jesus let them go. He did not stop them. He did not stop them saying, "Wait, you misunderstood! I only meant that you would eat a 'symbol' of my body; a 'symbol' of my blood." No, Jesus did not say that. He did not stop them.

Even the apostles did not understand <u>how</u> He was going to give them his Body and Blood to eat, but they believed.

At the Last Supper, Jesus took bread and wine and declared of it, "This is my Body; this is my Blood. Take this all of you and eat it; drink it." And just as God commanded that the Jews celebrate the Passover Meal every single year, Jesus commanded, "Continue to do this in memory of me."

The Mass is the New Passover Meal. This is how all people, Jews and Gentiles alike, enter into the New and Everlasting Covenant. The Mass is celebrated every single day.

Catholics are obligated to celebrate the Holy Sacrifice of the Mass every single Sunday and Holy Days of Obligation, but can come daily if they choose.

How long have Catholics believed in the True Presence of Christ in the Eucharist? Always!

In the year 110 AD St. Ignatius wrote: "The heretics abstain from the Eucharist and from prayer, because <u>they do not confess that the Eucharist is the Flesh of our Savior Jesus Christ</u>, Flesh which suffered for our sins and which the Father, in His goodness, raised up again."

In the year 150 AD, St. Justin Martyr wrote: "<u>We call this food Eucharist and it is truly the Flesh and Blood of Jesus.</u>"

God feeds the world with His very Life. We take and eat it and we are given the strength to strive to become like Him: holy, good, and kind. The Eucharist is nourishment for our souls. We need it in order to be holy. We need holiness in order to get to Heaven.

We are not earthly beings who experience temporary spiritual moments. We are spiritual beings who are experiencing a temporary earthly life.

Protestants may say: <u>Well, in John chapter 6 verse 63 Jesus says, "It is the spirit that gives life, while the flesh is of no avail. The words that I have spoken to you are spirit and life."</u> So you see Jesus was only talking spiritually. He meant that it would be a "symbol" of His body and blood.

If that is true, then why did they all walk away? If they were only going to eat a symbol of His Flesh and Blood, what's the big deal? Why did they stop following Him that day? And why did they say, "How can this man give us his flesh to eat?" They would have said, "How can this man give us a symbol of his flesh to eat?" Moreover, since when does the word 'spirit' mean the same thing as 'symbol?' Where else in Scripture does the word 'spirit' mean symbol?

And why did He say in verse 64 "But there are some of you who do not believe."? What's not to believe if it's just a symbol? See, Jesus meant what He said. The people would have to eat His very Flesh and drink His very Blood and they could not accept it.

So Jesus turned to His disciples and said, "Do you also want to leave?" Simon Peter answered, "Master, to whom shall we go? You have the words of eternal life.

The apostles did not understand either, but nevertheless, they believed.

What Jesus meant by verse 63 was that we have to believe with our spirit; with our faith because our earthly flesh cannot believe on its own. That is still true today. To believe in the True Presence of Christ in the Eucharist takes faith. If we rely only on our earthly understanding, we will have trouble.

Bible Verses to Reference on this subject:
John 6:35-71—Jesus promised His real Flesh and Blood as our
    true food
Matt 26:26ff. (Mark 14:22ff, Luke 22:17ff.)—Jesus fulfilled His
    promise by instituting the Eucharist
1 Cor 10:16—receiving Eucharist is participating in Christ's
    Body and Blood
1 Cor 11:23-29— receiving unworthily is to be guilty of

profaning His Body and Blood

Ex 12:8, 46—Paschal Lamb had to be eaten

John 1:29—Jesus called "Lamb of God"

1 Cor 5:7—Jesus called "Paschal Lamb who has been sacrificed"

John 4:31-34; matt 16:5-12—Jesus talking symbolically about food

1 Cor 2:14-3:4—explains what "the flesh" means in *John 6:63

Psalm 14:4; Is 9:18-20; Is 49:26; Mic 3:3; 2 Sam 23:15-17; Rev 17:6, 16—to symbolically eat and drink one's body and blood is to assault and persecute

XV.   Confession

Criticism: Catholics think they have to confess their sins to a priest when they should go directly to God instead.

The truth is that we <u>can</u> go directly to God. We can confess our sins to God at home and we should. We should examine our conscience every night and confess our sins to God and then say the "Act of Contrition." But do we?

The truth is that most of us sin daily and hardly give it any thought. The sins that we commit daily are usually venial sins or lesser sins. They can easily be forgiven by confessing them in prayer and praying the "Act of Contrition".

Venial Sins can also be forgiven by going to Mass and receiving the Eucharist or by doing acts of penance.

So why do we as Catholics go to a priest? When we are born, we do not have God's Life in our soul. When we are baptized we receive God's Life for the first time. God places His very Life in our soul. When we commit a Venial Sin, we wound God's Life in our soul. We harm our relationship with Him. This type of sin is easily forgiven.

But when we commit a Mortal Sin, we do not simply wound God's Life in our soul, we destroy it. We completely destroy the Life of God in our soul. He no longer dwells inside of us. So how can we get the Life of God back into our souls?

Just as it took a sacrament to put God's Life inside of us the first time (Baptism), it takes a sacrament (Reconciliation) to restore God's Life inside of us once we have committed a Mortal Sin. The Sacrament of Reconciliation restores God's Life to our souls.

This sacrament also calls us to humble ourselves and admit that we can do better. God cannot dwell where there is sin. We cannot be close to Him when our souls are full of sin.

The Church encourages us to confess even Venial Sins because they can build and lead us into Mortal Sin. Plus when we receive this sacrament, we receive God's grace, God's Life, into our souls. It gives us a special strength to avoid sin in the future.

All sacraments are here to make us holy and all sacraments achieve that. The Bible tells us that only those who are holy will enter Heaven.

The confession of sins goes all the way back to the time of Moses. The Jews even had special feast days when they all confessed their sins to the High Priest.

John the Baptist required the confession of sin before he would baptize a person. His was a Baptism of repentance.

Jesus gave His apostles the authority to forgive sins when He said, "Receive the Holy Spirit. Whose sins you forgive are forgiven, whose sins you retain are retained."

In the Book of James it is written, "Confess your sins to one another," immediately after it tells us to call for a priest to heal us.

Bible Verses to Reference on this Subject:
Matt 9:2-8—Son of Man has authority to forgive sins
John 20:23—whose sins you forgive or retain are forgiven or
    retained
John 20:22—breathed on them, "receive Holy Spirit" (recalls

Gen 2:7)

2 Cor 5:17-20—given us the ministry of reconciliation

James 5:13-15—prayer of presbyters (priests) forgives sin

James 5:16—confess your sins to one another

Matt 18:18—whatever you bind or loose on Earth will be bound or loosed in Heaven

1 John 5:16—there is sin that is not deadly

XVI. Purgatory

<u>Criticism</u>: The Catholic Church thinks people go to a place called Purgatory, but when we die we go directly to Heaven or Hell. Purgatory is not in the Bible.

The word Purgatory is not in the Bible, but either is the word Trinity and we believe wholeheartedly in that.

The <u>doctrine of Purgatory</u> is in the Bible. The Bible teaches very clearly that there is a place where imperfect souls go to be made perfect in order to enter Heaven. The Catholic Church calls this place Purgatory.

First, the Bible teaches us that "Nothing unclean will enter Heaven" (Rev. 21:27). This means that no person with sin on their soul at the time of their death will enter Heaven.

Second, in Matt 12:32 Jesus says, "Whoever speaks a word against the Son of Man will be forgiven; but whoever speaks against the Holy Spirit will not be forgiven, <u>either is this age or in the age to come</u>."

From these words of Christ we learn that forgiveness of sin takes place in this life and in the life to come. If a person is in Hell there is no forgiveness; it's too late. If a person is in Heaven, there is nothing to forgive. Therefore there must be a third place, a place other than Heaven and Hell, where sins are forgiven. That place is Purgatory.

Moreover, God forgives the guilt of our sins, but still requires us to make reparation. In other words, God forgives our sins, but requires us to repair the damage that our sins caused.

This is evident in the Bible in 2 Samuel 11 and 12. David committed grave sin. First he committed adultery with Bathsheba and then David caused the death of Bathsheba's husband.

God sent the prophet Nathan to David to make him aware that God was very displeased. David immediately repented of his sin and God forgave David. But God still required a punishment. The child that resulted from David's union with Bathsheba would die.

Purgatory is that place where a person can make reparation for their sins if they did not make up for them while on earth. Purgatory is the place where a person can go to become holy and perfect so that he can enter Heaven.

Scripture clearly teaches that only the perfectly holy will enter Heaven: Matthew 5:48 "Be perfect as your Heavenly Father is perfect." 1Peter 1:15-16 "As he who called you is holy, be holy yourselves in every aspect of your conduct for it is written, be holy because I am holy." Hebrews 12:14 it says, "Strive for peace with everyone and for that holiness <u>without which no one will see the Lord</u>."

Then Scripture describes what happens in Purgatory: 1Corinthians 3: 14-15 "If the work which any man has built on the foundation survives, he will receive a reward. If any man's work is burned up, he will suffer loss, though he himself will be saved, but only as through fire."

<u>Bible Verses to Reference on this Subject</u>:
Matt 5:48—be perfect as your Heavenly Father is perfect
Heb 12:14—strive for that holiness without which we cannot see
    God
James 3:2—we all fall short in many respects
Rev 21:27—nothing unclean shall enter Heaven

1 John 5:16-17—degrees of sins distinguished

James 1:14-15—when sin reaches maturity it gives birth to death

2 Sam 12:13-14—David, though forgiven, still paid a penalty for his sin

Matt 5:25—you will not be released until the last penny is paid

Matt 12:32—sin against Holy Spirit unforgiven in this age or Next

Matt 12:36—account for every idle word on judgment day

2 Mac 12:44-46—Judas Maccabees atoned for the dead to free them from sin

1 Cor 3:15—suffer loss, but saved as through fire

1 Pet 3:18-20, 4:6—Jesus preached to the spirits in prison

2 Tim 1:16-18—Paul prays for dead friend, Onesiphorus

1 Cor 15:29-30—Paul mentions people baptizing for the dead

Source Cite

CCC-The Catechism of the Catholic Church Second Edition; English translation of the Catechism of the Catholic Church for the United States of America copyright © 1994, United States Catholic Conference, Inc.

The Shroud of Turin
Information on the Shroud of Turin was obtained from the following sources:

Turin Shroud Center of Colorado PO Box 25326, Colorado Springs, CO 80936; www.shroudofturin.com

Report on the Shroud of Turin; John H. Heller; 1983 Houghton Mifflin, Boston.

Dr. August Accetta; The Shroud Center of Southern California; Forensic Research.

Father Francis J. Peffley; "The Passion of Christ in Light of the Holy Shroud of Turin"; Lighthouse Catholic Media © 2009.

Chapter III: God's Covenant With You
Scott Hahn, A Father Who Keeps His Promises, St. Anthony Messenger Press, Cincinatti, Ohio, 1998.

Jeff Cavins, "The Great Adventure Bible Timeline," Ascension Press, 2005.

Chapter V: Confirmed in the Church
"The word Catholic was first written in the year 110 by St. Ignatius of Antioch in his letter to the Smyrneans."

Jurgens, William A, The Faith of the Earyly Fathers, Volume I, The Liturgical Press, Collegeville, Minnesota, 1970

Mead, Frank S.; Hill, Samuel S.; Handbook of Denominations in the United States, Abingdon Press, Nashville TN, 2001

Weidenkopf, Steve; Schreck, Alan, EPIC A Journey Through Church History, Ascension Press, West "Chester, Pennsylvania, 2009

Graham, Henry G., Where We Got the Bible Our Debt to the Catholic Church, Catholic Answers, El Cajon, CA, 1997

Hensley, Ken, "Scripture Alone-The Rest of the Story," Saint Joseph Communications, West Covina, CA, 2003

Hensley, Ken, "Luther-The Rest of the Story," Saint Joseph Communications, West Covina, CA, 2007

Althaus, Paul, The Theology of Martin Luther, Fortress Press, Minneapolis, MN, 1966

DeWette, Wilhem, Martin Luther's Briefe Send Schreiben Und bedenken, Vollstanig Vol 3, Martin Luther, Johann Karl Geidemann; op, cit., III, 61

Lortz, Festgabe Joseph, Reformation Schicksal Und Auftrag, Vol 1, Bruno Grimm, Baden Baden, 1958

Chapter IX: The Sacrament of Eucharist

www.akhlah.com, Passover Seder Steps

Hahn, Scott, "The Fourth Cup," Saint Joseph Communications, West Covina, CA, 2005

Hannan, Archbishop Philip, "Her Life After Death," Focus Worldwide of New Orleans, Covington, LA

Pitre, Brant, Jesus and the Jewish Roots of the Eucharist, Doubleday, New York, 2011

Chapter XI: The Holy Sacrifice of the Mass

Sri, Edward, A Biblical Walk Through The Mass Understanding What We Say and Do in the Liturgy, Ascension Press, West Chester, Pennsylvania, 2011

Jurgens, William A, The Faith of the Earyly Fathers, Volume I, The Liturgical Press, Collegeville, Minnesota, 1970**Chapter**

XVII: Purgatory and Indulgences

An Unpublished Manuscript on Purgatory, The Reparation Society of the Immaculate Heart of Mary, INC., Baltimore, MD, 1967. Nihil obstat, Rev. Msgr. Carroll E. Satterfield, S.T.D., Censor Librorum. Imprimatur, His Eminence, Lawrence Cardinal Shehan, Archbishop of Baltimore, December 26, 1967

Bishops' Committee on the Liturgy, National Conference of Catholic Bishops, The Handbook of Indulgences Norms and Grants, Catholic Book Publishing Corp., New York, 1991

Chapter XVIII: Hell

Van Den Aardweg, Gerard J.M., Hungry Souls, Saint Benedict Press, LLC and TAN Books, Amsterdam, 2009

Hahn, Scott; Ray, Steven; Casey, Fr. Bill, "What Every Catholic Needs to Know About Hell," Saint Joseph Communications, West Covina, CA, 2005

Chapter XX: Catholic Morality

Fergusson Study, New Zealand, LifeNews.com, November 3, 2009

Mitchell, Bill, <u>Adultery: Statistics on Cheating Spouses,</u> www.examiner.com, December 4, 2009

McKinley, Irvin, www.mckinleyirvin.com, Divorce Statistics, October 30, 2012

The Center for Disease Control, National Center for Health Statistics, The U.S. National Vital Statistics Report, April 2010, EWTN News, "Record Percentage of U.S. Children Born out of Wedlock," Washington, D.C., April 11, 2010

Poverty, U.S. Census Bureau, American Community Survey, 2007-2009 data, http://factfinder2census.gov

Coulter, Ann, <u>Guilty: Liberal Victims and Their Assault on America,</u> Crown Publishing Group, 2009

Chapter XXI: We are Simply Stewards

USCCB, "Stewardship and Teenagers, The Challenge of Being a Disciple, USCCB Publishing, Washington, D.C., 2007

Chapter XXII: Mary, Mother of God; Our Mother; And Advocate

Emerich, Ven. Anne Catherine, <u>The Life of Jesus Christ And Biblical Revelationsas recorded by the journals of Clemens Brentano,</u> Tan Books and Publishers, INC., Rockford, Illinois, 1979